AGING
Stability and Change in the Family

AGING

James G. March, Editor in Chief
Graduate School of Business
Stanford University
Stanford, California

Aging: Biology and Behavior, edited by James L. McGaugh and Sara B. Kiesler

Aging: Social Change, edited by Sara B. Kiesler, James N. Morgan, and Valerie Kincade Oppenheimer

Aging: Stability and Change in the Family, edited by Robert W. Fogel, Elaine Hatfield, Sara B. Kiesler, and Ethel Shanas

AGING

Stability and Change in the Family

Edited by

ROBERT W. FOGEL
Department of Economics
Harvard University
Cambridge, Massachusetts

ELAINE HATFIELD
Departments of Sociology and Psychology
University of Wisconsin–Madison
Madison, Wisconsin

SARA B. KIESLER
Department of Social Science
Carnegie-Mellon University
Pittsburgh, Pennsylvania

ETHEL SHANAS
Department of Sociology
University of Illinois at Chicago Circle
Chicago, Illinois

ACADEMIC PRESS
A Subsidiary of Harcourt Brace Jovanovich, Publishers
New York   London   Toronto   Sydney   San Francisco

NOTICE: The project that is the subject of this report was approved by the Governing Board of the National Research Council, whose members are drawn from the Councils of the National Academy of Sciences, the National Academy of Engineering, and the Institute of Medicine. The members of the Committee responsible for the report were chosen for their special competences and with regard for appropriate balance.

This report has been reviewed by a group other than the authors according to procedures approved by a Report Review Committee consisting of members of the National Academy of Sciences, the National Academy of Engineering, and the Institute of Medicine.

The National Research Council was established by the National Academy of Sciences in 1916 to associate the broad community of science and technology with the Academy's purposes of furthering knowledge and of advising the federal government. The Council operates in accordance with general policies determined by the Academy under the authority of its Congressional charter of 1863, which establishes the Academy as a private, nonprofit, self-governing membership corporation. The Council has become the principal operating agency of both the Academy of Sciences and the National Academy of Engineering in the conduct of their services to the government, the public, and the scientific and engineering communities. It is administered jointly by both Academies and the Institute of Medicine. The Academy of engineering and the Institute of Medicine were established in 1964 and 1970, respectively, under the charter of the Academy of Sciences.

This project was supported by Grant No. NO1-AG-8-2111, awarded by the National Institute on Aging.

ACADEMIC PRESS, INC.
111 Fifth Avenue, New York, New York 10003

United Kingdom Edition published by
ACADEMIC PRESS, INC. (LONDON) LTD.
24/28 Oval Road, London NW1 7DX

Library of Congress Cataloging in Publication Data
Main entry under title:

Aging--stability and change in the family.

    Proceedings of a symposium held in Annapolis, Md.,
Mar. 22-24, 1979.
    Includes bibliographies and index.
    1. Aged--United States--Family relationships--
Congresses. 2. Aged--Government policy--United States--
Congresses. 3. Aged--United States--Sexual behavior--
Congresses. I. Fogel, Robert William. II. March,
James G. III. National Research Council (U.S.).
Committee on Aging. IV. National Institute on Aging.
HQ1064.U5A6364   305.2'6   81-12804
ISBN 0-12-040003-0   AACR2
ISBN 0-12-040023-5 (pbk.)

PRINTED IN THE UNITED STATES OF AMERICA

81 82 83 84   9 8 7 6 5 4 3 2 1

COMMITTEE ON AGING

Contents

1

Overview on Aging: Some Biomedical, Social, and Behavioral Perspectives

ROBERT N. BUTLER

I

FAMILY ROLES AND BEHAVIOR

2

Problems and Promises in the Social Psychology of Intergenerational Relations

GUNHILD O. HAGESTAD

3
The Changing Nature of Life-Cycle Squeezes:
Implications for the Socioeconomic Position of the Elderly   47
VALERIE KINCADE OPPENHEIMER

4
Aging and Becoming an Elder:
A Cross-Cultural Comparison   83
JOHN W. M. WHITING

5
Historical Change in the Household Structure of the
Elderly in Economically Developed Societies   91
DANIEL SCOTT SMITH

6
Remarriage and Intergenerational Relations   115
FRANK F. FURSTENBERG, JR.

15
Aging and Sexuality and the Myth of Decline   317
STEPHEN J. WEILER

Appendix A
Stability and Change in the Family, March 22–24, 1979, Annapolis, Maryland   329

Appendix B
Reviewers   331

List of Contributors

Numbers in parentheses indicate the pages on which the authors' contributions begin.

ROBERT N. BUTLER (1), National Institute on Aging, 9000 Rockville Pike, Bethesda, Maryland 20205

PATRICK E. CONNOR (233), School of Business, Oregon State University, Corvallis, Oregon 97331

FRANK F. FURSTENBERG, JR. (115), Department of Sociology, The University of Pennsylvania, Philadelphia, Pennsylvania 19174

WILLIAM GRIFFITT (301), Department of Psychology, Kansas State University, Manhattan, Kansas 66506

GUNHILD O. HAGESTAD (11), College of Human Development, The Pennsylvania State University, University Park, Pennsylvania 16802

TAMARA K. HAREVEN (143), Department of History, Clark University, Worcester, Massachusetts 01610 and Center for Population Studies, Harvard University, Cambridge, Massachusetts 02138

ELAINE HATFIELD* (253), Departments of Sociology and Psychology, University of Wisconsin–Madison, Madison, Wisconsin 53706

*Present address: Department of Psychology, University of Hawaii at Manoa, Honolulu, Hawaii 96822

HAROLD H. KELLEY (275), Department of Psychology, University of California, Los Angeles, Los Angeles, California 90024

VALERIE KINCADE OPPENHEIMER (47), Department of Sociology, University of California, Los Angeles, Los Angeles, California 90024

VIRGINIA P. RENO (185), National Commission on Social Security, 330 C Street, S. W., Washington, D. C. 20201

ETHEL SHANAS (211), Department of Sociology, University of Illinois at Chicago Circle, Chicago, Illinois 60680

DANIEL SCOTT SMITH (91), The Newberry Library, The Family and Community History Center, 60 West Walton Street, Chicago, Illinois 60610

MARVIN B. SUSSMAN (211), Department of Individual and Family Studies, College of Human Resources, University of Delaware, Newark, Delaware 19711

JANE TRAUPMANN (253), Center for Research on Women, Wellesley College, Wellesley, Massachusetts 02181

W. KIP VISCUSI (169), Department of Economics, Northwestern University, Evanston, Illinois 60201

STEPHEN J. WEILER (317), Department of Psychiatry and Behavioral Sciences, State University of New York, Stony Brook, New York 11794

JOHN W. M. WHITING (83), Department of Anthropology, Harvard University, Cambridge, Massachusetts 02138

Foreword

This book is one of three volumes examining some possible social and behavioral science research perspectives on aging. The others are: *Aging: Social Change*, edited by Sara B. Kiesler, James N. Morgan, and Valerie Kincade Oppenheimer; and *Aging: Biology and Behavior*, edited by James L. McGaugh and Sara B. Kiesler. The papers were solicited by the Committee on Aging of the National Research Council in response to a request from the National Institute on Aging.

The reason for the request was uncomplicated. As the phenomena of aging become more salient to private lives, effective research on aging becomes more critical to public policy and personal understanding. Most analyses suggest that there will be more money for research on aging over the coming years and that shifts in research funding will be incentives for shifts in research attention. Past experience warns, however, that although financial resources are necessary for an outstanding research program, they are rarely sufficient. In order for a public agency to influence the direction of important research, it must entice the community of scholars not only with money but also with a sense of the challenges and opportunities that the field provides. It must influence the individual professional enthusiasms that collectively determine the allocation of significant research creativity. In such a spirit, the National

Institute on Aging asked the National Research Council's Committee on Aging to organize a series of workshops at which experienced gerontologists and other social and behavioral scientists might discuss research ideas of possible relevance to future work on aging.

Organizing and implementing the workshops and the resulting volumes have involved many members of the research community. The 14 members of the Committee on Aging, the 65 contributors to the volumes, the 63 other participants in the workshops, and the 80 colleagues who reviewed the papers submitted for the volumes all contributed their time and expertise. In many cases, this represented a considerable personal commitment. On behalf of the committee, I want to thank this large band of generous colleagues, and particularly the editorial group of Robert W. Fogel, Elaine Hatfield, Sara B. Kiesler, James L. McGaugh, James N. Morgan, Valerie Kincade Oppenheimer, and Ethel Shanas. With no personal gain and little glory, they did the job. At the usual risk of promoting ordinary behavior into heroics, I calculate the professional fees foregone as being on the order of $1,000,000 and happily record the amount as a grant from the research community to the Academy and the Institute.

For most of the scientists who participated in this effort, however, the activity has had little connection to eleemosynary instincts. What more could a reasonable person ask from life than that it provide a few opportunities to exchange ideas with people who have some? The willingness of important research scientists to write papers for these volumes attests to the intellectual stimulation they found in fundamental research questions about aging. On behalf of my research colleagues, therefore, I want to thank the National Institute on Aging and the National Academy of Sciences for their parts in creating some occasions for such pleasures.

In particular, we owe a debt to some Washington colleagues. The original request to the Academy came from Robert N. Butler, Director of the National Institute on Aging, to David A. Goslin, Executive Director of the National Research Council's Assembly of Behavioral and Social Sciences. Both of them, as well as Betty H. Pickett, former Associate Director of the extramural collaborative research program of NIA, Matilda White Riley, Associate Director of NIA for social and behavioral research, and Shirley P. Bagley, health scientist administrator at NIA, contributed considerably to the climate of support that sustained the effort.

In addition, there was a small, tolerant staff in Washington. Elaine McGarraugh of the Committee on Aging and Christine L. McShane of the Assembly of Behavioral and Social Sciences managed the many details of bringing the papers together for the books. They cajoled an unlikely crew of widely scattered contributors with patient humor and peristaltic persistence and edited the volumes for the Academy with the sweet and sour sense and firmness that distinguish good editors. The one indispensable person, however, was Sara B. Kiesler. Before she left to return to academe, she served as study director for the project. Without her exceptional professional breadth and imagination, as well as her high style of dealing with ideas and people, the committee would have been unable to function. She deserves primary credit for having brought it all together.

As usual, it is necessary to exonerate all of these people, as well as the United States government, the National Academy of Sciences, the Assembly of Behavioral and Social Sciences, the National Institute on Aging, and innumerable universities from responsibility for what the individual authors say. The sensible things they have written are doubtless attributable to their colleagues and to the Committee on Aging. But the foolish things are their own.

JAMES G. MARCH, CHAIR
Committee on Aging

Preface

Despite its heavy load of evolutionary and traditional social functions, the family is a popular concept. Families are personally important to individuals and, generally, have proved adaptive to modern requirements. The idea of the family is a reference point for people. A family represents love, security, and certain values even if, in reality, one's own family is mean-minded and distant. Families also have wider meaning as a cohesive social force. They connote responsibility, especially toward the very young and very old. People believe that families are the group of first and last resort. It is therefore normal that we should study families as a primary force in the lives of elderly people and in aging.

The topic of this volume, *Aging: Stability and Change in the Family*, derives from our opinion that families are enduring and flexible. The family as a fundamental social unit has adjusted to vast changes in the social order and to differences among societies. The pervasiveness of the family suggests how useful it must be. In detail, however, the role of families for older people is unclear. Families have never before taken on so many different forms and altered responsibilities. To understand these new patterns and their effects is a difficult but important task for research.

The authors of the chapters in this volume were asked to grapple with three primary issues. The first concerns the functions of the family for older people. Because the role of the family in the life-cycle has changed, some of the authors dealt with the functions of the family in the entire life-span. A second issue concerns the apparent growing influence of government on the well-being of older people. New research may reveal how government policies affect families, and whether there are family patterns that run too deep to respond to such external factors. Some of this research may reveal where there is room for improving the quality of life of older people within the context of families of the future. The final issue dealt with in the book concerns close relationships and families. Personal ties are correlated with the physical and mental well-being of older people and with the responses of others to them. But the basis of the correlation is not well understood. We hope that by studying the close relationships of older people we will eventually understand how relationships within and outside families affect the welfare of their older members.

The idea of this volume originated in 1978 with the Committee on Aging of the Assembly of Behavioral and Social Sciences at the National Research Council. The committee, chaired by James G. March of Stanford University, worked on this project in cooperation with David A. Goslin, Executive Director of the Assembly, and the leading individuals from the sponsoring federal agency, Robert Butler, Betty Pickett, and Matilda Riley of the National Institute on Aging. A workshop entitled "Stability and Change in the Family" was held March 22–24, 1979, in Annapolis, Maryland. It was planned by a group consisting of the editors of this volume, James G. March, and members of the Committee on Aging, Sidney W. Mintz, and Jacquelyne J. Jackson. The discussants and reviewers (whose names appear in Appendix A and Appendix B, respectively) were an important source of ideas and provided feedback to the authors. Elaine McGarraugh was administrative associate to the committee and organizer-in-chief of the many reviews and revisions of the papers. Christine L. McShane read and edited every paper in this volume. The editors are very grateful to these many colleagues.

AGING
Stability and Change in the Family

chapter 1

Overview on Aging:
Some Biomedical, Social,
and Behavioral Perspectives

ROBERT N. BUTLER

In the twentieth century, life expectancy of the average American has increased by more than 50%. Basic improvements in sanitation, immunization, and medical care have resulted in a decrease in the number of deaths during infancy, childhood, and, for women, the childbearing years. Only 20% of all newborns in 1776 lived into their sixties, compared with over 80% in 1980. Life expectancy at birth for the total population has jumped from 48.2 years at the turn of the century to 73.2 years in 1978.

This triumphant increase in survivorship prompted the federal government to create the National Institute on Aging (NIA) in 1974, as part of the National Institutes of Health. The NIA's mission is to support, conduct, and promote social and behavioral—as well as biomedical—research on aging. That the United States Congress judiciously gave the institute such a broad mandate reflects the complex nature of the aging process. Its various manifestations and underlying mechanisms must be addressed by the best fundamental, scientific, and scholarly concepts and methods.

The National Institute on Aging was pleased to support the Committee on Aging, chaired by James G. March of Stanford University and directed by Sara B. Kiesler of Carnegie-Mellon University, under the auspices of the National Research Council's Assembly of Behavioral and Social

1

AGING
Stability and Change in the Family

Sciences. It has been a privilege, too, to be involved in its major work-shops on stability and change in the family, the elderly of the future, and the relationship of biology and behavior in aging, the results of which are offered in these volumes.

STABILITY AND CHANGE IN THE FAMILY

Changes in the demographic profile of the U.S. population—partic-ularly the increase of three-generational and multigenerational families—have given rise to much speculation about the role of the family. Those caught up in a romanticized portrayal of years past sometimes create the impression that something quite destructive has happened to the family. It is argued that the elderly were venerated in ancient and not-so-ancient societies, and they still are in "primitive" and oriental cul-tures. The extended family is cited as a powerful umbrella of warmth and support.

In reality, historians, sociologists, and others know that the extended families of the past were in large part the result of high fertility. These families were characterized by many siblings, uncles, and aunts but not necessarily many generations. There simply were not a great many sur-vivors. One indication of this fact is that in the 50 years from 1920 to 1970, the likelihood for a 10-year-old youngster to have two living grand-parents has risen from 40 to 75%.

The extended multigenerational family of this century offers a new kind of opportunity for care and support. In some parts of the United States, we are already witnessing a formalized network of family support as families band together to help relatives no longer able to care for themselves because of the devastating and destructive course of organic brain diseases. Senile dementia of the Alzheimer's type, the most com-mon form of irreversible organic brain disease and perhaps the fourth or fifth leading cause of death in the United States, is marked in its extreme form by disorientation, confusion, severe mental impairment, destruction of the personality, urinary and fecal incontinence, and the high likelihood of a need for institutionalization. Because the patient may remain physically robust while intellectually devastated, it may become very difficult for the family to provide proper care at home. We are beginning to see the growth of various organizations in the United States and in Canada to assist and offer information to relatives of Alzheimer's disease victims and to sponsor research that might lead to new knowledge to prevent and treat that disorder.

The family as an activist organization has also resulted in formal networks wherein friends, relatives, and older people themselves become effective advocates for the rights of the elderly, in some cases monitoring nursing homes and other health and social service programs that serve elderly clientele. Oregon and Detroit have developed models for such family organizations.

There are, of course—and there always have been—problems in families and problem families in which there are conflicts, feelings of guilt, and even brutality. On the basis of a study of victimization and the elderly conducted in Washington, D.C., in the late 1960s by the Washington School of Psychiatry, the "battered old person syndrome" is described (Brostoff *et al.* 1972), in which the domestic life of some older people is marked by physical brutality, without respect to social or economic class.

In addition to raising a number of questions on the role of the family, increased survivorship demands that we take a closer look at the older woman, who throughout most of her adult life is typically the major caregiver in the family support system. Peter Uhlenberg (1979) has noted the changing character of the life of the American woman. In 1870, only 44% of all women in the United States who survived past 15 years of age ever experienced what we now think of as the normal course of the life-cycle; that is, growing up, marrying and having children, watching their children grow up and leave home, growing older, becoming widowed, aging, and dying. Today, American women have a life expectancy at birth of 77.1 years and generally outlive men by 8 years. Therefore, this is not only a century of old age, but also a century of older women.

Because of the different life expectancies of the sexes, many of the problems as well as the opportunities of old age pertain to older women. Women constitute some 75% of the residents of nursing homes, for example, largely because they outlive those who might have cared for them in their old age. The elderly women in these last few decades of the twentieth century suffer an additional handicap. The cohort born from 1905 to 1910—those who had their main childbearing years at the height of the severe American economic depression of the 1930s—has been called a low fertility cohort. Of this cohort 22% had no children, 20% had only one, and still another 20% had two children.

Social and behavioral research studies such as those supported by the National Institute on Aging can do much to enhance our understanding of the ways in which families of various racial, ethnic, and cultural groups function. Such studies might also help in the development of the data bases that will rid us of misconceived notions of old age and allow us to promote effective public policy. We hear a good deal now about the "graying of America"; I have used that phrase myself in an effort to sensitize the American public to the striking changes in the age composition of our society. We must be careful, however, about the negative attitudes attached to phrases like the "graying of the health budget." While the Medicare and Medicaid programs have had an impact on skyrocketing national health expenses, the fact that health costs are now accumulated in later life is due in large part to the postponement of illness and related health costs from earlier years. Demographic research might alleviate misunderstandings about the costs associated with old age as well as fears that liberalization of Medicare home care benefits might lead to increased drains on the federal treasury, as those families that currently provide for elderly relatives request federal support. I know of no evidence to support this fear. In fact, this has not been the experience in those European countries that have provided more generously for home health care.

THE ELDERLY OF THE FUTURE

When we talk about the elderly of the future, we obviously cannot do so in a vacuum. The control of childhood diseases as well as improvements in the treatment of infectious diseases, cardiopulmonary diseases, and cancer demand that we take the time to reevaluate old age as a normal, natural stage of the life-cycle. While to this point I have emphasized the needs of an aged population, we might do better to consider the needs of an *aging* population. Although by the year 2030 as much as 20% of the United States' population will be 65 years of age or older, the majority will be under 65; the overall median age will be 37.6 years. Clearly, we must look to the implications of a changing age structure on problems in the areas of labor, housing, and health care.

Paralleling the social needs of a population with a changing age structure is an increased interest in gerontology and geriatrics. In order to enhance the quality of life of older people, we must also develop the knowledge to treat and prevent the diseases that currently interfere with normal, healthy aging. Gerontology or research on aging offers a new approach to diseases in an effort to retain or restore those physiologic and behavioral functions altered with the passage of time. We have already found that the immune system weakens with age, thus making the body more susceptible to viruses, bacteria, and noxious environmental agents. A close look at normal aging may help us isolate age-related changes in the immune system and the central nervous system as well as hormonal and regulatory capacities. Research in these areas might ultimately delay the onset or mitigate the severity of a variety of diseases and disabilities that become more frequent with age.

Geriatrics is the branch of medicine that deals with the complexities of old age, namely, multiple diseases, changes in the expression of illness, and alterations in such functions as pain reaction and temperature response. Geriatric medicine refers not only to this body of knowledge, but also to a needed change in the negative attitudes and the lack of information that prejudice many doctors, nurses, and other health providers who work with elderly patients. It is not enough to have financing mechanisms like Medicare to meet the medical needs of older people when formal training programs do not include material on basic aging and clinical geriatrics. Incorporating this information into medical school curricula will guarantee that the health care system will respond more effectively to older people of the future.

Studies by research gerontologists of healthy volunteers living in the community—ranging from youth to old age—provide a practical means for understanding normal aging and gaining a glimpse of the elderly of the future. The National Institute of Mental Health's human aging studies (1955–1966), the Duke University studies (1955 through the present), and the Baltimore longitudinal study of aging (1958 through the present) are among those that have examined aging by identifying types and rates of change in the same individuals over time.[1] Many misconceptions regarding age have disappeared as a result—including the misguided notions that all intellectual functions automatically decline with age and that cerebral blood flow and oxygen consumption show decrements in relationship to age alone. It may also be possible for gerontologists to capitalize on any of the 40 longitudinal studies conducted in the United States, particularly since the 1920s, many of which are still active. Some, such as the famous Framingham study in Massachusetts, began as community studies of risk factors. Others, such as the Terman "gifted child" study and the Oakland-Berkeley studies, began as developmental studies of children in the 1920s.[2]

While we cannot precisely predict social changes of the future, we must not restrain our imaginations. The idea that prosthetic devices might compensate for lost physical functions in the elderly is just one example

---

[1] For the NIMH human aging studies see Birren et al. (1971), Granick and Patterson (1971); for the Duke University studies see Palmore (1970, 1974); for the Baltimore longitudinal study of aging see Butler (1977).

[2] For the Terman "gifted child" study see Terman et al. (1925), Burks et al. (1930), Terman and Oden (1947), Terman (1959); for the Oakland-Berkeley studies see Block and Hann (1971), Elder (1974).

of the potential of technology. As Paul Valery wrote, "The responsibility of the educated is to prepare man for what has never been."

BIOLOGY AND BEHAVIOR OF THE ELDERLY

The interrelationship of biology and behavior is no less crucial in old age than at any other time. The need for multidisciplinary research is apparent as we make plans for studies on nutrition and aging, drugs and aging, and sleep problems of the aged, to name only a few. Perhaps most exciting, however, is the interaction of biomedical and psychosocial factors in the debate on the possibilities of life-span extension. In this area, in particular, issues of feasibility are closely linked with those of the desirability and the necessity for socioeconomic reconstruction that would follow.

One might wonder which is more restrictive—our limited intellects or our finite lives. Our understanding of the human brain has begun to increase at a rapid pace with the explosion of new research findings in the area of neuroscience. Not long ago, senility was thought to be an inevitable untreatable manifestation of cerebral arteriosclerosis. We now know that this is not so; in fact, preliminary findings suggest that an enzyme replacement therapy somewhat analogous to the use of L-dopa in the treatment of Parkinson's disease might one day be used to arrest the symptoms of Alzheimer's disease. It was also once thought that the functions of damaged brain cells were irretrievably lost; yet research supported by NIA indicates that undamaged brain cells can compensate for damaged ones in transmitting nerve signals. In much the same way, our understanding of the mechanisms of longevity and senescence is contingent on far-reaching advances in molecular biology, genetics, and biochemistry.

Although advances in the basic sciences have the potential for providing a robust extended life-span, we must also look at the other influences that act on mental and physical health. What, for example, is the effect of environmental stress on health and disease? What is the impact of boredom and adventure on the quality of life? How does physiology relate to sexual behavior?

Aging research in the areas of biology, medicine, and the social and behavioral sciences is likely to offer rich rewards in the next several decades. The need for such research is compelling, considering the extraordinary demographic changes in the United States' population and the staggering health costs that public policymakers associate with old age. The likelihood of some success is reflected in the fascinating and scholarly scientific questions that are being formulated, including increased attention to well-defined epidemiological studies of disease in old age. The 1981 White House Conference on Aging, the 1982 United Nations World Assembly on Aging, and the Resolution on Aging of the World Health Organization will all include a major emphasis on the broad range of research disciplines needed to develop an understanding of normal human aging. We expect the social and behavioral sciences to play a major role in all of these initiatives. Solving the problems of old age requires the concurrent application of the latest and best information available from the biological sciences, clinical medicine, and studies of personal and social behavior.

REFERENCES

Birren, J. E., Butler, R. N., Greenhouse, S. W., *et al.,* eds. (1971) *Human Aging I: A Biological and Behavioral Study.* National Institute of Mental Health, ADAMHA, Publication No. (ADM) 77–122. Washington, D.C.: U.S. Department of Health, Education, and Welfare.

Block, J., in collaboration with Hann, N. (1971) *Lives Through Time.* Berkeley, Calif.: Bancroft Books.

Brostoff, P. M., Brown, R. B., and Butler, R. N. (1972) "Beating up" on the elderly: Police, social work, and crime. Public Interest Report No. 6. *International Journal of Aging and Human Development* 3:319–322.

Burks, B. S., Jensen, D. W., and Terman, L. M. (1930) *Genetic Studies of Genius, Volume 3. The Promise of Youth: Followup Studies of a Thousand Gifted Children.* Stanford, Calif.: Stanford University Press.

Butler, R. N. (1977) Research programs of the National Institute on Aging. U.S. Department of Health, Education, and Welfare *Public Health Reports, 92(1):3–8.*

Elder, G. H., Jr. (1974) *Children of the Great Depression.* Chicago: University of Chicago Press.

Granick, S., and Patterson, R. D., eds. (1971) *Human Aging II: An Eleven-Year Followup Biomedical and Behavioral Study.* National Institute of Mental Health, ADAMHA, Publication No. (ADM) 77–122. Washington, D.C.: U.S. Department of Health, Education, and Welfare.

Palmore, E. B., ed. (1970) *Normal Aging: Reports from the Duke Longitudinal Studies, 1955–1969.* Durham, N.C.: Duke University Press.

Palmore, E. B., ed. (1974) *Normal Aging II: Reports from the Duke Longitudinal Studies, 1970–1973.* Durham, N.C.: Duke University Press.

Terman, L. M. (1959) *Genetic Studies of Genius, Volume 5. The Gifted Group at Mid-Life.* Stanford, Calif.: Stanford University Press.

Terman, L. M., assisted by Baldwin, B. T., Bronson, E., Devoss, J. C. *et al.* (1925) *Genetic Studies of Genius, Volume 1. Mental and Physical Traits of a Thousand Gifted Children.* Stanford, Calif.: Stanford University Press.

Terman, L. M., and Oden, M. H. (1947) *Genetic Studies of Genius, Volume 4. The Gifted Child Grows Up.* Stanford, Calif.: Stanford University Press.

Uhlenberg, P. (1979) Demographic change and problems of the aged. Pp. 153–166 in M. W. Riley, ed., *Aging from Birth to Death: Interdisciplinary Perspectives.* Boulder, Col.: Westview Press.

PART I

FAMILY ROLES
AND BEHAVIOR

Problems and Promises
in the Social Psychology
of Intergenerational Relations

GUNHILD O. HAGESTAD

INDIVIDUAL, COHORT, AND GENERATION

This chapter outlines recent demographic and cultural changes that have created a new context for intergenerational ties, and it argues that these changes call for new approaches to the study of such ties. Specifically, I argue that we must approach intergenerational relations on a social–psychological level in order to pursue questions that cannot be answered on an aggregate level, through the analysis of life-course patterns of birth cohorts or through census information on households.

The family offers the social scientist a unique social arena, in which members of different generations, with different historical anchorings, meet in long-term bonds. It is an arena in which lives are structured and interwoven, in which meanings are created in a blending of historical forces, family realities, and individual needs and resources. Studying family relationships across generations promises new insights into how individual lives are shaped, how social change is mediated, and how long-term primary group ties are maintained. This area of study also offers problems and challenges. The family presents an intersection of three types of time and change: individual life time, family time, and historical time (Aldous 1978b, Hareven 1977). Thus, if we are interested

11

AGING
Stability and Change in the Family

in how changing individuals relate in family bonds across generations, we are likely to ask questions that incorporate three distinct levels of analysis.

The necessity of keeping levels of analysis clear is evident with regard to the central concept of this chapter, that of generation. The term *generation* has been used to cover a number of underlying concepts (Bengtson and Cutler 1976, Troll 1970). In this discussion a distinction is made between two kinds of temporal locations and group membership. The term *generation* refers to lineage position within families, whereas *cohort* refers to individuals born at a particular point in historical time—people who are likely to share "life imprints" of historical events (Rosow 1978, Ryder 1965).

A central argument in my discussion is that while the family represents a unique opportunity for exploring linkages between these two concepts of generation, it is essential for us as researchers to keep in mind that family members do not file into generation by cohort (Troll 1970, Troll and Bengston 1979). This fact is often neglected when we examine cohort patterns in the general population and seek to develop hypotheses about their consequences for intergenerational relations in families. The grandparent generation currently includes individuals ranging in age from their upper thirties to the nineties, members of drastically different birth cohorts. High school students still live in a baby boom environment, as the last of the large postwar birth cohorts are coming of age. However, students who spend their days in crowded high schools may go home to quite different generational environments. If they are last-born children, they have baby boom parents; if they are first born, their parents are post boom. Families formed between the mid-1940s and the late 1950s may witness a cohort gap within their younger generation: those who were adolescents or young adults in the late 1960s and those who were too young to have their lives affected by historical events of that tumultuous decade.

It is essential for us to recognize that each family lineage creates its own set of cohort combinations. The more generations we add, the greater the variety of patterns across families. Precisely because of the extensive interfamily variance in cohort combinations, we cannot build a social psychology of generations on cohort data, although trends observed on an aggregate level certainly may suggest questions to pursue on a social–psychological, family level.

The last decade or so has given us a great deal of work on life patterns of various birth cohorts. Inspired by anthropological work on age grading, social scientists studying Western industrial societies have investigated the sociocultural structuring of individual lives, the process through which lifetime is divided into culturally recognized units and cohort members are channeled into social roles. In this process, lifetime becomes translated into social time, and chronological age becomes social age (Elder 1975, Neugarten and Hagestad 1976). A major focus in this work on the social patterning of lives has been on life-course patterns: the timing and sequencing of major role transitions. Another emphasis has been on age-related or stage-related expectations which create opportunities and constraints for cohort members as they pass through a given life phase (Riley *et al.* 1972). In addition to looking at transitions in individual lives, we have looked at family careers and critical phases in the development of the family system, much as we would do on the individual level. Thus, we have looked at patterns of timing in major family transitions, such as marriage, or the transition from a preparental to a parental phase.

Much of the work on individual and family transitions has examined normative patterns, in two senses of the word normative. First, comparing different birth cohorts, we have looked at statistical norms, mostly central tendencies, in the timing of major role transitions (e.g., Glick 1977). Second, we have tended to assume that the statistical norms tell us something about social norms. In other words, we see these transitions as guided by cultural timetables and age-related norms (Baltes 1979, Neugarten and Moore 1968).

Modal patterns of timing in family role transitions can be used for discussions of life course, comparing the structuring of individual lives across cohorts, or they may be viewed as critical phases in the development of family systems. In the latter case, we are focusing on historical trends in the family life-cycle (Aldous 1978a, Glick 1977, Hareven 1977). A "family development" approach to the social psychological study of the family builds on these modal patterns and assumes an orderly sequence of family transitions that present "developmental tasks" for the family system and its members at various stages of the family cycle (e.g., Duvall 1957, Hill and Rodgers 1964, Hill and Mattessich 1979, Rodgers 1973).

Recent social and demographic changes have pointed to limitations of past work on the structuring of individual and family time and have also suggested promising new avenues for future work. First, in face of recent trends in the patterning of individual and family time, it appears increasingly difficult to treat the unfolding of individual and family "careers" as orderly, irreversible progressions of transitions, particularly if our focus is on adults. Second, we have become increasingly aware that in comparing patterns of role transitions across cohorts, we need to examine variability as well as modal patterns (Uhlenberg 1974, Neugarten and Hagestad 1976). In other words, we must pay attention to intracohort as well as intercohort contrasts.

Examination of intracohort variance may yield a number of benefits. Non-normative patterns are likely to provide insights regarding the presence and strength of cultural norms. Furthermore, it may suggest proximal environmental factors that are strong predictors for individual life outcomes. Because of recent historical work (Demos and Boocock 1978, Elder 1974, Hareven 1978) we have increasingly become aware that the life course is shaped not only through a set of distal societal factors, such as age-related norms and historical events. A powerful proximal social force is found in the family, probably the strongest producer of intracohort variance. In the family sphere, multiple cohort effects are translated into family meaning and personal significance, and individual life trajectories are shaped by an intimate yet complex interweaving of lives across generations.

Before we can discuss challenges currently confronting researchers interested in issues surrounding generation and cohort and their relationship to life course and family development, we need to review some recent changes in the sociocultural context that gives shape to individual and family time.

THE PATTERNING OF INDIVIDUAL LIFE TIME

Since the pioneering overview by Cain (1964), we have seen a steadily increasing interest in the social patterning of individual life time. In reviewing the last decade or so of this work, Smelser and Halpern (1978) argue that "in our life time, some stages of life have been truncated, while others have been created [p. 311]." They further state that "in all cases age norms have been redefined and each phase made more distinct [p. 311]." I believe most scholars in this area would agree with the first part of their statement, but the latter part would generate considerable disagreement.

The early part of the twentieth century saw the general recognition of adolescence. Later in the century, a new stage was being discussed, that of youth. Recently, new differentiations have begun to be made within the second half of life. Middle age has now been clearly delineated, owing not only to increasing longevity and improved health but also to the altered rhythm of events in the family cycle. Still another division seems to be appearing, that of the young–old and the old–old (Neugarten 1974). The young–old phase has emerged, again because of increasing longevity, but also because of the drop in age of retirement. Thus, we seem to have general agreement that life time has become more differentiated, as Smelser and Halpern suggest. However, one would not find unanimity on their point regarding age-related norms and distinctiveness of aging grading. While it is commonly argued that the first three decades of life have become more structured and uniform, many writers would suggest that the later decades of life have shown increasing variance in life patterns, complexity, and, sometimes, lack of clear cultural structuring.

I would like to briefly examine current arguments about age grading and uniformity of patterns in various stages of life, and then look at the extent to which some of the present generalizations are cohort-bound and likely to change in the future.

The First Decades of Life: Increasing Uniformity?

In much recent discussion of the first decades of life, there is a theme of greater uniformity and clearer age grading. In the case of childhood, it is argued that children's social milieux have become more uniform, both on an intrafamilial and interfamilial level (Uhlenberg 1978). Within families, there are a number of effects stemming from the reduction in family size and the closer spacing of children. With siblings being close in age, they are likely to be born roughly within the same period of their parents' adulthood, sharing roughly the same parental resources. Furthermore, the pattern of older children being caretakers, or "assistant parents" for their younger siblings, so common in the nineteenth century (Hareven 1977), is becoming increasingly rare.

Across families, the decreased variance in fertility patterns, both in terms of family size and child spacing, has diminished earlier contrasts among family groups. It is also argued that, with successive cohorts of this century, parents have become more homogeneous: A steadily growing proportion of them has been native-born, with a high school education or more, leading an urban life, reading the same child-care manuals (Bronfenbrenner 1961, Uhlenberg 1978). Furthermore, it is pointed out that the relative influence of the parent in the socialization of children has declined with the growth of public education, the rise of day care and early childhood education, and the pervasive influence of mass media. In sum, it is argued that systematic variance in child-rearing due to social class, region, and subculture has declined, and that "family idiosyncrasies" have less chance of showing up. Thus, we have had a "homogenization of childhood." It is also argued that the early years are more stable and worry-free now than in the nineteenth and early twentieth centuries. In particular, the results of dramatically reduced mortality are pointed out (Uhlenberg 1978).

Discussions of the transition into adulthood have also pointed to a new uniformity. Two themes emerge in recent writing on this life phase. First, it is shown that the transition into adult roles has become increasingly compressed and synchronized. While the passages used to be gradual, one at a time, they now take place in a shorter time period, with more overlap between transitions. Second, it is demonstrated that timing patterns show clearer modalities, with birth cohorts showing decreasing age variance in such patterns. This new uniformity is seen to be a result of a shift from family considerations, norms, and controls to general cultural age norms. Modell *et al.* (1976) state: "Transitions are today more contingent, more integrated because they are constrained by a set of formal institutions. 'Timely' action to 19th century families consisted of helpful response in times of trouble; in the 20th century timeliness connotes adherence to a schedule [p. 30]."

Late Adulthood: Flexibility, Complexity, and Diversity

In quite marked contrast to discussions of early life, in which increased uniformity is the theme, stand recent discussions of later adulthood, especially the last decades of life. A number of writers have argued that while the first decades of life may have become "overstructured" and show a great deal of uniformity, late adulthood is "understructured," shows little synchronization among role transitions, and has a perplexing number of possible life patterns. Rosow (1976) compares early adulthood when "life is mainly structured by social duties" with old age, when "life is shaped by individual choice and personal initiative [p. 467]."

The lack of uniformity and the complexity of patterns in late adulthood are related to a number of factors: the multidimensionality of age systems, the lack of orderly progression in them, a general blurring of age demarcations, and the interruption and resumption of careers.

Recent discussion of life course patterns in adulthood has emphasized the complexity of social age systems in our culture, since different institutional spheres have different timetables and expectations regarding age-appropriate behavior. The consequence for the life course is that age-related changes in roles are not synchronized, especially not in later adulthood. Roth (1963) described the life course as "an interacting bundle of career timetables," and Elder (1975) speaks of "interdependent life paths which vary in synchronization."

With regard to adulthood, it is increasingly hard to insist that life paths follow a pattern of orderly, linear progression. Careers are interrupted and restarted, and individuals make "loops" in the age system. Thus, it is possible to become a social age peer of persons who are not chronological age peers. Guemple (1969) calls this type of phenomena *renewal activities*. Examples of such loops would be a woman who becomes a college freshman at the age of 45, or a man who starts a new family at the age of 50.

In addition to changes in role patterns, generations have witnessed a general "younging" of life-styles, with the young and the middle-aged sharing leisure activities, dress and hairstyles more than earlier. A couple of decades ago, stores had major dress departments for "the mature woman." Today these departments have for the most part vanished, or they are serving women much older than was previously the case. Casual clothes, jeans, and sportswear have led to a general "democratization" of dress and a diminishing of visible age differences. Indeed, in what must be a historically unique situation, there can indeed be cases in which it is difficult to distinguish a mother from her daughter, just as TV commercials have wanted us to believe for years. The similarity between mothers and daughters goes beyond appearance and vigor. A new kind of social age peership is now entering the intergenerational picture. We are seeing mothers and daughters sharing the student role or starting out together in an occupational role; fathers and sons sharing the role of retiree, or the role of father of a young child.

This social age peership, I would argue, owes more to flexibility in the second part of adulthood than in early adulthood. When parents and children become social age peers, it is likely to be because the parent engages in "renewal activities," more commonly than because the child is engaged in "acceleration activities" (Neugarten and Hagestad 1976). However, the latter can also happen, particularly between the middle and older generations. Examples would be early retirement for the son; early widowhood for the daughter.

A lessening of normative structuring with increasing age has also been seen as the consequence of another phenomenon: the emergence of new age statuses and role relationships for which there are no or few culturally shared expectations. Laslett (1977), in a discussion of the history of aging in Western countries, concluded that "our situation remains irreducibly novel; it calls for invention rather than imitation [p. 181]." In many instances, we seem to have "cultural lag," a situation in which our culture has not quite kept up with demographic realities.

When Gloria Steinem turned forty and a TV interview marked the occasion, her interviewer remarked that she did not "look forty." Steinem's reply was, "What's forty supposed to look like?" The reporter had no answer, and seemed to reflect a general puzzlement over what Bernard (1975) has called a new species: the new middle-aged woman. Cultural uncertainty regarding new life stages is reflected in popular literature. When we had a recognition of youth as a stage, there was a wave of books advising parents how to deal with this new breed. Now, the best-sellers address the new adulthood: for example, *Passages; My Mother, Myself; You and Your Aging Parents.*

Particularly in the case of women, it has been common to argue that we have created new life phases, such as the "empty nest" years, for which there is little cultural recognition and few guidelines for what to become (Blau 1973, Lopata 1966, Parsons 1942). Rosow (1974, 1976) has presented careful analyses of how new patterns in late adulthood demonstrate that status and role can be "out of step," a possibility not allowed for in such classical discussion as that by Linton (1936). Thus, Rosow and others argue that when new, formerly nonexistent, statuses are created or appear, a set of expectations may not be associated with them. Nye (1974) speaks of *emergent roles*, Rosow (1976) uses the term *tenuous roles*. This, of course, means that relationships between role partners have few structurally given guidelines—a theme that reemerges in discussions of intergenerational relationships, to which I return later.

New Discontinuities

Recently, a new source of variance and discontinuity has emerged: the dramatic increase in the interruption of marital careers. Current estimates predict that in recent marriage cohorts, nearly one-third of the couples will eventually divorce (Bureau of the Census 1979a, Glick 1979). Even though divorce may not markedly affect most of the traditional life-cycle measures (Norton 1980), it certainly represents interrupted marital careers and structural reorganization. Facing recent trends, authors who have demonstrated greater uniformity in life course patterns over the last century (Modell *et al.* 1976, Uhlenberg 1974, 1978) warn that the tide may turn—we may enter a new era of instability and decreasing uniformity. Thus, the cohorts born in the early 1950s may go down in history as having had the ideal childhood, growing up in a sea of tranquillity between disruptions due to mortality and disruption due to divorce. Their parents, some of whom were marked in early life by the Depression, had learned the value of family stability and cohesion and helped produce a pattern of uniformity and stability (Elder 1974).

Thus, much of our thinking about life and family stages, most of which was developed after 1950, may have been inspired by this temporary tranquillity, one which may never be equaled again. Children born in the 1970s may grow up with disruption and changes similar to those experienced by their grandparents and great-grandparents. In the cohorts born early in this century, family disruption was common, owing to high mortality. Uhlenberg (1978) estimates that among individuals born in 1910, fewer than 50% survived to the age of 15 without having experienced the death of a parent or a sibling. About one in eight of them lost one or both parents before the age of 15. Currently, 19% of children under the age of 18 live in one-parent households, and it is estimated that if current trends persist, 45% of children born in the 1970s will spend some time in a one-parent home before the age of 18 (Bureau of the Census, 1979a). Children who have spent part of their early years with an intact parental pair, a second part in a single-parent household, and a third part in a reconstituted family are not going to fit the uniform picture of childhood. Thus, the future may bring less uniformity and stability for the younger generations, too.

The recent trends in family dissolution and reconstruction have also demonstrated how individual lives are intimately interwoven in the family and how much of one's life context—the constraints and opportunities it presents—are created by generational membership.

The Interaction between Life Careers

When the lives of family members, within and across generations, were structured by economic interdependency and cooperation, the interrelated nature of their life careers was hard to overlook. The family set constraints on individual choice and life decisions, as we have seen in discussions of transitions to adulthood (Hareven 1977, Hogan 1978, Modell *et al.* 1976). Under a system of primogeniture, the oldest son did not fully come of age and could not marry and start a family until his father died or relinquished ownership of the farm. In nineteenth century New England, late-born children were unable to start their own families because of responsibilities for aging parents (Ankarloo 1978, Hareven 1977). Maybe because of the general ideological emphasis on freedom and autonomy in the twentieth century, we have neglected the rather impressive extent to which families still provide constraints and opportunities within and across generations, through an intricate interweaving of life careers.

"Voluntary" life decisions and transitions by one family member creates "involuntary" changes for others in what Riley and Waring (1976) call counter-transitions. We have ripple effects, because of the intimate interconnections of roles and lives. Marriage in one generation creates in-laws in another. Parenthood creates grandparenthood. Voluntary childlessness may create involuntary grandchildlessness. "Voluntary" divorce leaves children to be raised "involuntarily" in single-parent homes and creates "ex-relationships."

We have generally neglected the fact that a status transition that is voluntary and a result of individual choice for family member A may not be so for member B, who also goes through a transition as a result of A's action.

Furthermore, A's patterns of timing set limits on B's options, often across several generations. The timing of marriage and parenthood in two generations influences the possibilities that members of the third generation will know their grandparents. The decision to have children close in age may produce siblings who tax their parents' resources as a "bunch." An example is a family who may have several children in college and several weddings within a 5-year period. Furthermore, as adults, these siblings may face constraints and stresses simultaneously, and therefore may not serve as effectively for mutual support as they might if they were more spread in age and life stage. Their similarity in life stage and resources available also makes it more complicated to sort out responsibilities for aging family members.

Not much work has been done on "timing, spacing and arrangement of events—within and across the life paths [Elder 1978, p. 27]" and the interrelations among these phenomena. Oppenheimer (1974) speaks of a "life-cycle squeeze," created by a lack of balance between a father's earning power and the economic needs of maturing children, arguing that such a squeeze might be a major factor in a mother's decision to enter the labor market.

Recently, we have started to discuss another type of squeeze: that experienced by members of the middle generation in three-generation families who at the same time may find themselves faced with parents needing care and attention, and young-adult offspring who need support in establishing themselves as adults (Silverstone and Hyman 1976, Streib 1972). Clearly, timing coincidence has a great deal to do with the extent to which being in this bridge generation is experienced as an overload of demands. When middle-aged persons feel a generational crunch, it is a result of the combined stresses, vulnerabilities, and strengths of three generations: the need for support by children seeking to establish themselves as adults; mid-life psychological, career, and health changes in the parent; and increased need for sustenance by the grandparents. These family resource and vulnerability constellations reflect the long-term effects of timing patterns in several generations and in several spheres of life. If we think that the individual life course patterns are complex, the complexity becomes perplexing if we think of the family as an intersect of multiple life paths. Not only do we have "an interacting bundle of timetables," we have interacting bundles! In an enormous matrix of life contingencies—past, present, and future—each family, each lineage, creates its own interwoven web, a unique pattern.

Summary

To sum up my discussion so far: I have argued that an emphasis on modal patterns and orderly career progressions has limited applicability in the study of adult lives, due to a number of factors: The complexity of age systems, blurring of age status lines, the lack of clear normative guidelines, and the interruption and resumption of careers. Thus, when we move across adulthood, life patterns become increasingly varied and complex, and it is increasingly difficult to find typical patterns in role transitions and people's *life stations,* to use Kingsley Davis's (1949) term. Therefore, on the individual level, it has been argued that a comprehensive theory of the life course is impossible, because the number of observable patterns in unmanageable (Clausen 1972, Rosow 1976).

Since families consist of interacting, changing individuals, family relationships, particularly among adults, show an impressive array of possible patterns. Hess and Waring (1978) conclude that: "With the passage of time, so much diversity arises in family groups that possibly no two sets of parents and children in the society—or even in the same family— have traveled parallel paths [p. 267]."

In light of this complexity, it may be increasingly necessary for us to study the generational interior of families; a microcosm in which life patterns and outcomes are created. Let us briefly examine how this social arena has been affected by recent sociocultural change.

THE CHANGING SOCIAL CONTEXT OF INTERGENERATIONAL BONDS

Demographic Change

Due to dramatic reduction of mortality, general life expectancy has jumped from less than 50 in the year 1900 to nearly 73 in the late 1970s. However, the changes in mortality have been quite different for men and women, with what is referred to as "the mortality gap" widening over the same time period. As a consequence, the average woman can now expect to live nearly 8 years longer than the average man. The difference in life expectancy in 1900 was 2.8 years (Bureau of Census 1978).

Decreased mortality coupled with decreased fertility has produced "the graying of America," a steadily growing proportion of the population who fall in the age categories over 65. Over the last two decades, we have seen a related phenomenon: a dramatic increase in the number of individuals in advanced old age, 80 years or older.

As a result of changes in mortality and fertility patterns, the intergenerational picture of American families has changed dramatically over recent decades. A number of factors are involved in the change:

1. The acceleration of generational turnover
2. The increased age homogeneity within and between generations
3. The rise of multigenerational families
4. The emergence of long-term intergenerational bonds between adults

As a result of an overall trend toward earlier marriage, smaller families, and closer spacing between children, we have witnessed a decrease in what Ankarloo (1978) labels the "reproductive span": the ages of men and women at the birth of their first grandchild. "The quickening of the family life cycle" (Neugarten and Moore 1968) has accelerated generational turnover. Furthermore, recent patterns of childbearing have produced a new age homogeneity in the nuclear family. Siblings increasingly regard each other as age peers in adulthood. Furthermore, age differences between generations have decreased. The generational acceleration, coupled with the increase in general life expectancy, will make multigenerational families increasingly common. As a result, we are faced with some new phenomena. Of particular importance for the present discussion is the emergence of long-term intergenerational bonds between adults and the possibility of social age peership between generations.

With life expectancy now past 75 for women, parents and children will often have more than 50 years of life overlap. The majority of those years will have adults on both sides of this intergenerational relationship. Since about one-third of women now can expect to survive past the age of 85, many mothers will live close to what used to be considered the span of two generations after their children have reached adulthood. The opportunity for relations between adults will also be increasingly common between noncontiguous generations: between grandparents and grandchildren. Since entry into grandparenthood now is typically a mid-life phenomenon (Troll 1971, Wood and Robertson 1976), this intergenerational tie may span 3 or 4 decades, with 1 or 2 of them involving a relationship between adults.

As a consequence of the phenomena discussed above, it follows that increasingly, parents and children may grow old together. Troll *et al.* (1979) estimate that among individuals 65 or older, 1 out of 10 has a child who is 65 or older. Furthermore, with the sex differential in life expectancy, a number of mothers will actually outlive their sons. Currently, it is estimated that among women who bear a son in their early twenties, close to one out of five will survive that son (Metropolitan Life 1977). Thus, barring drastic changes in age differences between spouses or in mortality patterns, an increasing number of families will go through a stage with two generations of retirees, followed by a stage with two generations of widows. One thing is sure: families will mirror the change in age composition witnessed on a societal level; they will become increasingly top-heavy as opposed to bottom-heavy, with a steadily growing number of members surviving to old age. Some of them will survive to advanced old age and will, most likely, require a period of increased care and attention.

In looking at the new intergenerational constellations in Western industrial society, particularly among adults, a number of authors have rewritten Simmel's classic question: "How is society possible?" Instead they ask: How are intergenerational bonds possible? Rosenmayr (1978, p. 4) asks: "The family has survived the various stages of the industrial revolution. . . . Will it also survive the 'psychological revolution?' " Hareven (1977, p. 68) wonders: "Is the family unable to tolerate the demographic stability it has finally achieved?"

Questions regarding the maintenance of long-term intergenerational ties center on the issue of integration. To use Landecker's (1951) terminology, recent discussions have focused on cultural and normative integration—the extent to which we have a set of shared normative expectations regarding such ties—and functional integration—the issue of mutual interdependence.

Normative Regulation

In arguments that run parallel to those seen in writing on the life course, discussions of the family in historical perspective conclude that family life has become less regulated by societal norms and community control. It has become a more self-contained social group, setting its own norms in its own private sphere (Aries 1977, Gadlin 1977). Burgess and Locke (1945) labeled this general historical change as one from institution to companionship, a steady moving away from the nineteenth-century situation in which relationships between husbands and wives, parents and children "were based on socially sanctioned mutual obligations that transcended personal affection and sentiment [Hareven 1977, p. 64]."

In addition to discussions of a general decline in the normative regulation of family life, we find mention of "cultural lags" similar to those discussed in the section on individual lives. Again, we find family relationships, across generations, that are new and have caught us somewhat off guard. In some cases, we do not even have language to fit the new phenomena. We are stuck with the peculiar phrase "adult children." It is even harder to talk about "adult grandchildren." Or how about "ex-granddaughter-in-law"? The awkwardness in part reflects the fact that not until recently was it common for the lives of grandchildren and grandparents to have so much overlap; grandparents may have grandchildren who are married, and possibly parents themselves. We also lack terminology to cover new relationships created by divorce chains and family reconstitution (Bohannan 1970). Cherlin (1978) has argued that remarriage is an incomplete institution, presenting few clear normative guidelines.

Research on grandparenthood finds little consensus on the rights and duties of this role (Robertson 1977). We therefore are not surprised to find a great variety in styles of grandparenting (Neugarten and Weinstein 1964, Wood and Robertson 1976).

In all of these discussions there is recognition that for some family status relations, there may not be an active, viable role relationship. The meaning of the relationship is not culturally, structurally provided; it has to be created. Turner (1970) writes

> The two major functions of assistance and companionship are generally accepted . . . but the manner in which they are to be carried out and the proper limits on their exercises are not clearly defined in American culture. Because of the privacy barrier and because of the lack of clear definition, the implementation of these functions is . . . a precarious matter. . . . *Each family must develop a somewhat idiosyncratic pattern* [pp. 424–425; emphasis added].

In general discussion of social roles and role relationships, it would be argued that the less that cultural consensus regarding expectations can be found in connection with a given status, the more variance one will find in the enactment of the role in society (Komarovsky 1973). However, if we look at the actual, concrete relationship between role partners, we find more stable, agreed-on expectations than what is found on a societal, structural level. The role partners, striving for a minimal sense of structure and predictability in their interactions, will negotiate a set of mutual expectations in a process of role negotiation (Goslin 1969, Strauss 1978, Turner 1970). These authors would suggest that in a complex, pluralistic society, a Durkheimian–Parsonian view of social roles as structural givens is not a useful one, since so many normative expectations emerge from social interaction in particular social subdomains.

As was discussed in the introduction, it has been common to see the careers of parents and children as an orderly progression of stages and to assume that "each stage in the parent–child cycle involves a distinctive set of prescribed age roles [Turner 1970, p. 407]." Again, this assumption appears problematic, particularly in relationships between adults.

If we combine these arguments with those presented in the discussion of the structuring of individual lives, we reach the generalization that adults in the family now confront each other in relationships for which there is no historical precedence and minimal cultural guidance, while they individually find themselves in life stages that also have few culturally shared expectations attached to them. In sum, we have a case of individuals in ambiguous life stages interacting in ambiguous relationships. Hess and Waring (1978) conclude that as a result of all these factors, intergenerational relationships among adults are anomic: "Clear normative prescriptions are lacking at the same time the range of choices of what to do is expanding [p. 242]."

I would argue that adults in intergenerational relationships may find themselves in a situation demanding negotiation skills previously not called for, since they to a large extent have to create the structure and meaning of their bond.

As researchers, we need to focus on the interactional level, where an ongoing process of socialization is taking place: "an interactional confrontation between developing individuals, in which those factors leading to continuity and those leading to change are negotiated [Bengtson and Black 1973, p. 209]." Thus, we are seeing socialization not primarily as the transmission of expectations, but the creation of them. Similarly, the negotiation of stability and change involves the creation of family culture as well as the conveyance and restatement of it.

It has been common to argue that as a result of the loosening of societal control and the greater emphasis on individual needs and sentiment, family relationships have become more discretionary in nature. Rosenmayr (1978), Schneider (1968), and Turner (1970) suggest that we see kinship status as a latent potential, for which real, viable relationships may or may not develop. Paine (1969) and Hess and Waring (1978) suggest that kin relations have become more like friendship relations. As a result, there is some concern about their stability and strength. Hess and Waring (1978) ask, "Are voluntary intergenerational ties viable?" This brings us to the issue of functional integration. Do intergenerational ties today, particularly among adults, have a sufficient basis of interdependence and reciprocity to maintain them? Or, as Kreps (1977) asks: "Will there be sufficient mutuality of interest to hold them together?"

New Patterns of Interdependence

INTERGENERATIONAL EXCHANGES

The family is no longer a corporate economic unit, with economic cooperation as the cornerstone of family cohesion and solidarity. Individual choices, such as decisions about when to marry and leave the family of orientation, used to be guided by the needs of the corporate unit. The twentieth century has freed generations from many of these economic interdependencies, through child labor laws, the mobility of an urban–industrial society, and a new emphasis on intragenerational economic cooperation with two spouses working. Social security, pension plans, and social welfare programs have made the old increasingly economically independent of the young (Modell *et al.* 1978). Thus, within less than a century, we have moved away from a situation in which economic factors were the center of intergenerational organization, often spanning three generations of workers, to one in which only one generation out of three or four may be active in the economic sphere.

Instead of economic cooperation, emotional bonds now form the basis of family solidarity and cohesion (Smelser and Halpern 1978). Using Turner's (1970) terminology, we can say that there has been a shift from task bonds to response bonds. Bettelheim (1961) describes "a balance sheet of interaction that is no longer economic, but largely emotional [p. 78]." Emotional needs of individual members have taken on new significance for the establishment and maintenance of relationships. However, two decades of research on intergenerational relations among adults have suggested that exchanges across generations still involve tangible and intangible resources, and that balance sheets of interaction have become exceedingly complex, spanning several generations and multiple domains of exchange. We have found that family members still share goods and services (Adams 1968, Troll and Bengtson 1979, Hill *et al.* 1970) and serve one another as reliable sources of continuing human contact, emotional support, and confidant relationships (Babchuk 1978,

Shanas 1979, Shulman 1975, Townsend 1957). This research has also pointed to the uniqueness of the parent–child bond (Lopata 1978). Even though economic interdependence is less important as a basis of inter-generational cohesion now than was the case in the nineteenth century, we need to keep in mind that parents and children start out with a prolonged period of economic dependency. Furthermore, although we may have witnessed a general decline in normative structuring of family bonds, the first 2 decades of the parent–child relationship do have in-stitutionalized as well as informal norms regulating it. Several authors have argued that in a society in which the norm of reciprocity (Gouldner 1960) is generally accepted, the early years of the parent–child bond set a powerful precedent: an "implicit bargain" (Sussman 1976). Rosenmayr (1978) discusses the importance of viewing reciprocity across more than two generations—as a continuous chain:

> The chain of intergenerational bonds reaches a balance—if at all—only if viewed over more than two elements in the chain. The exchange that occurs within the family is never reciprocal with identical individuals, but functions as a transfer process. Parents who have yielded benefits to their children are not "adequately" rewarded by these children, the latter instead yield benefits to their offspring. . . . The exchange between generations is chronically one-sided, only transfer as an infinite process creates a balance.

Hill *et al.* (1970) have also discussed the necessity of viewing patterns of reciprocity across more than contiguous generations. Furthermore, these authors illustrate how the balancing of exchanges occurs across spheres of exchange. For example, the middle generation may provide material support to the young, in exchange for contact and emotional support.

In summary, despite the reduced importance of economic cooperation as a basis of intergenerational cohesion, it still represents one aspect of a complex, multifaceted matrix of exchange, the balancing of which may occur across generations and across resource domains.

In addition to creating bonds through a complex web of contact and exchange, shaped by the needs and resources of several generations, families also write their own unique histories.

BONDS OF SHARED EXPERIENCE AND MEANINGS

The long life overlaps between adult family members present new opportunities for the formation of what Turner (1970) calls *crescive bonds*. His term refers to bonds that evolve over time, through the continuing interaction among particular individuals. These bonds are primarily shaped not by social norms or roles, but by the accumulation of common experience: "As two or more persons have a succession of shared experiences, they develop a wider and more firmly rooted common conception of reality—setting them apart from others, who have not been part of the same experience circle [Turner 1970, p. 82]."

Often, family rituals will reiterate and reinforce this experience circle. Through informal chats, toasts, and speeches on family occasions, such as holidays, weddings, and funerals, past events are relived and their shared meaning restated.

Families not only engage in a continuous writing and rewriting of their family history and individual biographies, they also interpret changes in the wider society. Elder (1974), more than any other recent scholar, has shown how effects of historical events, such as the Great Depression, are filtered through a family lens. Thus, the personal meaning of societal change often depends on family meanings: concrete effects on family resources and interpretations of what took place. Elder (1974) demonstrates how economic deprivation altered family life and individual orientations. In my own interviews with elderly Pennsylvania residents, I found a number of accounts that reflected little perceived impact of the Depression, again because of family factors. One respondent said: "The Depression? No . . . it was rough on other people . . . it didn't change things for us. Things were always rough for us. We didn't have nothing to lose."

The new overlap between adult lives in the family provides a longer shared history and a greater fund of common life experiences, through the sharing of adult roles, living through historical events, and encountering individual and family events. It also presents the task of creating a common base of expectations, values, and orientations in the face of multiple life trajectories and a changing society. This ongoing negotiation will be discussed shortly, but first, I would like to explore some additional ways in which families mediate between individuals and the wider social context.

TRANSCENDING AGE GROUP AND COHORT

In discussions of both youth and the elderly, strong concerns have been voiced about increasing age segregation in our society. The Panel on Youth of the President's Science Advisory Committee (1973) discussed problems resulting from the increased age homogeneity of nuclear families and educational settings, suggesting that as a result of these new institutional arrangements, young people are being deprived of valuable socialization experiences. Lofland (1968), in a discussion of "youth ghettos," adds the concern that by spatially separating members of different age groups, we encourage the development of age stereotypes. In their study of aging in three industrial societies, Shanas *et al.* (1968) point to age segregation as a key problem.

In bringing generations together, families offer unique opportunities to transcend a single age group and cohort. The family gives some freedom from age-related norms regulating individual behavior. As is discussed by Parsons (1955) for the young nuclear family, intergenerational bonds give license to break away from norms regarding age-appropriate behavior. The presence of children allows adults of all ages to do "childish" things: skip, fly kites, be curious, giggle. Children also allow sanctioned opportunities for touching, often a problem for the old in a culture that allows physical intimacy in a few narrowly defined interactional contexts. Furthermore, the family offers a unique life-span reflector: members observe others in life phases that they themselves have moved through—or anticipate the joys and sorrows of phases yet to come, by watching significant others who are currently going through them.

By bringing together members of different age groups, families also serve a cohort-bridging function, through which historical contrasts produced by a changing society are reduced and softened.

For example, in interviews with middle-aged parents in the early 1970s, I found many of them discussing how the 1960s would have been much more frightening and incomprehensible without having their children to interpret the events. Similarly, I found that mothers reported changes in views of sex roles as a result of discussions with children who were in college. Among the 120 middle-aged mothers I studied, nearly three-fourths reported instances of influence from their young-adult children, usually on questions regarding a changing social context: work, life-style, and social issues.

Recently, the importance of adult offspring as mediators to bureaucracies for elderly parents has been given considerable attention (Shanas and Sussman 1977). What is becoming clear is that when we move our focus from the young nuclear family to relations among adult family members, the family serves bridge functions that go far beyond the instrumental functions outlined in Parsons and Bales (1955). Long-term, intense, and complex intergenerational relationships form interactional bridges between age groups and cohorts, thus modifying contrasts and conflicts that exist in society at large, softening them through interwoven lives, shared meanings, personal knowledge, and long-term reciprocities. On the other hand, there are times at which historical cohort contrasts are not dealt with. Such instances give us opportunities to study mechanisms used by families to maintain and protect highly valued bonds.

THE MAINTENANCE OF TIES

The investment individuals have in maintaining family ties is reflected in the lengths to which they will go in the protection of such ties. In some of my own work on intergenerational dyads, I have been struck by the *interaction management*, to use Goffman's term, that family members use to maintain their relationships.

One mechanism used is what I would call the creation of demilitarized zones: silent, mutually understood pacts regarding what not to talk about. One grandson said about his relationship with his grandfather: "We are careful what we talk about. We don't want to rock the boat [Hagestad 1978]."

A second mechanism used by families is to pick one's fights (Troll 1972). Issues that really matter and that might constitute a threat to the relationship if conflicting views fully emerge are avoided, but steam is let out over something that does not matter so much.

A third mechanism is the manipulation of interactional settings. Many of the people we interviewed could tell you exactly the conditions under which they got along smoothly with certain family members: alone, engaging in a particular shared activity, or with other people as buffers. There is evidence that in some families, grandchildren serve as buffers, making interactions more smooth between parents and grandparents.

SUMMARY

There is rich evidence that for most people, young and old, family bonds across generations meet a multitude of needs, some of them new. As Hess and Waring (1978) conclude after taking a probing look at intergenerational relations among adults: "A need for community, intimacy, and solidarity based on kinship remains a compelling impulse of the human spirit [p. 268]." There is still strong evidence that the majority of Americans do not want to give up the security and the obligations described so well by Robert Frost in "The Death of the Hired Man":

> Home is the place where, when you have to go there,
> they have to take you in.

However, many questions remain to be asked regarding the nature and quality of intergenerational relations. The researcher is faced with ample uncharted territory, both in terms of substantive issues and methodological strategies.

NEEDED EXPLORATIONS

Substantive Issues

In large part because of arguments presented by sociologists in the first part of this century (e.g., Ogburn and Nimkoff 1955, Parsons 1949, 1955), it became a political task to address the relative isolation of the old in American families. That became the Hydra that Shanas, and many researchers like her, set out to fight. I believe we now should consider the beast slain. More than a decade of large-scale research shows high rates of contact as well as considerable exchange of goods and services between parents and adult offspring (Adams 1968, 1970, Hill *et al.* 1970, Litwak 1960, Shanas 1979, Shanas *et al.* 1968, Sussman 1965, 1976). It is now time to turn to some questions raised by their work.

THE PROBLEM OF ASYMMETRY

Because much of this research has focused on the old, we may have a problem of asymmetry. Often, we ask if the old have seen one child over a given period of time. We do not ask about all children. Thus, if we started in the middle generation and asked how many of them had seen a parent, we would get a less cohesive picture, with lower rates of contact. Methodological implication of the asymmetry problem are raised below. It would seem that the time has come to do a study of children who do not keep in touch, individuals who tend to operate outside intergenerational webs. So far, they have had little chance of being recruited in surveys of intergenerational relations. We also need to focus attention on interpersonal resources and support among childless adults.

THE CONSEQUENCES OF HAVING
NO DIRECT VERTICAL LINKAGES

Practically all of our research on the modified extended family is research on ascendant–descendant kin, or the ties between parents and children (Gibson 1972, Lopata 1978). What happens to the intergenerational bonds of individuals who do not have a ready-made link: those who never married and those who married but do not have children? It has been found that unmarried individuals have significantly stronger sibling ties than those who marry (Adams 1967, Shanas 1979). Some preliminary work I have done in Pennsylvania indicates that, in many cases, the close sibling is also single. Thus, we may have a strong horizontal tie, but no strong vertical tie.

In my exploratory research, I found that many single older adults had built their own long-term reciprocities. Over their adult years, they had extended significant assistance to siblings and their offspring. Sometimes, they would remark, "You know, she is really like a daughter to me." One might hypothesize that the most vulnerable older person may be widowed and childless. His, more likely her, long-term reciprocity investment has been in a horizontal tie, one which may not last through old age. The extent to which single and childless elderly feel intergenerationally integrated needs to be addressed, as does the extent and nature of family substitution among such individuals.

Currently, we have a unique opportunity to investigate some of these questions empirically, as birth cohorts with extremely high rates of childlessness move into old age. Among married women born between 1900 and 1910, nearly one-fifth remained childless (Glick 1977). These cohorts also had a somewhat higher proportion who never married. Research on the cohorts born early in this century could also shed light on the frequency with which the middle generation may find themselves facing obligations not only to parents but also to aging aunts and uncles with no children. This brings me to a third question in need of exploration, namely, conditions under which kin obligations constitute overload and strain.

THE COSTS OF KIN-KEEPING

I would think that it is precisely because of the uniqueness of direct vertical ties, those from parent to child, that the middle generation may find themselves in a stressful bridge position. They have two generations who have claims on their time and resources, material and emotional, precisely because they find themselves in two intergenerational role relationships for which there are some cultural norms regarding obligations. Furthermore, they often serve as facilitators of wider intergenerational contact, such as that between grandparents and grandchildren (Robertson 1975). If, as is often argued, women are the kin-keepers (e.g., Bahr 1976) one would expect more signs of kin-keeping overload among women than men in middle age. On the other hand, women are more likely to be involved in complex intergenerational exchanges across multiple domains. Thus, although they may feel pressured by kin-keeping tasks, they may also be receiving more emotional support, particularly from daughters, than are their husbands and brothers (Aldous and Hill 1965, Babchuk 1979, Hagestad and Snow 1977, Troll and Bengtson 1979).

QUALITY OF TIES AMONG ADULTS

The quality of bonds between adult men and women and their parents deserves much more attention than it has received so far. First, there are some peculiar voids in the parent–child literature. After the voluminous research on early childhood and adolescence, we seem to drop the relationship and not pick it up until the parents are old and the children are middle-aged. The quality of ties, and especially patterns of reciprocal socialization, in the 20–30-year period between these two stages is grossly underexamined. Ironically, we know more about the influence of infant and mother than we do about this process between adults in their 30s and their parents.

Second, research on grandparents also has distinct limitations. For example, the ages of grandparents and their grandchildren are seldom dealt with as important variables. It seems quite possible that we would have a dramatically different picture of the grandparent role if we studied it in relationships between adults. As an example, I would like to mention the common generalization that the grandparent role is essentially a maternal one. In a recent study of young adults and their grandparents in the Chicago area (Hagestad 1978, Hagestad and McDonald 1979), we found striking differences between grandfathers and grandmothers, with the former being significantly more instrumental in their relationship with grandchildren. Grandfathers also distinguished much more between grandsons and granddaughters than did grandmothers. Finally, these data suggest that there is considerable more cohort-bridging between grandchildren and grandmothers than between young people and their grandfathers. In relationships with granddaughters who were young adults in the 1970s, grandfathers appeared to have difficulties overcoming gaps created by cultural change, particularly the redefinition of male and female roles.

These contrasts between current cohorts of grandmothers and grandfathers suggest a number of research questions in the general area of socialization. As was already noted, socialization has increasingly been seen as an ongoing process of negotiation.

INTERGENERATIONAL PATTERNS OF SOCIALIZATION

As was mentioned earlier, discussions of socialization have shifted from an emphasis on transmission to an emphasis on negotiation. This shift has in part occurred because we have come to see socialization as a process through which shared expectations are created. Thus, literature on socialization also reflects a change from a unidirectional to a reciprocal view. We now view the process as one in which both sides undergo change, and recent literature on parents and children has asked how the young socialize their elders.

We need to study the creation and maintenance of family ways and family themes in multigenerational families. In what areas of life are such themes likely to show up? Who are the main negotiators? One would expect that these family cores of orientations and behaviors represent influence from the old to the young. Now that we have recognized influence from the young to the old, we need to ask what life domains are open to such influence. In other words, what types of attitudes and orientations are open to cohort-bridging? Are some members of the older generations more open to influence from the young? As was discussed above, some of my own work suggests that women, because of their long-term, complex interaction with the young, may be more likely to receive influence from their children and grandchildren than are men. Where is lineage influence stronger than cohort influences from nonfamily peers? How are differential influences from maternal and paternal lineages sorted out? Work by Bengtson (1975) and Thomas (1973) indicates that value domains vary significantly in the extent to which one is likely to observe family or cohort influence. How idiosyncratic are families in their ways of negotiating and the products of their negotiations? If each family creates its own unique themes, research on value similarity and expectations across generations cannot use a set of standard measures of values or attitudes, the way we have tended to go about asking such research questions. To sum up: We need to ask questions about the process and products of intergenerational socialization as well as factors associated with them. What types of family constellations, structural and interpersonal, produce the greatest similarities and the strongest family themes across generations? Under what conditions do we see reciprocal influence between young and old?

Another set of questions necessitating an awareness of unique family constellations deals with ways in which family members' lives interconnect.

THE INTERWEAVING OF LIVES

Neither traditional life course analysis nor a family development perspective can capture the intimate interconnections of life matrices in the family. Through such interconnections, across several generations, each family lineage creates its own set of tasks, its own constellations of opportunity and constraints. Indeed, we may want to rewrite Burgess' and Locke's (1953) classic definition of the family as a unit of interacting personalities to be a unit of interacting lives, because the interrelatedness of life careers across generations transcends personal knowledge and face-to-face interaction. This interweaving can be approached in several

areas: patterns of timing, constellations of tangible and intangible resources, and developmental tasks.

Elder (1977) suggests that we study family transmission of timetables.
For example, we may ask if there are some families who for generations
are early or late in such role transitions as job entry, marriage, and
parenthood. Do we see evidence of family norms that are likely to produce nonmodal patterns, compared with general cohort patterns?

Recent work has presented a strong argument for the need to study
life events in a total life context (Danish *et al.* 1980). We now need to
take the logical next step and recognize that people's coping abilities and
available supports are influenced not only by a constellation of events
but also by a family constellation of events, affecting individuals and
their significant others. For example, an older woman might become
widowed at a time when her son has had a heart attack and another child
is going through a divorce. These events not only spell out an accumulation of traumas, but they may also disrupt support systems that
could otherwise be counted on.

An experience of overload among the middle-aged is likely to be
produced by factors in three or four generations: the needs of one or
two generations of elderly, the needs and resources of the young, and
the number of available siblings in the middle generations as well as their
tangible and intangible resources (Smith 1981).

We know very little about how family members produce developmental milieux for one another. How are the identity issues of adolescence affected by parents who seem to be struggling with similar issues
in their own lives—or by watching a loved grandparent slip into senility?
Does the presence of a young adult grandson who is seeking guidance
in educational and occupational decisions make a difference in a grandfather's retirement adjustment? How are aged individuals affected by
surviving their children? Does it make a difference in individual adjustment to become a grandparent at 36 compared with 60?

How is the sense of accomplishment and freedom, often described
in studies of middle-aged women, affected by having all one's children
experiencing marital breakups? How many parents are currently in that
situation? The study of divorce and its aftermath offers opportunities to
examine a host of questions regarding the strength of bonds among adults,
patterns of socialization, intergenerational exchanges, and the interconnections of lives.

CONSEQUENCES OF MARITAL INSTABILITY

The dramatic increase in divorce will not only disrupt horizontal ties,
namely those between husband and wife; it may also threaten vertical

ties. Between parents and young children, there is usually a legal custody arrangement, by which one parent (the mother in 90% of cases) will have much more contact with the child than the other parent. What happens to the parent–child bond when the child of the divorcing couple is an adult? Do adult offspring feel that they have to take sides when their parents part? Are patterns of help and support affected by late-life divorce? Does the divorced middle-aged and old person receive more or less support from kin? And what happens to the parents of divorce, a totally neglected category? What is the effect on parents' sense of backing and security when their adult children divorce and are likely to face economic strain—particularly daughters (Hagestad and Smyer 1980, Smyer 1979)? With the disruption of a focal horizontal dyad, will we see a new strenthening of vertical bonds? Much has been made of the strength of the mother–daughter bond, stressing women as kin-keepers. Will the increased disruption of marital bonds increase the importance of this bond for family stability and continuity?

How many families will have two generations of divorced individuals? Will the increase in divorce lead to more multigenerational homes, because of the financial difficulties in maintaining an independent household? Are we, as Hess and Waring (1978) suggest, going to see a refilling of the nest in more families in the future?

What happens to grandparent–grandchild ties following divorce? If preliminary research is correct, generations of children may be deprived of the opportunity to really know one set of grandparents: those on the noncustodial side. This would seem to confirm what has been suggested by studies of grandparents: that the amount of contact, maybe even the quality of the relationship, between grandparents and grandchildren depends on the mediation of the middle generation, the parents. However, we would expect the age of grandchildren to be an important variable here. Will grandparents take more initiative in maintaining the tie when the link is not operating properly? Remarriage and reconstituted families present a new set of intergenerational questions not dealt with yet (Furstenberg 1979). Are children in these families more likely to see their step-grandparents than their noncustodial grandparents? What happens to family reunions when the father in the middle generation remarried a woman the same age as his daughter and has a second family the same age as his grandchildren? Will widowhood following a second marriage be more or less traumatic than when it occurs in a first marriage? Do noncustodial parents who have a distant relationship with their children following the divorce reestablish contact as they grow older and the children mature?

Many of the questions regarding the effects of divorce and family reconstitution will start with a very simple query: How common is a certain family pattern? This brings us to methodological issues, such as choosing a unit of analysis, sampling, and research design.

Methodological Challenges

DEVELOPING FAMILY PARAMETERS

Those of us who have done research on three-generational families are often asked about the representativeness of our samples (see Bytheway 1977). The answer has to be that we do not know because we have minimal baseline knowledge about family constellations across more than two generations. Indeed, even our knowledge about parents and children is limited by our tendency to use either individual or households as units of analysis. Thus, we have a fundamental lack of parameter estimates for family patterns beyond young nuclear families. For example, we do not really know how common four- and five-generation families are, and how many of them have members of all generations living in the same community. We do not know the frequency of families with several childless elderly members, or how many relatives they have in the younger generations. We have no estimates of how often several or all siblings in the same family have experienced divorce.

For a number of purposes, we could use demographic data on families, not individuals or households. We need information on family age structures across several generations, their population pyramids, and dependency ratios. These types of data, which could be grouped into main types or patterns, are important for predictions regarding supports, housing, and needed services. They would also give researchers an anchoring, enabling them to judge the representativeness of intergenerational samples or make decisions about how to draw stratified samples to pursue questions regarding specific subgroups of families or individuals. Studies of fertility patterns have already pointed to the necessity of considering generational factors within the family in addition to cohort trends. Preston (1976) compares number of children among women in their forties at two points in recent history: 1940 and 1970. He points out that while the average number of children rose during that period, women were having, on the average, half as many children as were in their families of orientation. Preston concludes that while members of the recent cohort had higher birth rates than their parents' cohort, they nevertheless had much lower fertility than the parents themselves. To my knowledge, no large-scale research has been done on fertility patterns across three or more family generations.

In work relating to family patterns of dependency and support, we still rely mostly on cohort data. (For examples, see Gelfand *et al.* 1978,

Treas 1977.) That is clearly a good place to start, but we have to be aware of the limitations and the possible fallacies in such data. Often, predictions regarding needed support and services are based on manipulations of cohort parameters. Modal three-generational pictures are created by starting with a given birth cohort as the first, or oldest, "generation," assuming the second "generation" to be born 25 years or so later, and the third roughly 50 years after the first. Thus, generational constellations are constructed by piling three composite cohort pictures on top of each other, translating cohort averages into generational averages. We now have produced a new twist to ecological fallacy.

An approach building on cohort parameters has three distinct shortcomings: First, it disregards the fact that people do not file into generation by cohort. Second, it does not allow for the existence of family norms, resources, and constraints, which influence lineage patterns of timing, family size, and flow of support. Such family factors would be reflected in rate of generational turnover and the age composition of lineages. Finally, it does not allow us to examine what I, for lack of a better term, will call family bundles, within and across generations. For example, we know the proportion of a given cohort who never married, or married but remained childless. We do not know how often these individuals had siblings or other members of their generation who took the same life-course route. For questions regarding support systems in old age, that is important information. In my pilot study of never-married Pennsylvania residents born between 1900 and 1910, I found the majority of them to have at least one sibling who remained single. Nearly half the respondents were living with a sibling at the time of the interview. In one case, a spry, alert woman in her seventies gave a moving account of how she had felt compelled to move into a nursing home with her sister, who had suffered a massive stroke. The two of them had lived together all their adult lives and considered themselves inseparable.

Family bundles may not occur only in life-course patterns, produced by family norms and resource constellations; they may also be found in an accumulation of life events and clusters of trauma. For example, family membership may bring multiple cases of serious illness or death of significant others. These bundles could in part be due to genetic factors, such as vulnerability to degenerative disease and certain types of cancer. However, there is also the possibility that they reflect vulnerabilities created by accumulated family stress through which psychological and material resources have been overtaxed. In an ongoing study of divorce in middle age (Hagestad and Smyer, 1980) we have been struck by how many of our respondents relate stories of multiple family traumas. In addition to experiencing divorce, several of them have families in which a parent and a sibling died and they themselves or a sibling had life-threatening illness—all over the span of 5 years or less. In this study, as so often is the case, we have no way of knowing the extent to which our respondents are part of an extreme group, coming from families with unusually high stress levels, because we do not know how common such bundles are in the general population of middled-aged men and women.

When I suggest that we initiate population surveys in which we gather data on family lineage units across several generations, I am certainly not arguing that we abandon cohort data on aggregates of individuals. Rather, the two approaches would complement one another. Cohort comparisons would suggest phenomena to look for in family generations. Data on age structures of families, by main patterns, would give us an indication of the utility of creating composite cohort picture of the type discussed above. What we know from existing research is that if we select families with three generations of adults, we are likely to end up with considerable age (and therefore cohort) overlap between the two older generations. In surveys on three-generation families—one in California by V. Bengtson, one in Minnesota headed by R. Hill, and one in Chicago by G. Hagestad and colleagues—age ranges within the two older generations are 30 years or more, and a substantial age overlap exists across these two groups (e.g., both grandparents and parents in their sixties). Because of sex differences in age at marriage, the area of age/cohort overlap between the two generational groups is likely to consist of grandmothers in the oldest generation and fathers in the middle generation.

SAMPLING

The extent to which the age and cohort overlap between generational groups presents a headache to researchers depends on their questions. If the research problem deals with the relative influence of age, cohort, family stage, and generational membership, it should be a major concern. In the best of all worlds, such research would want to work with carefully stratified samples, matching respondents on age, family stage, and generational status. However, as is evident in an exchange between Bytheway (1977) and Hill (1977) recently, meeting such criteria is easier said than done. For one thing, common problems of refusals are magnified in multigenerational survey research, since the researcher needs the cooperation of several family members. In the three studies cited above, a minimum of four volunteers from each family had to be recruited.

UNIT OF ANALYSIS

How can one obtain data on family lineages across several generations? Normally, we would rely on methodological individualism in the data-gathering phase. In other words, we would use individuals in probability samples from the general population as informants about their maternal and paternal lineages, much the way anthropologists have done in their work on kinship (e.g., Schneider 1968). A new set of challenges faces the researcher in the data analysis phase of work on generations. We are still in the early stages of developing data analysis schemes for the creation of family systems data. All too often, we end up treating the generations as aggregates, and the family, the interlocking of members in relationships, gets lost in the computer.

In most of the data analysis from the Minnesota study, grandparents, parents, and grandchildren are treated as unrelated groups, a data treatment that obviated the cost and effort of locating families in which members of all three generations agreed to be interviewed.

Bengtson (1975) has done some innovative work, comparing the relative impact of family and cohort membership, but so far this study has not presented an overall discussion with family across all three generations as the unit of analysis.

In the study from Chicago, we are focusing much of our analysis on dyads. Each of the four family members were interviewed about two of the others. Thus we have reciprocal data across intergenerational pairs, such as grandfather and grandson. This strategy has its headaches, too. First, there is the question of whether one can combine dyad pictures into family lineage pictures— a problem that gets into central questions of reduction and emergence in social research. Second, we are faced with the asymmetry problem, mentioned earlier in this chapter. Since we are interested in the degree of consensus and shared perceptions in different intergenerational dyads, we need to keep in mind that in some pairs, the two partners have quite different frames of reference. For a grandchild, there is only one paternal grandfather; for the grandfather, the grandson he is discussing may be one of 20 grandchildren. We would therefore expect greater detail in description and better recall in the grandchild's report than in that from the grandparent, quite aside from possible age-related differences between the two. In addition to the asymmetry problem, researchers with an interest in the extent of shared views across generations in the same family soon realize that standard statistical procedures for measuring agreement, such as measures of association, do not serve this purpose.

SUMMARY

Drawing on a variety of sources, this chapter examines the interweaving of human lives through intergenerational ties in the family. It argues that the family group offers a unique opportunity for contact, support, and influence across age groups and cohorts. One factor that makes such ties unique is their unprecedented duration, the long-term overlapping of lives, especially among adults. This duration is a promise and a challenge. It creates the potential for a sense of continuity and stability, based on a pool of common experiences, shared meanings, and long-term reciprocities in a rapidly changing world. The challenge is to find a common base of expectations in the face of changing individuals who have different life vulnerabilities and strengths and different historical experiences and who find themselves in relationships for which our culture presents few normative guidelines. Thus, individuals in such relationships need to engage in an ongoing negotiation of the basis of their bond: its intensity, its scope, and its expectations. Furthermore, multiple lives in multiple relationships within family generations are interwoven in a web of unrecognized interdependencies, a complex matrix of lives spanning several generations. Given the range of possible life combinations and interweaving, it is increasingly hard to speak of typical intergenerational patterns on a societal, aggregate level.

Families are cultural units in which norms, symbols, and meanings are created; they bring together members of different cohorts in their own unique combinations; and they create their own clusters of life patterns, crises, and resources. Therefore, they have to be studied as units in their own right, through a social psychological approach to family lineage groups. Such a social psychology of intergenerational bonds holds a rich promise of new insights into the shaping of individual lives, the mediation of social change, and the maintenance of long-term primary ties. It also challenges us as researchers to explore new avenues in terms of the questions we ask, the level on which we ask them, and the tools with which we pursue them.

REFERENCES

Adams, B. N. (1967) Interactional theory and the social network. *Sociometry* 30: 64–78.

Adams, B. N. (1968) *Kinship in an Urban Setting.* Chicago: Markham Publishing Company.

Adams, B. N. (1970) Isolation, function, and beyond. American kinship in the 1960's *Journal of Marriage and the Family* 32:575–597.

Aldous, J. (1978a) *Family Careers: Developmental Change in Families.* New York: John Wiley.

Aldous, J. (1978b) Family Careers Over Time. Address given at the University of Notre Dame, September 22, 1978.

Aldous, J., and Hill, R. (1965) Social cohesion, lineage type, and intergenerational transmission. *Social Forces* 43:471–482.

Ankarloo, B. (1978) Marriage and family formation. Pp. 113–133 in T. K. Hareven, ed., *Transitions.* New York: Academic Press.

Aries, P. (1977) The family and the city. *Daedalus* 106:227–235.

Babchuk, N. (1978) Aging and primary relations. *Aging and Human Development* 9:137–151.

Babchuk, N. (1979) Primary Ties of Older Men. Paper presented at the annual meetings of the Gerontological Society, Washington, D.C.

Bahr, H. M. (1976) The kinship role. Pp. 61–79 in I. F. Nye, H. M. Bahr, S. J. Bahr, J. E. Carlson, V. Gecas, S. McLaughlin, and W. L. Slocum, eds., *Role Structure and Analysis of the Family*. Beverly Hills, Calif.: Sage Publications.

Baltes, P. B. (1979) Life-span developmental psychology: Some converging observations on history and theory. Pp. 255–279 in P. B. Baltes and O. G. Brim, eds., *Life-Span Development and Behavior*, Vol. 2. New York: Academic Press.

Bengtson, V. L. (1975) Generation and family effects in value socialization. *American Sociological Review* 40:358–371.

Bengston, V. L., and Black, O. (1973) Intergenerational relations: Continuities in socialization. Pp. 208–235 in P. Baltes and W. Schaie, eds., *Life-Span Developmental Psychology*. New York: Academic Press.

Bengtson, V. L., and Cutler, N. (1976) Generations and intergenerational relations: Perspectives on age groups and social change. Pp. 130–159 in *Handbook on Aging and the Social Sciences*. New York: Van Nostrand Reinhold Company.

Bengtson, V. L., Olander, E., and Haddad, A. (1976) 'The generation gap' and aging family members: Toward a conceptual model. Pp. 237–263 in J. F. Gubrium, ed., *Time, Self, and Roles in Old Age*. New York: Behavioral Publications.

Bernard, J. (1975) *Women, Wives, Mothers*. Chicago: Aldine.

Bettelheim, B. (1961) The problem of generations. In E. H. Erikson, ed., *Youth: Change and Challenge*. New York: Basic Books.

Blau, Z. S. (1973) *Old Age in a Changing Society*. New York: New View Points.

Bohannan, P. (1970) Divorce chains, households of remarriage, and multiple divorcers. Pp. 127–139 in P. Bohannan, ed., *Divorce and After*. New York: Doubleday.

Bronfenbrenner, U. (1961) The changing American child: A speculative analysis. *Journal of Social Issues* 17:6–18.

Bureau of the Census (1978) *Social and Economic Characteristics of the Older Population*. Current Population Reports, Special Studies Series P-23, No. 85. Washington, D.C.: U.S. Department of Commerce.

Bureau of the Census (1979a) *Divorce, Child Custody and Child Support*, by R. Sanders, and G. B. Spanier, Current Population Reports, Series P-23, No. 84, Washington, D.C.: U.S. Department of Commerce.

Bureau of the Census (1979b) *Prospective Trends in the Size and Structure of the Elderly Population, Impact of Mortality Trends, and Some Implications* by J. S. Siegel, Current Population Reports, Special Studies Series P-23, No. 78, Washington, D.C.: U.S. Department of Commerce.

Burgess, E. W., and Locke, H. J. (1945) *The Family: From Institution to Companionship*. New York: American Book Company.

Burgess, E. W., and Locke, H. (1953) *The Family*. New York: American Book Company.

Bytheway, B. (1977) Problems of representation in the three generation family study. *Journal of Marriage and the Family* 39:243–250.

Cain, L. D., Jr. (1964) Life course and social structure. Chapter 8 in R. F. Faris, ed., *Handbook of Modern Sociology*. Chicago: Rand McNally.

Cherlin, A. (1978) Remarriage as an incomplete institution. *American Journal of Sociology* 84:634–650.

Clausen, J. A. (1972) The life course of individuals. Pp. 457–514 in M. W. Riley, M.

Johnson, and A. Foner, eds., *Aging and Society: A Sociology of Age Stratification*, Vol. 3. New York: Russell Sage Foundation.

Danish, S. J., Smyer, M. A., and Nowak, C. A. (1980) Developmental intervention: Enhancing life-event processes. In P. B. Baltes, and O. G. Brim, Jr., eds., *Life-Span Development and Behavior*, Vol. 3. New York: Academic Press.

Demos, J. and Boocock, S. S., eds., (1978) *Turning Points. American Journal of Sociology* Supplement.

Davis, K. (1949) *Human Society*. New York: Macmillan.

Duvall, E. (1957) *Family Development*. Philadelphia, Penn.: Lippincott.

Elder, G. H., Jr. (1974) *Children of the Great Depression*. Chicago: University of Chicago Press.

Elder, G. H., Jr. (1975) Age differentiation and the life course. In A. Inkeles, J. Coleman, and N. Smelser, eds., *Annual Review of Sociology I*. Palo Alto, Calif.: Annual Reviews.

Elder, G. H., Jr. (1977) Family history and life course. *Journal of Family History* 2:279–303.

Elder, G. H., Jr. (1978) Approaches to social change and the family. Pp. 1–38 in J. Demos and S. S. Boocock, eds., *Transitions*. American Journal of Sociology Supplement.

Furstenberg, F. F. (1979) Recycling the family: Perspectives for a neglected family form. *Marriage and Family Review* 21(3):12–22.

Gadlin, H. (1977) Private lives and public order: A critical view of the history of intimate relations in the United States. Pp. 33–72 in G. Levinger, and H. Raush, eds., *Close Relationships: Perspectives on the Meaning of Intimacy*. Amherst, Mass.: University of Massachusetts Press.

Gelfand, D. E., Olsen, J. K., and Block, M. R. (1978) Two generations of elderly in the changing American family: Implications for service. *The Family Coordinator* 27:395–403.

Gibson, G. (1972) Kin family network: Overheralded structure in past conceptualizations of family functioning. *Journal of Marriage and the Family* 34:13–23.

Glick, P. C. (1977) Updating the family life cycle. *Journal of Marriage and the Family* 39:5–13.

Glick, P. C. (1979) *The Future of the American Family*. Current Population Reports, Series P-23, No. 78, Washington, D.C.: U.S. Department of Commerce.

Goslin, D. A. (1969) Introduction. Pp. 1–21 in D. A. Goslin, ed., *Handbook of Socialization Theory and Research*. Chicago: Rand McNally.

Gouldner, A. W. (1960) The norm of reciprocity: A preliminary statement. *American Sociological Review* 25:161–178.

Guemple, D. L. (1969) Human resource management: The dilemma of the aging Eskimo. *Sociological Symposium* 2:59–74.

Hagestad, G. O. (1978) Patterns of Communication and Influence between Grandparents and Grandchildren in a Changing Society. Paper presented at the 9th World Congress of Sociology, Uppsala, Sweden.

Hagestad, G. O., Cohler, B., and Neugarten, B. L. (in preparation). *The Vertical Bond: Communication and Influence in Three Generations of Urban Families*. Monograph.

Hagestad, G. O., and McDonald, M. (1979) What Grandfather Knows Best. Paper presented at the annual meetings of the Gerontological Society, Washington, D.C.

Hagestad, G. O., and Smyer, M. A. (1980) Midlife Divorce: Implications for Parent-Caring. Paper presented at the annual meeting of the American Orthopsychiatric Association, Toronto, Canada.

Hagestad, G. O., and Snow, R. (1977) Young Adult Offspring as Interpersonal Resources in Middle Age. Paper presented at the annual meeting of the Gerontological Society, San Francisco, California.

Hareven, T. K. (1977) Family time and historical time. *Daedalus* 106:57-70.
Hareven, T. K., ed. (1978) *Transitions: The Family and the Life Course in Historical Perspective.* New York: Academic Press.
Hess, B. B., and Waring, J. M. (1978) Parent and child in later life: Rethinking the relationship. Pp. 241-273 in R. M. Lerner and G. B. Spanier, eds., *Child Influences on Marital and Family Interaction.* New York: Academic Press.
Hill, R. (1977) Response to Bytheway. *Journal of Marriage and the Family* 39:251-252.
Hill, R., Foote, N., Aldous, J., Carlson, R., and MacDonald, R. (1970) *Family Development in Three Generations.* Cambridge, Mass.: Schenkman.
Hill, R., and Mattessich, P. (1979) Family theory and life-span development. In P. Baltes and O. Brim, Jr., eds., *Life-Span Development and Behavior,* Vol. II. New York: Academic Press.
Hill, R., and Rodgers, R. H. (1964) The developmental approach. Pp. 171-211 in H. T. Christensen, ed., *Handbook of Marriage and the Family.* Chicago: Rand McNally and Company.
Hogan, D. P. (1978) The variable order of events in the life cycle course. *American Sociological Review* 43:573-586.
Komarovsky, M. (1973) Some problems in role analysis *American Sociological Review* 38:649-662.
Kreps, J. (1977) Intergenerational transfers and the bureaucracy. Pp. 21-34 in E. Shanas and M. Sussman, eds., *Family, Bureaucracy, and the Elderly.* Durham, N.C.: Duke University Press.
Landecker, W. S. (1951) Types of integration and their measurement. *American Journal of Sociology* 56:332-340.
Laslett, P. (1977) *Family Life and Illicit Love in Earlier Generations.* Cambridge, England: Cambridge University Press.
Linton, R. A. (1936) *The Study of Man.* New York: Appleton-Century-Crofts.
Litwak, E. (1960) Geographical mobility and extended family cohesion. *American Sociological Review* 25:385-394.
Lofland, J. (1968) The youth ghetto. *Journal of Higher Education* 39:121-143.
Lopata, H. Z. (1966) The life cycle of the social role of the housewife. *Sociology and Social Research* 51:5-22.
Lopata, H. Z. (1978) Contributions of extended families to the support systems of metropolitan area widows: Limitations of the modified kin network. *Journal of Marriage and the Family* 40:355-375.
Metropolitan Life Insurance Company (1977) Current patterns of dependency. *Statistical Bulletin* 58:10-11.
Modell, J., Fustenberg, F. F., Jr., and Hershberg, T. (1976) Social change and transitions to adulthood in historical perspective. *Journal of Family History* 1:7-32.
Modell, J., Furstenberg, F. F.,Jr. and Strong, D. (1978) The timing of marriage in the transition to adulthood: Continuity and change, 1860-1975. Pp. 120-150 in J. Demos and S. S. Boocock, eds., *Turning Points. American Journal of Sociology* 84, Supplement.
Neugarten, B. L. (1974) Age groups in American society and the rise of the young-old. *Annals of the American Academy* 415:187-198.
Neugarten, B. L., and Hagestad, G. O. (1976) Age and the life course. Pp. 35-55 in R. Binstock, and E. Shanas, eds., *Handbook of Aging and the Social Sciences.* New York: Van Nostrand Reinhold Company.
Neugarten, B. L., and Moore, J. W. (1968) The changing age status system. Pp. 5-21 in B. L. Neugarten, ed., *Middle Age and Aging.* Chicago: University of Chicago Press.

Neugarten, B. L., and Weinstein, K. K. (1964) The changing American grandparent. *Journal of Marriage and the Family* 26:199–204.

Norton, A. J. (1980) The influence of divorce on traditional life cycle measures. *Journal of Marriage and the Family* 42:63–69.

Nye, I. F. (1974) Emerging and declining roles. *Journal of Marriage and the Family* 36:238–245.

Ogburn, W. F., and Nimkoff, M. F. (1955) *Technology and the Changing Family.* Boston: Houghton Mifflin.

Oppenheimer, V. K. (1974) The life cycle squeeze: The interaction of men's occupational and family life cycles. *Demography* 11:227–245.

Paine, R. (1969) In search of friendship: An exploratory analysis in "middle class" culture. *Man* 4:505–524.

Panel on Youth, President's Science Advisory Committee. (1973) *Youth: Transition to Adulthood.* Washington, D.C.: U.S. Government Printing Office.

Parsons, T. (1942) Age and sex in the social structure *American Sociological Review* 7:604–616.

Parsons, T. (1949) The social structure of the family. Pp. 173–201 in R. Anshen, ed., *The Family: Its Function and Destiny.* New York: Harper.

Parsons, T., and Bales, R. F. (1955) *Family: Socialization and Interaction Process.* New York: The Free Press.

Preston, S. H. (1976) Family sizes of children and family sizes of women. *Demography* 13:105–114.

Riley, M. W., Johnson, M. E., and Foner, A., eds. (1972) *Aging and Society, A sociology of Age Stratification,* Vol. 3. New York: Russell Sage Foundation.

Riley, M. W., and Waring, J. (1976) Age and aging. In R. K. Merton and R. Nisbet, eds., *Contemporary Social Problems,* 4th ed. New York: Harcourt Brace Jovanovich.

Robertson, J. F. (1975) Interaction in three-generation families, parents as mediators: Toward a theoretical perspective. *International Journal of Aging and Human Development* 103–109.

Robertson, J. F. (1977) Grandmotherhood: A study of role conceptions. *Journal of Marriage and Family* 39:165–174.

Rodgers, R. (1973) *Family Interaction and Transaction: The Developmental Approach.* Englewood Cliffs, N.J.: Prentice-Hall.

Rosenmayr, L. (1978) A View of Multigenerational Relations in the Family. Paper presented at the 9th World Congress of Sociology, Uppsala, Sweden.

Rosow, I. (1974) *Socialization to Old Age.* Berkeley: University of California Press.

Rosow, I. (1976) Status and role change through the life span. Pp. 457–482 in R. E. Binstock and E. Shanas, eds., *Handbook of Aging and the Social Sciences.* New York: Van Nostrand Reinhold Company.

Rosow, I. (1978) What is a cohort and why? *Human Development* 21:65–75.

Roth, J. A. (1963) *Timetables.* Indianapolis, Ind.: Bobbs-Merrill.

Ryder, N. (1965) The cohort as a concept in the study of social change. *American Sociological Review* 30:843–861.

Schneider, D. M. (1968) *American Kinship: A Cultural Account.* Englewood Cliffs, N.J.: Prentice-Hall.

Shanas, E. (1979) Social myth as hypothesis: The case of the family relations of old people. *Gerontologist* 19:3–9.

Shanas, E., and Sussman, M. B. (1977) *Family Bureaucracy and the Elderly.* Durham, N.C.: Duke University Press.

Shanas, E., Townsend, P., Wedderburn, D., Friis, H., Milhøj, P., and Stehouwer, J. (1968) *Old People in Three Industrial Societies.* New York and London: Atherton and Routledge Kegan Paul.

Shulman, N. (1975) Life cycle variations in patterns of close friendship. *Journal of Marriage and the Family* 37:813–821.

Silverstone, B., and Hyman, H. K. (1976) *You and Your Aging Parents.* New York: Pantheon Books.

Smelser, N. J., and Halpern, S. (1978) The historical triangulation of family, economy, and education. Pp. 288–315 in J. Demos and J. Boocock, eds., *Turning Points. American Journal of Sociology* 84, Supplement.

Smith, L. (1981) Meeting Filial Responsibility Demands in Middle Age. Unpublished M.A. Thesis, Pennsylvania State University.

Smyer, M. A. (1979) Divorce and Family Support in Later Life: Emerging Trends and Issues. Paper presented at the annual meetings of the American Psychological Association, New York.

Strauss, A. (1978) *Negotiations.* San Francisco, Calif.: Jossey-Bass.

Streib, G. F. (1972) Older families and their troubles: Familial and social responses. *Family Coordinator* 21:5–19.

Sussman, M. B. (1965) Relationships of adult children with their parents in the United States. Pp. 62–92 in E. Shanas and G. Streib, eds., *Social Structure and the Family: Generational Relations.* Englewood Cliffs, N.J.: Prentice-Hall.

Sussman, M. B. (1976) The family life of old people. Pp. 218–243 in R. H. Binstock, and E. Shanas, eds., *Handbook of Aging and the Social Sciences.* New York: Van Nostrand Reinhold.

Thomas, L. E. (1973) Correspondence Between Related Generations on a Range of Attitudes and Values: An Attempt to Map the Domain. Paper presented at the annual meeting of the American Psychological Association, Toronto, Canada.

Townsend, P. (1957) *The Family Life of Old People.* New York: Free Press of Glencoe.

Treas, J. (1977) Family support systems for the aged. *The Gerontologist* 17:486–491.

Troll, L. E. (1970) Issues in the study of generations. *Aging and Human Development* 1:199–218.

Troll, L. E. (1971) The family of later life: A decade review. *Journal of Marriage and the Family* 33:263–290.

Troll, L. E. (1972) Is parent–child conflict what we mean by the generation gap? *The Family Coordinator* 21:347–349.

Troll, L. E., and Bengtson, V. L. (1979) Generations in the family. Pp. 127–161 in W. R. Burr, R. Hill, F. I. Nye, and I. L. Reiss, *Contemporary Theories about the Family*, Vol. 1. New York: The Free Press.

Troll, L. E., Miller, S. J., and Atchley, R. C. (1979) *Families in Later Life.* Belmont, Calif.: Wadsworth Publishing Company.

Turner, R. H. (1970) *Family Interaction.* New York: John Wiley and Sons, Inc.

Uhlenberg, P. R. (1974) Cohort variations in family life cycle experiences of United States females. *Journal of Marriage and the Family* 36:284–292.

Uhlenberg, P. R. (1978) Changing configurations of the life course. Pp. 65–95 in T. Hareven, ed., *Transitions.* New York: Academic Press.

Wood, L., and Robertson, J. F. (1976) The significance of grandparenthood. Pp. 278–304 in J. F. Gubrium, ed., *Time, Role, and Self in Old Age.* New York: Human Sciences Press.

chapter 3

The Changing Nature of Life-Cycle Squeezes: Implications for the Socioeconomic Position of the Elderly

VALERIE KINCADE OPPENHEIMER

For some time now, I have been investigating sources of pressures within families for additional income. For convenience's sake, I have referred to these pressures as economic squeezes, defined as those situations in which the cost of achieving or maintaining an accustomed or desired life-style exceeds the income currently available to do so. According to this definition, economic squeezes have three essential components: (1) the family's (or individual's) life-style aspirations; (2) the cost of these aspirations; and (3) the income currently available to achieve the aspirations, given their costs. If these three components are in balance, then by definition no economic squeeze exists. However, if one or more of the components is or becomes seriously out of balance with the others, then economic squeeze situations should be observable. These, in turn, may produce behavioral responses such as marriage and/ or birth postponement, reduced fertility, wives' going out to work, and so on. A variety of family behaviors could be profitably investigated using an economic squeeze approach. My general strategy has been to investigate structural sources[1] of such squeezes, how these vary among

[1] "Structural sources of economic pressure" means pressures that arise out of the basic social and economic organization of a society. This organization is assumed to be relatively stable, though changes will, of course, be occurring over time. Hence, stability is partly a function of the time frame employed.

47

Copyright © 1981 by Academic Press, Inc.
All rights of reproduction in any form reserved.
ISBN 0-12-040003-0 0-12-040023-5(p)

different population groups, and changes in the three components over time that may result in an intensification or amelioration of squeezes.[2] In my own empirical research, I have focused particularly on women's economic behavior. This has been an especially interesting problem because the employment of married women outside the home was relatively uncommon in the United States during the first 40 years of the twentieth century. However, since 1940, the extent of married women's labor force participation has increased enormously, as has its relationship to the family cycle (Oppenheimer 1970). In trying to explain wives' employment, it makes sense to use husbands' incomes as a means of analyzing how the income component can affect the severity of squeezes and thereby influence wives' economic behavior. However, one need not limit one's consideration to just the husband's income; one could analyze squeezes including all possible forms of family income in the income component. Furthermore, although I have focused on an economic squeeze model as a device for analyzing wives' changing economic roles, such a model has considerable potential value for exploring a wide range of socioeconomic and demographic behaviors and situations. The theoretical implications that can be drawn from this model for the socioeconomic situation of the elderly are the focus of this chapter.

LIFE-CYCLE SQUEEZES

Starting with the notion of economic squeeze situations, this chapter focuses on "life-cycle squeezes"—squeezes that are a product of the interaction of rather basic life-cycle patterns associated with family and work behavior. These age-related patterns can vary among subgroups in the population. They also change over time—either temporarily, due to transitory fluctuations in a variety of conditions affecting income, costs, or aspirations, or, more permanently, in response to long-run secular changes. Nevertheless, life-cycle patterns have, I think, sufficient stability to be counted as social phenomena worth investigating.[3]

[2] For earlier publications dealing with these issues, see Oppenheimer 1979, 1976, and 1974. The problem is dealt with in considerable length in a forthcoming book, tentatively titled: *Work and the Family: A Study in Social Demography*. Academic Press.

[3] The term *life-cycle squeeze* was coined by Wilensky who uses it to refer to what I have called the *second life-cycle squeeze* (Wilensky 1963, Estes and Wilensky 1978). For other discussions of various life-cycle squeezes, their determinants and consequences, whether or not they always employ this term, see Gove *et al.* 1973, Heberle 1941, Easterlin 1973, 1978, Schorr 1966.

The basic notion of a life-cycle squeeze is that age-related changes in men's incomes are not always well synchronized with the cost of the life-style aspirations associated with different stages of the family cycle. Three major life-cycle squeezes are important to distinguish in modern American society. The first occurs early in adulthood when young couples are trying to set up households suitable for child-rearing. A squeeze situation may arise at this stage because, on the one hand, setting up a household often involves considerable capital investments in housing and consumer durables. On the other hand, young men's earnings, regardless of occupation, are usually very low and also frequently rather unstable (Oppenheimer 1974, 1976, 1979). This is to be expected, of course, since this is a period in the life-cycle when extensive human capital investments are often still being made and are being paid for at least partly by foregone earnings (Becker 1975). It is also a time when young men are vulnerable because of low seniority and lack of experience and when considerable occupational experimentation occurs.

The second identifiable squeeze period in contemporary American society arises when there are adolescent children in the home. Evidence on the cost of children indicates that it rises with the number and ages of the children, although there may be some economies of scale (Oppenheimer 1974, 1976, Espenshade 1973, U.S. Bureau of Labor Statistics 1968). Hence, costs peak when children are the most expensive to maintain but not yet making major financial contributions on their own, that is, during adolescence. Yet the earnings of fathers do not increase so rapidly at this stage of their career cycle—compared with younger men with younger, less expensive children at the same point in time or compared with their own past (Oppenheimer 1976).

At least one additional life-cycle squeeze seems intrinsic to the socioeconomic organization of contemporary Western society. This is the economic squeeze that often occurs when a husband and his wife, if she has been working, retire from market employment. This is the third squeeze at old age when income may drop precipitously because of the loss of earnings. The severity of the third squeeze should, like that of the first two, vary markedly among socioeconomic groups. As a consequence, it should engender different types of behavioral modifications, not only at the time of its occurrence but also earlier, in anticipation of the potential economic difficulties of the postretirement period.

In sum, it seems reasonable to posit that three life-cycle squeeze periods are a common feature of modern American society, though their nature may vary among different subgroups in the population. Furthermore, the severity of these squeezes should not only affect wives' economic behavior, but also encourage other types of adjustments to such

economic pressure points, if only because wives' economic behavior is
one among several related responses to economic stress. For example,
the employment of young women in response to the first squeeze, or in
anticipation of it, may have demographic as well as economic implications
if it is accompanied by postponed marriage and postponed or foregone
childbearing. And the employment of women over 40 years old may
affect the nature of their interaction with elderly relatives and the type
of assistance it is possible to supply.

Even though the three life-cycle squeezes have been defined in terms
of three different stages in the life-cycle of couples (or individuals), it
is important to emphasize that the impact of each of these squeezes and
how individuals and families attempt to deal with them not only affect
the couples involved but others as well, both within and outside the
family and kin group. Moreover, the severity of any one squeeze and
the ways devised to cope with it may impinge on later squeezes or the
different squeeze stages other family members are concurrently experiencing. For example, in considering three-generation families, the ability of the middle-generation to provide aid (monetary or otherwise) to
an older generation in the third squeeze period may be reduced if the
middle generation is experiencing a particularly severe second squeeze[4]
at the same time. This, in turn, may also impair the middle generation's
ability to help provide for its own third squeeze period. Some of these
possibilities are discussed later in this chapter. However, the point to
be made here is that the three squeezes and how people deal with them
are interrelated, not only in terms of how the squeezes are experienced
in sequence over the life course of a particular couple (or individual) but
also in terms of their simultaneous interrelationship to family and kin
who are concurrently at different points in the life-cycle, including different squeeze periods. Hence, whether one's major interest is in people
in life-cycle stages as temporally distinct as the marriage and family
formation period on one hand, and old age, on the other, such a model
argues for the analytical importance of simultaneously dealing with the
problem of families at various stages of the family cycle. Focusing too
exclusively on the elderly per se may not be the best way of fully
understanding their social and economic positions and role in the context
of the family and kin as important social groups. In addition, an understanding of how various factors change the nature and severity of earlier
squeezes ought to help us understand how the character of the third
squeeze may change over time.

---

[4] Or the reverse may be the case. The ability of the parents to prepare their children
for a similar or higher station in life can be impaired by extensive obligations to elderly
kin.

Occupational Differences in Life-Cycle Squeezes

Though the three life-cycle squeezes may be intrinsic to contemporary American society, there is also evidence that the nature and severity of the squeezes varies among subgroups in the population. As a consequence, the behavioral responses to actual or potential squeeze situations may also vary. In this chapter I focus on one major source of group differences in life-cycle squeezes: occupational differences in the age pattern of men's earnings—the age-earnings profile. Rather marked occupational differences in the age-earnings profiles of men are observable and seem to be of long standing in American society. This suggests that certain types of family strategies may have developed as an adaptation to these earnings patterns as well as to other long-standing socioeconomic and demographic features of society. Finally, some of the basic conditions to which these strategies represent an adaptive response have themselves been changing over time which in turn has permitted, encouraged, or "forced" certain changes in the type of family strategies that have been commonly observed in the past.

A useful way of conceptualizing the problem of variations in the economic position of men over the life course is in terms of age, period, and cohort effects. This is really an essential approach in any analysis of change involving age-related variables.[5] Age effects are those factors in which an individual's age plays an important role. For example, I have been discussing two types of age effects: family cycles and career cycles. In the case of career cycles, age-related patterns of human capital investment and the returns from these investments are one important example of a career-cycle effect producing age differentials in earnings.

If we can think of age effects as relatively stable patterns associated with age, cohort and period effects provide the highly dynamic elements that temporarily, and sometimes permanently, modify the age effect. Period effects refer to the influence of the historical period on the behavior or characteristics of respondents at the time the observations are being made. For example, cyclical fluctuations in the business cycle may affect earnings, the birth rate, the marriage rate, and so on in a particular year. Cohort effects are those that are tied to a particular birth cohort and that continue to influence its characteristics over time.

Given this conceptualization of the problem, I will use well-known occupational differences in cross-sectional age-earnings profiles as a very

[5] A basic problem is that age, period, and cohort effects are often confounded. For example, a comparison of different age groups at one point in time will confound age with cohort effects, since there is no way to determine whether age differentials in a variable—fertility, for example—reflect solely an age effect or intercohort differences. For a discussion of these problems see Ryder 1965, Schaie 1967, Mason et al. 1973, Glenn 1976.

TABLE 3.1
Median 1959 and 1969 Earnings of White Men, by Type of Occupation and Age
(in 1969 Dollars)[a,b]

	1959			1969		
	White collar		Blue	White collar		Blue
Age	Upper	Lower	collar	Upper	Lower	collar[c]
			Median earnings[d]			
18–24	3997	2908	2929	5113	3286	3202
25–34	8289	6422	6160	10,387	8256	7682
35–44	10,400	7364	6724	13,358	9612	8425
45–54	10,537	6952	6250	13,811	9485	8109
55–64	10,197	6387	5516	12,537	8418	7161
			Ratio of peak median earnings to those at different ages			
18–24	2.64	2.53	2.30	2.70	2.93	2.63
25–34	1.27	1.15	1.09	1.33	1.16	1.10
35–44	1.01	1.00	1.00	1.03	1.00	1.00
45–54	1.00	1.06	1.08	1.00	1.01	1.04
55–64	1.03	1.15	1.22	1.10	1.14	1.18

[a] From subsamples of white men, aged 18–64, in nonfarm occupations, drawn from the original
1/1000 sample from the Public Use Samples of the *1960 Census of Population and Housing* and from a
3/1000 sample from the Public Use Samples of the *1970 Census of Population and Housing, County
Group, 5% Sample.*
[b] For the basis of this classification system see Oppenheimer 1974 and 1977.
[c] Includes service occupations.
[d] The age group at which the highest, or peak, median occurred in each occupational group is
underlined.

rough indicator of occupational differences in the age or career-cycle
effect on earnings. These are occupational differences in age patterns
of earnings that have been repeatedly observed in numerous cross-sectional snapshots.[6] Examples of these patterns are presented in Table 3.1.
It is useful to distinguish three general types of occupations or occupational careers in this respect. First, there are relatively high-level
white-collar occupations. A number of professional, managerial, and
sales occupations fall into this group. The age pattern of earnings in
these occupations is usually characterized by a steep age-earnings profile—very low earnings in youth with rapid and sharp rises in earnings

[6] This approach, of course, ignores the role of period and cohort factors affecting
differences among occupations and over time in the actual experience of different cohorts,
but it is relatively persistent patterns that I wish to deal with in this chapter. For a
discussion of additional roles of period and cohort factors, see Oppenheimer (1976, 1979).
Also ignored in this chapter are how the earnings patterns that individuals actually experience over their life course are affected by occupational mobility.

for successive age groups and a "peak" at relatively older ages; earnings for older workers remain relatively high. In contrast to this well-known pattern for higher-paying occupations, the age-earnings profile of men in most blue-collar occupations is typically rather flat. Although the earnings of young adult men in the 18–24 group are quite low, earnings rise considerably for the 25–34 age group and increase slightly more to peak for men in the relatively young 35–44 age group. The earnings of older men—particularly those in the 55–64 age group—are often quite poor relative to those of younger men.

Between these two extremes are a number of white-collar occupations that, on one hand, are usually characterized by a relatively flat age-earnings profile, often resembling that of craft workers. On the other hand, the families of men in such occupations tend to have relatively high life-style aspirations, especially with regard to the education of their children. As a result, they may often be caught in a "lower white-collar squeeze" if they attempt to rely on the husband as the major, if not exclusive, source of income (Oppenheimer 1979).

In sum, men who remain in high-level occupations or move into them can expect considerable increases in income over most of the career cycle. Those in occupations with low peak earnings have been in the unenviable position of expecting relatively modest increases in income owing purely to the occupationally related career-cycle factor. Furthermore, since median incomes peak at a relatively early age, men in such occupations risk earlier deterioration of income unless other factors intervene (rising real earnings in occupations, overtime pay, upward mobility, etc.). In short, age-related shifts alone seem to bring very different changes in earnings among these occupational groups.

ADAPTIVE FAMILY STRATEGIES

To the extent that these contrasting occupational age–earnings profiles reflect a certain historical stability, they are indicative of some of the different kinds of constraints under which families must function. Combined with other exogenous factors, these constraints tend, I believe, to lead to a number of different adaptive behavioral responses that I term *family strategies.*

Some Basic Assumptions

When socioeconomic subgroups or whole societies regularly encounter a variety of circumstances over which they have little or no control, it is to be expected that certain types of adaptive strategies might evolve over time. In this instance, it is family strategies that are of interest. Moreover, owing to the nature of these exogenous factors, operating singly or together, some strategies have a greater adaptive value than others. Second, not only might these strategies develop in response to certain external constraints, but also any particular strategy that is adopted can be expected to impose its own additional constraints on behavior. Third, one might expect all strategies to have certain vulnerabilities. By looking at the vulnerabilities of different strategies as well as the constraints they impose, we may achieve a better understanding of both the sources of stress that lead to change and the direction this change is likely to take.

I will roughly define an adaptive family strategy as one that on average promotes the replacement (or even the multiplication) of the family unit over generations at the same or a higher socioeconomic level.[7] In doing so, it safeguards the family against crises by either preventing them or in some way ameliorating their negative consequences. As a corollary, such an adaptive strategy promotes the maintenance or improvement of the customary level of living of the family unit and its individual members over the "life" of the unit. Moreover, the notion of adaptive family strategies does not imply that the utility of some individuals in the family unit or of the family unit as a whole is maximized. If anything at all is being maximized in this formulation, it is the chances that a particular type of unit will reproduce itself. Hence, it is in a sense evolutionary success that is being maximized rather than utility or happiness or the chances for the development of a just society. Nevertheless, if certain strategies involve considerable "disutilities" for various (or all) family members, then they will be a source of considerable built-in stress that may lead to behavioral modifications, depending on changes in the nature of the various exogenous constraints. Hence, the structurally based dis-

---

[7] The concept of adaptive family strategies under discussion here has a number of similarities to Louise Tilly's notion of family strategies. She argues that "the concept of strategies implies objectives. What objective did the families examined pursue? Quite simply, they strove to promote nuclear family survival over the cycle of family expansion and contraction. . . . It was this goal which informed family responses to economic structure and change, to political intervention in or impact on their adjustment to economic realities. How families pursued this goal differed, then, according to both structural and historical factors [1979a, p. 139]." The main difference in our approaches seems to be that I place somewhat greater stress not just on survival but on the maintenance or improvement of socioeconomic status within and across generations and, in addition, on the notion of strategies as evolved cultural patterns as well as possibly rational strategies of individual families. However, I am not at all sure that my approach to the problem of family strategies is not also implied in Tilly's formulation (see also Tilly 1979b).

utilities of any strategy provide one of the sources of vulnerability to which it is subject.

The notion of an adaptive strategy does not necessarily imply that all or even most of the individuals conforming to such a strategy have individualistically planned it in a relationalistic, decision-making process. Rather, I am using the concept more in the way that biologists do when they discuss biologically adaptive behaviors in an evolutionary sense of the term. The behavioral pattern may be adaptive and hence persist as a cultural pattern because of its "success." Many individuals, however, may follow a given strategy for entirely nonrational reasons or rational reasons unconnected with the adaptive value of the strategy. In other words, the notion of an "adaptive (or nonadaptive) family strategy" is the observer's evaluation of a behavioral pattern and does not necessarily imply that the actors involved perceive of it as a strategy, although some, or many, may do so, of course.

The rough typology of family strategies that follows makes no pretense of being exhaustive and hence applicable to all societies at whatever point in time we may observe them. Indeed, it represents a very preliminary effort to develop a particular kind of analytical approach. A major limitation on its generalizability, for example, is that it will focus only on those societies in which wage and salary earnings of men are the norm rather than a nonmarket–based subsistence economic activity. Nevertheless, the discussion should have historical relevance in European and American societies, although it will only be possible to deal somewhat superficially with the historical implications of this conceptual approach.

In general, my conception of family strategies is that they are common behavioral or cultural patterns that provide a template, so to speak, on which individuals model their behavior. Some of these patterned behaviors may be largely a result of normative constraints, but this is not necessarily true. Hence, it is useful to treat the role of social norms as an empirical issue rather than an essential prime ingredient of all family strategies.

At its heart, this analysis of different types of family strategies focuses on problems intrinsic to age-related patterns of both men's earnings and family behavior. For one thing, as we have seen, the earnings of young men are usually relatively (and absolutely) very low. This is one major factor in the first life-cycle squeeze, in that low earnings make it difficult to set up an independent adult existence at a young age. If such an independent adult existence also involves marriage, the establishment of a household suitable for child-rearing, and the start of childbearing, on the basis of the young men's earnings alone, the difficulties are compounded still further. On the other hand, too extensive a postponement of marriage and children also entails certain risks. One is that such delays may result in the heaviest child-care costs occurring when the career-cycle effect on husband's earnings is no longer positive but may actually be neutral or even negative. In short, too prolonged a postponement of family formation in response to the low earnings of youth increases the risk of intensifying the second squeeze, other things being equal. Hence, it is of great interest how family strategies deal with the competing risks of the various life-cycle squeezes and how these risks change over time.

Let us consider, in turn, the situation of men who spend much of their working lives in high-level white-collar occupations, blue-collar occupations, and lower-level white-collar occupations. What has typically been the nature of at least some of the constraints that affect their family life, and what are some examples of the types of strategies that may represent a more or less successful adaptation to these varying constraints? Furthermore, how have these constraints and the types of strategies appropriate to them changed over time? Although most of my own research has been concerned with the exploration of the first two life-cycle squeezes, I will attempt in this discussion to suggest the relevance of the analysis of constraints and adaptive strategies to the third squeeze. Here, however, the discussion often becomes rather speculative.

HIGHER-LEVEL WHITE-COLLAR WORKERS

Ignoring period and cohort effects for the moment, the age-earnings profile of men who spend much of their working lives in high-level white-collar occupations is likely to be quite steep—rising sharply from very low earnings in youth to a peak at a relatively late age with little or no decline in earnings for the older age groups. Hence, this is a career trajectory for which, on the basis of husbands' age-earnings profiles alone, the most economically vulnerable point occurs early in adult life. What types of family strategies might be adaptive for such a career trajectory, keeping in mind that, by definition, one goal of an adaptive family strategy is to maintain or improve on socioeconomic status within and across generations?

The type of adaptive strategy that might evolve as a necessary concomitant of a career trajectory typical of high-level occupations[8] should

---

[8] Of course, such a career trajectory may be almost impossible to achieve without also following certain behavioral strategies. Hence, the career trajectory is not necessarily an exogenous variable.

depend, in part, on whether the man's family of procreation is usually entirely dependent on his occupationally derived income or whether and when additional sources of income are also available, such as from the wife or children or in the form of transfer payments of one sort or another.[9]

If men going into such higher-level, late-peaking occupations are expected to be the sole support of their families, then marriage postponement is one obvious adaptive mechanism for dealing with the low-earnings period of youth. This not only postpones the heavy economic responsibilities involved in setting up a household until a man is more established (thus reducing the severity of the first squeeze) but also leads to a postponement of the second squeeze period until the husband's earnings are at their peak. What effect such marriage postponement by the man may have on completed fertility is another matter, however, and depends on a number of other factors as well. One is the age of the wife he ultimately marries and another is the use and effectiveness of marital fertility control measures. If little marital fertility control is exercised and the man marries a relatively young woman, then the couple's ultimate surviving family size might be quite large—just how large being partly a result of fecundity levels and the mortality risks faced by the husband, wife, and children at the time period in question. On the other hand, if marriage postponement for such men also involves a relatively late marriage for their wives as well, then completed family size may well be reduced. Finally, if marital fertility can be reliably controlled, then ultimate family size might be quite moderate, whatever the age of the wife at marriage. Furthermore, one might anticipate that "high-quality" children—the kind necessary to maintain status over generations—

---

[9] By and large, it seems rather unlikely that such children can make much of a socioeconomic contribution to their families of orientation while they are still children or even as young adults. This is because, if socioeconomic status is to be maintained across generations, then the children, like their fathers, will typically be involved in a career trajectory for which their relative income position in youth is very low. Moreover, since such careers often involve extensive investments in human capital before the actual start of work in a given occupation, the age at actual entry into the job may well be relatively late. Hence, the cost of raising children to achieve or assume a comparable socioeconomic status to that of their parents will be higher for parents at a high socioeconomic level, and these costs may extend into early adulthood. This will vary, however, depending on the extent to which the locus of human–capital investments is weighted more toward on-the-job training or toward formal schooling, for which there may be higher direct costs, which are more likely to be borne by the parents. Moreover, even if the parents do not plan to make extensive investments in human capital for all their children—for example, for girls— the relative economic contribution such children could make by working would be correspondingly very low because of their low level of human–capital attainments. In the case of daughters, moreover, there are indications that the cost of seeing that they marry well is not necessarily minor for high socioeconomic groups.

are expensive and that except for families that are very wealthy indeed, the cost of such children promotes family size restrictions by couples in higher-level socioeconomic groups.

Historical as well as contemporary examples of some of these strategies are not hard to find. Banks's fascinating description of the Victorian middle classes is actually a description of two of the strategies described (Banks 1954). As he points out, for these socioeconomic groups, it was considered imperative for newly married couples to set themselves up in a style appropriate to their social station in life. However, the only way of accomplishing this feat was to postpone marriage until the husband's income was sufficiently high (Banks 1954, Chapter III). In this way, the difficulties of the first life–cycle squeeze could be avoided. In fact, Banks essentially captures the logic of my life-cycle squeeze argument as follows:

> This calculation of life chances, so typical of the middle classes at this time, was directly related to the career structure of the older professions. At twenty-two or twenty-five years of age a middle-class lawyer or doctor could predict with a fair degree of accuracy what sums of money the men of his profession were likely to earn at various periods of their lives. Unlike the working man whose maximum was reached early on in adulthood, the middle-class man could anticipate a steady series of income increases in the future stretching out before him at least until middle age; and at the same time he need not expect to be susceptible on the income side to considerable fluctuations of an adverse kind due to the cycle of trade. Postponement of marriage, therefore, was a judicious policy, for a higher income would almost certainly be his in the course of time [1954, p. 199].

Banks goes on to point out, however, that while marriage postponement was a long-accepted family strategy, historically it had not also involved a limitation of births within marriage as well. However, he argues that the cost of children rose considerably in the latter half of the nineteenth century—especially due to the need to educate them more extensively as well as more expensively (Banks 1954, Chapter XI). Thus, during the nineteenth century, numerous changes led to the expansion of different types of occupational opportunities for middle-class sons. However, this expansion in opportunities had its price, creating considerable increases in the cost of children to parents. For example, the abolition of patronage in the civil service provided newly affluent middle-class families with the opportunity to place their sons in positions previously barred to them because of their lower socioeconomic backgrounds. To take advantage of the new opportunities, however, their sons had to receive the education of a gentleman and also survive through several lean years early in the occupational career (Banks 1954, p. 183).

In the lower middle classes, there was also a drive to extend the education of sons in order for them to obtain commercial posts. Hence, rather than putting their sons into an apprenticeship for a trade, such families maintained them through a more extensive schooling (Banks 1954, pp. 192–193). It thus became increasingly difficult to maintain the high standard of living to which the middle classes had become accustomed, prepare their children for a similar or higher station in life, and have large families as well. For these reasons, among others, Banks argues that in the English middle classes control of marital fertility became more common later in the nineteenth century (Banks 1954, Chapter XII).

As far as twentieth-century patterns are concerned, I have recently been engaged in research on white couples in the 1960 and 1970 Public Use Samples, which indicates that a later timing of marriage and childbearing by higher as compared with lower occupational groups persists, although there was a considerable decline in the age at marriage and family formation since the late nineteenth and early twentieth centuries (Oppenheimer, forthcoming). However, more recent data from the Current Population Survey indicate that, after a decline in the age difference of mothers at the birth of their first child for white-collar as compared with blue-collar mothers, it has again increased. Thus, in the case of the cohorts of women born in 1935–1939, the proportion of wives who had their first child by age 25 was 75% for wives of white-collar men and 82% for the wives of blue-collar men—a difference of only 7 points. In the case of the cohorts of 1945–1949, the percentage having their first child by age 25 was only 59% for white-collar wives compared with 80% for blue-collar wives—a 21 point difference (U.S. Bureau of the Census 1978, Table 12). How much these differences are due to differences in age at marriage and how much due to the timing of the first birth after marriage in unclear.[10] All this supports the notion that upper white-collar couples' major point of vulnerability is early in adult life, making their age at marriage and at the birth of the first child particularly sensitive to shifts in the economic climate.

In sum, given the age–earnings profile of men in these occupations, strategies that involve postponement of marriage and childbearing have considerable adaptive value. However, this is partly because of the favorable age effect on earnings for middle-aged and older men in these occupations. Postponed childbearing not only eases the severity of the

[10] Another family strategy that men going into late-peaking occupations might adopt would involve medium-young ages at marriage and at the birth of the first child. Such a strategy would be made possible by the availability of sources of income other than the husband or wife—income transfers from parents, the G.I. bill, subsidized housing, student loans and scholarships, etc.

second squeeze. In fact, it probably leads to a more optimal timing of the second squeeze. Another advantage of postponed fertility, at least, is that it facilitates the employment of wives during the first squeeze period, thus helping to ease its severity.

We might briefly consider the situation of such couples when they reach their sixties and older. What types of strategies were likely to have emerged to deal with this life-cycle stage? By and large, such couples ought to be able to avoid the third squeeze altogether, although their position is not entirely invulnerable. Since earnings peak late for men in high-level occupational groups, such couples (or one survivor, at least) should enter old age with a much greater economic advantage than other socioeconomic groups. And especially in the past, for many the high income of the middle and later working years has been derived from the ownership or part ownership of a business so that retirement need not lead to a significant net income loss. Even in a period such as the present, in which self-employment is becoming increasingly rare, the accumulation of income-producing assets should be an important and practical strategy for such families in order to permit the maintenance of living standards during the retirement years. Parenthetically, it would also be interesting to investigate the timing of the death of the affluent elderly in relation to the second and even the third squeeze period of their children. For example, what role might inheritance have or have had in affecting the ease or difficulty with which successive generations dealt with the different squeezes? In general, however, it does not appear likely that the potential third squeeze would pose serious problems for such socioeconomic groups, barring a major war or depression. The major vulnerability is perhaps to inflation, although even here the assets of such groups might be expected to keep pace with inflationary trends. However, inflation would tend to encourage such families to acquire assets that do appreciate in value rather than to rely exclusively on income sources that were more fixed, such as retirement benefits.

BLUE-COLLAR WORKERS

The Nature of the Constraints

Turning now to the case of manual occupations, the age–earnings profile of such men—especially those in the lower-level blue-collar and service occupations—places very different types of constraints on the types of family strategies that have been historically feasible. Of particular importance is the fact that the age–earnings profile of men in these jobs exhibits sharp increases in earnings only in youth (Table 3.1).Earnings peak early, therefore, and may actually deteriorate with increasing age if depreciation in human capital occurs or if a man loses his job and with it the accrued advantages of operating in a stable internal labor market. As a consequence, the actual ability of such men to increase their earnings over time rests more heavily on such factors as upward occupational mobility and/or positive period or cohort factors that would offset a neutral or possibly negative age effect on earnings—and one that starts relatively early in adulthood.[11] However, many of these possible sources of improved earnings seem less predictable at the early career stage than the age-effect on earnings that can be roughly estimated by individuals on the basis of interage comparisons. In fact, over time, some cohort factors may have systematically worked to the economic disadvantage of older men. For example, the long-run trend in increased educational attainment has meant that older men were usually at a considerable educational disadvantage compared with younger men.

In sum, from the point of view of developing an adaptive family strategy, an early-peaking and rather flat age–earnings profile creates certain rather severe constraints. Such men are caught in a dilemma: The period between the very low and uncertain earnings of youth and the start of a possible negative age effect can be rather short. If, in response to the first squeeze difficulties, marriage and childbearing are considerably delayed, then the costs incurred by raising a family will also be postponed to a point in the husband's career cycle at which his earnings position may be relatively poor—and, perhaps more important, much more uncertain. In addition, postponement may increase the economic vulnerability of elderly couples or the widowed. To the extent that the elderly are heavily dependent on their children for economic and other types of aid, then child postponement increases the risk that no or few children will be sufficiently launched economically to provide much assistance. In short, marriage and child postponement in response to the first squeeze may exact a price among these men and their families that it does not for those in occupational careers that regularly involve a steeper age–earnings profile, including greater income security in the middle and later years.

With a continuing process of industrial development, however, historical shifts have occurred in the kind of penalties lower-level manual

---

[11] Some cohorts may have a life-long advantage or disadvantage because of their cohort size; see Easterlin (1978) for this argument. The secular growth in real earnings is an example of a period effect that enhances the positive age effect at younger age-transitions and offsets a negative or neutral age effect for older-age transitions. Inflation, of course, may greatly erode this positive period effect, as has been the case in recent years.

workers risk as a consequence of delays in family formation. For one thing, the nature of manual employment has been changing considerably over the years. In the nineteenth century, unskilled and semiskilled workers were a more important segment of the labor force and were more commonly employed in jobs in which physical strength was of much greater importance than it is today. Of course, when physical strength is extremely important, it tends to operate to the disadvantage of somewhat older men. In addition, the more highly skilled manual labor force typical of the latter half of the twentieth century is one that has probably achieved a greater amount of firm-specific human capital training. Such training increases the employer's investment in the worker and hence presumably helps provide greater job security.[12] Furthermore, as educational attainment gradually approaches an asymptote, we are starting to observe fewer intercohort differences in educational attainment. As a result, in contrast to earlier in the twentieth century and perhaps the nineteenth century as well, somewhat older men are now at much less of an educational disadvantage compared with younger ones.

Another important change is the considerable improvement in morbidity and mortality conditions over the years of adults as well as of children. The working conditions under which blue-collar workers labored were, by and large, much more dangerous and more unhealthy in the past than they are at present. Furthermore, general adult morbidity and mortality conditions were worse in the nineteenth and early twentieth centuries. For example, Jacobson estimated that of the cohort of white men born in 1840 in the United States, as few as 66% of those who survived to age 20 also survived until age 55; only 59% survived to age 60 (Jacobson 1964, p. 44). On the other hand, the current United States life table for white men indicates that under the mortality conditions of 1976, 88% of those surviving to age 20 would live to age 55 and 81% to age 60 (U.S. National Center for Health Statistics 1978, pp. 5–11). However these are mortality figures for all white men and hence will overstate the survivorship chances of lower socioeconomic groups.

In sum, as a consequence of the generally higher mortality conditions of the nineteenth century and early twentieth century, which were probably higher still for lower socioeconomic groups, there was a much greater chance then than now that husbands would die or be disabled for manual work before all their children had reached adulthood. For example, Uhlenberg estimates that only 52% of the children in the relatively recent birth cohort of 1870 in the United States both survived

---

[12] On the other hand, rapid technological development may make some previous on-the-job training obsolete.

to age 15 and had their parents survive as well, compared with 92% for the cohort of 1950. In the case of those children who did survive to age 15, 28% of the cohort of 1870 were likely to have lost one or both parents by that age compared with 4% for the cohort of 1950. The chances of losing just a father for children surviving to age 15 was 18% for the cohort of 1870 but only 3% for the cohort of 1950 (Uhlenberg 1978, p. 79). Of course, these are national figures and hence do not accurately reflect the experience of working-class families—especially the poorer segments of this group.[13]

A third historical trend that will increase the job, and hence the economic, security of older workers has been the growth of large protected internal labor markets plus other sources of institutionalized job protection for workers over age 35 or 40 (Oppenheimer 1979).

Finally, there has been the increase in the sources of income other than the current earnings of family members. These include, in the United States, the growth of the social security system, unemployment insurance, health insurance, disability compensation, and pension plans as well as a variety of public welfare measures. Such sources of income provide at least two important types of income support—in crises that occur during the prime economically productive years and in retirement when earnings are very low or nonexistent. Hence, they provide a type of economic cushion that was largely unavailable to most manual workers in the earlier stages of industrialization.

As a result of these factors that improve the economic position of blue-collar men in the middle and later years, the penalties of postponed marriage and childbearing and of low fertility as well should have been declining over the years, though some of the benefits of this decline may not have been apparent until well after the Great Depression. Whether these trends also indicate a rise in the advantages of postponement is another matter, however.

Let us now go on to consider a variety of family strategies that would represent adaptive responses to an early-peaking and relatively flat earnings profile. Some of these strategies are probably more appropriate to an earlier historical period than to the last quarter of the twentieth century. However, it is extremely helpful to consider possibly adaptive strategies of the past as well as those of the present so that we can achieve a better understanding of developmental changes in family strategies and why these may have occurred. Moreover, as it turns out, the historical literature on the socioeconomic conditions of working-class

---

[13] They will also probably reflect a later age at the birth of the last child for the earlier time period.

families and on their demographic behavior have been very much concerned with some of the same factors involved in the family strategies under discussion here and hence is well worth discussing at some length.

Adaptive Strategies

In general, a pattern of relatively early marriage and early childbearing seems like the most adaptive family strategy, given the age–earnings profile of many blue-collar workers. This would be particularly true the earlier the age at peaking and the more uncertain were the income-producing capabilities of men over age 35 or 40. However, how young an age at marriage is possible will depend in part on the extent to which young men can achieve some employment security, and this will vary according to the business cycle and long-run trends affecting the full-time entry of men into stable occupational careers. The advantage of early marriage and early childbearing, once the young man can settle down to a regular job, is that his heaviest child-care responsibilities may either be over or are being shared by older children before the age effect on his earnings becomes neutral or even negative.

Within the general strategy of early marriage and childbearing, there are several variant patterns, depending on a number of factors such as mortality conditions, family size, and the economic role of children and wives. In one variant, children may provide an important source of family income, especially if they stay in the home until they marry. In that case, relatively large families are functional. This seems like a pattern most appropriate to the nineteenth and early twentieth-century period of industrialization. However, it is still important to consider this strategy. Understanding the reasons for its declining significance can give us a better idea of the changing constraints that have, I think, led to substantial postwar modifications in adaptive family strategies. Given a strategy in which children make important monetary contributions, although family size may be large, the work of children, while they are adolescents or in young adulthood, may compensate for both the large family size and the waning abilities of the father to be the economic mainstay of the family. As a consequence, the family's economic position may be relatively favorable when adolescent and young adult children are in the home, in spite of the low earnings of the young and possibly deteriorating earnings of the father. Several incomes plus economies of scale may produce a level of living for all above that which individual workers could produce for themselves independently. Under these circumstances, there may be no second squeeze at all but just one long first squeeze while the family is setting itself up and raising enough children to an age when at least some of them can be economically productive.

If children are an important source of family income, then high infant and childhood mortality would also favor a strategy of early childbearing as well as a large completed family size. To the extent that the family's economic well-being depended, in part, on the earnings of children supplementing those of the father, or substituted for them in the case of the loss of his earnings, then high infant and childhood mortality may delay the time when enough children have survived to make such a contribution. That is, high mortality among the young reduces the reproductive efficiency of families in the sense of their ability to produce a given number of surviving children within a relatively brief time period.

Multiple-earner families would also have had the advantage of reducing the vulnerability of the family to severe income loss, should the father die or be incapacitated. However, the greater the postponement of childbearing, the more likely the family would experience the loss of the husband's earnings before many of the offspring had reached working age. This, in turn, would have an extremely negative effect on the family's economic position.

In sum, in a family economy in which nonfamilial sources of income are few and not very adequate, in which childhood and adult mortality is high, and in which children make an important economic contribution, early marriage and childbearing will probably increase the chances of families raising their children to economically productive ages while the husband is still alive and capable of employment himself, or at least before the probability of his making a significant income contribution greatly diminishes. However, such a strategy does not seem very conducive to the employment of married women outside the home, as their home productivity would be fairly high.

A number of historical studies have paid considerable attention to many of these issues and provide substantial support for the idea that such strategies were common and, moreover, seemed to provide an appropriate adaptation to the circumstances under which many manual workers had to function in an earlier period of industrialization. The data from England are particularly illuminating in this respect as they indicate an early awareness by some scholars of life-cycle variations in the economic situation of families. Rowntree's 1898 study of working-class families in York and the more recent study by Anderson of families in nineteenth-century Lancashire are especially noteworthy in this respect (Rowntree 1922, Anderson 1971).

Rowntree divided the population studied using a measure of poverty based on an estimate of a minimum budget for the basic necessities for

families of different sizes and composition (Rowntree 1922, Chapter 4).
All families with an income below the amount appropriate to their size
and composition were considered to be in a state of poverty. Approximately 15% of the working-class population in his study (10% of the
population of York) were classified below the poverty line (Rowntree
1922, p. 144). After classifying the population by its relationship to the
poverty line, Rowntree attempted to determine the reasons for their
poverty. He estimates that for about 44% of the families it was because
the husband was dead or not working regularly for one reason or another.
For 13% of the families, it was because of a family size of five or more
children.[14] However, in 44% of the cases it was simply because the
husband's wages were low (Rowntree 1922, p. 153). Most of such men
were laborers (73%) and other ·unskilled workers (Rowntree 1922, pp.
165–166).[15]

What is particularly pertinent about Rowntree's analysis is that he
looked at poverty in life-cycle terms. Thus, he argues

> The life of a labourer is marked by five alternating periods of want and
> comparative plenty. During early childhood, unless his father is a skilled
> worker, he probably will be in poverty; this will last until he, or some of his
> brothers or sisters, begin to earn money and thus augment their father's wage
> sufficiently to raise the family above the poverty line. Then follows the period
> during which he is earning money and living under his parents' roof; for some
> portion of this period he will be earning more money than is required for
> lodging, food, and clothes. This is his chance to save money. If he has saved
> enough to pay for furnishing a cottage, this period of comparative prosperity
> may continue after marriage until he has two or three children, when poverty
> will again overtake him. This period of poverty will last perhaps for ten years,
> i.e., until the first child is fourteen years old and begins to earn wages; but
> if there are more than three children it may last longer. While the children
> are earning, and before they leave the home to marry, the man enjoys another
> period of prosperity—possibly, however, only to sink back again into poverty
> when his children have married and left him, and he himself is too old to
> work, for his income has never permitted his saving enough for him and his
> wife to live upon for more than a very short time [1922, pp. 169–171].

[14] Nevertheless, these children may have turned into an economic asset once they
reached working age.
[15] According to Rowntree: "Allowing for broken time, the average wage for a labourer
in York is from 18s. to 21s.; whereas . . . the minimum expenditure necessary to maintain
in a state of physical efficiency a family of two adults and three children is 21s. 8d, or,
if there are four children, the sum required would be 26s. It is thus seen that *the wages
paid for unskilled labour in York are insufficient to provide food, shelter, and clothing
adequate to maintain a family of moderate size in a state of bare physical efficiency* [1922,
p. 166]."

Even more importantly, he points out that those observed to be in poverty at the time of the study represented:

> *merely that section who happened to be in one of these poverty periods at the time the inquiry was made.* Many of these will, in course of time, pass on into a period of comparative prosperity; this will take place as soon as the children, now dependent, begin to earn. But their places below the poverty line will be taken by others who are at present living in that prosperous period previous to, or shortly after, marriage. Again, many now classed as above the poverty line were below it until the children began to earn. The proportion of the community who at one period or other of their lives suffer from poverty to the point of physical privation is therefore much greater, and the injurious effects of such a condition are much more widespread than would appear from a consideration of the number who can be shown to be below the poverty line at any given moment [1922, pp. 171–172].

Rowntree's study provides a picture of a socioeconomic group whose economic fortunes, both positive and negative, are closely related to the number and ages of their children. If they do marry and have children they must as a consequence pass through a period of considerable absolute deprivation until several of the children are old enough to work and make an income contribution themselves. When that point is reached, however, the family may achieve a relatively favorable income position.

Anderson's study of mid-nineteenth-century Lancashire presents a somewhat similar picture of variations in the economic position of working-class families over the family cycle as well as of the important role of children in the family's economic well-being (Anderson 1971). For example, using Rowntree's primary poverty line, Anderson estimated the proportion of Preston families at various levels in relation to the poverty line. His general findings are that poverty status varied sharply by family-cycle stage. The highest proportion of families at or below the poverty line are those with several children at home but none employed (52% below the poverty line) and those in which some, but less than half, of the children were employed (31%). On the other hand, the highest proportions of families who were well above the poverty line are those in which half or more of the children were employed (82%), and those in which the wife was under age 45 and no children were in the home (51%) (Anderson 1971, p. 31). Anderson thus concludes that:

> In the later stages of the life-cycle, skilled factory workers in particular lived fairly comfortably by contemporary standards, many with family earnings of at least £3 per week. The earnings of children were thus crucial to the family's standard of living, though even they were of little help in the worst slump periods [1971, p. 32].

Anderson also points out that the earnings of wage workers of various sorts tended to peak early in life (Anderson 1971, pp. 23, 128ff). In the cotton industry, for example, he maintains that "peak earnings for men were reached by the mid-twenties at the latest" (Anderson 1971, p. 201). As a consequence, he argues:

> The high wages obtained by many men in the Lancashire towns made it easy for them to support themselves and at least a small family while relatively young. This early independence, coupled with the fact that subsequent expectations were likely to be of a fall rather than any much greater rise, of wages, seems to have persuaded most that it was safe and even best to marry young [1971, p. 132].

As evidence supporting this interpretation, Anderson cites the considerable differentials in the age at marriage of men in Preston, a manufacturing town, compared with rural areas in which coming into property was more important. For example, in 1851, while 94% of men aged 20–24 had never been married in rural Lancashire, only 69% of Preston men in this age group had not yet married. For men 25–34 years old, the proportion who had never married was still 50% for rural men but only 27% for Preston men (Anderson 1971, p. 133). Furthermore, he found that:

> early marriage was not just a matter of rural–urban differences. Areas where most of the population were agricultural labourers, and where, therefore, independence, such as it was ever likely to be, was attained quite young, had marriage ages only a little higher than those of the Lancashire towns. Conversely, rural areas like those of Lancashire, where independence came late because their agriculture was based on small farms, had delayed marriage, while towns relying on traditional artisan and trade occupations had more delayed marriage, and higher non-marriage rates [1971, p. 134].

A final aspect of Anderson's study that is relevant to this discussion has to do with the position of the aged. In his Preston sample of 1851, Anderson found that most of those noninstitutionalized persons aged 65 and older were living with one of their children—68% were living with a child, 13% with a spouse, and 5% with other kin. Only 6% were living alone (Anderson 1971, p. 139).[16] Furthermore, Anderson found that it was primarily the widowed who lived with children, as there was little evidence of a doubling up of married parents residing with children (Anderson 1971, p. 140). An advantage of such an arrangement was that

---

[16].The addition of the institutionalized to the table from which these figures came would hardly have changed the picture since Anderson estimated that only about six of the elderly from Preston were in institutions.

it saved on housing costs, on the investment in furniture (and thus eased both the first and third squeezes) and, in some cases, it provided young mothers with someone to look after her children if she worked (Anderson 1971, p. 141).

In sum, Anderson's study is consistent with the notion that for men in early-peaking, low-income occupations, early marriage and child-bearing was a common adaptive strategy. Furthermore, so was a pattern whereby the economic role of adolescent and young adult children was extremely important in helping families achieve a certain measure of prosperity in the latter part of the family cycle.[17] Finally, adult children were a major source of support for the widowed aged who could in exchange often still provide some useful functions in the household.

While both Rowntree and Anderson focused on poverty and its re-lationship to the family cycle, it ought to be possible to treat their analyses more generally. If the number and ages of children present have income and cost implications, changes in family composition over the family cycle will signify variations in the family's economic position, even if the process does not involve falling into or rising out of a state of poverty, however it is defined. Hence, the literature on how poverty is related to the family cycle can also tell us something about how economic affluence can vary over the life-cycle, even for families who never ex-perience poverty.

To my knowledge, demographic and economic historical research on American society has only recently begun to concern itself with a detailed examination of some of the factors involved in the type of family strat-egies under discussion here. The study by Michael Haines is a case in point (Haines 1979). The main focus of Haines's book is an investigation of the theory that a number of particular factors led to the earlier marriage and higher fertility observed among mining and heavy industrial popu-lations in nineteenth-century Europe and America. However, many of his findings and the causal factors he saw as important would hold for a large variety of manual occupations, not just those involved in heavy

---

[17] This implies the existence of some built-in conflict of interests between parents and children, with parents often desiring that at least some of the children make a more extended contribution to the parental household than the children themselves wanted to make (see Anderson 1971 and Ankarloo 1978). Normative constraints keeping young adult children in the home may then have promoted some delays in marriage earlier in the industrialization process. This suggests that as the economic role of adolescent and young adult children in the parental home declined, age at marriage would also decline if early marriage remained an advantageous strategy for young people in this socioeconomic group. There was, in fact, a long-run decline in the age at marriage in the twentieth century, especially for men, which has only just recently begun to reverse itself (see Modell et al. 1978).

industry or mining. Of particular interest is his analysis of the United States Commissioner of Labor Survey in 1889–1890 (Haines 1979, Chapter VI). This was a study of nine protected industries—bar iron, pig iron, steel, bituminous coal, coke, iron ore, cotton textiles, woolens, and glass—made in preparation for a debate over protective tariffs. Partly as a by-product of the study, information was obtained on the demographic characteristics, occupations, incomes, and expenditure patterns of 8544 families and their family members in these nine industries for 24 states in the United States and 5 European countries—Belgium, France, Germany, Great Britain, and Switzerland. Of the families in the sample, 98% were headed by men.[18]

Haines stressed the nature of the age–earnings profile, pointing to the early-peaking earnings profile of many manual occupations in the nineteenth century. He argued that an early-peaking pattern would tend to promote early marriage and early childbearing and a large completed family size for two major reasons: (1) young men could afford to marry and have children earlier and in greater numbers; and (2) since the husband's income prospects in later life were probably unfavorable or, at least, uncertain, large numbers of surviving children would act as an insurance policy, contributing to the support of the family while they were teenagers (Haines 1979, p. 225). Furthermore, Haines found from the labor survey that the economic role of children increased considerably in importance for older families. For example, in the United States sample of the 1889–1890 survey, the proportion of families with income from children rose from 12% for families with the head aged 30–39 to 51% where he was 40–49 and on up to 59% where he was 50–59. It was still 58% when the head was 60 and over (Haines 1979, p. 227).

As a consequence of the increase in the likelihood of children's contributing income as they reached working age combined with the declines in income of heads past age 40, the proportion of family income contributed by husbands was less for older men, while that of children was greater. For example, in the United States sample, the head's mean income went down from 92% of the total mean family income for families in which he was 20–29, to 67% when he was 40–49, to 56% when he was 50–59. When the head was 60 or older, his income was, as one might expect, even lower—47% of the total mean family income. On the other hand, the proportion of mean family income contributed by children rose with the age of the head—from 4% when the head was 30–39, to 24 and 31% when he was 40–49 and 50–59, respectively, rising to 34%

---

[18] For a discussion of the nature of the survey, see Haines (1979, Chapter IV) and Modell (1978).

when the head was age 60 or older. The results from the European samples were similar except that the relative contribution of the children was even greater (Haines 1979, pp. 226–227).[19]

In sum, historically, in the United States as well as in Europe, the middle-aged period of blue-collar male heads of families was, because of multiple earners, often one of relative prosperity for working-class households. But this was primarily because of the income contribution of children. Without that contribution and solely on the basis of the husband's income alone, the relative income position of older families would have been well below that of families of men in their thirties.

Changing Constraints and Changing Strategies

A family economic strategy that heavily relies on children's providing a considerable income contribution to the family is most practical if young people make relatively low levels of human capital investments, especially in formal schooling. When there is an increasing premium on extensive educational attainment, then this will postpone the period in which children can start to make significant contributions of money income to their families of orientation. Hence, children of families following this strategy in relatively industrialized societies would find themselves at a considerable economic disadvantage. Increasingly, however, laws governing the minimum school-leaving age have limited the ability of families to choose such strategies.[20] Nevertheless, these strategies, in families that adopt them, help explain how low socioeconomic status can persist across generations. In any event, they suggest that strategies that may be to the advantage of the family as a whole, or to the parents, need not maximize the long-run utility of the children and may put limits on their freedom to choose among a variety of their own lifetime utility-maximizing plans. Hence, this introduces one sort of stress into such an adaptation and, as a consequence, may represent a major vulnerability of the strategy.

In general, the rise in the school-leaving age that blue-collar children experienced during the twentieth century should signify the emergence of the second life-cycle squeeze for working-class families and the decline in the economic contribution of children to their families of orientation

---

[19] For an additional discussion of the possible economic role of adolescent and young children in the family in nineteenth-century America, see Katz and Davey (1978).

[20] For a brief discussion of trends in laws governing the school-leaving age and the use of child labor with the resulting changes in children's economic roles in the family in England and Europe, see Tilly and Scott (1978, Chapter 8).

(Oppenheimer, forthcoming, Chapter 9). Given such a trend, adolescent and even young adult children would increasingly consume much more than they produce. Furthermore, even if they should continue to contribute to their families of orientation once they did enter the labor force in a relatively permanent way, their overall economic contribution would be reduced by the fact that the number of years during which they would be making such a contribution is greatly reduced, unless they postpone marriage more than was the case in the past.

The twentieth-century emergence of the second squeeze for blue-collar families has a number of important implications for family strategies and the constraints under which they operate. For one thing, by definition, it raises the overall cost of children and this should lead to long-run changes in fertility, if nothing else. What is particularly of interest here, however, is that it raises the possibility of a pile-up or overlapping of squeezes. It is very unlikely that in one family, the experience of the first squeeze by the younger generation will coincide with the third squeeze period of their parents, thus greatly impeding family strategies of mutual aid. However, there is a much greater possibility that middle-aged parents in the second squeeze period may also have elderly parents in the third squeeze period. Since, in working-class households, the middle years are a time during which the husband's earnings are not rising rapidly, at least due to the age or career-cycle effect on earnings, then middle-aged couples with elderly parents and dependent or semi-dependent adolescent children may find themselves in quite an economic crunch. Furthermore, the couple's ability to prepare for its own third squeeze may be greatly hampered by extensive and simultaneous socioeconomic obligations to both parents and children.

The very real possibility of overlaps in squeezes and the pressures it places on traditional ways of dealing with the support of the elderly has a number of implications that would be worthwhile to investigate in more rigorous fashion. First, the overlap can be reduced if relatively early marriage and early childbearing remain common behavioral patterns among these socioeconomic groups. This has the additional advantage of timing the second squeeze before the age effect on the husband's earnings is negative, though presumably the negative effect is declining. Second, smaller families and early completion of childbearing would also help prevent the pileup of squeezes. The greater control of fertility that has become possible in recent years—especially the increasing practice of sterilization—should help make this strategy more feasible. Third, the emergence of the second squeeze combined with increased longevity in the later years and the high medical costs such longevity often entails decrease the possibility that middle-aged children can financially carry most of the economic burden of their aging kin themselves. In other words, the economic costs of the third squeeze will increasingly be borne collectively by the society as a whole and by the elderly themselves. This is, of course, what has been occurring with the growth of public transfer payments of one sort or another, pension plans, and the like.

Another advantage to an early end to childbearing is that it makes it easier for wives to make a significant and extended income contribution to the family economy after childbearing and the heaviest child-care activities are completed. Hence, one important possible adaptation to the emergence of the second squeeze for blue-collar families is for the market work of wives to substitute for the market work of their children. In fact, even though declining mortality and increased job security for older men has reduced the economic vulnerability of families dependent on a single income, the risks of such an economic arrangement still seem great when the main source of that income is in the form of earnings. Even if the chances of a husband's dying, being incapacitated, or losing his job have declined, there is still some chance of these events occurring, and the risk is probably higher in blue-collar families. Furthermore, if the marriage breaks up, an event whose probability has been rising rapidly over time, the wife and children are extremely vulnerable economically. Hence, this would greatly increase the importance of the wife's being able to make a monetary contribution to the household, given the declining economic importance of children.

While a strategy of early marriage and early completion of childbearing combined with a more extensive involvement of wives in the latter part of the family cycle seems to be one that was characteristic of many blue-collar families (and white-collar families, too) in postwar America, it exhibits certain basic vulnerabilities. Some of these have eased in recent years, but others have probably increased. As a consequence, this may not be a highly stable long-run strategy, although it may offer many short-run benefits. For one thing, it requires a successful early completion of childbearing. Hence, in historical periods in which fertility control is imperfect, such a strategy is likely to break down for many of the families attempting to follow it. To the extent that it does, being able to rely on older children or other kin seems like an important backup to such a strategy. However, in recent years improved contraception, legalization of abortion, and the option of sterilization have all made it possible to plan one's reproductive behavior with far greater certainty than existed in the past. Hence, these developments have greatly increased the feasibility of this strategy.

There are still, however, significant risks in any strategy that places some reliance on the wife's returning to the labor force after a considerable lapse of time devoted to childbearing and child-rearing. Much depends on her ability to find a job at that time. However, if the couple embarked on marriage and childbearing at an early age, especially if the wife were very young, then her initial level of human capital attainment might be relatively low. Hence, the practicality of such a strategy would seem to depend in part on some minimum level of human capital investment. This, in turn, should involve a later age at the initiation of childbearing than would be necessary if the family were not planning for her to have a later economic role outside the home. As a result, it may be difficult for many families to switch to such a strategy midway through the family cycle. This probably puts certain breaks on the speed with which a strategy of this kind might evolve over time, even if it is destined to become very widespread. It also puts a floor on how young an age at marriage might emerge.

Another factor to consider is that the feasibility of a strategy of delayed economic activity depends on the availability of jobs for the wife returning to the labor force. This strikes me as an extremely vulnerable point in such a strategy because of the uncertainty couples must necessarily feel about the future labor market opportunities for women. Perhaps in time of rapidly expanding job opportunities for women, such as the postwar period in the United States, these circumstances might inspire sufficient confidence to embark on such a lifetime plan. However, this does not seem to be something families could always count on. Certainly, recent trends in the demand for workers in occupations filled mainly by women suggest how inadequate and unreliable the demand in these jobs is to make it possible to plan a lifetime work pattern with any degree of certainty (Oppenheimer 1972). This is clearly a rather different situation from the strategy that may tie the age at marriage to the ability of young wives to find jobs. Predicting job conditions 1 or 2 years hence may have certain risks but how much greater are the risks of making such predictions 10 or 15 years into the future? Hence, if families start to plan to rely on wives' labor force participation, then this should operate to regularize their work involvement—not only to increase women's level of human capital attainment, and hence their wage, but also to provide them with more employment security.

If, in response to the emergence of the second squeeze, wives' paid employment develops into a regular feature of the adaptive strategy of many blue-collar families, this has implications for the third squeeze as well. On the one hand, wives' employment can help increase the resources that couples will have available in order to cope with their own third squeeze through the accumulation of assets and/or pension benefits.[21] Furthermore, it may increase the financial ability of middle-aged couples to help aged kin. On the other hand, the regular employment of the wife reduces the amount of time she would have available to provide services for or interact with elderly kin. This implies that the elderly will increasingly rely on the purchase of goods and services by one means or another rather than on intrafamilial transfers that heavily rely on direct inputs of time.

LOWER-LEVEL WHITE-COLLAR WORKERS

Let us close with a brief consideration of the situation of middle- and lower-level white-collar workers, the constraints under which they operate, and the type of adaptive strategies that are likely to develop.

In some respects, the socioeconomic position of the families of men in medium- and lower-level white-collar occupations is unique. If one assumes that they desire their children to achieve a socioeconomic position comparable to or better than their parents, then children must typically remain in white-collar occupations.[22] However, if this is the case, then the educational attainment of offspring should at least equal that of their parents. In fact, it should probably be greater, since there is evidence that a higher educational attainment of offspring is increasingly necessary just to replicate the status of the parental generation. This implies a relatively late school-leaving age for the children of such families. While the school-leaving age may have been increasing over time, a relatively late age at school completion also seems to have been characteristic of this group at an earlier stage of industrialization.[23] This suggests that even in times past the second life-cycle squeeze was characteristic of lower-level white-collar occupations, though not necessarily of blue-collar occupations. That is, young white-collar sons (and daugh-

---

[21] See Treas 1981, for a more extensive discussion of the possible impact of wives working on the economic position of the elderly. She points out that according to current laws, the increased social security advantages of a wife's working are not great. Of potential greater importance would be pension benefits, if the wife were eligible. This, of course, would require women to have a more extensive work history pattern than has been typically characteristic of wives until quite recently.

[22] That is, if one takes status as well as income into consideration. In addition, maintaining a white-collar status may be considered important in order to provide a stepping-stone to higher-level white-collar occupations, if not for oneself then for one's children.

[23] For some discussion of this, see Banks (1954, pp. 192–193), Kaestle and Vinovskis (1978, p. 171), Katz and Davey (1978, pp. S110–S111). See also Oppenheimer (forthcoming).

ters, too, probably) would be able to make much less of an early contribution to their families than the blue-collar children of blue-collar
families. The contribution such white-collar offspring could make would
start later and probably only achieve significance if there were later
marriage.[24] Marriage delays were also likely if on-the-job training and
achieving a secure position added more time to the late job-entry stage
before a sufficient measure of economic security were achieved.

In short, the cost of children to white-collar families—even those at
moderate or lower-paying levels—was relatively high and the relative
economic contribution these children might make was probably small.
At the very least, it was delayed. On the other hand, the age earnings
profile of such white-collar workers does not appear to favor very late
childbearing, since earnings peak early in these occupations, as in blue-
collar occupations, though there is probably greater late-career security
for white-collar than for blue-collar men. However, the earnings of white-
collar men are often below that of men in several blue-collar occupations
(Oppenheimer 1974). Hence, implied in the interaction of the age pattern
of child-care costs and that of the husband's earnings is a relatively
severe second squeeze—one that, if anything, has intensified over time.

What types of family strategies might represent an adaptive response
to the constraints under which these medium- and lower-level white-
collar couples have been operating, and have these been observed empirically? First, given the late school-leaving age, one would expect to
observe a later age at marriage than that observed for manual workers,
though not so late as for the professions, whatever the level. Second,
the wives of such men should have a more significant economic role than
the wives of either high-level white-collar or blue-collar men, since children's economic role was limited. Otherwise, the family's socioeconomic
position would rest entirely on the husband's earnings, with all the risks
this might entail. In an earlier historical period, this may have involved
relatively lengthy employment by the wife before marriage and/or before
childbearing to help set up the family in a style deemed appropriate.
More recently, it also includes the extensive employment of the wife
after children are in school, if not before. In my own study of the 1960
and 1970 Public Samples, I certainly observed that the labor force participation of lower-level white-collar wives was among the highest of all
occupational groups considered—overall and net of other factors such
as education and husband's income (Oppenheimer, forthcoming).

---

[24] For evidence that marriage delays among lower-level white-collar workers were probably true in the past, see Katz and Davey (1978, pp. S112–S113).

Certain fertility patterns should also be characteristic of families of men in such lower-paid white-collar occupations. Given the relatively high cost of children and their limited economic value during childhood and adolescence combined with the flat age–earnings profile of the father, this socioeconomic group should be most highly motivated to limit family size in general and to be particularly sensitive to changes in apparent economic life chances or the cost of children.[25] With regard to timing, this is a more difficult question. However, one would expect some delays in childbearing, when fertility control is possible, to permit a greater economic contribution by the wife and the setting up of an independent household at a desired standard of living. However, if fertility is low, then childbearing, once started, might best be completed soon if the wife expects to return to the labor force (or remain in it) in order to maximize her economic contribution.

IMPLICATIONS

There are a number of implications one can draw from this preliminary discussion of family strategies and the changing constraints under which they operate and which they also impose on family and economic behavior. First, the growing importance of extensive schooling for children has undoubtedly intensified (and in some cases created) the second life-cycle squeeze. This should have affected families of men throughout the occupational spectrum. At the lower occupational levels, a growing premium on graduating from high school has considerably raised the school-leaving age of young people and, in the process, has probably postponed entry into the labor force except in a fairly casual manner. As one rises in the occupational scale, attending and graduating from college has become increasingly important in the United States. And for some socioeconomic groups, professional or postgraduate training of some sort is considered essential for an occupational career.

[25] For example, in my study of the 1960 and 1970 Public Use Samples the mean number of children ever born to the wives of clerical and medium and lower-level sales workers who were aged 45–54 in 1960 (and hence aged 14–24 at the start of the Great Depression) was only 1.87 and 1.91 respectively compared to 2.34 for the wives of all husbands aged 45–54 in 1960. However, for the cohorts who were aged 45–54 in 1970 (and who therefore reached young adulthood in a time of much greater prosperity), the mean number of children ever born rose to 2.49 for clerical workers and 2.57 for the medium and lower-level sales workers. This was still below the overall mean of 2.70 but the gap was much smaller in 1970 than in 1960 (Oppenheimer forthcoming).

In the case of families of men in white-collar occupations, all this has probably led to still further delays in an already late launching date for one's children and, in the process, increased the costs of raising children. In the case of working-class families, however, the prolongation of the child-dependency burden has probably had a somewhat different effect on the nature of intergenerational transfers of income at this stage of the family cycle. For these families, if older children have increasingly become an economic drain on parents, then a family strategy that seems to have been fairly common in the past has ceased to be generally practical. This is the pattern of adolescent and young adult children remaining at home, working, and contributing to the support of the family.

A major consequence of the widespread emergence of the second life-cycle squeeze as an important feature of modern industrial society is the increased probability that overlaps in squeezes will occur. Since the second squeeze period is likely to be experienced by couples in the middle adult years, this is also a period in which such couples may have elderly parents or other elderly kin with whom they have traditionally had ties of mutual assistance. In short, the difficulties of the third squeeze may impinge on the children of the elderly at the same time the children are themselves experiencing the second squeeze. Such cross-pressures may, in turn, impair their ability to aid elderly parents or to support children through the education process, or both. It may also impede their ability to plan for their own third squeeze period.[26]

Adaptations to the widespread emergence of the second squeeze also have implications for the situation of couples (or the widowed) in the third squeeze period. Relatively low fertility is one obvious adaptive response since it reduces the severity and often the length of the second squeeze period. It also increases the feasibility of wives' paid employment substituting for the economic contribution of adolescent and young adult children in times past. However, these adaptations, in turn, imply that fewer children will be available to help elderly parents, though this is somewhat offset by increased survivorship of those children that are born (Soldo 1981). In addition, if wives' employment becomes an important family strategy for maintaining an economic homeostasis in the family, then this suggests that older families will benefit from the increased work experience of the wife earlier in the life-cycle. However, it also implies that the ability of women to provide unpaid services to kin may be curtailed due to their increased involvement in paid em-

---

[26] Thus an interesting research project would be to explore the possible squeeze impac of variations in the number and timing of children.

ployment. Hence, family (or societal) strategies of dealing with the aged should increasingly rely on the purchase of goods and services to be supplied by non-kin of one sort or another. This, of course, seems to have taken place.

In sum, a life-cycle squeeze model should have considerable utility for the study of the socioeconomic position of the elderly, even though such a model was not developed with this purpose in mind. However, its potential utility does not lie in identifying a third squeeze per se. After all, this merely attaches a label to a well-known economically difficult period. Rather, the potential contribution of the approach lies in an increased understanding of, first, how earlier squeezes impinge on the third squeeze and, second, how adaptations to these earlier squeezes and shifts in their character also have implications for those in the third squeeze period. In short, to the extent such an approach is fruitful in the study of the elderly, it indicates the essential value of basic research on the family, whichever age group is currently of particular concern from the point of view of public policy.

REFERENCES

Anderson, M. (1971) *Family Structure in Nineteenth Century Lancashire.* Cambridge, England: Cambridge University Press.

Ankarloo, B. (1978) Marriage and family formation. Pp. 113–134 in T. K. Hareven, ed., *Transitions: The Family and the Life Course in Historical Perspective.* New York: Academic Press.

Banks, J. A. (1954) *Prosperity and Parenthood: A Study of Family Planning Among the Victorian Middle Classes.* London: Routledge and Kegan Paul.

Becker, G. S. (1975) *Human Capital,* 2nd ed. New York: National Bureau of Economic Research.

Bureau of Labor Statistics (1968) *Revised Equivalence Scale for Estimating Incomes or Budget Costs by Family Type.* Bulletin No. 1570-2. Washington, D.C.: U.S. Department of Labor.

Bureau of the Census (1978) *Trends in Childspacing: June 1975.* Current Population Reports, Series P-20, No. 315. Washington, D.C.: U.S. Department of Commerce.

Easterlin, R. A. (1973) Relative economic status and the American fertility swing. Pp. 170–223 in E. Sheldon, ed., *Family Economic Behavior.* Philadelphia: J. B. Lippincott.

Easterlin, R. A. (1978) What will 1984 be like? Socioeconomic implications of recent twists in age structure. *Demography* 15:397–432.

Espenshade, T. (1973) *The Cost of Children in Urban United States.* Population Monograph Series No. 14. Berkeley, Calif.: Institute of International Studies, University of California.

Estes, R. J., and Wilensky, H. L. (1978) Life cycle squeeze and the moral curve. *Social Problems* 25(February):277–292.

Glenn, N. (1976) Comment on "Some methodological issues in cohort analysis of archival data." *American Sociological Review* 41:900–904.

Gove, W. R., Grimm, J. W., Motz, S. C., and Thompson, J. D. (1973) The family life cycle: Internal dynamics and social consequences. *Sociology and Social Research* 57:182–195.

Haines, M. (1979) *Fertility and Occupation: Population Patterns in Industrialization*. New York: Academic Press.

Heberle, R. (1941) Social factors in birth control. *American Sociological Review* 6:794–805.

Jacobson, P. H. (1964) Cohort survival for generations since 1840. *Milbank Memorial Fund Quarterly* XLII(July):36–53.

Kaestle, C. F., and Vinovskis, M. (1978) From fireside to factory: School entry and school leaving in nineteenth-century Massachusetts. Pp. 135–185 in T. K. Hareven, ed., *Transitions: The Family and the Life Course in Historical Perspective*. New York: Academic Press.

Katz, M. B., and Davey, I. E. (1978) Youth and early industrialization in a Canadian city. Pp. S81–S119 in J. Demon and S. S. Boocock, eds., *Turning Points: Historical and Sociological Essays on the Family*. Chicago: University of Chicago Press.

Mason, K. O., Mason, W. M., Winsborough, H. H., and Poole, W. K. (1973) Some methodological issues in cohort analysis of archival data. *American Sociological Review* 38:242–248.

Modell, J. (1978) Patterns of consumption, acculturation, and family income strategies in late nineteenth-century America. Pp. 206–240 in T. K. Hareven and M. A. Vinovskis, eds., *Family and Population in Nineteenth-Century America*. Princeton, N.J.: Princeton University Press.

Modell, J., Furstenberg, F. F., Jr., and Strong, D. (1978) The timing of marriage in the transition to adulthood: Continuity and change, 1860–1975. Pp. S120–S150 in J. Demos and S. S. Boocock, eds., *Turning Points: Historical and Sociological Essays on the Family*. Chicago: University of Chicago Press.

Oppenheimer, V. K. (1970) *The Female Labor Force in the United States: Demographic and Economic Factors Governing Its Growth and Changing Composition*. Population Monograph Series No. 5. Berkeley, Calif.: Institute of International Studies, University of California.

Oppenheimer, V. K. (1972) Rising educational attainment, declining fertility and the inadequacies of the female labor market. Pp. 305–328 in C. F. Westoff and R. Parke, Jr., eds., *Demographic and Social Aspects of Population Growth*. Vol. 1 of the Research Reports of the Commission on Population Growth and the American Future.

Oppenheimer, V. K. (1974) The life-cycle squeeze, The interaction of men's occupational and family life cycles. *Demography* 11:227–245.

Oppenheimer, V. K. (1976) The Easterlin hypothesis: Another aspect of the echo to consider. *Population and Development Review* 2:433–457.

Oppenheimer, V. K. (1977) The sociology of women's economic role in the family. *American Sociological Review* 42:387–406.

Oppenheimer, V. K. (1979) Structural sources of economic pressure for wives to work: An analytical framework. *Journal of Family History* 4:177–197.

Oppenheimer, V. K. (forthcoming) *Work and the Family: Study in Social Demography*. New York: Academic Press.

Rowntree, B. S. (1922) *Poverty: A Study of Town Life*. London: Longmans, Green and Co.

Ryder, N. (1965) The cohort as a concept in the study of social change. *American Sociological Review* 30:843–861.

Schaie, K. W. (1967) Age changes and age differences. *The Gerontologist* 7:128–132.

Schorr, A. (1966) The family life cycle and income development. *Social Security Bulletin* 29(2):14–25.

Soldo, B. J. (1981) The living arrangements of the elderly in the near future. In S. B. Kiesler, J. N. Morgan, and V. K. Oppenheimer, eds., *Aging: Social Change*. New York: Academic Press.

Tilly, L. A. (1979a) Individuals' lives and family strategies in the French proletariat. *Journal of Family History* 4(Summer):137–152.

Tilly, L. A. (1979b) The family wage economy of a French textile city: Roubaix, 1872–1906. *Journal of Family History* 4(Winter):381–394.

Tilly, L. A., and Scott, J. W. (1978) *Women, Work, and Family*. New York: Holt, Rinehart and Winston.

Treas, J. (1981) Women's employment and its implications for the status of the elderly of the future. In S. B. Kiesler, J. N. Morgan, and V. K. Oppenheimer, eds., *Aging: Social Change*. New York: Academic Press.

Uhlenberg, P. (1978) Changing configurations of the life course. Pp. 65–97 in T. K. Hareven, ed., *Transitions: The Family and the Life Course in Historical Perspective*. New York: Academic Press.

U.S. National Center for Health Statistics (1978) *Life Tables: Vital Statistics of the United States, 1976*. Vol. II, Section 5. Washington, D.C.: U.S. National Center for Health Statistics.

Wilensky, H. L. (1963) The moonlighter: A product of relative deprivation. *Industrial Relations* 3:105–124.

chapter 4

Aging and Becoming an Elder: A Cross-Cultural Comparison

JOHN W. M. WHITING

To set the family and the life-cycle in its social context, a system quite different from the one that most of us are familiar with will be briefly described. Since my wife and I have been doing fieldwork in Kenya during the last decade and have worked most intensively on Ngecha, a Kikuyu village 20 miles (32 km) from Nairobi, I have chosen Kikuyu culture as an exemplar of a highly developed age set, age grade system. Since this system is no longer functional, I have had to reconstruct it as it existed in 1890 just before Christian missionaries, Western schooling, Pax Britannica, and an influx of British farmers radically changed it.

The data in the following description are from the old men and women informants living in Ngecha,[1] from early ethnographic reports (see bibliography), and especially from a monograph written by the late Jomo Kenyatta (1953). Kenyatta begins his monograph with the following statement:

---

[1] Interviews on traditional Kikuyu culture with the Ngecha elders were carried out by John Herzog with the assistance of Kikuyu students from the University of Nairobi. Frances Cox and Ndung'u Mberia carried out a study of changes in the role of elders since 1900.

AGING
Stability and Change in the Family

Copyright © 1981 by Academic Press, Inc.
All rights of reproduction in any form reserved.
ISBN 0-12-040003-0 0-12-040023-5(p)

The Kikuyu tribal organization is based on three most important factors, without which there can be no harmony in the tribal activities. For the behavior and the status of every individual in the Kikuyu society is determined by the three governing principles which we will categorically enumerate here. The first is the family group (*mbari* or *Nyomba*), which brings together all those who are related by blood; namely a man, his wife or wives and children and also their grand- and great-grandchildren. The second is clan (*moherega*) which joins in one group several *mbari* units who have the same clan name and are believed to have descended from one family group in the remote past. . . .

The third principal factor in unifying the Kikuyu society is the system of age-grading (*riika*). As we have seen, the *mbari* and the *moherega* system help to form several groups of kinsfolk within the tribe, acting independently; but the system of the age-grading unites and solidifies the whole tribe in all its activities. . . .

Almost every year, thousands of Kikuyu boys and girls go through the initiation or circumcision ceremony and automatically become members of one age-grade (*riika rimwe*) irrespective of *mbari*, *moherega* or district to which individuals belong. They act as one body in all tribal matters and have a very strong bond of brotherhood and sisterhood among themselves [pp. 3, 4].

The *mbari*, which Kenyatta translates as "family group," consisted of a group of patrilineally related families residing in the same locality. If a new community was being established, the *mbari* might be limited in size to a patriarch and his married sons, their wives, and children. In older communities they might occupy a whole ridge and number in the thousands. The elementary families in a *mbari* were called *nyumba* ('a man, his wife or wives, and their unmarried children'). When a son married he ordinarily built his house near that of his father, thus forming a patrilocal compound (*mucii*). Large *mbari* might also be subdivided into *itura*, 'a collection of dispersed homesteads forming a closely knit microcommunity.' These microcommunities were often further aggregated into a larger unit, the *rugongo* or ridge. This was the largest meaningful localized administrative unit based on kinship (Muriuki 1974, pp. 35–36).

The compound (*mucii*) was not a simple structure. Each wife had her own domain (*nyumba*), which was symbolized by her hut and included herself and her children but ordinarily not her husband, her co-wife, or her sons and daughters-in-law. Thus each co-wife of the patriarch and each son's wife or wives had her own hut and hearth. Although a man when he was first married would ordinarily sleep in his wife's hut, he would, usually after the birth of his second child, move into a special house (*thingira*) built in the compound for men and older boys.

The clan system (*moherega*) needs little further discussion. Compared with the local lineage (*mbari*) and the age sets (*riika*) it had few important functions. There are nine clans, each named after a daughter of Gikuyu and Moombi, the Adam and Eve of Kikuyu mythology. The clans had no political, economic, or ceremonial functions, nor was there a strict rule of clan exogamy.

The age set system, however, needs further elaboration. As Kenyatta indicated, each boy and girl becomes a member of the age set that consists of all individuals circumcised on a given year. These age sets are named after some current event such as "shillingi"—the year that the British introduced shillings as currency: This would probably have been the name of my age set had I been born a Kikuyu. Age set mates are supposed to help one another as siblings during the remainder of their lives. I found that when I introduced myself to a Kikuyu elder he was much more interested in establishing what my age set would have been than in the fact that I came from America or was an anthropologist.

The rite that was highlighted by circumcision for the male and clitoridectomy for the female took place when a boy was between 16 and 18 years old and when a girl was between 10 and 14. For both sexes, this ceremony marked the transition into a sequential series of statuses or age grades that stretched throughout life.

For the girls, the ceremony marked her as a marriageable woman. Marriage—or, more properly, the bearing of her first child, which occurred at about the age of 19—marked the transition to the next stage. The initiation of her oldest child was the next marker, and the initiation of her youngest child the last, after which she was an old woman. Certain privileges and responsibilities were attached to these statuses. During her maidenhood, she lived at home and helped her mother with domestic chores, made friends with other members of her own and adjacent age sets, and flirted with young men not tabooed by the incest barrier. Although coitus was forbidden, interfemoral intercourse was permitted and even thought to be a necessary part of training for later married life. After marriage, she moved to her husband's house, which was always in a different hamlet (*mbari*) and often in a different district. Her role as wife and mother was arduous since she not only had to raise children but was also responsible for gardening and seeing to supplies of wood and water for the household. A woman who was polygynously married shared the task of providing for her husband with her co-wife or co-wives. From genealogies taken in a Kikuyu village in 1969 (Whiting and Herzog, n.d.) more than half the women born before 1920 had one or more co-wives during the course of their married lives. Only 1 in 10 of the women born in the 1940s were polygynous.

At the initiation of her oldest child, a woman was ceremonially initiated into the *nyakinyua* as a junior member of the female council of elders, which was responsible for ensuring that the women of her location carried out their duties during the important rituals such as female initiation, marriage, birth, and death.

When a woman reached menopause, and particularly after her youngest child had been initiated, she would continue her duties on the council but she would be relieved of most of her domestic duties. She would no longer have to feed a large family but could expect help from her sons and daughters-in-law, who would be living nearby. She also was not expected to behave with the decorum expected of women in their childbearing years and was free to make ribald jokes and ostensibly flirt with young men.

The stages through which a man passed during the course of his life were even more highly structured and clearly marked. These are in sequence that of junior warrior, senior warrior, junior elder, senior elder, and finally ritual elder. As previously stated, a young man was initiated into the status of junior warrior when he was about 16 years old. At that time, he became the member of an army set or regiment that consisted of all the age sets formed during a 9-year period. Each regiment took the name of the oldest age set, had regimental songs, war cries, and distinctive designs on their shields. It also chose a political leader, a chief composer, and organizer of songs and dances. For 6 years, a man was considered a novice under the direction and tutelage of members of his regiment who had graduated to senior warriorhood. This change of status was accomplished by payment of two goats to the council of elders and participation in a public ceremony. As a senior warrior, a man became a member of the council of senior warriors, which was responsible for the defense of the country against territorial expansion and theft of cattle, sheep, and goats by Masai and other hostile neighbors—even sometimes against other Kikuyu. Junior warriors were usually assigned front-line duty if they had proved themselves competent. The senior warriors were more often the strategists, but they continued to carry the spear and shield, which was a mark of their status. Due to the high birth rate of the Kikuyu, scouting for new land was another task often assigned to warriors.

Fighting and scouting took up by no means all or even most of a warrior's time. When not thus engaged, they spent their time dancing, singing, and playing competitive games with other members of their age set. A most important occupation consisted of forming into small groups and visiting age mates in neighboring villages. Here they were graciously welcomed and fed by the mothers of their age set brothers and took the opportunity to carry on sexual affairs with the sisters of their hosts who, being members of a different lineage (*mbari*), were not interdicted by incest rules. They were not, however, permitted to marry until they had graduated to the next stage—that of junior elder.

It is not until their late twenties that men could marry and begin to learn the role of an elder. Again, they were obliged to pay one male goat or sheep to the senior council of elders and were publicly initiated into the status of elder, junior grade. However, according to Kenyatta, "They are not yet elders; they are learners of the *kiama's* ('senior council') procedures. The *kamatimo* ('junior elders') act as messengers to the *kiama,* and help to skin animals, to light fires, to bring firewood, to roast meat for the senior elders, and to carry ceremonial articles to and from the *kiama* assembly [1953, p. 193]."

During this novitiate period, the junior elders still carried a spear and shield but were primarily concerned with raising a family and learning to be an elder. They joined the warriors in battle only if needed. For the most part, their time was divided between meeting with the senior elders, tending their flocks and herds, and helping their wives with the gardening.

It was not until their oldest son was initiated as a junior warrior that men took the next step up the age grade ladder. At this time, a man joined the *kiama kia mataathi,* 'the council of peace.' Since they did not marry until their late twenties, this step would ordinarily be taken in the mid forties. The ceremony of induction was the most elaborate rite of passage since circumcision. On becoming a senior elder, the spear and shield were replaced by a staff of office, which from then on was carried on all public and ceremonial occasions. Senior elders were responsible for settling disputes, performing rituals, and debating political issues with other members of the council.

Those who were particularly well qualified by virtue of their wisdom and political skills were elected to represent their local (*mbari*) council on larger—ridge or district—councils.

Representation on the larger councils was governed by another principle designed to prevent the accumulation of power by any one individual, descent group, or territorial group. Kikuyu males all belonged to one of two "generations"—*Maina* or *Mwangi*. Membership was assigned at birth on the basis of alternating generations. Father and son belonged to different generations. Grandfather and grandson belonged to the same generation. The right to sit on the larger councils was governed by generation membership, which alternated every 30 years. The changeover took place at an elaborate Kikuyu-wide ceremony. The last of these took place in 1898, when the *Maina* generation stepped down and the *Mwangi* generation took over the "reins of government." The changeover ceremony that was to have occurred in the late 1920s was prohibited by the British. Some modern Kikuyu thinkers hold that the recent growth of a Kikuyu elite would have been impossible if the alternating generation system were still in effect.

When a man's last son was circumcised—he would then be in his sixties—he entered the last and, according to Kenyatta (1953, p. 196), most honored status. He was then initiated into the *Kiama kia maturanguru* ("religious and sacrificial council"). Members of this council had the exclusive right and responsibility of officiating at the religious ceremonies that took place under the sacred tree.

From this brief and idealized description of the Kikuyu life-cycle, the following features emerge:

1. Each stage in life is clearly defined and ritually marked at each step, and the roles required of the occupants of each stage are clearly specified.
2. A period of role learning precedes the two most important stages. One must pass through the novitiate stage of junior warrior before becoming a senior warrior. A similar sequence applies to junior and senior elders.
3. The age set system establishes a same age/same sex support group that remains in effect throughout the life-span.
4. Both men and women interact more and are more intimate with members of their age set than with their spouses. Husbands and wives sleep in the same hut only during the first years of marriage.
5. A socially meaningful status is assigned to the aged of both sexes.
6. The local community consisting primarily of male members of a patrilineage together with their wives and children has generational depth and continuity. It provides a strong hierarchical support group that complements the age set.

Ethnographic materials describing how problems are solved elsewhere in the world can often give a useful perspective on our own society. Unless one takes the ethnocentric position that solutions by preindustrial peoples are quaint but irrelevant for modern life, they can serve to shake the biases of those who focus exclusively on their own society.

The title assigned to me for this chapter is "Aging and Becoming an Elder." From the perspective of Kikuyu culture, our society has the former—aging—but not the latter—elderhood. Although there are numerous particularistic statuses that are open to some older people, such as a church elder or chairman of the board, the only universalistic status occupied by everyone over 65 is that of senior citizen. Unlike the Kikuyu, there is no formal preparation for this status. One does not become a junior senior citizen apprenticed to and instructed by senior senior citizens. Furthermore, there is no public ceremony that proclaims that one has become a senior citizen, nor is there a staff of office or change of costume proclaiming this status. In fact, many try to deny that they have reached this stage of life.

It should also be noted that we measure age by a calendar, whereas the Kikuyu use a more sociologically relevant yardstick. For a Kikuyu man, marriage makes him eligible for the status of a novitiate or junior elder, but the attainment of senior eldership must wait upon the initiation of one's eldest son, and ritual eldership upon the initiation of one's youngest son. Eldership for Kikuyu females is also defined by a woman's position in the reproductive cycle.

The Kikuyu elders were expected to play an important role in the society. Senior elders were the peacekeepers and judges. The ritual elders, who were the age of our senior citizens, were responsible for carrying out the most sacred of the rituals. The senior citizen in our society has no such assignment. In fact, his or her status is sociologically and psychologically retrogressive. With social security benefits, medicare, and medicaid he or she becomes at least partially a dependent of the state.

Occupational retirement may correspond in time with becoming a senior citizen. This is often celebrated by a retirement dinner given by friends and colleagues. If this is supposed to be a rite of passage it is a very peculiar one. Van Gennep (1910) argues persuasively that all such rites have three phases: (1) a preliminal period during which one is symbolically separated from a previous status; (2) a liminal period or transitional stage; and (3) a postliminal phase during which one is incorporated and officially accepted into the new status. Retirement dinners generally focus on the preliminal phase. There is no definition of the new status, no instruction as to the behavior expected of a retired person, and certainly no group of retired people waiting to accept and welcome the retiree. At my recent retirement dinner, I was able to say that either retirement was not a rite of passage or Van Gennep's analysis of ritual was wrong.

When a Kikuyu elder left the community, he or she could expect to find someone in the same age set who was expected to treat him or her as a sibling. This support group was distributed throughout Kikuyuland. No such support group is available to our senior citizen. High school or college classmates, sorority sisters, fraternity brothers, or occupational colleagues are small groups that are highly localized. Except for the brotherhood and sisterhood of all people, our support groups are highly particularistic.

Finally, and perhaps most important, few senior citizens in our society live in the community in which they were born. The practice of neolocal residence indicates that a young couple ordinarily sets up residence and raises their family in a community other than that in which either was born and brought up. During this period, they generally develop a support group composed of parents of their children's classmates, colleagues, and sometimes neighbors. Many couples, upon retirement and the marriage of their children, make still another move—to Florida, Southern California, or some other warm climate community of other retired people. Here they have to start afresh to find supportive friends.

This discussion may seem to be a plea for the acceptance of a "utopian" system of age grades, age sets, and permanent multigenerational microcommunities and gerontocracy. Such is not the case. Such a system is incompatible with a complex industrialized society such as our own. It may be, however, that some of the features of our society that have been illuminated by contrast with the Kikuyu might be modified, but contrast with a single case is quite inadequate. Other life-cycle strategies that have been reported in the ethnographic literature should be explored so the dimensions can be further identified and the economic and political constraints can be better understood. To my knowledge, there has been no cross-cultural studies of the life-cycle as a whole. There have been many parts of it such as early childhood, adolescent initiation, and Simmons's cross-cultural study of the aged. The results of these studies should be put together and new sources explored. I would like to suggest that this committee promulgate and support such a project.

REFERENCES

Cox, F. M., and Mberia, N. (1977) *Aging in a Changing Village Society.* Washington, D.C.: International Federation on Ageing.

Kenyatta, J. (1953) *Facing Mount Kenya: The Tribal Life of the Gikuyu.* London: Secker and Warburg.

Muriuki, G. (1974) *A History of Kikuyu, 1500–1900.* Nairobi: Oxford University Press.

Simmons, L. (1945) *The Role of the Aged in Primitive Society.* New Haven, Conn.: Yale University Press.

Van Gennep, A. (1910) *The Rites of Passage.* Translated by M. B. Vizedon and G. L. Chaffee (1960). Chicago: University of Chicago Press.

Whiting, B., and Herzog, J. (n.d.) Unpublished field notes.

chapter 5

Historical Change in the Household Structure of the Elderly in Economically Developed Societies[1]

DANIEL SCOTT SMITH

Specifying and understanding the relationships between old people and their families in past societies are challenging and important tasks. Historians have only recently begun to study older populations. Entering a field already explored by other social scientists, they encountered a variety of theoretical discussions relevant to their own inquiries. Characteristically, the historians adopted one or another of these perspectives to design their research and to organize their findings. At the same time, the catholicism and empiricism of the tradition of historical study shaped their works. Time and space were given expansive specifications. To understand the present, historians instinctively sensed that they must go back not a decade or generation but centuries, and that they had to examine the family relationships of the elderly in a diversity of cultures. Historians also attempted to discover a data source that would provide maximal comparability over time and among societies. Research has thus

[1] The research underlying this paper was supported by the National Institute on Aging, Grant AG 00350-02. Michel Dahlin, Mark Friedberger, and Janice Reiff assisted in the research on the 1880 and 1900 U.S. samples. Hans Christian Johansen (University of Odense), Andrejs Plakans (Iowa State University), and Ethel Shanas (University of Illinois at Chicago Circle) generously supplied unpublished data for use in this paper.

concentrated on the study of family relationships from information on households.

Although historical documentation of the household structure of the elderly remains incomplete at present, contrasting the extant record with the theoretical perspectives can yield insights about both history and theory. This preliminary assessment is the chief purpose of this chapter. The first section outlines three major theoretical notions pertinent to the subject and briefly discusses the categories and problems of interpretation of data on households. The apparent conflicts among the perspectives define what needs to be known empirically; the constructs thus supply a useful heuristic framework. The second part employs the available historical evidence to fill in the desired framework. Three more realistic propositions emerge to clarify the historical record and to modify the theoretical constructs. The final section of the chapter surveys and comments on three important problems suggested by the realistic propositions.

THE THREE PERSPECTIVES

Modernization and Postmodernization

Once upon a time, in traditional societies, people lived in extended families; now they live in nuclear families. In between came (in older versions) the industrial revolution or (in newer terminology) modernization. Old people enjoyed security, status, and power in traditional societies in part because their age made them dominant within their families. Modernization or industrialization involved proletarianization, urbanization, greater geographic and social mobility, and the rise of individualism. These developments destroyed the extended family and the advantaged position of the elderly.

Some versions of this interpretation concentrate on changes that have occurred in the twentieth century in Western societies. Among these are the rising proportion of the population in older age groups, the impact of compulsory retirement, the emergence of mass affluence, and the development of the welfare state as an alternative to the family. This is the postmodernization or advanced-industrial variant of the model.

If this orientation is completely correct, then the situation of the elderly in currently advanced societies should be roughly similar as should their position in traditional, preindustrial societies. This theory, in short, predicts little variation over space but great change over time.

Demographic Determinism

In all human societies, past and present, mean household size has been remarkably small. Multigenerational households are never universal and, more frequently, comprise only a distinct minority among all households. Demographic constraints—a steep age structure produced by high fertility, large variance in fertility, and high mortality—explain the striking similarity in household structure in all traditional societies. Since no golden age of the extended family for old people existed, there could not have been a major transition as predicted by the modernization model. The secular decline in vital rates ironically implies that a larger proportion of the population in demographically advanced (low fertility and mortality) societies can enjoy the possibility of an extended family or household. Generally, however, this perspective emphasizes little variation over either time or space.

Cultural Continuity

As a primary group, the family embodies a set of meanings whose definition is extraordinarily important to individuals in all societies. People will maintain a whole range of family practices, regardless of major demographic changes, economic transformations, and ideological revolutions. The nuclear family, for example, does not fit modern societies any better than alternative ways of conceptualizing organizing family relationships. In the distant past, usually before written records existed, different cultures developed divergent ways of organizing family structure. Although there may be functional reasons why a particular type of family structure evolved in a given society, the important point for this argument is that whatever exists, persists. Family structure is primarily a cultural phenomenon, a set of intimate relationships robustly resistant to change. This perspective thus predicts great variation in household structure over space but little change over time.

Discussion

The first perspective derives from classic sociological theory that has attempted to define and understand, most often by means of dichotomous ideal types, the great transformation under way in Western society since the early nineteenth century. "From extended to nuclear" is the familial analogue of "from status to contract" and "from *Gemeinschaft* to *Gesellschaft.*" The demographic emphasis reflects a later orientation in sociology and anthropology: the search for various universal features in human relations and in human societies and the development of functional explanations to account for the commonalities. With its origins in anthropology and linguistics, the emphasis on cultural continuity is still more recent. Based on relativistic assumptions about cultures, this orientation uses language to locate universals in the human mind.

No bibliographical citations are provided for these three interpretations, for no scholar would subscribe completely to any of them. Although there is some truth in each position, they are now polemical arguments, more often cited by their opponents than by their proponents; they have become straw men. Not only do competing social science theories reflect different orientations (often ideological in origin) and the distinctive concerns of the times of their formulators; they also provide answers to quite distinct questions and are not, when fully understood, actually competing. The theoretical literature is most significant for identifying the important issues. I hope in this chapter to transcend the straw men and resultant pseudocontroversies by explicitly not regarding them seriously as explanations but as constructs that inform us as to what needs explanation. In this case, the three perspectives supply an empty matrix that needs to be filled with historical evidence.

TIME

Data from three eras—premodern, modern, and postmodern—are required. Scholars agree that the sustained per capita economic growth is the proper division between the first two periods. The modern versus postmodern distinction is more ambiguous and controversial; the contrast should perhaps be labeled industrial versus advanced–industrial. We can avoid this terminological problem for Western societies by comparing the nineteenth century with the era after World War II. Whether this periodization is important for the history of the elderly is, of course, an empirical question.

CULTURAL SPACE

If the modernization perspective requires us to examine change over centuries, the cultural continuity argument informs us that an adequate theory cannot rest on the experience of a single society. Three major cultural family systems may be documented with historical evidence on household structure.

Household structure is a narrower phenomenon than family structure.

The latter might be defined through the diversity, frequency, and meaning of interactions between persons biologically or fictively related by blood or marriage. It is difficult and sometimes impossible for the historian to study that expansive definition of family structure. The patterns of co-residence enumerated by census-takers and other list-makers should not be confused with this broad conception of family structure. Who lives with whom supplies an operationalizable index of family structure. In terms of relative availability of data over time and space, the household must be regarded as the basic building block of the comparative history of the family. Furthermore, sharing living space is not a trivial matter for individuals. The study of household structure is at least as central to larger issues as such possible alternatives as family law, inheritance practices, child-naming patterns, and marriage contracts. Without the index of the household, this chapter about the history of the family of the elderly would lack an empirical section.

That data exist does not prove that they have meaning. There is, however, considerable evidence that a correspondence exists between household structure and family structure. My earlier work on Massachusetts has convinced me that a conjugal family system prevailed during the colonial era and became even more pronounced during the nineteenth century. The evidence for this conclusion comes from the range of kin recognized in wills, the names parents gave and did not give their children, and the emphasis on the centrality of marriage in law, and Puritan writings on the family. For example, if men had children, they almost never gave anything in their wills to anyone except their wives and children; a man also did not name a son for his brother, unless the son's uncle had no children. As the culture linked marriage to the economic independence of men, people overwhelmingly lived in conjugal or nuclear households, although taking in a widowed mother was not uncommon. Their writings about the family neglected the subject of household composition; they seemed to have held quite precise ideas about family statuses (what it meant to be a wife, a father, a head of household) and family relationships (husband–wife, parent–child).

The study of household structure involves the interpretation, classification, and analysis of the persons clustered together on listings. It is not always clear if the people listed together lived under one roof, ate together, worked together, or were merely a unit to be taxed by authorities. Slaves, for example, are listed at the bottom of the households of white Marylanders in 1776. A widow in early Massachusetts living in the same house as her married son was sometimes enumerated as a separate head of family if her autonomy had been established in her late husband's will. Although she was a dependent of her son, her rights to that dependence could be sustained in court. Who lived with whom in the past obviously depends on what was meant by both the enumerators and the enumerated. Historians appear to have been quite careful in using household lists; other sources are usually exploited to determine the meaning behind the lists.

Focusing on the households of the older population has two additional disadvantages. Because of high fertility, old people were relatively scarce in the past. For the era before national census-taking, one must rely on listings for localities. Thus, only 297 persons over age 64 from five communities are available from all of England before 1800. Local listings in the premodern era, as in Maryland in 1776, often do not provide information on relationship to head; kin ties must be inferred from surnames and ages of persons in the household. Finally, since previous research on the history of the household has concentrated on mean size (Laslett 1972), the data typically are not tabulated by age. (Anderson 1972 is a rare exception.)

Social gerontologists and historians use different schemes of household classification. The typology of the gerontologists depends on a set of priorities in the coding of family structure. Living with a married child has precedence over all arrangements; living with an unmarried child has precedence over living with another relative (other than spouse), which has precedence over living with an unrelated person, which, finally, has precedence over living alone or, if married, living with a spouse (Shanas *et al.* 1968). Historians of the family use the number of marital units in a household to define its structure. The main types are (Laslett 1972): (1) nuclear: one married couple living with or without unmarried children or a widow(er) living with unmarried children; (2) extended: a nuclear household plus individuals from another marital unit, for example, a brother or widowed mother of the head; (3) multiple: a household with two or more married couples; (4) no family: a household without a marital unit but containing related persons (e.g., coresident unmarried siblings); and (5) solitary: living alone, sometimes defined to include living with nonkin such as servants or boarders.

Although these household classification schemes are not directly comparable, each distinguishes among the three types of family structures (systems) documented for both normative ideals and actual behavior of people. These types and their historical locale are (Laslett 1977) defined below.

1. Conjugal: The married couple defines the family unit, and households in this system have only one marital unit or, on occasion, one couple and another relative, for example, a widowed mother.

The existence of the ideal and the reality of the conjugal family has been attributed to societies in northwestern Europe.

2. Stem: The family line, not marriage, provides the key to kinship. Couples in each generation attempt to preserve the continuity of the "house." Although households ideally contain two married couples (a married parent and a married child), there is only one couple per generation. A widowed mother living with a married child is also consistent with the stem pattern. Although the stem structure existed in parts of Europe, Japan provides the most striking case.

3. Joint: The family is a corporate entity including married siblings. A household with an old person would typically have two or more married siblings. A joint understanding of the family may be found in the cultures of eastern Europe and China. Students of the Chinese family designate these types as "grand families" (Hanley and Wolf 1978).

It is difficult, of course, to define family types in an unequivocal yet comprehensive manner (Pasternak 1976). For some analytical purposes, a set of prerequisites as to inheritance rules, economic activity, etc. might be advantageous (Verdon 1979), but such elaborate specifications limit comparative analysis to a few cases. The conjugal, stem, and joint types are suited to the subject addressed—the historical evolution of the family structure of the elderly in economically developed societies. Some scholars have argued that conjugal households have predominated in the populations of all societies, while others claim that different forms of domestic organization existed in significant proportions in some cultures. The types and the societies they include provide a genuine problem for empirical historical analysis.

DEMOGRAPHIC VARIABLES

Since demographic factors influence the distribution of household types in a population, we must define three different concepts.

1. Incidence in the population is the least desirable indicator. Demographic parameters affect the proportion of households with three generations, with earlier marriage, for example, increasing the possible incidence (Mendels 1978). Many studies, however, report only a distribution of household types for the entire population.

2. Here age-specific incidence refers to the households of persons aged 65 and over. Age-specific incidence is more comparable among societies; in a society with earlier marriage, however, old people

will be more likely to have only married children. Since coresidence
of married old people with their married children is the distinguish-
ing characteristic of nonconjugal family systems, nuptiality patterns
affect the incidence of stem and joint households in the older
population.
3. Although age-specific propensity is the best measure for assessing
   rules of behavior, it is often difficult to estimate and is rarely
   reported. Age-specific propensity measures, for example, the percentage of old people who are grandparents who live with grandchildren. Unfortunately, it is usually not known what proportion
   of old people have living grandchildren. More frequently the percentage with living children is known or can be indirectly estimated.

THREE REALISTIC PROPOSITIONS

The three perspectives provide the framework of Table 5.1. Northwestern Europe, Japan, and eastern Europe represent the historic areas
of conjugal, stem, and joint families, respectively. The preindustrial era,
the stage of industrialization, and the current, advanced–industrial era
delineate the time parameter. Stages of the demographic transition
roughly correspond to the time periods; demographic controls must also
be introduced for the columns, since these family types also have characteristic patterns of nuptiality.

Realistic Proposition 1

The best predictor of differences in the household structure of the
elderly among economically advanced societies today is the pattern extant before industrialization/urbanization/modernization.
The results for Japan (see Table 5.2 and, for detail, Appendix Table
5.A1) provide the most striking support for this contention. Four of five
Japanese over age 64 lived with their children in 1973 and three in five
lived with married children. Although some historians of the Japanese
household (Nakane 1972, Hayami and Uchida 1972) stress its small size
and simple structure, the idea of the household (*ie*) in Japan conforms
to the stem ideal. Although the Japanese ideal differs from Chinese and
Indian models, the emphasis is strongly on the continuity of the household over generations. The incidence of the three-generation household
in the entire population is much higher in the Tokugawa period (1615–1868)
than in premodern northwestern Europe. The frequency of parent–child

TABLE 5.1

Framework and Evidence for the Historical Study of the Household Structure of the Elderly

Variables	Cultural space: Type of family system			Demographic characteristics
	Conjugal	Stem	Joint	
A. Periodization				
Premodern	Rural Denmark in 1787, 1801 England before 1801 Maryland, 1776		Kurland, Latvia, 1797	High fertility and mortality; small percentage of the aged in the population.
Modern	U.S., 1880, 1900 Preston, England, 1851		Poland, 1966 Yugoslavia, 1969	Declining mortality and fertility; a somewhat older population
Postmodern	United States, 1962, 1975 Britain, 1962 Denmark, 1962	Japan, 1972		Low fertility and mortality; 10% or more over age 65
B. Historical regions	Northwestern Europe	Japan	China, Eastern Europe	
C. Distinctive demographic parameters	Late marriage; low maximum of complex households	Earlier marriage; greater complexity possible, especially with first-son succession	Earliest marriage; greatest possible complexity	

TABLE 5.2
Summary of Living Arrangements of Population over Age Sixty Four

Place and date	Sample size	Percentage who have living children	Percentage living with Children	Percentage living with Married child
United States, 1975[a]	5,756	82	14	5
1962[b]	2,442	82	25	10
1952[c]	17,661	—	33	
1900[d]	3,001	85	61.4	26.5
1880[d]	1,500	—	60.7	25.0
Maryland, whites, 1776[e]	99	—	58–64	—
Denmark, 1962[b]	2,446	82	18	4
Rural Denmark, 1801[f]	464	c.75	56.0	29.5
Rural Denmark, 1787[f]	369	—	55.0	28.5
Britain, 1962[b]	2,500	76	33	12
Preston, Lancashire, 1851[g]	194	c.67	68.0	32.5
Preston environs, 1851[g]	249	—	48.1	18.5
Five places in England, pre-1801[h]	297	—	46.1	16.5
Postenden, Latvia, 1797[i]	94	65	41.5	24.2
Sweden, 1956[j]	—	—	11	—
West Germany, 1958[k]	821	80	32	—
Milan, Italy, c. 1958[l]	1,958	—	41.8	8.3
Poland, 1966[l]	2,693	86	48	31
Yugoslavia, 1969[l]	2,645	86	48	38
Israel, western origin, 1967[l]	793	—	26	15
oriental origin	349	—	58	25
Japan, 1972[m]	—	96	81	60

[a] From Shanas 1978.

[b] From Shanas et al. 1968, table VII–1, p. 186.

[c] From Steiner and Dorfman 1957, table 3.6, p. 22. Includes children aged 21 and over; women married to men under age 65 are excluded from sample.

[d] From national samples of the noninstitutionalized population. This research is supported by Grant AG 00350-02 of the National Institute on Aging; Smith (1978) provides details on the samples.

[e] From Brumbaugh 1915. Data from Prince George's County, I, pp. 1–17; Frederick County, I, pp. 198–232; and Harford County, II, pp. 122–137, 142–193.

[f] Tabulated from printouts on households kindly supplied by Hans Chr. Johansen. See Johansen 1972, 1978.

[g] From Anderson 1972, table 7.8, p. 225.

[h] From Laslett 1976, table 8, p. 111.

[i] From Plakans 1978, table II, p. 11.

[j] From Burgess 1960. Sample limited to those aged 67 and over.

[k] From Baumert 1962, table 2, p. 421.

[l] From Shanas 1973, table 1, 2, p. 507.

[m] From Palmore 1975, table 4.2, p. 39.

coresidence in the 1972 survey of the elderly is so high that one doubts that it could have been still higher in the Tokugawa era.

Demographically (Hajnal 1965) and familially (Laslett 1977) northwestern Europe in the preindustrial era was unique: late marriage, especially for women, with a high proportion never marrying; higher marital fertility; and a very high proportion of conjugal or nuclear households among all households. Eastern Europe was at the other extreme—very early marriage for both sexes and high proportions of nonnuclear households. Central Europe was probably closer to northwestern Europe and southern Europe to eastern Europe, albeit with considerable variation among localities within these broad areas.

The results for Europe in the 1950s and 1960s nicely correspond to these traditional differences. The countries with the lowest proportions of old people living with children include Sweden (11%), Denmark (18%), the United States (25% in 1962, 14% in 1975), and Great Britain (33%). Coresidence of old people with children was distinctly higher in both Poland and Yugoslavia (48% in each case). In between, come West Germany (32%) and Milan, Italy (42%). The differential between older Jews of western origin (26%) and nonwestern origin (58%) in Israel is also consistent with an emphasis on the continuity of household patterns between the preindustrial era and the present.

Perhaps cultural continuity is not the entire explanation. Current differentials among countries might be attributed to the level of economic development as indexed by per capita income. Housing shortages in the socialist countries of eastern Europe, the inadequacy of pensions in Japan, or the relative poverty of nonwestern-origin Jews in Israel might also be advanced as explanations. It is naive, however, to believe that people in the nonwestern world are merely westerners with less money and less constituent-oriented governments. The concentration on industrial development in both eastern Europe and Japan may have been facilitated by the cultural tradition of intergenerational coresidence of old people with their children. The family, to invert Mills's (1959, p. 10) classic definition of the sociological imagination, is an institution that can channel public issues into private troubles. The most serious criticism of this proposition is that cross-sectional differentials provide an unreliable basis for making generalizations about historical development; the converse of that argument is also true.

Realistic Proposition 2

The household structure of the older population changed relatively little during the early and middle phases of modernization and industrialization.

The remarkable similarity between the distribution of household types in rural Denmark in 1781 and 1801 and the United States in both 1880 and 1900 provides the best evidence for this contention. The distinctive household characteristic of the conjugal family system was present in both preindustrial Denmark and the industrial United States; married old people tended to live with unmarried children, and unmarried (i.e., mostly widowed) old people tended to live with married children (see Table 5.A1).

Although some scholars have written about the United States in 1900 as if it were a traditional, rural society (Nimkoff 1962), nearly every indicator of modernization—urbanization, per capita income growth, fertility decline, and level of literacy—points to a process of rapid change under way already for more than half a century (Brown 1976). Rural Denmark in 1787 and 1801 also provides a realistic example of a Western preindustrial society. Nearly half of the heads of families in the entire population were farmers, mainly lease-holding tenants, more than a quarter were cottagers, and about one in eight were artisans (Johansen 1972). The small sample from Maryland in 1776 is not so adequate since family relationships had to be inferred and since the slave population is excluded from the tabulation. The standard image of Western preindustrial society also excludes such American innovations as slavery. Not many Americans in 1900 were of Danish origin, but then the ancestors of many Americans in that year also were not Americans in the eighteenth century.

Realistic Proposition 3

The household structure of the older population has changed dramatically in the twentieth century in Western societies.

In both 1880 and 1900, more than three in five persons aged 65 and over in the United States lived with their children. By 1962, the proportion coresiding with children had dropped to one in four and, by 1975, to one in seven. One may guess that the change in household structure of the elderly in Britain and Denmark is also a twentieth-century development. The twentieth-century timing is consistent with the other major discontinuities in the history of old people—the rising fraction of the aged in the total population, the decline in rates of labor force participation by older men, and the development of welfare policies such as social security. The modern–postmodern or industrial–advanced–industrial dichotomy appears to be central to the history of old people in Western societies (Achenbaum and Stearns 1978).

The framework outlined in Table 5.1 represents an advance over the limited truth in the three perspectives. Although there has been a before-

and-after (Laslett 1976) in the history of the household structure of the elderly in Western societies, that transition was not coincident with the breakthrough to modern, industrial civilization in the nineteenth century. Although continuity in household structure during that century supports the cultural argument, change finally did occur. Even if a similar massive transition is not inherent in, for example, the Japanese case, it is also true that no culture today is isolated. Western family values have been resisted, but they have also seemed attractive to persons in other cultures (Goode 1970, Caldwell 1978, Ransel 1978). Still, the labels could be incorrect; perhaps the change should be identified with the particular region, the West, and not with such general categories as postmodern or advanced–industrial. The straw man of demographic determinism is just that, representing a confusion of what is significant for the entire population with what is relevant to a small fraction who are old enough to have both married children and grandchildren.

THREE EMPIRICAL PROBLEMS

Table 5.1 is designed to outline the long-run comparative picture and to suggest what work needs to be done. The apparent regularities therein are not unimportant. That 64% of Taiwanese who had a married child between the ages of 20 and 39 lived with a married child in 1973 does not seem so surprising (Freedman et al. 1978). Policymakers concerned with curtailing rapid population growth will find it significant that historically fertility changes more easily than family structure. Since research into the history of the elderly is only beginning, I can only outline three important areas in this chapter.

1. The origin and persistence of the distinctive premodern patterns of household structure
2. The curvilinear hypothesis that early industrialization and urbanization produced a higher incidence of coresidence of older people and their children
3. The mixture of considerations underlying the dramatic decline in the coresidence of the elderly with their children in the United States in the twentieth century

Premodern Discontinuity and Continuity

Since the characteristic patterns of households are so persistent over time within societies, examples of change therefore become very interesting. Cross-cultural data suggest that nonnuclear household organization does have correlates, being more common in settled agricultural societies than in hunting–gathering or urban–technological ones (Blumberg and Winch 1972). Several scholars have uncovered hints of major transitions within the premodern period.

Mean household size in Suwa County, Shinano Province, Japan, fell sharply from 7.04 to 4.25 between 1671–1700 and 1851–1870 (Hayami and Uchida 1972). The number of married couples in households with at least one married couple declined from 1.66 to 1.20 over the same interval. In all periods, the proportion of three-generation households fluctuated around 30%. These trends, not elaborated on by the authors of the study, are consistent with a shift from a joint to stem structure.

The European historical record provides examples of a shift to the northwest European demographic pattern. Monter (1979) documents an upward shift in marriage age in the fascinating case of post-Calvin Geneva. If Geneva shifted from the southern European regime, the Baltic area appears to have moved from the eastern European to the northwest European model during the nineteenth century. The Baltic provinces of Russia in 1897 had non-Russian levels of marital fertility and age at marriage (Coale et al. 1979) and mean household size was only 4.8 (Plakans 1976). Plakans's work in progress on the soul-revision (fiscal census) of 1797 points to a quite different pattern—very large households (a mean size of 17 persons), early marriage, and nonnuclear household organization.

Two noteworthy points appear in the comparison (see Table 5.3) of household structure for persons age 65 and over in the United States in

TABLE 5.3
Comparison of the Household Structure of the Population Aged Sixty Five and over on Forty Serf Estates in Kurland (Latvia) in 1797 and the United States in 1900[a]

	Males		Females	
Type of household	Kurland 1797	U.S.A. 1900	Kurland 1797	U.S.A. 1900
Solitary	15.8%	5.8%	30.0%	8.5%
Nuclear	48.8	57.3	25.6	39.2
Extended and no family	7.4	29.6	22.1	47.2
Multiple	28.0	7.5	22.3	5.2
Sample size	1177	1508	945	1493

[a] Kurland sources: Unpublished results furnished by Andrejs Plakans, Department of History, Iowa State University. (See Plakans 1978.) United States sources: National sample of noninstitutionalized population. (See Smith 1978.)

1900 and people in the same age group located on 40 serf estates in Kurland (Latvia) in 1797. In Latvia, there were more multiple households and, more surprisingly, a higher proportion of old persons living without kin (Plakans 1978). One should not exaggerate, as Laslett (1976) argues, the extent of coresidence of old people with their kin in the preindustrial era; a larger fraction of old people in rural Denmark in 1787 and 1801 lived apart from kin than in the United States in 1900. Very high proportions of multiple families were, however, a distinctive feature of serf societies in eastern Europe (Czap 1978), and solitary residence was unusual. At present, it is unknown whether the abolition of serfdom in Latvia in the 1820s resulted in a nuclear household pattern or a small, kin-based, complex household; the mean size of 4.8 in 1897 is compatible with the predominance of either form.

If one can find hints of change in characteristic household structures within preindustrial societies, the literature is even more rich in illustrations of continuity. The incidence of the complex household in Yugoslavia, including the famous *zadruga*, may be as common in the recent past as in the nineteenth century or, for that matter, the medieval period (Hammel 1972, Halpern and Anderson 1970). The Bulgarian village of Dragalevtsy, located on the outskirts of Sofia, provides a particularly striking case of continuity. In 1935, some 60% of the households in the village had three or more generations. By 1974, after the abolition of private ownership of farmland and the integration of the population into the economy of the capital, 61% had three or more generations (Sanders 1977).

The continuity in living arrangements may conceal important shifts in the content of family relationships; household structure may be an insensitive index of family structure. Anthropologists have a great advantage over historians, whose respondents are dead, and over survey researchers, who limit their reports to narrowly quantifiable aspects of behavior. The anthropological tradition stresses the interpretation of the meanings underlying behavior. Robert J. Smith (1978) studied the Japanese village of Kurusu in 1952 and 1975. By the latter date, reports Smith, "The parents and children of Kurusu obviously feel they rarely understand one another [p. 190]." Despite the vast changes in economic life and subtle shifts in the meaning of family relationships, the ideal of intergenerational coresidence persists. A young woman is quoted for the ideal:

It's best for a young couple and the husband's parents to live separately—but not too far apart—until the first baby comes. Then the young couple can move in with the parents. I think the trend to living separately went too far.

Now the generations are moving closer together and both children and parents
are more willing to adjust and make compromises than they were until recently
[Smith 1978, p. 191].

Such views may be merely rationalizations, functional substitutes for
"adequate public welfare and pension programs for the elderly [Kii
1976]." Or they may be persistent value preferences, transcending mun-
dane economic necessities. Although one must not reify the index of
household structure into the larger concept of family structure, the preferences of the young woman quoted above are reflected in the actual
living arrangements of the elderly in Japan today.

Industrialization and the Curvilinear Hypothesis

In his important study of the Lancashire textile city of Preston, Anderson (1971, 1972; see also 1977) reversed the modernization argument
that associates industrialization with the decline of complex household
formation. Coresidence of old people with children in Preston in 1851
was more common than in either the preindustrial period or the present
in England. Retaining the moral thrust of the modernization perspective,
Anderson argued that coresidence occurred on the basis of calculation
rather than norms; older people, particularly widows, were useful in
caring for the children of a working mother.

There are several reasons for supposing that old people may have
been more likely to live with children and other kin during the nineteenth
century. Declining mortality increased the proportion of old people with
surviving children. In rural areas where the household was a unit of
economic production, separate residence (or separate listing) might have
been more common than in cities; in urban–industrial settings, on the
other hand, people worked outside the home for employers who were
not kin. During the early phases of urban growth, housing was scarce
and expensive. Finally, a characteristic of current kinship among the
working classes, the close linkage between mothers and daughters, may
be part of the urban world of the nineteenth century (Sweetser 1966,
Bott 1971). Although inheritance and farm succession structured kinship
along male, father–son lines in rural areas, affect was more important
in the city.

The evidence currently available for the United States during the
nineteenth century does not support the curvilinear interpretation. Data
on household headship may be used as a proxy measure for household
structure; widows who head their households are less likely to live with
married children than widows who are not household heads, and only

those listed as heads can live completely alone. The most representative evidence comes from a one-in-five sample of the 1840 Census of Revolutionary War Pensioners (Bureau of the Census 1841). This volume lists both the old person and the household head; headship may thus be ascertained and, if the old person were not the head, one knows if she or he lived with a person who had the same surname. Only 22.5% of widows aged 75 and over (standardized on the 1900 age-distribution of the over 74 population) headed their household in 1840; by 1900 the figure had increased to 28.8%. Thus, there was a slight trend toward independent residence among very old widows during the nineteenth century, a shift consistent with a probable tendency of men to leave their property to their widows rather than to their children. The important subject of inheritance practices has not, however, been sufficiently studied.

Rural–urban differentials may also be cautiously used to make inferences about trends. Some 14.2% of married old people in places over 2500 population in 1900 lived with married children, while in rural areas the figure was 17.8%. Old unmarried people were more likely to live with their married children—some 32.1% in urban areas compared to 39.6% in rural places. Since the city drew widowed, single, and kinless old people who had no place or opportunity in rural areas (Reiff *et al.* 1980), these slight urban–rural differences should not be emphasized.

More suggestive is the differential in living with married sons in contrast to living with married daughters. Old unmarried people were marginally more likely to live with married daughters in urban areas (20.1%) than in rural places (17.2%); urban unmarried old people, however, were much less likely to live with married sons (12.1%) compared with rural unmarried persons aged 65 and over (22.4%). Thus the urban shift to the parent–daughter tie was associated with a sharp decrease in coresidence of old people and married sons. This cross-sectional pattern for 1900 is also evident in the comparison of the 1962 national sample with that for 1900. Some 11% of unmarried old people in the United States in 1962 (compared with 18% in 1900) lived with married daughters, while only 4% lived with married sons (contrasted also to 18% in 1900.) Since we do not have adequate samples before 1880, we cannot address the specific issue of the effects of the first phase of industrialization and urbanization. No change in household composition occurred, however, in Bertalia, a parish lying outside the city of Bologna, Italy, during its period (1880–1910) of initial urbanization (Kertzer 1978). Although change in the household structure of the elderly during the nineteenth century in the United States was probably slight, the direction of change was consistent with the modernization perspective rather than the curvilinear hypothesis.

The Transformation of the Household Structure of the Elderly in the United States during the Twentieth Century

Although the change in living arrangements of the elderly in the United States has accelerated since 1950 (Kobrin 1976a, 1976b), that movement was under way in the first half of the century. The percentage of men aged 65 and over living as parent-of-head declined from 16.3 to 10.9 between 1900 and 1940; the figures for women are 34.2 and 23.0 for the two dates. By 1970, only 4.3% of men and 12.7% of women aged 65 and over were living as the parent of a head of household.

The decline in the coresidence of old people and their children was primarily due to changes in the propensity to form these types of households rather than to shifts in demographic structure. The proportion of old persons with no living child has increased only slightly, from 15% of women in 1900 to 18% of both men and women in 1962. Earlier marriage age and a shorter time span of fertility do imply that old people in recent years are less likely to have an unmarried child with whom they could reside; this is particularly important for married old people who were more likely to live with single rather than married children in 1880 and 1900. The change in the quantity and timing of fertility has, however, only a very small impact on the coresidence of the widowed with children. In 1900, the number of surviving children barely affected the probability of a widowed woman living with a child; some 79% of widows aged 65 and over with one living child in that year lived with that child, while those widows with five or more living children were coresident with a child in nearly 90% of the cases (Smith 1979).

Without a decline in the propensity for coresidence, the proportion of households with three generations or more in the entire population would have sharply increased after 1930 (Kobrin 1976a). The ratio of the population 65 and over to the population in the age-groups occupied by their children has risen dramatically. Similarly, the decrease in male labor force participation at older ages (again, particularly marked in the 1930s when participation of men aged 65 and over dropped from 58.2% to 41.5%) would also have increased the frequency of multigenerational households (Brennan et al. 1967, p. 19). Nongainfully employed old men in 1900 were distinctly more likely to live as dependents of children than those men who still had occupations. The social security system emerged at precisely the right time to dampen these effects produced by changes in age-structure and labor force participation.

Both social commentators and scholars disagree about the larger implications of the decline in the propensity for old people to live with their children during the twentieth century. In social science, as on Wal

Street, there are bulls and bears (Berliner 1977). Historians aspire to be owls, wisely flying over time, rather than optimistically grazing in the fields of survey research or pessimistically foraging in the forests of classic sociological theory.

The bulls emphasize that old people in the United States today live near and frequently interact with their children; old people are not isolated from kin (Shanas *et al.* 1968). Separate residence for old people and their children alleviates the tension and conflicts inherent in sharing space. Intergenrational relationships today are perhaps more harmonious than ever in the past (Anderson 1977), and social security has reduced the need for generations within a family to struggle over the allocation of income.

The bears speculate differently. While producing tension and conflict, coresidence also generates a more genuine closeness. Furthermore, change in the household structure of the older population is not an isolated development in the American family. The bears can draw connections between that movement and the continuing exponential rise in divorce (Preston and McDonald 1979), the ongoing sexual revolution among teenagers (Zelnik and Kantner 1977), the rise in the incidence of primary individuals in all age-groups (Kobrin 1976b), and other changes in American family behavior. Bullish critics of this position argue that the "modern" familial glass is still more than half full (Bane 1976). The dispute is thus between the bulls who emphasize current cross-sectional patterns and the bears who focus on the direction and extent of recent change.

While this historical owl leans toward the bulls in the short run, he must favor the bears over the long-term future. Perhaps the most significant thing one learns from studying the history of the family is how slowly it changes; a decade or two is but a moment in its glacial evolution. Since the family changes slowly, the owl must be impressed by the rapidity and recent origin of the transformation of the living arrangements of the elderly in the United States. The bulls could, however, invoke a historical explanation for the recent shift; it might be regarded as a consequence of the long-standing conjugal emphasis of the family system of northwestern Europe. Behind that peculiar understanding of the family, however, is a general cultural tendency toward individualism (Macfarlane 1979). Thus, the recent change from living-with to living-near may be an ongoing process with living-completely-apart being the ultimate terminus. The middle-aged children of old people today grew up in a society in which a majority of old people lived with children; young persons now are growing up in a society in which a majority of old people live near their children.

The historian may fail in his role as a prophetic owl he will have ample company. His job narrowly is to figure out what happened in the past(s) and how past patterns compare and relate to the present. To accomplish this task, he requires salient data, a technical knowledge of intervening or confounding factors, and a sense of what are the crucial forces for change and continuity. Information on the household structure of the elderly has supplied the first need. Demographic processes—the impact of nuptiality, mortality, and fertility on indices of household composition—are the most important control variables. Modernization in this story provides the irresistible force for change in all human relationships. Cultural preferences for particular definitions of the family make that institution the agent of continuity, an immovable object. When the irresistible force encounters the immovable object, the result, in history as in literature, is a complex, extended drama with an uncertain outcome.

APPENDIX

TABLE 5.A1
Historical and Comparative Data on the Living Arrangements of Persons Aged Sixty-Five and Ove

	United States				Denmark		
Household type	1975	1962	1900	1880	1962	Rural 1801	R 1
I. Married persons							
(1) With spouse only	84%	79%	28.6%	25.2%	82%	31.9%	29
(2) With married daughter	2	1	7.4	6.6	1	6.8	3
(3) With married son		1	8.6	6.6		10.4	9
(4) With unmarried child	10	15	42.4	44.1	14	35.9	37
(5) With other relative	4	3	7.5	10.3	0	4.0	4
(6) With nonkin	2	1	5.6	7.1	3	11.2	16
Sample size	3005	1335	1532	757	1399	251	21:
II. Unmarried persons							
(1) Living alone	66%	48%	11.4%	9.0%	61%	8.9%	8
(2) With married daughter	7	11	18.8	20.7	7	13.6	2.
(3) With married son		4	18.7	16.3		30.5	2.
(4) With unmarried child	10	18	27.0	27.2	15	15.5	1:
(5) With other relative	13	12	13.4	11.8	7	8.0	4
(6) With nonkin	3	6	10.8	15.0	10	23.5	2.
Sample size	2751	1107	1468	744	1107	213	15

a For sources see references to Table 5.2.   (con

5.A1
ued

Household type	Britain		Japan 1972	Poland 1966	Yugo-slavia 1969	Israel 1967	
	Before 1801	1962				Western origin	Oriental origin
rried persons							
With spouse only	44%	68%	15%	50%	49%	82%	47%
With married child	6	5	79	22	33	4	10
With unmarried child	43	23		19	11	12	41
With other relative	7	3	5	3	5		
With nonkin		1	1	6	2	2	2
mple size	119	1211	—	1263	1392	508	204
nmarried persons							
Living alone	17%	43%	9%	30%	32%	50%	23%
With married child	24	19	83	38	44	35	47
With unmarried child	21	18		16	8	9	21
With other relative	38	13	6	9	8		
With nonkin		6	2	7	8	6	9
mple size	178	1289	—	1451	1192	285	145

REFERENCES

Achenbaum, W. A., and Stearns, P. N. (1978) Essay: Old age and modernization. *Gerontologist* 18(June):307–312.

Anderson, M. (1971) *Family Structure in Nineteenth Century Lancashire*. Cambridge, England: Cambridge University Press.

Anderson, M. (1972) Household structure and the industrial revolution: Mid-nineteenth-century Preston in comparative perspective. Pp. 215–236 in P. Laslett, ed., *Household and Family in Past Time*. Cambridge, England: Cambridge University Press.

Anderson, M. (1977) The impact on the family relationships of the elderly of changes since Victorian times in governmental income-maintenance provision. Pp. 36–59 in E. Shanas and M. B. Sussman, eds., *Family, Bureaucracy, and the Elderly*. Durham, N.C.: Duke University Press.

Bane, M. J. (1976) *Here to Stay: American Families in the Twentieth Century*. New York: Basic Books.

Baumert, C. (1962) Changes in the family and the position of older persons in Germany. In C. Tibbitts and W. Donahue, eds., *Social and Psychological Aspects of Aging*. New York: Columbia University Press.

Berliner, J. S. (1977) Internal migration: A comparative disciplinary view. Pp. 443–461 in A. A. Brown and E. Neuberger, eds., *Internal Migration: A Comparative Perspective*. New York: Academic Press.

Blumberg, R. L., and Winch, R. F. (1972) Societal complexity and familial complexity: Evidence fo the curvilinear hypothesis. *American Journal of Sociology* 77(March):898–920.

Bott, E. (1971) *Family and Social Network: Roles, Norms, and External Relationships in Ordinary Urban Families*, 2nd ed. London: Tavistock Publications.

Brennan, M. J., Taft, P., and Schupack, M. B. (1967) *The Economics of Age*. New York: W. W. Norton.

Brown, R. D. (1976) *Modernization: The Transformation of American Life, 1600–1865*. New York: Hill and Wang.

Brumbaugh, G. M., ed. (1915) *Maryland Records*. Baltimore, Md.: Williams and Williams.

Bureau of the Census (1841) *A Census of Pensioners for Revolutionary or Military Services*. Washington, D.C.: Secretary of State.

Burgess, E. W. (1960) Family structure and relationships. In E. W. Burgess, ed., *Aging in Western Societies: A Comparative Study*. Chicago: University of Chicago.

Caldwell, J. C. (1978) A theory of fertility: From high plateau to destabilization. *Population and Development Review* 4(December):553–578.

Coale, A. J., Anderson, B., and Härm, E. (1979) *Human Fertility in Russia Since the Nineteenth Century: The Demographic Transition in a Different Historical Context*. Princeton, N.J.: Princeton University Press.

Czap, P., Jr. (1978) Marriage and the peasant joint family in the era of serfdom. Pp. 103–123 in D. Ransel, ed., *The Family in Imperial Russia*. Urbana, Ill.: University of Illinois Press.

Freedman, R., Moots, B., Sun, T., and Weinberger, M. B. (1978) Household composition and extended kinship in Taiwan. *Population Studies* 32 (March):65–80.

Goode, W. J. (1970) *World Revolution and Family Patterns*. New York: Free Press.

Hajnal, J. (1965) European marriage patterns in perspective. Pp. 101–143 in D. V. Glass and D. E. C. Eversley, eds., *Population in History*. London: Edward Arnold.

Halpern, J. M., and Anderson, D. (1970) The Zadruga: A century of change. *Anthropologica* 12(1):83–97.

Hammel, E. (1972) The Zadruga as process. Pp. 335–374 in P. Laslett, ed., *Household and Family in Past Time*. Cambridge, England: Cambridge University Press.

Hanley, S., and Wolf, A. (1978) Comparable Measures and Standard Formats for East Asian Demography and Family History. Unpublished memo, University of Washington, Seattle.

Hayami, A., and Uchida, N. (1972) Size of household in a Japanese county throughout the Tokugawa era. Pp. 473–515 in P. Laslett, ed., *Household and Family in Past Time*. Cambridge, England: Cambridge University Press.

Johansen, H. C. (1972) Some aspects of Danish rural population structure in 1787. *Scandinavian Economic History Review* 20(1):61–70.

Johansen, H. C. (1978) The position of the old in the rural household in a traditional society. Pp. 122–130 in S. Åkerman, H. C. Johansen, and D. Gaunt, eds., *Chance and Change: Social and Economic Studies in Historical Demography in the Baltic Area*. Odense, Denmark: Odense University Press.

Kertzer, D. I. (1978) The impact of urbanization on household composition: Implications from an Italian parish (1880–1910). *Urban Anthropology* 7(Spring):1–23.

Kii, T. (1976) Aging in Japan: Policy Implications of the Aging Population. Unpublished Ph.D. thesis, University of Minnesota.

Kobrin, F. (1976a) The fall in household size and the rise of the primary individual in the United States. *Demography* 13(February):127–138.

Kobrin, F. (1976b) The primary individual and the family: Changes in living arrangements in the United States since 1940. *Journal of Marriage and the Family* 38(May):223–239.

Laslett, P., ed. (1972) *Household and Family in Past Time*. Cambridge, England: Cambridge University Press.

Laslett, P. (1976) Societal development and aging. Pp. 87–116 in R. H. Binstock and E. Shanas, eds. *Handbook of Aging and the Social Sciences*. New York: Van Nostrand Reinhold.

Laslett, P. (1977) Characteristics of the western family considered over time. *Journal of Family History* 2(Summer):89–116.

Macfarlane, A. (1979) *The Origins of English Individualism*. Cambridge, England: Cambridge University Press.

Mendels, F. (1978) Notes on the age of maternity. *Journal of Family History* 3(Fall):236–250.

Mills, C. W. (1959) *The Sociological Imagination*. New York: Oxford University Press.

Monter, W. (1979) Historical demography and religious history in sixteenth-century Geneva. *Journal of Interdisciplinary History* 9(Winter):399–427.

Nakane, C. (1972) An interpretation of the size and structure of the household in Japan over three centuries. Pp. 517–543 in P. Laslett, ed., *Household and Family in Past Time*. Cambridge, England: Cambridge University Press.

Nimkoff, M. F. (1962) Changing family relationships of older people in the United States during the last fifty years. Pp. 405–414 in C. Tibbitts and W. Donahue, eds., *Social and Psychological Aspects of Aging*. New York: Columbia University Press.

Palmore, E. (1975) *The Honorable Elders: A Cross-Cultural Analysis of Aging in Japan*. Durham, N.C.: Duke University Press.

Pasternak, B. (1976) *Introduction to Kinship and Social Organization*. Englewood Cliffs, N.J.: Prentice-Hall.

Plakans, A. (1975) Seigneurial authority and peasant family life: The Baltic Area in the eighteenth century. *Journal of Interdisciplinary History* 5(Spring):629–654.

Plakans, A. (1976) Familial structure in the Russian Baltic provinces: The nineteenth century. Pp. 346–362 in W. Conze, ed., *Sozialgeschichte der Familie in der Neuzeit Europas*. Stuttgart, Germany: Ernst Klett Verlag.

Plakans, A. (1978) The Familial Contexts of Old Age in a Serf Community. Paper presented at the annual meetings of the Social Science History Association, Columbus, Ohio.

Preston, S. H., and McDonald, J. (1979) The incidence of divorce within cohorts of American marriages contracted since the Civil War. *Demography* 16(February):1–26.

Ransel, D., ed. (1978) *The Family in Imperial Russia*. Urbana, Ill.: University of Illinois Press.

Reiff, J. L., Dahlin, M. R., and Smith, D. S. (1980) Rural push and urban pull: Work and family experiences of older black women in southern cities, 1880–1900. Forthcoming in S. Harley, ed. *The Urban Experiences of Afro-American Women: A Social History*. Boston: G. K. Hall & Company.

Sanders, I. T. (1977) Dragalevtsy household members then (1935) and now. Pp. 125–133 in H. L. Kostanick, ed., *Population and Migration Trends in Eastern Europe*. Boulder, Colo.: Westview Press.

Shanas, E. (1973) Family–kin networks and aging in cross-cultural perspective. *Journal of Marriage and the Family* 35(3).

Shanas, E. (1978) Final Report. National Survey of the Aged. A Report to the Administration on Aging.

Shanas, E., Townshend, P., Wedderburn, D., Friis, H., Milhoj, P., and Stehouwer, J. (1968) *Old People in Three Industrial Societies*. New York: Atherton Press.

Smith, D. S. (1978) A community-based sample of the older population from the 1880 and 1900 United States manuscript census. *Historical Methods* 11(Spring):67–74.

Smith, D. S. (1979) Life course, norms, and the family system of older Americans in 1900. *Journal of Family History* 4(Fall):285–298.

Smith, R. J. (1978) *Kurusu: The Price of Progress in a Japanese Village, 1951–1975.* Stanford, Calif.: Stanford University Press.

Steiner, P. O., and Dorfman, R. (1957) *The Economic Status of the Aged.* Berkeley and Los Angeles, Calif.: University of California Press.

Sweetser, D. A. (1966) The effect of industrialization on intergenerational solidarity. *Rural Sociology* 31(June):156–170.

Verdon, M. (1979) The stem family: Toward a general theory. *Journal of Interdisciplinary History* 10(Summer):87–106.

Zelnick, M., and Kantner, J. F. (1977) Sexual and contraceptive experience of young unmarried women in the United States, 1976 and 1971. *Family Planning Perspectives* 9(2):55–71.

chapter 6

Remarriage and Intergenerational Relations[1]

FRANK F. FURSTENBERG, JR.

Once ignored and unappreciated, the life course perspective has recently become a popular way of wedding history, sociology, and psychology. This approach to the study of social behavior has been particularly appealing to students of the family, who, until recently, have been prisoners of the present tense. Informed by a temporal perspective on the family, some researchers have begun to look at the changing construction of the life course (Baltes and Brim 1979, Elder 1978, and Riley 1979). In this chapter, I shall present some preliminary observations on the restructuring of kinship ties after conjugal disruption and their consequences for relations between the generations.

It is my intent to explore the implications of emerging changes in the kinship system that have resulted from an unprecedented increase in the incidence of divorce and remarriage. The reader should be forewarned that much of the discussion that follows about the nature of these changes, especially their implications for intergenerational contact, is speculative and intended to provoke further empirical inquiry. The data

[1] The research on which this paper is based was supported by a grant from ACYF, #90-C-1767, "Recycling the Family: Experiences in Remarriage," through the Center for Research on the Acts of Man, Inc.

presented here are drawn from a series of case studies and should be regarded merely as illustrative.

At the outset of this discussion, it is well to say that the operating principles of kinship in American society are only dimly understood. With only a few significant exceptions, anthropologists have generally ignored the workings of the American kinship system. (Significant contributions have been made by Parsons 1943, Schneider 1968, Adams 1968, Farber 1973, Stack 1974.) In fact, we know far less about the rules of contemporary kinship in our society than we do about those in many exotic cultures.[2]

Complicating our ability to describe and account for the variability of kinship patterns in contemporary society is the flux within the current system. For example, the general decline in fertility and the increase in childlessness in particular may be altering the availability of kin resources. Similarly, some observers have argued that the growth of welfare institutions may be weakening the basis of intergenerational exchange (Elder 1974, Hareven 1978, Sawhill 1978). Whether or how particular demographic, economic, and political developments have modified American kinship practices has not been established with any degree of precision. And even assuming that patterns of kinship behavior have been altered by the profound institutional transformations that have taken place in contemporary American society, it does not necessarily follow that fundamental understandings about kinship have been revised as well (Schneider 1968). Evidence is lacking on whether shifts occurred in classifications of kin, notions of closeness and distance, or expectations attached to specific kin relations in response to organizational changes within the family.

---

[2] Contributions by family sociologists to the study of American kinship patterns have a curiously negative quality. What we have learned about the kinship system has been largely derived from a lingering debate over the appropriateness of Talcott Parsons's (1943) characterization of the American family as an *isolated nuclear* unit. He first used this term in 1943 and later elaborated upon it in several essays depicting kinship patterns in the United States and Western society in general. In retrospect, it is difficult to understand how this ill-defined phrase generated so much controversy. I suspect that, stripped of the technical meaning that Parsons intended, the image of isolation had peculiar resonations for family sociologists in the immediate postwar era. If one rereads the literature of this period, a strong sense of nostalgia can be detected in the descriptions of family life. Parsons's phrase undoubtedly had an unsettling effect; hence, it must have been reassuring to discover empirically that the nuclear family was not nearly so "isolated" as Parsons's term seemed to imply. Thus, it seems that Parsons may have been used as a convenient straw man, a foil for rediscovering the vitality of the family in American society at the very time when fears were spreading that the family was in deep trouble.

The extraordinary increases in divorce and remarriage rates that have come about over the past half century present an interesting case study in which to explore conceptions of kinship, rules of kinship behavior and the possibility of change in either of these two domains. This chapter examines whether and how patterns of divorce and remarriage are likely to restructure our notions of kinship and the functioning of the kinship system in American society.

CHANGING PATTERNS OF DIVORCE AND REMARRIAGE

It is undoubtedly true that enormous change has taken place in the behavior of Americans. While remarriage has never been rare in this country and, in fact, was nearly as prevalent in the nineteenth century as today, it was almost invariably in response to widowhood. Indeed, only since World War I has there been a sizable number of divorced persons in the United States. It was not until after World War II that divorce became common enough to challenge the ideal of lifelong marriage. And only within the past decade has that challenge reached the point where the stigma associated with divorce has vanished or been greatly attenuated. Sequential marriage has become not only a possibility but also a realistic alternative to permanent conjugal commitment (Bureau of the Census 1977).

Even in the absence of data showing a corresponding shift in attitudes toward marriage, the change in behavior during the last century is impressive. Although the ratio of marriages to divorces in any given year declined steadily during the latter part of the nineteenth century, it was not until the 1880s that the figure fell below 20 to 1. By the end of World War I, this figure had dropped below 10 to 1; it declined to below 4 to 1 after World War II and then turned upward for a time. In the 1970s, the ratio of marriages to divorces plummeted again and stands at approximately 2 to 1 today (Vital and Health Statistics 1973).

These changing ratios provide little sense of the expectation of divorce over the lifetime of an individual. Various projections have been constructed, built on the assumption that the current divorce rates will remain at their present level. Glick and Norton (1977) estimate that approximately two out of five marriages will end in divorce, while Preston (1975) figures that the rate may reach even higher proportions. Both these projections ignore those marriages that will end in separation but in which no official divorce procedures are instituted.

Most divorced people eventually remarry. Overall, approximately four out of every five people who dissolve their marriages enter another union. Men are more susceptible to remarriage than women, largely because they occupy a more favorable position in the marriage market. Age, too, figures importantly in the probability of remarriage. When divorce occurs before age 30, the chances of remarriage are extremely high. Recent figures reveal that almost 80% of women who divorce before age 25 will remarry in 5 years (Vital and Health Statistics 1980). Indeed, individuals who divorce at an early age have a higher probability of remarrying than single persons of the same age do of marrying (Jacobson 1959).

Nearly as impressive as the figures depicting an increasing likelihood of divorce and remarriage are the data describing the timing of these events in the life course. The pace of recycling the family has quickened to a remarkable degree. The median intervals from marriage to divorce and from divorce to remarriage have both been declining rapidly, resulting in a much lower age at remarriage today than occurred several decades ago. In the early part of this century, the interval between divorce and remarriage was nearly 10 years longer on the average than today. The typical remarrier today is in his or her late twenties or early thirties.

Extrapolating from these figures on the incidence and timing of divorce and remarriage, we can get some crude ideas of how they are likely to affect the experience of children growing up in families. In the 1920s, approximately a third of the couples who divorced had children; today three out of five do (Vital and Health Statistics 1970, Bureau of the Census 1979). Children may be a less powerful deterrent to divorce today for a variety of reasons: family size is smaller; women are better equipped to manage motherhood on their own; and parents have been reassured by experts that maintaining an unhappy marriage for the sake of the children is ill-advised.

While there are no reliable accounts of the proportion of children who are affected by divorce and remarriage, Bane (1979) estimates that approximately 40% of all children born today will experience a divorce or separation in their family before they reach age 18. As previously indicated, remarriage in these families generally occurs swiftly (half of all younger divorced women remarry within 3 years). Consequently, we might expect that about a fourth of all children growing up today will have more than two parents before they reach age 18. If present trends continue unabated, this figure will climb even higher in the future as current birth cohorts encounter more parental divorce at an early point in life. Rates of redivorce have also been going up in recent years, increasing the prevalence of even more complex kinship structures (with three, four, and even more parents).

IMPLICATIONS OF REMARRIAGE FOR KINSHIP RELATIONS

To the extent that we have thought about the significance of these trends for the working of the kinship system, our attention has largely focused on their meaning for children, particularly regarding their intellectual and social development (Herzog and Sudia 1971, Hetherington *et al.* 1977, Longfellow 1979, Zill 1980). There has been far less interest in exploring the implications of these changing patterns of marriage on adults in the middle and later years of life.

There is, of course, an obvious corollary to the observation that a substantial number of children will grow up with more than two parents. Many adults will have the experience of rearing children who do not reside with them, or of residing with children who are not their offspring. Whether and how these facts will alter the concept of parenthood we can only speculate at this point, as we have not collected the kind of anthropological and sociological data that might permit a rigorous assessment. Certainly it would be misguided to extrapolate from cultural images of step-parentage in the past. Until quite recently, the term meant the replacement of a parent, whereas today it typically implies the adding on of a parent. There is little or no research on the cultural or sociological features of reconstituted families that bears on the question of how parents collaborate when they live apart or on how the intricate relations between parents and step-parents are established, a phenomenon that has no historical precedent in Western society.[3]

The question of the changing meaning of parenthood becomes even more intriguing when considered from a temporal perspective. How are generational linkages affected by divorce and remarriage? A key feature of the conjugal family in our society is that it is the principal domestic unit. The meaning of "close family" must derive in part from spatial proximity as well as from conceptions close genetic or blood ties, as Schneider (1968) has pointed out. To what extent does the residential

---

[3] One exception might be noted to the absence of interest in the functioning of complex family structures, particularly those involving participation of step-parents and surrogate parents. Both historical and a large number of contemporary studies of Afro-Americans reveal culturally variant family structures that involve collaboration between resident and nonresident parents and caretakers. For excellent historical treatment of the black family, see Gutman (1977). The contemporary literature is almost too vast to introduce. Several important starting points may be found in Staples (1978) and Hill (1977).

separation of parents and children in early life attenuate their emotional bonds in later life? If information is lacking on the effect on close family relations of divorce and remarriage, we know even less about the impact on kinship bonds that span more than a single generation or cut laterally across a generation. Does the universe of relatives expand because individuals retain both their "old" and "new" relations? Or does it contract because they lose their "former" relatives and cannot cement ties to kin acquired in later life?

PREVIOUS RESEARCH ON KINSHIP RELATIONS AFTER DIVORCE

When I first became interested in the problem of how kinship relations are restructured after divorce and remarriage, I made a rather cursory survey of the literature. My point of departure as textbooks on marriage and the family, as I have accumulated quite a collection of these specimens from enterprising publishers. Although my analysis of the existing literature was not exhaustive, I was struck by the almost complete absence of references to remarriage in recent family texts. If they mentioned the subject at all, most writers dwell on the prospects of conjugal success in a second marriage. By and large, family sociologists ignored the implications of remarriage for kinship relations (Furstenberg 1979).

Abandoning the textbooks, I researched the literature on remarriage and kinship ties. To say the least, the result was unrewarding. My search revealed only one empirical study that explicitly addressed the issue of relations among kin after remarriage (Anspach 1976) and two studies that examined the impact of divorce on patterns of kinship (Rosenberg and Anspach 1973, Spicer and Hampe 1975). I shall say more about these studies shortly. Several reviews of the literature note the paucity of research on this subject (Bohannon 1971, Cherlin 1978). For example, Walker et al. (1977, p. 281), in the most extensive survey of the literature on remarriage, observe: "An additional shortcoming in the research literature is the lack of a focus on relationships of remarriage family household members with relatives and friends connected through a former marriage. Very few studies examine step-relationships with the extended and friendship network outside the remarriage household."

One of the rare exceptions to the generalization in Walker et al. is a perceptive essay by Paul Bohannon (1971) on the aftermath of divorce (see also Mead 1971). In a brief comment on the complex social configurations resulting from remarriage, Bohannon introduces the notion of a "divorce chain," the social links that are created by successive marriages. Bohannon contends that this arrangement might be viewed as a new extended family form, the modern equivalent to the multigenerational family unit. Unfortunately, Bohannon said little about the implications of this kinship constellation for the individual or society.

Finding little of substance in the literature on remarriage, I turned to studies on kinship and intergenerational relations in hopes of finding some related research. Several investigators, Adams (1971), Sussman (1976), and Troll et al. (1979), have reviewed the existing studies in some detail but uncovered little of relevance to the subject of family reconstitution. In fact, one of these reviewers, Lillian Troll (1979, pp. 126–127), has commented in a recent book on the strategic importance of conducting research on the way that kinship patterns are affected by divorce and remarriage: "Most writers refer only to the in-law adjustment problems of young married couples; few note the adjustment problems of middle-age parents and even older grandparents to the new families introduced into kin networks upon each new marriage in the family." Troll (p. 130) goes on to comment about the complexity of kin networks among remarried families, where not only parents and siblings are added but also grandparents, uncles, aunts, and cousins. "We know so little about kinship relations among reconstituted families that we cannot even speculate about them."

Marvin Sussman (1976), noting the sharp increase in divorce and remarriage, speculates on how these changes may affect patterns of intergenerational exchange. Like Troll, Sussman reasons that multiple marriages inevitably enlarge the pool of potential kin, just as is true in large extended families. "The promise of an inheritance," Sussman writes, "may provide motivation for family members to invest in a relationship with the elderly person," while the elder in turn "has a greater field of relatives from which to choose." In effect, Sussman is making an argument similar to the one advanced by Bohannon. Remarriage enriches the kinship network and may, to some extent, offset the impact of declining fertility on the stock of effective kin.

Interestingly enough, the few empirical investigations of how kinship relations are restructured after divorce and remarriage have failed to consider this possibility. Indeed, each has emphasized the contraction of kinship contacts and the diminution of intergenerational exchange, probably because they focused on the period immediately after divorce. Rosenberg and Anspach (1973), in a study of working-class kinship patterns in Philadelphia, discovered that formerly married participants maintain, if not increase, contact with close kindred (parents, siblings, and spouses of siblings) following a divorce. By contrast, they interacted with significantly fewer members of their former mate's kindred (affines) in the period after divorce. Approximately a quarter of the widows and a fifth of the divorced listed their former spouse's kin in the pool of available relatives compared with three-fifths of the currently married. Following Schneider, the authors argue that the recognition of affinal relations as "kin" is optional in American society. So the dissolution of the marriage usually nullifies kinship consciousness, weakening effective ties (see Weiss 1975). The diminution of affinal ties is offset in part by the strengthening of bonds with blood relations: "The normative pattern of treating close and spouse's kindred equally is reflected in patterns of interaction as long as the marriage is intact. But upon the disruption of marriage, one's former spouse's kindred are not subjectively considered as kin by most respondents [p. 87]."

There is one serious shortcoming in this study: Kinship links are traced exclusively on an individual basis, ignoring those contacts that might appear if the family were taken as the unit of analysis. Specifically, the Rosenberg–Anspach these that the maintenance of affinalisties depends on the preservation of the conjugal bond excludes the possibility that children constitute another link that is less easily erased. After all, children remain members of their absent parent's kindred. Accordingly, a potential conflict arises between the interests of adults and their children. The extinction of former relations places children in jeopardy of being disconnected from a significant portion of their kindred.

Another study of kinship interaction after divorce, conducted by Spicer and Hampe, highlights this point. While based on a smaller and less representative sample exclusively of divorces, the findings strongly corroborate the results obtained by Rosenberg and Anspach. Divorced men and women reported distinctly less contact with the relatives of their former spouse after the break of their marriages (based on retrospective accounts). At the same time, contact with consanguineal kin increased slightly, especially among women who presumably relied on their parents and siblings for material and emotional support after divorce. Despite the finding that relations with affines diminished following divorce, the data collected by Spicer and Hampe reveal a tremendous amount of variation in amount of contact among respondents and their former in-laws. This finding also recurs in the Rosenberg-Anspach study described above.

Spicer and Hampe (1975) consider several explanations for the variability in kinship interaction after divorce. The most promising explanation revolves around the role children play in linking adults with their former affines. The presence of children in the household more than doubled the likelihood of continued interaction. As the authors conclude:

> from the viewpoints of the former affines and the children, they are connected to one another by a consanguineal relationship . . . creat[ing] a feeling of obligation on the part of the divorcee to continue interaction with the former affines so that the children will know their consanguineal relatives on that side of the family [p. 118].

In sum, parents often apply a different set of standards in recognizing and relating to kin if they are looking out for a child's interest from that they apply if they are merely expressing their own preferences. Even when children are not a consideration, it should be noted that some parents will elect to regard their former affines as kin.

A critical question, left unanswered by these two studies, is what, if any, changes take place in the event of remarriage? Does a second marriage result in a further withering away of kinship contacts with affines from the initial union? If so, are any provisions made for continuing the links between children and their kindred, or are these ties replaced by step-kin, the blood relations of the child's residential stepparent? Only one study could be located that even addressed these questions; it is an investigation by Donald Anspach (1976), which is billed as a preliminary study to generate hypotheses.

Anspach interviewed a sample of mothers in Portland, Maine, of whom 47 were divorced, 37 were remarried, and 35 were in their first marriages, collecting information on the number of available kin, contacts with these relations, and perceived changes in kin contact following divorce and remarriage. His results assume a predictable form. Approximately four-fifths of each marital status grouping reported contact during the preceding week with close kindred who were living in the same area, a figure that seems to correspond with those in other studies on patterns of kinship interaction (Shanas 1973). In line with the findings of the previous two studies, divorced and remarried persons perceive a decline in social relations with their former spouse's close kin, though approximately a third of each group reported seeing at least one member of their ex-husband's family in the preceding week. Significant for our discussion, Anspach also discovered that the patterns of interaction with the present spouse's family among women in their first and second marriages were identical. About three-quarters of each had seen a family member. In short, the remarried were like the divorced in regard to their previous spouses and the once-married women in regard to their current spouses.

When Anspach examined patterns of help and assistance, much the same pattern emerged. Relative to married women, divorced women suffered a distinct disadvantage with regard to the availability of resources. While they received as much, if not slightly more, aid from their close kindred, only a fourth got some form of assistance from the immediate family of their former spouse. Married and remarried women generally received help from both their own and their spouse's close relatives, though women in both groups were more dependent on their own kindred. Again, it is interesting to observe the relatively advantageous position of the remarried women. Compared with the women in their first marriages, they received an even greater measure of assistance from their own family and the family of their spouse. Moreover, approximately a third received aid from their former spouse's kindred, a figure slightly higher than the one reported by the divorced women. Of course, despite the investigator's attempt to match the various samples in demographic and socioeconomic features, these results may be attributable to differences other than marital status, for example, proximity to kin. Nevertheless, we must at least entertain the possibility that remarriage intensifies and enhances kin support, a supposition on which I will elaborate later in this chapter.

In attempting to explain the variation in contact with paternal kindred, Anspach observes that the role of the absent father is critically important. When the parents break off or drastically curtail interaction after divorce, relations with paternal kin decline accordingly, resulting in an imbalance in a child's kinship network. By withdrawing from his role as the child's sponsor, the father weakens the child's link to his or her paternal kin. Anspach's data show that maternal kin are much more likely to be favored when the father is seen infrequently and figure more equally when the father maintains his ties to the family.

This study, like the two previous investigations, emphasized the disadvantage to the child whose parents are divorced, especially in the event that the nonresidential parent (typically the father) severs contact and fails to link his children to their paternal kin. But a less dire interpretation can be fashioned from the existing data, an interpretation that is more in line with the argument advanced earlier in this chapter. To a surprising extent, bilateral kinship ties are maintained after divorce and even after remarriage. Though divorce unquestionably restricts the child's access to relatives on one side of his or her family (usually the father's), this result is far from inevitable. Moreover, when remarriage occurs—and this event is highly likely—the child appears to enjoy a certain advantage. Ties with the father's family do not dissolve even after new links are established with the step-parent's family.

The impact of divorce and remarriage on the senior or grandparent generation may also have favorable as well as unfavorable consequences. Of course, the situation for the relatives of the residential parent is not problematic, at least regarding the level of exchange. If any shift occurs at all, it is probably in the direction of intensifying interaction as the divorced parent is forced to rely more heavily on the support of kin in the aftermath of divorce. By contrast, the relatives of the nonresidential parent may stand to lose out when the parent is not present in the home to serve as a direct link to the child. However, we have seen that relatives of the nonresidential parent frequently maintain contact with the child, especially when custody of the child is shared to some extent. The preliminary data assembled by previous researchers, in fact, may have understated the extent of interaction between children and the relatives of their noncustodial parent because they did not expect to find much contact occurring.

Without dwelling on the methodological limitations of these studies, I should mention the obvious fact that each of the studies considered was designed in such a way as to stress the imbalance in the child's kinship network. By examining only interaction between the adults and former affines, they failed to consider the possibility that kin members may relate independently to the child. Moreover, by looking only at frequent (daily or weekly) contact, the results discount the fact that relations may be confined to monthly visits or may be concentrated at vacation times. Finally, considering only close kindred, as two of the three studies did, the results underestimate the maintenance of kin ties to former affines. The only investigation (Spicer and Hampe 1975) that did not look only at contact with close kindred found a substantial amount of interaction with more distant relatives (aunts, uncles, etc.). All of these criticisms probably would not alter the conclusion that conjugal dissolution creates some imbalance in the child's kinship network, an imbalance favoring the relatives of the residential parent; however, it would correct the impressions created by these studies that divorce virtually obliterates half of the child's kinship network.

In the next section of this chapter, I will examine in greater detail the mechanisms that preserve the generational ties between the child and his or her relatives and the pressures brought to bear on residential parents to deal with their former in-laws (that is, their children's kin). I shall try to illustrate the stake various parties hold in maintaining existing kinship ties.

At the same time, another set of incentives operate on the family of remarried persons, leading to the incorporation of new relations into the kinship network. Specific pressures are brought to bear on the extended family to reach out to step in-laws and their children. The case studies suggest that extended kin may find it difficult to maintain close ties with relatives who remarry if they insist on treating their newly acquired relations as nonkin. Just as refusing to recognize a kinperson's spouse as a "relative" may impair bonds within the kindred, slighting the step-child may produce a similar rupture within the bloodline. Studying the pressures brought to bear on the extended family to incorporate the new spouse and his or her children provides a fascinating example of how individuals pass from strangers to kin.

THE RESTRUCTURING OF KINSHIP TIES
AFTER REMARRIAGE: A CASE STUDY

In 1979, I was given a grant to follow up the participants in a local study of separation and divorce initiated 3 years earlier by Graham Spanier of Pennsylvania State University. In 1977, Spanier had inter-viewed some 200 individuals living in Centre County, Pennsylvania, who had recently dissolved their marriages. In collaboration with Spanier, I planned to relocate these individuals several years later when it might be expected that about half would have established a new relationship.

As part of the process of preparing for the follow-up survey, I carried out a series of 24 qualitative case studies of couples living in Philadelphia who had been recently remarried. It is these cases to which I will refer in the latter part of this chapter. The subjects of this pilot study were located from marriage records in Philadelphia. It should be clear, how-ever, that the people with whom we have talked are neither representative nor typical of remarried couples in general: they are a self-selected sample of persons who are willing to share their experiences. As such, it is not surprising to find that they are predominantly middle-class and well ed-ucated, a fact that should be kept in mind throughout the following discussion.

When conducting the interviews, I resisted the dictates of my disci-pline and deliberately refrained from asking structured questions. Rather I converse with the subjects about a wide range of topics relating to the transition from divorce to remarriage. Most participants, relieved of the burden of answering structured queries, responded rather fully and sin-cerely, sometimes even enthusiastically, to what were often nebulous questions. In some respects, the collaborators in this pilot study may be thought of as informants in the sense in which anthropologists are accustomed to using that term.

Preserving Kinship Ties

In the preceding discussion, I have identified certain organizational features of our family system that might predispose members of a conjugal network to retain ties with one another after divorce. Schneider and Cottrell (1975) make the point that the boundaries of kinship are flexible; that is, relationships are, to a very large extent, discretionary. There is, as they put it, no specific "rule of closure." The optional nature of the system means that divorce can occur without necessarily nullifying existing kinship ties based on a preexisting marriage. Individuals have, therefore, a choice of whether or not to "be related" when they are no longer connected by an intact marriage. I might, for example, consider my ex-sister-in-law a member of my family either because she was my brother's wife, because she is my nephew's mother, or merely because I feel close to her. In the discussion that follows, I try to show why individuals, especially if they are parents, have a stake in preserving relations with affines (relatives by marriage) following a divorce. I will argue that when children are involved, there are certain structural pressures working to preserve ties between former family members even when sentiments might dictate the discontinuation of relationships.

Let us look first at the problem posed earlier of the mechanisms operating to preserve kinship ties with the family of the nonresidential parent as well as some of the circumstances that undermine the continuity of relationships. When asked about the amount of contact they had with their former in-laws, most informants explained that they saw less of them, often because they were no longer living in the same locality. However, during other parts of the interview, it became clear that members of their former spouse's family had figured critically in their lives in the very recent past.

CASE 1

This is part of an interview with a formerly married husband and his second wife, married for the first time. The man, whom we call Robert, had one child (Robbie) who lived with his former wife (Irene), who had remarried and subsequently separated. During Irene's marriage, she left the country, leaving the child with her mother.

Husband: I don't see that she's (his former wife) changed so much.
Wife: Can you believe that she never wrote to him and said that she was sending that child home, alone?

Interviewer: How did you find out?
Wife: His grandmother called Robert. Robbie's grandmother. Irene's mother. His mother-in-law called him.
Husband: And she said she was going to Washington to pick him up.
Interviewer: That suggests that you have maintained some kind of relationship with her . . . at least she's still responding to you as a family member.
Wife: . . . for the child. They legitimately like him (presumably the husband), see, and it's because of her that I think it's been a much more communicative type of thing about Robbie . . . . What information you get about Robbie comes from his mother-in-law.
Husband: (after some further clarification) . . . they (his in-laws) want to be very friendly. And I think Robbie's grandmother has been in some ways more concerned and more motivated to take care of him than his mother has. (Husband goes on to describe how the grandmother and the estranged parents went to see a psychologist to coordinate plans for the child.)

CASE 2

This is part of an interview with remarried husband and his second wife, who had not been previously married. The couple live with children from the husband's first marriage who came to live with them after their mother was hospitalized for emotional problems.

Husband: (recounting the period when he assumed custody of the children): Then there would be periods when she would want to see the kids every third weekend or something . . . that was fine with me. She really tried to be a good mother, within the limits of what she was capable of doing. She frequently took them to her parents, and they are pretty decent people, so I had confidence that they were going to be ok. I was honestly glad to get rid of them for the weekend, it was great occasionally.

Both of the informants quoted above depict the grandparents (their former in-laws) as the child's protectors, a characterization that I suspect is not unusual in families that have experienced a divorce. Particularly if relations with in-laws were amicable before the breakup of the marriage, the grandparents or sometimes the child's uncles or aunts (the in-laws' siblings) can serve as emotional intermediaries between children and their separated parents. In Case 1, the mother-in-law plays a central role in bringing the father back into the family constellation. (Interestingly, the present wife, after searching for a term, finally resorts to the designation of mother-in-law, even though that same term could also be used to describe her own mother's relationship to her husband.) The grandmother, by virtue of her own relationship to the child, is in an especially strategic position to intercede on behalf of the child, reminding the absent parent of his rights and obligations. And once the father assumed a more active presence in child-rearing, the child began to have more contacts with the father's family as well.

In the second case, the grandparents are serving a surrogate role for the mother, incapacitated by illness. By doing so, they relieve the father of exclusive parental responsibilities and at the same time provide a direct bridge between the children and their maternal relatives. It was through visits with the grandparents that the children maintained contact with their uncles and aunts.

The patterns described above do not apply to all the families we studied. One woman, for example, who experienced a bitter separation with her husband, reported that her parents would not permit her ex-husband near their home even though he had custody of the children. She agreed with her ex-husband that her parents were being "asinine," but our informant explained that her parents did not want to expose their children "to a face from the past." Even though her family avoided contact with their former son-in-law, the daughter arranges for them to see their grandchildren when they visit her.

Children are, as anthropologists have reminded us, a form of social property. Except under rare circumstances, custody arrangements recognize the interests of both parents (and indirectly, their families), though the division does not typically stipulate an even share. Involvement of extended kin may serve to impress upon the various parties a sense of mutual rights and obligations. The grandparents assume an especially critical role in preserving family claims after the marriage contract between the parents is terminated. They often represent the interests of the absent parent, reminding both their former in-laws and their grandchildren that ties to the absent parent endure. The grandparents are often in an especially advantageous position to link the child to other family members of the kindred. Thus, by threatening to break lineage ties, a divorce may have the paradoxical consequence of invoking family ties. Grandparents may become guardians of the family line.

Quantitative studies of patterns of visitation, unless explicitly designed to discover diverse accommodations, are likely to miss the part of the action that takes place among family members formerly related by marriage. Since children retain consanguineal ties to both parents and hence to their retrospective families, the estranged couple are predisposed to acknowledge some type of relationship to their former affines, though the precise nature of this relationship remains unspecified. In a few cases, the bond between the parent and his or her former in-laws continues as if the divorce had never occurred. More typically, the relations between the two parties are more perfunctory, maintained merely for the "children's sake."

All the principals involved, the parents, their respective close kindred, and the children, have a stake in not disrupting the generational ties. The parents, whatever the degree of enmity between them, are usually willing to concede that it is in the child's best interests not to destroy kinship connections that might be emotionally and materially important to their offspring, both at present and in the future. Informants who had little good to say about their former spouse frequently acknowledged the legitimate rights of their ex's family to see the child. And, often they went out of their way to promote continued relations with the extended family, arranging weekend or vacation visits.

Of course, the grandparents serve the residential parent's interests in another way as well. In many cases, they continue to lend assistance, relieving the parent of some of the burdens of child care. Several informants who were residing with their children explained that they tended to see their former in-laws when they dropped their children off for a visit. In several instances, it appears that their in-laws' house was a neutral zone where the previously married couple could carry on their common business of parenting. Because of the benefits derived by the parents, the grandparents (and other relatives as well, by inference) held a secure position within the family so long as they performed a "helping role."

Interestingly, the helping role that the grandparents performed vis-à-vis their former son-in-law or daughter-in-law and their grandchildren probably served to strengthen their bond to their own child. Grandparents who have only an ancillary part to play in the family when the couple is married become much more important to their children when a divorce takes place. Men turn to their parents for child-care support; women may do likewise and may seek financial aid as well. Divorce increases the level of exchange as it serves the parents' interests to involve the older generation.

All of this is not to say that divorce ultimately promotes harmony in the extended family. Obviously, as the quantitative data show, on balance divorce complicates relations between the generations, especially adults and their former in-laws. Strains are particularly likely to occur when the in-law relationship was weak to begin with or when the senior generation took active part in the divorce process. What I have tried to suggest is that there may be a response within the family system offsetting these potential rifts that works in the opposite direction, promoting continued relations between the generations. In sum, divorce does not inevitably disadvantage the senior generation either vis-à-vis their grandchildren, their own children, or even their former in-laws. Considering the latter instance, it is possible that when in-laws provide help to an estranged spouse, she or he may respond with devotion and gratitude, strengthening long-term family obligations.

Augmenting the Kinship Network

Relationships with new kin are not mandatory, but they are permitted and even encouraged. Although children have no blood ties to their stepparent's kindred, they are connected to them by marriage. Culturally, they are permitted to think of these relations as equivalents to their blood relatives, and the evidence that I have collected thus far indicates that they frequently do. Our kinship system allows for an unlimited number of siblings, uncles, aunts, cousins. With the possible exception of marriage, there are no closed sets in our kinship categories. While we are accustomed in our society to having only two parents and four grandparents, these categories, too, are potentially elastic. I have quoted at some length below a section from an interview with a remarried woman, describing the situation of her daughter, who is living with her father, who is now remarried. She is telling about the child's initiation into a new kinship network.

Interviewer: What about other relatives, I mean, she now has a fairly extensive set of . . .

Woman: Yeah, she loves that. She loves it. Like they went to Minnesota for a week, and she got to meet 15 different relatives, and now, I don't know what that makes, 4 or 5, 10 sets of grandparents I think, and I don't know how many sets of aunts and uncles, and she would describe every single one of them to me and how nice they were

	and what they gave her and what they did. She loves it. She loves the attention.
Interviewer:	So . . . she has four sets of grandparents now?
Woman:	Well, she would, wouldn't she? I mean, if she's got four parents . . . my parents are alive and Art (present husband) has a father alive but not a mother. Jerry (former husband) has both his parents alive and Carol (former husband's wife) has both her parents alive, so she really has seven.
Interviewer:	Does she have a relationship with Art's father?
Woman:	Yeah, and I think it's pretty nice. Not . . . we don't see him that often, but he's very good to her and she's very friendly to him, and they have a sort of tickle kind of relationship.
Interviewer:	What does she call him?
Woman:	Well, we're working on that. Sometimes it's Pop-pop, and Grandpa, it comes out most, but not Samuel, not by his first name or anything like that . . . . I think it's kind of nice to have the name of grandpa or grandfather or something like that. And I guess she has enough of those. (laughter)
Interviewer:	And then she sees something of Carol's family?
Woman:	They all went up there for a family reunion at Christmas time, but at Thanksgiving, Henny (the child) went to Syracuse just to see them, Pop-pop and Nana or whatever, I can't remember what it's called now.
Interviewer:	And does Art have any brothers and sisters around?
Woman:	Leslie, Art's sister . . . Henny's very fond of Leslie, sort of a female kind of relation . . . big-sister sort of a thing and she sends her special things and stuff. (She goes on to describe a more distant relationship that her child has with a brother of her husband whom he doesn't see very often.) Well, she didn't acquire too much with Art and I. No. But with Jerry and Carol, I mean, they lived together for a year or two before. But they didn't branch out into all the familial kind of stuff until they'd really gotten married. So, really, since April, she's met everybody in the chain. So that is a real onslaught of people.
Interviewer:	Has that meant any decline in her contact with your family, or . . .
Woman:	I think so . . . because, well, it's not like my parents are her only grandparents so they're very special and sort of

a sacred entity or something. I mean, she can go to any level for love and attention now, that kind of attention.

Interviewer: Do your parents feel any sense of diminution in their relationship with her?

Woman: No . . . you see, my mother and father have three new children. (Her mother remarried 12 years ago) so it wasn't a real grandmother situation, I mean.

This conversation serves to illustrate a number of themes that came up in the interviews when subjects were questioned about how remarriage had altered their own and their children's kinship networks. It was generally assumed that they and their children would annex the current spouse's family so long as the new parent had active ties with his or her relatives. With respect to family, the rule seemed to be that what is mine is thine. Accordingly, children were encouraged if not required to develop kinship names for their new relatives, most importantly the grandparents. In turn, there was some active pressure put on elders to treat the children as grandchildren. Even with the step-parent's active sponsorship, the process of incorporation was not automatic. One step-parent described, with a certain trace of bitterness, how her parents slipped her step-son some money for Christmas while giving their biological grandchild a toy. Although she felt it was understandable in view of the limited contact which had taken place between the child and her parents, the informant was determined not to allow the situation to be repeated in the future.

This particular case notwithstanding, there is little question that from the point of view of the child, the process of family augmentation is usually a real boon. As in the case quoted previously, the child has additional doting grandparents, uncles, and aunts, and additional cousins. To convert Bohannon's phrase, a "remarriage chain" develops which can become quite complex. In the case I have cited, it later surfaced in the interview that Carol, the step-mother, had been previously married as well. Henny, it turns out, went along with her step-sister on the weekends when Carol's child visited her grandparents. Our informant casually mentioned that "those grandparents have been actively involved in Henny, too." It turned out that both Carol's former husband and his father were doctors and had treated Henny during a recent illness. The remarriage chain, it would appear, extends the child's network, but also spans a number of families, creating indirect connections among a large universe of individuals. As I shall elaborate in the conclusion of this chapter, the ties established through remarriage chains create a support system for the child even when kinship is not directly invoked or acknowledged.

Moreover, a much larger pool of relatives exists for the child from which gratifying and supportive relations may be selected. As suggested by the case just mentioned, some of these relatives may drop out of the child's kinship world due to conflicting obligations or geographical distance. Second-order affinal relations may also be more fragile and less resistant to dissolution if and when second marriages end. For example, a set of siblings, whom we interviewed shortly after the breakup of their mother's second marriage, were divided on whether they considered their step-father (whom they had never even lived with) a relative. The oldest replied that she thought he was a relative but the youngest thought he was more like "a friend"; and, he added, "I guess 'cause you don't see him as much as you see Katherine" (his stepmother who now lives with him). Interestingly, at a later point in the interview, this same child, when asked to list his relatives, included the parents of his step-father as his grandparents.

Acknowledgment of kinship may never develop or may be rescinded if the marital link is broken and contact ceases. This pattern is evident in many of the black families who participated in my study of adolescent childbearing. Ties with the biological father frequently survived limited contact, whereas relations with step-fathers were transient unless the man resided in the home or had done so for an extended period of time (Furstenberg 1976, Furstenberg and Talvitie 1980).

Our data are far too sketchy at this point to supply any detail about the process involved in acquiring new relatives through marriage. Most of the parents I spoke to did not view the situation as highly problematic, and the few children we have interviewed confirm this impression. When asked how it feels to get new relatives, one child explained: ". . . you just press a button and it's there all of a sudden." At the same time children are sensitive to the distinctions between "old" and "new" relations, sometimes using the term *real* to describe their consanguineal kin. When speaking of her step-mother's siblings, a teenager explained: " . . . their children aren't as much cousins as like friends." (In fact, they were technically uncles and aunts but she regarded them more like her cousins.) She went on to explain: "We've only known (them) like 2 years of our lives so we can't be like intimate, you know, like our real cousins."

It would appear that relations acquired by marriage are automatically eligible to be relatives—"like pressing a button"—but may not be considered as kin unless there is some intimate contact over an extended period. In this respect, the same general rules are applied in deciding whether persons are relatives when remarriage takes place as might occur when any marriage takes place (Schneider 1968). In making the determination, the child is not acting entirely independently. As we indicated earlier, there is pressure on extended relatives to incorporate the child in the family; so, too, we might expect parents to exert pressure on their children to "adopt" the same persons whom they consider as relatives. In effect, the children are being pressed to acknowledge the conjugal ties between the biological and step-parent. If they refuse to regard their step-parent's kin as their relatives, the children are implicitly denying their own ties to their step-parent and ultimately rejecting the legitimacy of the marriage that brought about their new family situation. Should this occur, it would, no doubt, create a serious rift between parent and child, forcing the parent to choose between cognatic and conjugal loyalties.

There was no case in the pilot study in which a child refused to acknowledge his or her step-parent's relations. Probably such instances are more likely to arise when the children are older and hence less willing to "adopt" a new family. In general, I suspect it happens less frequently than is portrayed in popular treatments of reconstituted families. The permissive feature of the system, which allows the child to add on new relatives without relinquishing ties to existing relations, undoubtedly dampens the potential of conflict and rivalry between the old and new families. This is not to say that competition between families does not develop but that the absence of a zero-sum rule means that existing relatives will not necessarily lose out, except perhaps on specific ritual occasions such as Thanksgiving or Christmas Day.

Not only is the kinship system elastic, it is also relatively unspecific in defining the nature of family obligations outside the nuclear unit. Thus, for example, there are no exact requirements prescribing how often relatives must see one another. Contact between kin can be infrequent without jeopardizing their status as relatives (more probably so than among friends). As is suggested in the conversation quoted earlier, re-married couples may initially take some pains to sponsor their children in their own families and invent special kinship designations for signif-icant relations. However, it probably does not require more than episodic visits to reinforce these family ties. This means that the child can absorb and be absorbed by a fairly substantial number of relations. If he or she already has cousins, there is a place for more cousins. If not, the child can rather quickly learn what it means to have a cousin.

One contemporary feature of American families that probably makes the adaptation to remarriage relatively easy for both adults and children is the declining birth rate. The fact that fewer children are being born and intervals between the generations lengthening, should promote greater receptivity to the acquisition of new relations. Older people, particularly if their offspring are childless, might be expected to welcome the addition of grandchildren even if they arrive by an unconventional route. Similarly, children may appreciate supplemental grandparents, especially if their own are not easily accessible. As I shall amplify in the conclusion, remarriage has the consequence of distributing a diminishing pool of children among a larger circle of adults. For children, it means being connected, albeit sometimes only weakly, to a great number of adults who are prepared to treat them as kin.

To be sure, remarriage complicates the child's world. One point that arose in several interviews is that generations become blurred by remarriage (more so than is the case in first marriages). An 11-year-old slyly announced with some amusement that his new uncle was younger than he. "I mean, they're too young to be uncles," his sister explained. The 11-year-old volunteered that he was good friends with his new relative, whom he regarded more like a "cousin." Age boundaries normally associated with kinship categories were being violated.

In many respects, remarriage recreates a kinship configuration that disappeared several generations ago. Higher death rates prior to this century created the necessity of family augmentation; kinship networks were made up of family fragments as individuals were incorporated into a household after the premature death of a parent or spouse. This frequently resulted in breaking down sharp generational boundaries. Similarly, large family size had the effect of widening the age range within families, as siblings (if not step-siblings) were typically spaced years apart. As family size diminished and siblings' ages became more uniform, cross-age contact within the family became less common. The growing pattern of divorce and remarriage may be reversing this trend by making family arrangements more complex and age heterogeneous again. As generations become less distinct in the everyday world of family life, the salience of generational boundaries in the larger society may decline as well.

DISCUSSION

In this chapter, I have explored the likely effects of divorce and remarriage on relations among extended kin generally and, more specifically, on interaction between generations within the family. The observations that I have offered should be treated as suggestions, not conclusions. They have not been substantiated by empirical investigation, and the data provided in the chapter are intended only for purposes of illustration. With these qualifications in mind, I would like to pull together some of the comments about the implications of remarriage for kinship relations that were scattered throughout the chapter and suggest some promising directions for future research.

It is worth reiterating that the upsurge of divorce and remarriage is a relatively novel trend. It may not continue; it could decline. Even if it does become a relatively permanent feature of our kinship system, it is not clear that it will retain the form it has today. One development that may be occurring already is a change in custody arrangements. In the twentieth century, though not in previous times, children have generally resided with the mother when marriages were voluntarily dissolved. Although it is not yet evident from official statistics (U. S. Bureau of the Census 1979), a trend toward shared custody may be emerging that could have profound implications for kinship relations after divorce. Much of the imbalance in kinship networks can be traced to the disappearance of the nonresidential parent, the child's main link to that side of his or her family. If both parents actively participate in raising the child, the child may not suffer any loss of parental sponsorship in the wider kinship network. Indeed, I have argued that marital disruption may promote active kinship ties outside the nuclear family as parents look to extended relatives for assistance and support in child care. The pattern of reliance on older family members for child-care assistance could create long-standing obligations to the senior generation, obligations that might be paid off in the later years of life. When grandparents have functioned as caretakers for their grandchildren, they may enjoy greater contact with kin in their later years of life (see the situation of the black family, Stack 1974, Jeffers 1967, Hill 1977). Thus, even when divorce is not followed by remarriage, it does not necessarily have the dire effects on relations among extended kin, the inference commonly drawn from the handful of existing studies.

Divorced people usually remarry. Contrary to some scholars who believe that remarriage replaces former kin with a new set of relatives (Mead 1971), I believe that parents and children will typically hold on to "old" relatives and at the same time acquire "new" ones. Our kinship system permits the augmentation of kin without relinquishing existing relations. And I have argued that it is generally in the interests of everyone to retain as many relatives as possible. The result is a structure that Bohannon labeled a "divorce chain," but that might more properly be referred to as a "remarriage chain." Whatever it is called, this configuration links (primarily through the child) former and present conjugal partners and their relatives.

This family chain has some potentially interesting features for the position of the child in the larger society. Of course, to the extent that he or she is connected to close kin and their relatives, the child will be afforded a good deal of support and assistance. Presumably a child with three or more parents and five or more grandparents, as well as additional kin in other categories, has an advantage over a child with fewer close relatives.

Granovetter (1973) argues that "weak ties," that is, social relations that are based on acquaintance rather than emotional intensity, are highly functional for the flow of information. All other things being equal, the more extensive the kinship network, the better situated a person is with respect to social and economic opportunities. An individual with a large number of weak ties has connections that are potentially useful resources, not only for times of crisis but also for meeting routine challenges such as looking for a job, seeking housing, or finding the name of a good dentist. The chain of relationships established by remarriage works to the benefit of both child and adult. With the increase of weak ties to a larger number of relatives, each stands to gain information and material resources. Instead of, or in addition to, knowing a "friend of a friend," each person in the remarriage chain may know a "relative of a relative."

When looked at from the vantage point of the larger society, the social structure generated by extensive remarriage has the consequence of increasing kinship ties and creating a network that offsets to some degree the decline in family size that has occurred in recent decades. People may have fewer relations by blood, but they may acquire a greater number through marriage(s). Another way of viewing this change is to say that a smaller number of children in the aggregate are being shared by a greater number of adults. This, of course, raises the possibility that relations will compete for the rights to the children, but it also means that a greater number of kin will feel obligated to care for and protect the child. The extent to which this added measure of adult input in the socialization process may result in a more favorable learning environment deserves some examination in future studies.

Remarriage establishes a greater number of intergenerational connections between children and their adult relatives and between parents and the senior generation. The interviews that I have conducted reveal that children's relations within their own generation were also expanded. Youngsters acquired step-siblings, cousins, and sometimes uncles and aunts who were approximately their age peers, who may serve as generational intermediaries for the child. This new system of allies may reduce the potential for sharp cleavages along distinct generational lines.

In considering the consequences of divorce and remarriage for kinship relations, I have ignored several problems that deserve mention. My emphasis throughout has been on recently remarried couples in their childbearing years. In contemplating the impact of family reconstitution on intergenerational ties, I have only alluded to a series of interesting questions that might arise were we to view the problem from a longitudinal perspective. For example, individuals might retain ties to former in-laws for a relatively short period after divorce but curtail relations sharply in the later years of second marriage. Relatives may relinquish claims gradually as contact diminishes, a pattern that would not show up unless the data were examined longitudinally. However, to use the language of exchange theory, relatives who played an instrumental role at the time of divorce may build up credits that are not quickly forgotten. The parent who provides her divorced daughter-in-law with emotional and material support until she is remarried may receive assistance from her and her children many years later. Clearly, then, researchers must be prepared to examine the process of family reformation over time if they are to do justices to the dynamics of divorce and remarriage.

In this chapter, I have dealt almost exclusively with the consequences of second marriage for kinship patterns among families still in their childbearing years. This is not a totally arbitrary decision, because the great majority of couples who remarry do so in their younger years. (More than three-fourths of all remarriers and four-fifths of those who remarry after divorce are under 45.) Nevertheless, it is both theoretically interesting and policy-relevant to examine remarriage later in the life course. I have focused on the impact of the attrition and addition of relatives on the senior generation, pointing out certain reasons why their role may be enhanced when divorce and remarriage occurs. But can we expect a reciprocal effect when it is the elderly who divorce and remarry? Certainly, this question deserves more attention that it has been accorded by gerontologists.

I have also not elaborated on the specific types of exchange that may be altered in the event of divorce and remarriage. For example, it is entirely possible that contact may be greatly disrupted by divorce and remarriage without a significant change in the flow of material resources; that is, inheritance patterns may remain unchanged. Similarly, I have contended that remarriage has the consequence of widening the child's kinship world, but it is conceivable that this widening occurs at the expense of diminishing the intensity of emotional contacts.

This leads me to a final caveat. Although it may have appeared so at times, it has not been my intention to depict divorce and remarriage as an attractive feature of family life in America. In considering the response to family reconstitution, I have stressed the potential for adaptation in our kinship system, arguing that remarriage presents possibilities as well as merely posing problems for family members. In making this assertion, I trust that I have not been either pollyannish or perverse.

REFERENCES

Adams, B. N. (1968) *Kinship in an Urban Setting*. Chicago: Markham.
Adams, B. N. (1971) Isolation, function, and beyond: American kinship in the 1960s. Pp. 163–185 in C. B. Broderick, ed., *A Decade of Family Research and Action*. Minneapolis, Minn.: National Council on Family Relations.
Anspach, D. F. (1976) Kinship and divorce. *Journal of Marriage and the Family* 38(2):323–330.
Baltes, P. B., and Brim, O. G., Jr., eds. (1979) *Life-Span Development and Behavior*, Vol. 2a. New York: Academic Press.
Bane, M. J. (1979) Marital disruption and the lives of children. Pp. 276–286 in G. Levinger and O. C. Moles, eds., *Divorce and Separation: Context, Causes, and Consequences*. New York: Basic Books, Inc.
Bohannon, P., ed. (1971) *Divorce and After: An Analysis of the Emotional and Social Problems of Divorce*. New York: Anchor Books.
Bureau of the Census (1977) Marriage, divorce, widowhood, and remarriage by family characteristics: June 1975. *Current Population Reports*, Series P-20:312(August). Washington, D. C.: U. S. Government Printing Office.
Bureau of the Census (1979) Divorce, child custody, and child support. *Current Population Reports*, Series P-23:84(June). Washington, D. C.: U. S. Government Printing Office.
Cherlin, A. (1978) Remarriage as an incomplete institution. *American Journal of Sociology* 84(November):634–650.
Elder, G. H., Jr. (1974) *Children of the Great Depression*. Chicago: University of Chicago Press.
Elder, G. H., Jr. (1978) Approaches to social change and the family. Pp. S1–S38 in J. Demos and S. S. Boocock, eds., *Turning Points: Historical and Sociological Essays on the Family*. Chicago: University of Chicago Press.
Farber, B. (1973) *Family and Kinship in Modern Society*. Glenview, Ill.: Scott, Foresman and Company.
Furstenberg, F. F., Jr. (1976) *Unplanned Parenthood: The Social Consequences of Teenage Childbearing*. New York: The Free Press.
Furstenberg, F. F., Jr. (1979) Recycling the family: Perspectives for researching a neglected family form. *Marriage and Family Review* 2(Fall).
Furstenberg, F. F., Jr., and Talvitie, K. G. (1980) Children's names and paternal claims: Bonds between unmarried fathers and their children. *Journal of Family Issues* 1(1):31–58.
Glick, P. C., and Norton, A. J. (1977) Marrying, divorcing, and living together in the U.S. today. *Population Bulletin* 32:5.
Ganovetter, M. S. (1973) The strength of weak ties. *American Journal of Sociology* 76(May):1360–1380.

Gutman, H. G. (1977) *The Black Family in Slavery and Freedom*. New York: Vintage Books.

Hareven, T. K. (1978) Family time and historical time. Pp. 57–70 in A. S. Rossi, J. Kagan, and T. K. Hareven, eds., *The Family*. New York: W. W. Norton & Company.

Herzog, E., and Sudia, C. E. (1971) *Boys in Fatherless Families*. Washington, D. C.: U.S. Government Printing Office.

Hetherington, E. M., Cox, M., and Cox, R. (1977) The aftermath of divorce. In J. H. Stevens, Jr. and M. Matthews, eds., *Mother–Child, Father–Child Relations*. Washington, D.C.: National Association for the Education of Young Children.

Hill, R. B. (1977) *Informal Adoption Among Black Families*. Washington, D. C.: National Urban League.

Jacobson, P. (1959) *American Marriage and Divorce*. New York: Rinehart.

Jeffers, C. (1967) *Living Poor: A Participant Observer Study of Priorities and Choices*. Ann Arbor, Mich.: Ann Arbor Publishers.

Longfellow, C. (1979) Divorce in context: Its impact on children. Pp. 287–306 in George L. and O. C. Moles, eds., *Divorce and Separation: Context, Causes, and Consequences*. New York: Basic Books, Inc.

Mead, M. (1971) Anomalies in American postdivorce relationships. Pp. 107–125 in P. Bohannon, ed., *Divorce and After: An Analysis of the Emotional and Social Problems of Divorce*. New York: Anchor Books.

Parsons, T. (1943) The kinship system of the contemporary United States. *American Anthropologist* XLV(January–March):22–38.

Preston, S. H. (1975) Estimating the proportion of American marriages that end in divorce. *Sociological Methods and Research* 3(May):435–460.

Riley, M. W. (1979) Age and Aging: From Theory Generation to Theory Testing. Paper presented at the annual meeting of the American Sociological Association, Boston, Massachusetts. (Forthcoming in volume edited by H. M. Blalock, Jr.)

Rosenberg, G. S., and Anspach, D. F. (1973) *Working Class Kinship*. Lexington, Mass.: Lexington Books.

Sawhill, I. V. (1978) Economic perspectives on the family. In A. S. Rossi, J. Kagan, and T. K. Hareven, eds., *The Family*. New York: W. W. Norton & Company.

Schneider, D. M. (1968) *American Kinship: A Cultural Account*. Englewood, N. J.: Prentice-Hall, Inc.

Schneider, D. M., and Cottrell, C. B. (1975) *The American Kin Universe: A Genealogical Study*. (The University of Chicago Studies in Anthropology Series in Social, Cultural and Linguistic Anthropology, No. 3.) Chicago: Department of Anthropology, University of Chicago.

Shanas, E. (1973) Family–kin networks and aging in cross-cultural perspective. *Journal of Marriage and the Family* 35(August):505–511.

Spicer, J. W., and Hampe, G. D. (1975) Kinship interaction after divorce. *Journal of Marriage and the Family* 37(February):113–119.

Stack, C. (1974) *All Our Kin*. Chicago: Aldine.

Staples, R. (1978) *The Black Family: Essays and Studies*, 2nd edition. Belmont, Calif.: Wadsworth Publishing Company, Inc.

Sussman, M. B. (1976) The family life of old people. Pp. 218–243 in R. H. Binstock, and E. Shanas, eds., *Handbook of Aging and the Social Sciences*. New York: Van Nostrand Reinhold Company.

Troll, L. E., Miller, S. J., and Atchley, R. C. (1979) *Families in Later Life*. Belmont, Calif.: Wadsworth Publishing Company, Inc.

Vital and Health Statistics (1970) Children of divorced couples: United States, selected years. Series 21:18(February). Washington, D. C.: U. S. Government Printing Office.

Vital and Health Statistics (1973) 100 years of marriage and divorce statistics: United States, 1867–1967. Series 21:24(December). Washington, D. C.: U. S. Government Printing Office.

Vital and Health Statistics, Advance Data (1980) Remarriage of women 15–44 years of age whose first marriage ended in divorce: United States, 1976. No. 58(February 14). Hyattsville, Md.: National Center for Health Statistics.

Walker, K., Rogers, J., and Messinger, L. (1977) Remarriage after divorce: A review. *Social Casework* 58(May):276–285.

Weiss, R. S. (1975) *Marital Separation.* New York: Basic Books, Inc.

Zill, N. (1980) *Happy, Healthy, and Insecure.* New York: Doubleday.

chapter 7

Historical Changes in the Timing of Family Transitions: Their Impact on Generational Relations[1]

TAMARA K. HAREVEN

The emergence of "old age" as a social, cultural, and biological phenomenon can best be understood in the context of the entire life course and of historical changes affecting it. The social conditions of children and adolescents in a given society are related to the way adulthood and old age are perceived in that society; and, conversely, the role and position of adults and of older people are affected by the treatment and role of people in earlier stages of life. A full understanding of the current trend toward the isolation and segregation of older people in contemporary American society would especially depend on a knowledge of the larger process of age segregation, which has affected different age groups.

The adaptation of individuals and their families to the social and economic conditions they face when they reach old age is contingent on the paths by which they reach old age. The differences in their respective

[1] This chapter was written while I was a recipient of a Research Career Development Grant from the National Institute on Aging. I am grateful to the NIA for its support. Some portions of this chapter were presented at the symposium of the American Association for the Advancement of Science in Houston in 1979, and were published in Kurt Back, ed., *Life Course: Integrative Theories and Exemplary Populations*. (Boulder, Colorado: Westview Press, 1980). I am also indebted to Raymond Smith, Mavis Vinovskis, and Robert Fogel for their comments.

143

AGING
Stability and Change in the Family

backgrounds, particularly the ways in which their earlier life experience and their cultural heritage have shaped their views of family relations, their expectations of support from kin, and their ability to interact with public agencies and bureaucratic institutions are crucial in determining their adaptability to conditions they encounter in "old age."

The family status and position that people experience in the later years of life is molded, therefore, by their cumulative life history and by the specific historical conditions affecting their lives at earlier points in time. For that very reason, the difference in the experience of various cohorts resulting from their location in historical time is critical for our understanding of their respective adaptation to old age (Riley *et al.* 1972).

The life-course approach links individual biography with collective behavior as part of an ongoing continuum of historical change. From such a perspective, older people are not viewed simply as a homogeneous group, but rather as age cohorts moving through history, each with its distinct life experiences, influenced by the historical circumstances it encountered earlier in life.

The life-course framework offers, therefore, a comprehensive, integrative approach, which steers one to interpret individual and family transitions as part of a continuous interactive process of historical change. It helps one view an individual life transition (leaving home or marriage, for example), as part of a cluster of other concurrent transitions and as part of a sequence of transitions affecting each other. It views a cohort as not only belonging to its specific time period, but also located in earlier times—its experience shaped, therefore, by different historical forces.

This chapter examines first the basic concepts of the life-course framework as they illuminate changing historical conditions affecting aging and the family. It next discusses the historical developments in the timing of life transitions as they affect the family status of older people. Finally, it presents a more detailed discussion of patterns of timing and generational relations among American families in the late nineteenth and early twentieth centuries, and implications of those patterns for generational relations in old age.

THE LIFE COURSE AS AN INTERDISCIPLINARY AND HISTORICAL CONCEPT

The interaction between individual development and collective family development, in the context of changing historical conditions, has only recently begun to attract the attention of researchers. Though the study of the individual life-span has for some time commanded the attention of psychologists, and though family development has been the domain of sociologists, it is only recently that an effort to examine these processes from a historical perspective has begun to mature. The application of developmental concepts to the past brought home the important realization that many aspects of human behavior, which social scientists had previously considered constant over time, have actually been subject to major historical changes. In this respect, historical research in recent years has had a similar impact on the study of human development as has anthropology; while anthropological research has shown that human development is relative to different cultures, historical research has demonstrated that it is time-bound.

As a result, the very focus of historical study has shifted. For historians, human development has ceased to be merely an explanatory framework for behavior in the past. Instead, the process of development itself has become a subject of historical investigation in its own right. Since it became clear that childhood, adolescence, youth, adulthood, middle age, and old age were not constant over time, the process of change in their respective definitions and experiences under different historical conditions have become important research subjects in themselves.

The historical study of aging from a life-course perspective is currently very much on the frontier of research. In their application of the life-course approach to past populations, historians have greatly benefited from the conceptual and methodological contributions of sociology, psychology, and economics. In their turn, historians can make certain contributions to other social sciences, which result from a historical, contextual view.

The life-course approach is interdisciplinary by its very nature: Its heritage combines several psychological, sociological, and demographic traditions. Drawing on life history analysis, on life-span psychology, on the sociology of age differentiation, and on the concept of cohorts as developed by demographers, it focuses on the interaction between individuals and collective timing of family transition as they are shaped by different historical conditions. It examines the synchronization of individual behavior with the collective behavior of the family unit, as they change over time and in their relation to external historical conditions (Elder 1978). The life-course approach is also historical by its very nature: Its essence is the interaction between "individual time," "family time," and "historical time."[2] It attempts to follow the move-

[2] Glen Elder has provided conceptual and methodological coherence to the life-course approach and has formulated it in a way that made it applicable to historical data (Elder 1978). The applicability of the life-course approach to historical data was explored in a series of interdisciplinary workshops sponsored by the Mathematics Social Science Board

ment of individuals through different family configurations and roles and is concerned with the determinants of timing patterns that affect these transitions (Hareven 1977). As Elder defines it, the life course encompasses "pathways" by which individuals move throughout their lives, fulfilling different roles sequentially or simultaneously (Elder 1978). In following such movements of individuals and families from one role or status to the next, or in the simultaneous balancing of roles, the life course is concerned with the process of such transitions under different historical conditions.

Three essential features of life-course analysis are particularly significant to an understanding of historical changes in the family: First, timing, which entails the synchronization of different individual roles over a person's career; second, interaction, which involves the relationship between individual life-course transitions and changing historical conditions; and finally, integration, which represents the cumulative impact of earlier life-course transitions on subsequent ones.

Timing

The life course concerns itself with two essential kinds of timing. First is the timing of transitions over an individual's career, particularly the balancing of entry into and exit from different roles. Second is the synchronization of seemingly individual transitions with collective family behavior. These aspects of timing cannot be understood without considering their interaction with external historical forces. For that reason, the use of the term *timing* in a historical population requires a specific definition that takes into account the historical context, since in the past, age itself was not the most critical aspect of the timing of life transitions.

On the individual level, the crucial question is how people plan and organize their roles over their life course and time their life transitions both on the nonfamilial as well as familial level, in such areas as entry into and exit from school or the labor force, migration, leaving home or

---

of the National Science Foundation, which Hareven directed. The workshops resulted in a volume that examined the timing of life transitions in the historical context of Essex County, Massachusetts, in the late nineteenth century (Hareven 1978a).

Initially, the family cycle approach as developed by Hill (1964) was valuable to historians because it provided a developmental approach to cross-sectional data (Hareven 1974). A more careful examination has shown, however, that the a priori stage did not always fit historical populations. The life-course approach takes a broader point of view—rather than focusing on stages, it examines the process of individual transitions as they relate to the family as a collective unit (Elder 1978, Hareven 1978d, see also Vinovskis 1977).

returning home, marriage, and setting up an independent household. Most important for an understanding of transitions into old age are the ways in which earlier life transitions are linked to later ones—the fact that the timing of marriage, for example, depends on the needs of aging parents.

The metaphor that captures best the interrelationship of individual transitions and changing family configurations is the movement of schools of fish. As people move over their life course in family units, they group and regroup themselves. The functions they adopt in these different clusters also vary significantly over their life courses. Most individuals are involved simultaneously in several family configurations, fulfilling different functions in each. A married person, for example, is part of both a family of origin and a family of procreation (occupying a different position and fulfilling a different role in each); in addition, such an individual also figures in his or her spouse's family of orientation, and in the spouse's kin network. When a son leaves home, his departure changes the configuration of his family unit. Depending on the status he held, his family might find itself less one breadwinner or less one dependent. When he marries and forms a new family unit, his roles and obligations differ from the ones he had in his parents' family. This seemingly individual move affects the collective conditions of at least three family units—his family of origin, his newly founded family, and his wife's family of origin. In situations in which remarriage follows death of a spouse or divorce, the new spouse's family enters the orbit of relationships, while the former spouse's family does not necessarily disappear completely. In case of divorce, especially, a woman would stop relating to her former husband's mother as her mother-in-law but may continue to relate to her as her child's grandmother. Thus, the multiplicity of familial relationships in which individuals are engaged changes over the life course, and along with these changes an individual's transitions into various roles are also timed differently. In this respect, age, although an important variable defining life transitions, is not the only one. Changes in family status and in accompanying roles are often as important as age, if not more significant.

Historical Timing

The second important feature of life-course analysis is the impact of historical processes on the timing of individual or family transitions. Life-course transitions are timed by the interaction of demographic, social, and economic factors as well as the influence of familial preferences. Fertility can abstractly account for the number of children born and the proportion of the life course spent on childbearing, but the commencement of childbearing and the spacing of children are determined (within biological limits) by personal decisions that are often governed by social and cultural values or prescriptions. Age at leaving home and age at marriage are similarly subject to complex interactions.

Social change has an important impact on timing in several areas. Demographic changes in mortality, fertility, and nuptiality affect the age configurations within the family and the length of overlap among family members over their lifetimes. Cultural changes in norms of timing and economic changes in the opportunity structure affect entry into the labor force, job availability, and, ultimately, retirement. Institutional and legislative changes, such as compulsory school attendance, child labor laws, and mandatory retirement, affect the transitions of different age groups in and out of the labor force.

In any examination of the timing of life transitions, the very question of "historical" or "social" changes in the life course requires more elaborate definition. "Historical change" is usually defined by nonhistorians as characterized by macrodevelopments, often represented by one specific major event, such as the Great Depression or a world war. But actually, the important contribution that historical research makes is in specifying and examining diachronic changes, which often have a more direct impact on the life course than macrosocial changes. Most important, historians can identify the convergence of socioeconomic and cultural forces, which are characteristic of a specific time period and which more directly influence the timing of life transitions than larger-scale or longer-term linear developments. For example, migration and changing local employment opportunities within a community can affect changes in the timing of life transitions more directly and dramatically than such momentous events as World War II.

Ryder has suggested that social change occurs when there is a distinct discontinuity between the experiences of one cohort and those of its predecessors (Ryder 1965). From a historical perspective, one would want to modify Ryder's assertion to argue that important historical discontinuities could also occur within the same cohort. For example, the cohort that reached adulthood during the Great Depression experienced major discontinuities in family and work lives, which were not only caused by historical events, but which also, in turn, may have catalyzed further social change. Or, consider the cohort that reached age 65 around 1910 and was faced with compulsory retirement. This cohort would have found mandatory retirement at a set age in one's work life far more traumatic than the cohort following it, which had come of age early in the twentieth century, when entry into and exit from the labor force were already becoming age-defined and legislated. At the same time, however, differences within cohorts are also of great significance. Variations in exposure to historical events by class and community background within each cohort would affect important differences between members of the same cohort. For example, within the same cohort, ethnic differences or differences in income, but especially historical experiences encountered earlier in their lives, would affect differences in their respective responses to when they reach "old age."

Cumulative Impact of Life Transitions

This leads us to the third feature of life-course analysis, the cumulative impact of earlier transitions on subsequent ones. Rather than following a static view of life experiences, a life-course approach views a cohort as an age group moving through history whose social experience is influenced not only by contemporary conditions but also by its experience of earlier life-course transitions. These transitions are affected in turn by a set of historical circumstances specific to their own time. This complex pattern of cumulative life-course effects can be grasped on two levels: First, the direct consequences of earlier life-course experiences on subsequent development must be taken into account.

Elder's *Children of the Great Depression*, one of the outstanding studies addressing these questions, documents the impact of depression experiences in childhood and early adulthood on subsequent adult experiences (Elder 1974). Within the same cohort of unemployed adults caught in the Great Depression, coping with unemployment differed not only in terms of the availability of resources such as personality, and family backgrounds, but also in terms of earlier transitions experienced—how long the individual had been working, whether his or her career had been continuous and stable or had already been disrupted.

Second, historical conditions that individuals encountered throughout their lives shaped their earlier life history and, therefore, also indirectly affected their transitions in the later years of life. This means that the social experience of each cohort is influenced not only by the external conditions at the particular point in time when it reaches "old age" but also by its earlier life experience as it was shaped by historical conditions at earlier points in time.

HISTORICAL CHANGES IN THE TIMING OF LIFE TRANSITIONS

The contours of the emergence of old age as a distinct stage of life were shaped by a larger historical process, involving the segmentation of the life course into specific developmental stages (Kett 1977, Hareven 1976, Fischer 1977, Keniston 1971, Neugarten 1968). New stages of life were only gradually recognized historically. Their characteristics were experienced first in the lives of individuals. They were subsequently recognized in the culture and, finally, were institutionalized and received public affirmation. Public recognition occurs through the passing of legislation and the establishment of agencies for the realization of the potential of people at a specific stage of life as well as for their protection within those stages. This is not to say that in earlier time periods there was no awareness of an individual's movement through a variety of age-related roles through life—it is to say merely that this awareness was not institutionalized.

The historical difference lies, however, in the recognition of distinct age-related stages of life, with their specific needs and societally recognized functions. To the extent to which it is possible to generalize about the historical emergence of stages of life, it appears that the "discovery" of such a stage is itself a complex process, since it involves the convergence of institutional and cultural factors in their formulation and acceptance. First, individuals become aware of the specific characteristics of such a stage in their private experience. The articulation of its unique conditions are then formulated by the professionals, and are eventually defined and followed in the popular culture. Finally, if the conditions peculiar to this stage seem to be associated with a major social problem, it attracts the attention of public agencies, and its needs and problems are dealt with in legislation and in the establishment of institutions aimed directly to meet its needs. Those public activities in turn affect the experience of individuals going through such a stage, and clearly influence the timing of transitions in and out of such a stage by providing public supports and, at times, constraints that affect timing.

In American society, childhood emerged as a distinct stage first in the private lives of middle-class urban families in the early part of the nineteenth century. The redefinition of the meaning of childhood and of the role of children was related to the retreat of the family into domesticity, the segregation of the workplace from the home, the redefinition of the mother's role as the major custodian of the domestic sphere, and the emphasis on sentimental as opposed to instrumental relations at the very base of familial relationships. As Philippe Ariés explained, the new child-centeredness of urban domestic families in Western Europe in the late eighteenth and early nineteenth centuries was also a response to two major demographic changes: the decline in infant and child mortality and the increase in the conscious practice of family limitation (Ariés, 1960). Having emerged first in the life of middle-class families and having become an integral part of their life-style, childhood as a distinct stage of development became the subject of the voluminous body of child-rearing and family advice literature. This literature popularized the concept of childhood and the needs of children, prescribed the means to allow them to develop as children, and called for the regulation of child labor.

The discovery of adolescence in the latter part of the nineteenth century followed a similar pattern to that of the emergence of childhood. While puberty in itself is a universal, biological process, the psychosocial phenomena of adolescence were only gradually identified and defined, most notably by G. Stanley Hall in the latter part of the nineteenth century. There is evidence that the experience of adolescence, particularly some of the problems and tensions associated with it, was noticed in the private lives of individuals reaching puberty during the second half of the nineteenth century (Demos and Demos 1969). The congregation of young people in peer groups and styles of behavior that might be characterized as a "culture of adolescence" were also observed by educators and urban reformers from the middle of the nineteenth century on. Anxiety over such conduct increased particularly in large cities, where the reformers warned against the potential threat of youth gangs. Adolescence as a new stage of life was articulated in the work of psychologists, particularly by Hall and his circle, and was also widely popularized in the literature. The extension of school age through high school in the second part of the nineteenth century, the further extension of the age limits for child labor, and the establishment of juvenile reformatories as well as vocational schools were all part of the public recognition of the needs and problems of adolescence (Bremner *et al.* 1969–1972).

The boundaries between childhood and adolescence on one hand and between adolescence and adulthood on the other became more clearly demarcated over the course of the twentieth century. The experience of childhood and adolescence became more pervasive among larger groups of the American population, as immigrant and working class families made their entry into the middle class. As Keniston has suggested, the extension of a moratorium from adult responsibilities beyond adolescence has resulted in the emergence of yet another stage—that of youth. However, despite the growing awareness of these preadult stages, no clear boundaries for adulthood in America emerged until much later, when "old age" became prominent as a new stage of life, and with it, the need to differentiate the social and psychological problems of "middle age" from those of "old age."

There are many indications that a new consciousness of "old age" along with institutional definitions and societal recognition emerged in the late part of the nineteenth and early part of the twentieth century. The convergence of an increasing volume of gerontological literature, the proliferation of negative stereotypes about old age, and the establishment of mandatory retirement represent the first moves in the direction of a public and institutional formulation of "old age" as a distinct stage of life.[3]

In the late nineteenth century, American society passed from an acceptance of aging as a natural process to a view of it as a distinct period of life characterized by decline, weakness, and obsolescence (Achenbaum 1978). Advanced old age, which had earlier been regarded as a manifestation of the survival of the fittest, was now denigrated as a condition of dependency and deterioration: "We are marked by time's defacing fingers with the ugliness of age [Anonymous 1893]." Writers began to identify advancing years with physical decline and mental deterioration.

In the beginning of the twentieth century, public concern for and interest in old age converged from various directions. In addition to physicians, psychologists, and popular writers, efficiency experts and social reformers were especially instrumental in attracting public attention to old age as a social problem. A variety of medical and psychological studies by industrial efficiency experts focused on the physical and mental limitations of old age. At the same time, social reformers began to expose the poverty and dependency suffered by many old people, as part of a general investigation of "how the other half lives," and to agitate for Social Security and social insurance (Hareven 1976).

Government recognition of old age evolved more gradually and began on the state level. By 1920, only 10 states had instituted some form of old-age legislation; all programs were limited in scope, and most of them were declared unconstitutional by the Supreme Court. Nevertheless, agitation for old-age security continued and finally culminated in the Social Security Act of 1935. It was not until the 1940s, however, that gerontology was recognized as a new medical field, and it was even more recently that social scientists identified old age as constituting a new and pressing human problem. Social definitions of age limits and public treat-

---

[3] On the periodization of "old age" in American history, Fischer (1977) has argued that changing perceptions toward old age had actually emerged in the late eighteenth and early nineteenth century.

ment through institutional reform, retirement legislation, and welfare measures represent the most recent societal recognition of this stage of life. The historical developments of the past half century have since contributed to the sharpening of the boundaries between old age and middle age. But the boundaries of adulthood itself are not yet sharply defined, and the transitions into middle age are still fuzzy. "Old age" is now recognized as a specific period of adulthood (Neugarten and Hagestad 1976).

More recently, rather than being viewed as a homogeneous stage, the concept of old age itself has been refined and subdivided into the "young old" and the "old old" in an effort to reflect developmental characteristics within the "elderly." Increasing consciousness of problems and crises related to middle adulthood, particularly as reflected in problems of parenting, has also resulted in the recognition of "middle age" as a distinct stage. On the public level, it has a formal beginning—age 65, at least as far as an individual's working life is concerned, and it is institutionalized by a rite of passage—retirement and eligibility for Social Security (Hareven 1976).

The conscious segmentation of the life course into publicly recognized stages and the preoccupation with their meaning has had significant implications for the relationships among age groups in American society, for patterns of age segregation within the family, and for the timing of life transitions.

The important connection between historical development and the emergence of such new stages has not been fully documented yet. The general contours of the pattern are beginning to emerge, however, with some clarity. Whether childhood, adolescence, youth, middle age, or old age were first experienced on the private, individual level or acknowledged on the public, collective level, their very appearance and increasing societal recognition have affected the timing of individual and family transitions in the past.

Not only has the very experience of these stages of life changed over time, but the timing of people's entry into such stages and exit from them and the accompanying roles involved in such timing have changed as well. For example, the existential as well as the institutional changes that have buttressed the extension of a moratorium from adult responsibilities have also affected the timing of both individual and familial transitions and have resulted in new pressures on families and individuals. Transitions at different points in the life course were interlocked and interdependent. Timing at one end of the life course affected timing at the other end, and vice versa. The postponement of the assumption of adult responsibilities, for example, would have meant longer residence of children in the household making no contribution to the family's economic effort, and a resulting increase in the state of "dependency" or "semidependency" as a typical experience of adolescence. At the other end, the recognition of old age as a distinct stage, and especially its imposition of discontinuity in the form of mandatory retirement, has had a serious impact on the timing of transitions in the family status of older people, leading to the emergence of dependency or semidependency in old age, and imposing tensions and demands on family obligations.

These large-scale societal developments as expressed in the discovery of new stages of life are reflected in changes in the timing of life transitions on the microlevel. Demographic changes in American society since the late nineteenth century have significantly affected the timing of life-course transitions and the age configuration within the family over the life of its members (Uhlenberg 1974, 1978, Hareven 1977). Important changes have also occurred in the synchronization of individual time schedules with the collective timetables of the family.

Demographic, economic, and cultural factors have combined to account for differences in the timing of such transitions as leaving home, entry into and exit from the labor force, marriage, parenthood, the "empty nest," and widowhood. As Uhlenberg suggests, over the past century, demographic developments have tended to effect greater uniformity in the life course of American families and have considerably increased the opportunities for intact survival of the family unit over the lifetime of its members (Uhlenberg 1978). As a result of the decline in mortality since the late nineteenth century, the chances for children to survive into adulthood and to grow up with their siblings and both parents alive have increased considerably. Similarly, the chances for women to survive to adulthood and to fulfill the normatively established script of their family lives—namely, marriage, raising of children jointly with a husband, and survival with husband through the launching stage (Uhlenberg 1974) have increased steadily between the late nineteenth century and the early twentieth century.

For women, these changes, combined with earlier marriage and earlier completion of maternal roles, have meant a more extended period of life without children in their middle years. At the same time, women's tendency to live longer than men has resulted in a protracted period of widowhood in later years of life. Men, on the other hand, because of lower life expectancy and a greater tendency to remarry in old age, normally remain married until death (Glick 1977). A comparison of different cohorts of white American women from 1870 to 1930 has thus shown that an increasing proportion of the population has entered prescribed family roles and, except for divorce, has lived out its life in family units (Uhlenberg 1974). Contrary to conventional assumptions, the American population has thus experienced an increasing uniformity in the timing of life-course transitions into family roles and survival through the entire family cycle.

The very demographic factors that are responsible for these continuities have also generated major discontinuities in the timing of life-course transitions over the past century. Such discontinuities were expressed in the timing of transitions into and out of family roles and work roles, and are closely related to the gradual segmentation of the life course into societally acknowledged stages, as previously discussed (childhood, youth, adolescence, adulthood, middle age, and old age).

The most significant expression of such discontinuities was evident most clearly in the timing of transitions to adulthood, especially in leaving home, marriage, family formation, and parenthood. As Modell et al. have shown (1976), over the past century, age uniformity in the timing of life-course transitions has been increasingly more marked. Transitions have become more rapidly timed and abrupt. By contrast to the nineteenth century, transitions from the parental home to marriage, to household headship, and to parenthood occurred more gradually and were timed less rigidly. In the late nineteenth century the time range necessary for a cohort to accomplish such transitions was wider, and the sequence in which transitions followed one another was not rapidly established. In the twentieth century, on the other hand, transitions to adulthood have become more uniform for the age cohort undergoing them, more orderly in sequence, and more definitive. The very notion of embarking on a new stage of the life course and the implications of movement from one stage to the next have become more firmly established. Most important, the timing of life transitions has become more regulated according to specific age norms, rather than in relation to collective needs of the family.

In the later years of life, transitions to the "empty nest," to widowhood, and out of household headship among urban populations in the late nineteenth century followed no ordered sequence, were not closely synchronized, and extended over a relatively long period of time. For most men surviving to old age, labor force participation and family status generally resembled those of their earlier adult years. Only at very advanced ages, when their capabilities were no doubt impaired by infirmity, did a substantial number experience definite changes in their household status. However, these men represented a minor fraction of their age peers. Because widowhood was such a common experience in their lives, older women did experience more marked transitions than men, although the continuing presence of adult children in the household meant that widowhood did not necessarily mark a dramatic transition to the empty nest (Chudacoff and Hareven 1979, Hareven 1981, Smith 1979).

In summary, the nineteenth-century pattern of transitions allowed for a wider age spread within the family and for greater opportunity for interaction among parents and adult children as well as among other kin. Demographic changes, combined with the increasing rapidity in the timing of transitions, the increasing separation between an individual's family of orientation and family of procreation, and the introduction of publicly imposed transitions, have converged to isolate and segregate age groups in the larger society. At the same time they have tended to generate new kinds of stresses on familial needs and obligations.

The most marked discontinuity has occurred in the middle and later years of life—namely, the emergence of the "empty nest" in a couple's middle age. The combination of earlier marriage and fewer children overall, with segregation of childbearing to the early stages of the family cycle and children's leaving home more uniformly earlier in their parents' lives, has resulted in a more widespread emergence of the empty nest as a characteristic of middle and old age (Glick 1977).

In contemporary society, the empty nest period comprises one-third or more of the married adult life-span. Glick concludes that the duration of this period has increased over the past 80 years by 11 years (from 1.6 years to 12.3 years): "The couple now entering marriage has the prospect of living together 13 years (without children) or more than one-third of the 44 years of married life that lay ahead of them at the time of marriage [Glick 1977, p. 9]." Growing sex differentials in mortality above age 50 have dramatically increased the ratio of women to men and made widowhood a more important feature in women's lives. In this respect, Uhlenberg (1978) has noted that the major change since the late nineteenth century has not been so much in the emergence of an empty nest but rather in the proportion of a woman's lifetime that this period encompasses. Earlier marriage and earlier completion of childbearing and child-rearing on one hand, and greater survival into older age on the other, have resulted in a higher proportion of a woman's life spent, first, with a husband but without children, and then alone, without either husband or children.

By contrast, in the nineteenth century, later age at marriage, higher fertility, and shorter life expectancy rendered different family configurations from those characterizing contemporary society. Thus, for large families, the parental stage, with children remaining in the household, extended over a longer period of time, sometimes over the parents' entire life. Since children were spread along a broad spectrum in families, younger children could observe their older siblings and near relatives moving through adolescence and into adulthood. Older siblings, in turn, trained for adult roles by acting as surrogate parents for younger siblings (Hareven 1977, 1982). Most important, the nest was rarely empty, as usually one adult child remained at home while the parents were aging.

FAMILY TIMING AND TRANSITIONS INTO OLD AGE

Demographic factors only partly explain the absence of an empty nest in the nineteenth century. As shown by the correlation of the children's age with that of the heads, children were present in the households of their aging parents not simply because they were too young to move out. Even when sons and daughters were in their late teens and early twenties, and therefore old enough to leave their parents' households, at least one child stayed on because it was customary for an adult child to remain at home to care for aging parents if there were no other source of assistance available. Autonomy in old age, partly expressed in household headship, hinged on some form of support from one or more working children in the household or on the presence of boarders. The transition into the later years of life was thus marked by the continued effort of aging parents to maintain the integrity of their family through the continued residence of at least one child at home.

Recent historical analyses of late nineteenth-century American communities suggest that older couples and especially aging widows who had children were more likely to reside with their children than with other kin or strangers.[4] Childless couples, or those whose children had left home, took in boarders and lodgers as surrogate kin. Widows, or

---

[4] The patterns of timing and household arrangements of older people reported here are based on the analysis of family and household patterns in select communities of Essex County, Massachusetts, in 1880 (Chudacoff and Hareven 1978a), a population sample for Providence, Rhode Island, from the 1860, 1870, and 1880 censuses (Chudacoff and Hareven 1979), and a sample from the 1900 census for Manchester, New Hampshire (Hareven 1982). The patterns found in these local analyses are consistent with the national picture emerging from the analysis of a cross-section of the older population in the United States from the 1900 census, a study carried out by Smith (1979). Any generalizations on this subject are necessarily limited by the cross-sectional data on which these studies are based. On one hand, the application of life-course questions to cross-sectional data has allowed us to infer longitudinal patterns, if only to a limited extent. Nor does census data provide insight into the quality of relationships. On the other hand, oral history interviewing for Hareven's study of Manchester, New Hampshire, has provided insight into familial norms and into the sense of familial obligations in generational relations. Most important, it has helped identify the areas of strain and conflicts in generational relations as parents were aging (Hareven and Langenbach 1978, Hareven 1978, Hareven 1982).

women who had never married and who were unable to maintain independent households, moved in with their relatives or boarded in other
people's homes (Chudacoff and Hareven 1979, Hareven 1982). Solitary
residence, a pattern that is becoming increasingly prominent among older
people today, was rarely experienced in the nineteenth century (Kobrin
1976).

As Taeuber (1969) described it, boarding and lodging provided a means
for the social equalization of the family. Young men and women in the
transitional state between leaving home and setting up their own household boarded with older people whose children had left home. In some
cases the function was reversed, and older people boarded in other
people's households.

Older people struggled to retain the headship of their own households,
rather than move in with their relatives and strangers. Nuclear household
arrangements were often broken or stretched, however, during parents'
dependency in old age, or during apparent housing shortages that made
it more difficult for newlyweds to afford separate housing. Thus, under
certain circumstances, some children either returned home with their
spouses to live with their aging parents, or other children, most commonly the youngest daughter remaining at home, postponed marriage,
in order to continue supporting older parents. Commitment to autonomy
was so pervasive that the commonly followed pattern was that of adult
children staying in their parents' household, rather than that of parents
moving in with their children. Even older widows, who were generally
the most vulnerable, continued to hold on to the headship of their household as long as they could. If there were no children available or able
to help, they took in boarders and lodgers. Once they were unable to
continue to maintain independent households, they, more frequently than
widowed men, eventually had to move into the households of relatives
or strangers (Chudacoff and Hareven 1978, 1979, Hareven 1981).

The rather powerful commitment to the continued autonomy of the
household and to the "nuclearity" of the family was clearly in conflict
with the needs of people as they were aging. In the absence of adequate
public and institutional means of support, older people were caught in
a conflict: On one hand they had to rely on the continued support from
their children and, on the other hand, they were committed to living in
nuclear households.

In the late nineteenth-century setting, the norms of familial assistance
and autonomy seemed to prevail over the age norms of timing. This is
precisely an area in which the historical difference with our times is
drastic. Life-course transitions in contemporary society have become
more strictly age related and more rigidly governed by age norms. Neu-

garten's definition of being "late" or "on time" in one's fulfillment of certain age-related roles reflects the standards of a society bound to age norms, while in earlier time periods, economic needs and familial obligations prevailed over age norms (Neugarten 1968). Thus, the current trend toward specific age-related transitions is closely related to the decline in instrumental relations among kin over the past century and their replacement by an individualized and sentimental orientation toward family relations. This trend has led to the isolation of the elderly and to increasing age segregation in American society.

The family was the central arena in which many of the life transitions were converging. Transitions that we could consider today as individual were actually collective and familial. They were either shared by a number of family members or, even if they involved strictly individual activity, such as the work life, they still affected the entire family as a unit, or at least several members within the family. Marriage, for example, was not merely subject to individual or couple decisions, but rather its timing hinged on the need of each partner's family of origin, particularly on the status of parents if they were aging.

Second, the family played a major role as the locus for most important economic and welfare functions. This central role of the family persisted even after the work place had been removed from the home and after many of the family's earlier educational, welfare, and social control functions had been transferred to other institutions under the impact of industrialization. Despite the growing tendency of middle-class urban families to serve as a retreat from the outside world and to concentrate on domesticity and child nurturing as the family's exclusive role, the majority of families in the larger society continued to function as economic units—indeed, often as work units. Families and individuals therefore had to rely heavily on kin relations as their very essential social base. Timing was a critical factor in the family's efforts to maintain control over its resources, especially by balancing the contribution of different members to the family economy. Thus, under the historical conditions in which familial assistance was the almost exclusive source of security, the multiplicity of obligations that individuals incurred over their life course was more complex than in the present setting of the welfare state, in which such responsibilities are primarily the domain of public agencies. (This is not to say that at present kin do not continue to fulfill such obligations, but major welfare functions that were earlier carried out by kin have been transferred to the public sector.)

Nineteenth-century family economy was out of necessity flexible because individual resources were precarious, and institutional buttressing slim or nonexistent. Family adaptation was crucial, therefore, in coping with critical life situations, or even with regular life-course transitions. The family was the most critical agent, both in initiating as well as in absorbing the consequences of transitions among individual members. Clearly, when viewed from this perspective, the essential aspect of the timing of a transition was not the age at which a person left home, married, or became a parent, but rather how this transition was related to those that other family members were undergoing and, especially, to the needs of parents as they were aging.

Under the economic conditions of the late nineteenth century, pressing needs and familial obligations took precedence over established norms of timing. The timing of early life transitions was bound up with later ones in a continuum of familial needs and obligations. More significant than age was the sequence or coincidence in which transitions were expected to occur. Modell *et al.* (1976) have also shown that even though nineteenth-century transitions to adulthood were more flexibly timed than today, they nevertheless followed a certain sequence: Marriage was conditioned on the establishment of a separate household and of means of self-support. The timing of life transitions was not so much governed by age norms as by family economic strategies and interdependence. It was also influenced by the economic opportunity structure in the community and was limited by institutional constraints, such as compulsory school attendance or child labor legislation. The absence of institutional supports, such as welfare agencies, unemployment compensation, and social security added to the pressures imposed on family members.

The timing of transitions along the life course converged around interdependence and mutual obligations among different family members. Individual life transitions were not always self-timed. In modern society, we are accustomed to thinking of most family roles and work careers as individual. Historically, most apparently individual transitions were treated as a family move and had to be synchronized with family needs. In addition to the ties they retained with their family of origin, individuals took on obligations toward their families of procreation and toward their spouses' families. The complexity of obligations cast family members in various overlapping and at times conflicting functions over the course of their lives. One role might gradually come to dominate while another receded in importance, but the alteration was not always a smooth one.

Historical changes in the nature of kin interaction have affected these patterns of kin assistance over the life course, tending to segregate and isolate older people. The increasing separation between the family of origin and the family of procreation over the past century, combined with a growing privatization of the family and the discontinuities along the life course discussed above, all occurred in the context of changes in the quality of kin relations. In the nineteenth and early twentieth centuries, family relationships were characterized by a higher degree of kin integration. Kin served as the most essential resource for economic assistance and security and carried the major burden of welfare functions, many of which fall now within the purview of the public sector. Exchange relationships among parents and children and other kin thus provided the major, and sometimes the only, base for security (Anderson 1971, Hareven 1978a).

The gradual erosion of instrumental kin relationships has tended to increase insecurity and isolation as people age, especially in areas of need that are not met by public programs. In examining this particular aspect of historical change, it is important to distinguish between the availability of kin and the nature of kin interaction and support systems. The major historical change was not the decline of coresidence, but rather involved functions that kin fulfilled. Recent historical studies have documented the multiplicity of functions of kin in the nineteenth century, especially their critical role in migration, job placement, and housing (Hareven 1978a) and in assistance in critical life situations (Anderson 1971). Contrary to prevailing theories, urbanization and industrialization did not break down traditional kinship patterns. There are thus many parallels between the role that kin fulfilled in the nineteenth and early twentieth centuries and patterns of kin assistance found by sociologists in modern American society (Sussman 1959, Litwak 1965, Shanas *et al.* 1968). Their studies, particularly that by Shanas, have emphasized the frequency of interaction among older parents and adult children and the flow of assistance to older people from their relatives. The difference lies, however, in the degree of integration with kin and the dependence on mutual assistance. While more intensive patterns of kin interaction have survived among first-generation immigrant, black, and working-class families, there has been an overall erosion of instrumental ties among relatives, especially in the almost exclusive dependence on kin for social security and support.

Contemporary studies insisting on the prevalence of kin assistance among older people have not documented the intensity, quality, and consistency of kin support that older people are receiving from their relatives. Until we have more systematic evidence in this area, it would be a mistake to assume that kin are carrying or should be expected to carry the major responsibility for assistance to older people. The current involvement of the elderly with kin, as Shanas *et al.* (1968) and others have found, represents a cohort phenomenon rather than a continuing historical pattern. The elderly cohort of the present has carried over into old age the historical attitudes and traditions that were prevalent when it was growing up earlier in this century, especially a strong reliance on relatives. It also has kin available, because of the larger family size of earlier cohorts. Future cohorts, as they reach old age, might not have the same strong sense of integration with kin, nor might there be sufficient numbers of available kin on whom to rely (Hareven 1978c). It would be a mistake, therefore, to leave kin to take care of their own at a time when the chances for people to do so are considerably diminishing. Nor should the historical evidence about the continuity in kin relations be misused in support of proposals to return welfare responsibilities from the public sector to the family without basic additional supports. An examination of the historical patterns reveals the high price that kin had to pay in order to assist each other in the absence of other forms of societal support. The historical precedent thus offers a warning against romanticizing kin relations, particularly against the attempt to transfer responsibility for children and the elderly back to the family without adequate governmental assistance.

THE CONTRIBUTION OF EXISTING HISTORICAL RESEARCH

The current state of historical knowledge on aging and on the family status of older people is still in its formulative stages, and cannot provide, therefore, a comprehensive picture of change over time. It has provided, however, valuable insights that help revise preconceived notions about the past and, by implication, about current conditions.

First, a historical life-course approach has warned us against what Riley calls "the reification of age" (Riley 1978). Historically, age itself has not been the significant factor in the timing of life transitions and in the definitions of old age. More important than age was family status, work status, and one's relationship to the community.

The existing historical evidence about family arrangements of older people suggests a continuity over time in the residential arrangement preferred by older people, which Rosenmayor defined as "intimacy from a distance." The commitment to autonomy on the part of older people has been a continuous theme in American society. The historical difference lies, however, in the ways in which such autonomy was achieved or sustained. Historically, the independence and self-sufficiency of older people was conditioned on assistance from relatives, especially from their own adult children. Currently, the double bind in which generations were caught has been alleviated to some extent by the welfare state, but the need for kin assistance persists.

The historical evidence regarding family relations of older people contradicts any myth about a golden age in the family relations of the aged in the past. In the colonial period, older people were as insecure as they are today, even though they were revered and accorded higher status (Demos 1978). The very fact that aging parents had to enter agreements with inheriting sons to secure old age supports in exchange for land suggests the potential tension and insecurity in such arrangements (Greven 1970, Smith 1973).

Nor did older people experience security and guaranteed support from their children in urban industrial society. While the evidence presented here suggests a strong interdependence among generations, one must not lose sight of the fact that familial supports for older people were strictly voluntary and were carried out at a high price. For that very reason, they were precarious and not always continuous.

The historical ambivalence and the potential conflict underlying support and sociability systems for older people has survived in America even after many of the functions of family welfare and support for the elderly were taken over by the public sector—a transfer culminating in the passage of social security legislation and in subsequent governmental welfare programs.

This shift of responsibility has generated considerable ambiguity in American society, particularly in the expectations for support and assistance for aging relatives from their own kin. On the one hand, it is assumed that the welfare state has relieved children from the obligation of supporting their parents in old age; on the other hand, these public measures are not sufficient in the economic area, nor do they provide the kind of support and sociability in areas traditionally provided by the family. It is precisely this ambiguity, and the failure of American society to consummate the historical process of the transfer of functions from the family to the public sector, that is one of the major sources of problems currently confronting older people.

REFERENCES

Achenbaum, A. W. (1974) The obsolescence of old age in America, 1965–1914. *Journal of Social History* 8:48–62.
Achenbaum, A. W. (1978) *Old Age in the New Land.* Baltimore, Md.: Johns Hopkins University Press.

Anderson, M. S. (1971) *Family Structure in Nineteenth Century Lancashire*. Cambridge, England: Cambridge University Press.

Anonymous (1893) Apology from age to youth. *Living Age* 193(14)January:170.

Ariés, P. (1960) *L'enfant et la vie familiale sous l'ance regime*. Paris. (Translated by R. Baldick as *Centuries of Childhood*. London, 1962.)

Bremner, R. J., Barnard, J., and Hareven, T. K. (1969–1972) *Children and Youth in America*, I–II. Cambridge, Mass.: Harvard University Press.

Chudacoff, H., and Hareven, T. K. (1978) Family transitions to old age. In T. K. Hareven, ed., *Transitions: The Family and the Life Course in Historical Perspective*. New York: Academic Press.

Chudacoff, H., and Hareven, T. K. (1979) From the empty nest to family dissolution. *Journal of Family History* (Spring).

Demos, J. (1978) Old age in early New England. In J. Demos and S. Boocock, eds., *Turning Points: American Journal of Sociology* 84(Supplement).

Demos, J., and Demos, V. (1969) Adolescence in historical perspective. *Journal of Marriage and the Family* 31:632–638.

Elder, G. (1974) *Children of the Great Depression*. Chicago: Chicago University Press.

Elder, G. (1978) Family history and the life course. In T. K. Hareven, ed., *Transitions: The Family and the Life Course in Historical Perspective*. New York: Academic Press.

Fischer, D. H. (1977) *Growing Old in America*. New York: Oxford University Press.

Glick, P. C. (1977) Updating the life cycle of the family. *Journal of Marriage and the Family* (February):5–13.

Greven, P. (1970) *Four Generations: Population, Land and Family in Colonial Andover, Massachusetts*. Ithaca, N.Y.: Cornell University Press.

Hareven, T. K. (1974) The family as process: The historical study of the family cycle. *Journal of Social History* 7:322–329.

Hareven, T. K. (1976) The last stage: Historical adulthood and old age. *Daedalus* (Fall):13–27.

Hareven, T. K. (1977) Family time and historical time. *Daedalus* (Spring): 13–27.

Hareven, T. K. (1978a) The dynamics of kin in an industrial community. In J. Demos and S. Boocock, eds., *Turning Points: American Journal of Sociology* 84 (Supplement).

Hareven, T. K., ed. (1978b) *Transitions: The Historical Study of the Family and the Life Course*. New York: Academic Press.

Hareven, T. K. (1978c) Historical changes in the life course and the family. In J. M. Yinger and S. J. Cutler, eds., *Major Social Issues: A Multidisciplinary View*. New York: The Free Press.

Hareven, T. K. (1978d) Cycles, courses, and cohorts: Reflections on theoretical and methodological approaches to the historical study of family development. *Journal of Social History* 12(1):97–110.

Hareven, T. K. (1982) *Family Time and Industrial Time*. Cambridge, England.: Cambridge University Press.

Hareven, T. K., and Langenbach, R. (1978) *Amoskeg: Life and Work in an American Factory City*. New York: Pantheon.

Hill, R. (1964) Methodological issues in family development research. *Family Process* 3(March):186–206.

Hill, R. (1970) *Family Development in Three Generations*. Cambridge, Mass.: Schenkman.

Keniston, K. (1971) Psychological development and historical change. *Journal of Interdisciplinary History* 21(Fall).

Kett, J. (1977) *Rites of Passage: Adolescence in America, 1790 to the Present*. New York: Basic Books.

Kobrin, F. E. (1976) The fall of household size and the rise of the primary individual. *Demography* (February):127–138.

Laslett, P., and Wall, R., eds. (1972) *House and Family in Past Time*. Cambridge, England: Cambridge University Press.

Litwak, E. (1965) Extended kin relations in an industrial democratic society. In E. Shanas and G. F. Streib, eds., *Social Structure and the Family: Generational Relations*. Englewood Cliffs, N.J.: Prentice-Hall, Inc.

Modell, J., and Hareven, T. K. (1973) Urbanization and the malleable household: Boarding and lodging in American families. *Journal of Marriage and the Family* 35:467–479.

Modell, J., Furstenberg, F., and Herschberg, T. (1976) Social change and transitions to adulthood in historical perspective. *Journal of Family History* 1:7–32.

Neugarten, B. L., ed. (1968) *Middle Age and Aging: A Reader in Social Psychology*. Chicago: University of Chicago Press.

Neugarten, B., and Daton, N. (1973) Sociological perspectives on the life cycle. In P. Baltes and W. K. Schaie, eds., *Life Span Development Psychology: Personality and Socialization*. New York: Academic Press.

Neugarten, B., and Hagestad, G. O. (1976) Age and the life course. In R. H. Binstock and E. Shanas, eds., *Handbook of Aging and the Social Sciences*. New York: Van Nostrand.

Riley, M. W. (1978) Aging, social change and the power of ideas. *Daedalus: Generations* (Fall).

Riley, M. W., Johnson, M. E., and Foner, A., eds. (1972) *Aging and Society: A Sociology of Age Stratification*. New York: Russell Sage Foundation.

Ryder, N. (1965) The cohort as a concept in the study of social change. *American Sociological Review* 30.

Shanas, E., Townshend, P., Wedderburn, D., Friis, H., Milhøj, P., and Stehouwer, J. (1968) *Old People in Three Industrial Societies*. New York: Atherton Press.

Smith, D. S. (1973) Parental power and marriage patterns: An analysis of historical trends in Hingham, Massachusetts. *Journal of Marriage and the Family* 35(August).

Smith, D. S. (1979) Life course, norms, and the family system of older Americans in 1900. *Journal of Family History* 4(Fall):285–299.

Sussman, M. B. (1959) The isolated nuclear family: Fact or fiction? *Social Problems* 6(Spring):333–347.

Taeuber, I. B. (1969) Continuity, change and transition in populations and family: Interrelations and priorities in research. In *The Family in Transition*. Fogarty International Center Proceedings, No. 3.

Uhlenberg, P. (1974) Cohort variations in family life cycle experiences of U.S. females. *Journal of Marriage and the Family* 34:284–292.

Uhlenberg, P. (1978) Changing configurations of the life course. In T. K. Hareven, ed., *Transitions: The Family and the Life Course in Historical Perspective*. New York: Academic Press.

Vinovskis, M. A. (1977) From household size to the life course: Some observations on recent trends in family history. *American Behavioral Scientist* 21:263–287.

PART II

FAMILY AND PUBLIC POLICY

chapter 8

An Assessment of Aid to the Elderly: Incentive Effects and the Elderly's Role in Society

W. KIP VISCUSI

A variety of government programs transfer cash or in-kind assistance to the elderly. These programs include efforts to which the elderly themselves have contributed through their payroll taxes or, less directly, through their income taxes. Most government assistance is in the form of cash through the Social Security and Supplemental Security Income programs or through the health insurance coverage provided by Medicare and Medicaid.

In the design of these aid programs, little attention has been devoted to their effect on the behavior of the elderly. The conditions for receiving assistance may alter one's actions, as in the case of income, asset, and residence requirements for aid. In some instances, such as housing for the elderly, the nature of the directed consumption effort will affect the behavior of the recipients.

The particular actions altered as a result of aid often are direct matters of concern. For example, if work penalties lead the aged to retire from the labor force, society may lose productive individuals, and the aged will have lower levels of income. The altered actions of the aged also may provide valuable information for policy design. If the beneficiaries are willing to contribute to the cost of medical care or public housing, one can be more confident that these commodities are valued by the recipient than if there were no cost sharing.

169

AGING
Stability and Change in the Family

The discussion begins with an analysis of the choice of the family structure and the role of government policy in these decisions. Although some of this discussion is necessarily speculative, my purpose is not to resolve the matter of the optimal family structure but to highlight the intractable problems involved in selecting policies of this type. The incentive effects of government policies are overviewed with special emphasis on programs that affect the family most directly. Although the actions taken by the elderly are often altered in response to government programs, this behavior is of interest wholly apart from potential inefficiencies that may be involved. In particular, the analysis indicates how information obtained from the elderly's actions can be used to target assistance more effectively. The final section summarizes the broader implications for policy.

CHOICE OF HOUSEHOLD STRUCTURE[1]

Although most of the elderly do not live with their relatives, substantial numbers do. Almost half of all unmarried elderly women and about one-third of single elderly men and married elderly live with relatives. About one-third of those elderly who live with their relatives bear at least their proportional share of the costs. The greatest dependency status is for single women, while for the married elderly it is the nonelderly relatives who often are subsidized.

The potential benefits of multiperson households, usually involving a spouse or one's relatives, are well known. As the economic theory of the family has shown, there are strong motivations for forming family units simply on the basis of the efficiency of the family as a productive unit (see Becker 1976). Services can often be provided more effectively on a joint basis, and many consumptive activities involve time inputs from more than a single individual. Several forms of in-kind assistance that are transferred by the government also are provided by the household unit, including medical care, shelter, and meals.

Nonelderly relatives also benefit in a variety of ways from the elderly, who assist in shopping, taking care of grandchildren, giving advice, and a variety of other activities summarized in Table 8.1. The diverse and widespread nature of this assistance suggests that the aged are quite active in the provision of services to nonelderly relatives. Even when these individuals do not share the same household, there appears to be

[1] Supporting data for this section are summarized in Viscusi (1979).

TABLE 8.1
Ways in Which the Elderly Help Their Children or Grandchildren[a]

	Respondent group		Ratio
Category	Elderly	Nonelderly	Column 1/ Column 2
Give gifts	90	85	1.06
Help out when someone is ill	68	57	1.19
Take care of grandchildren	54	42	1.29
Help out with money	45	35	1.29
Give general advice on life's problems	39	58	.67
Shop or run errands	34	30	1.13
Fix things around the house or keep house	26	22	1.18
Give advice on raising children	23	40	.58
Give advice on running a home	21	42	.50
Give advice on jobs or business matters	20	31	.65
Take grandchildren, nieces, or nephews into home to live	16	21	.76

[a] Reprinted from *The Myth and Reality of Aging in America,* a study prepared by Louis Harris and Associates, Inc. for The National Council on the Aging, Inc., Washington, D.C.©1975.

considerable contact. Overall, of those elderly who have children, 55% have seen their children within the last day or so, while 81% have seen them within the last week or two (see National Council on the Aging 1975).

The economic rationale underlying the formation of household units is straightforward and will be discussed here within the context of the choice by the elderly and another party (e.g., their children) to live in the same household. Since this relationship would be terminated if either party chooses to do so, the joint arrangement will prevail only if the two parties prefer this arrangement to its alternatives. This underlying aspect of behavior is uncontroversial. The possibility of preferences that are interdependent is not ruled out. A typical example of such interdependence is the case of an individual who would prefer to terminate the relationship if the other party were willing to do so, but otherwise is willing to continue.

Under rather broad circumstances, economists would conclude that the resulting arrangements are efficient (i.e., Pareto optimal). This household choice result is simply a variant of the Coase Theorem, which demonstrates the efficiency of a wide class of such bilateral bargaining arrangements.[2] Interdependence of the parties creates no particular dif-

[2] The classic article by Coase (1960) presents this result.

ficulties since the principal purpose of the Coase Theorem was to show that private bargains in cases of pollution and other externalities will be optimal.

The two principal requirements for efficiency are that there be no transactions costs to arriving at these bargains and that resources can be exchanged between the parties to compensate the other party for any loss in welfare due to a change in the course of action that would have been preferred if no such compensation were paid. This compensation need not be financial, as services within the household can be provided.

While this bilateral bargaining framework is instructive, within the context of family relationships it is likely to be quite costly to arrive at the types of implicit contracts associated with this theory. Most important is that as one moves from impersonal market transactions to relationships within the family, the role of transactions costs associated with arriving at solutions looms particularly large. These costs are unlikely to be symmetrical with respect to forming or dissolving relationships and are also likely to be inequitably divided between the parties.

Although social policies can potentially diminish such costs by shifting the decision from the parties themselves to the government, unless the direction and extent of the deviation of present arrangements from the socially optimal pattern is known with precision, one should be cautious in interfering with the choices of the individuals involved. Indeed, the principal implication of many of the chapters in this volume is that our knowledge of the relative welfare levels of individuals in different living contexts is still rather primitive. Even more rudimentary is our understanding of how altering the current structure of family relationships would alter the welfare of the affected parties.

Other considerations related to the effectiveness of the policy mix may lead one to consider intervention in this area. Society has instituted a number of programs to aid the aged, presumably because there is an externality to society at large from raising the elderly's welfare. If influencing household choice were a particularly effective mechanism for increasing the well-being of the aged, one might wish to utilize it.

Suppose, for example, that additional tax incentives or other benefits are provided to household units with the desired characteristics and that, as a result, a substantially greater number of elderly would reside with their children. The welfare of the nonelderly individuals whose choices are altered presumably is no worse than before since they have chosen to make this decision. The well-being of the aged may be increased substantially.

The difficulty with outcomes in the absence of such incentives is that neither the elderly nor society at large may be able to compensate the prospective nonelderly household members for the welfare gains that will accrue. The aged may be willing to incur higher Medicare decuctibles or forego public housing in return for a subsidy that would alter household choices in this manner. However, these funds are not provided on a discretionary basis to be shared by the household. Cash assistance is less susceptible to this difficulty than is in-kind aid.

A second limitation of individual choices is that the relative attractiveness of different household structures may depend on what everyone else is doing.[3] In particular, the relative rewards associated with the household choice are likely to depend on the household structures others have selected. For both non-elderly and elderly household members, the decision to live with one's relatives is likely to be more attractive if many other households of this type exist. If sufficiently large numbers of children choose to live with their parents, others will do so as well. However, if very few do, they will not live with their parents either.

The group externalities reflected in this situation do not simply represent a desire to keep in step with one's neighbors, as in the case of consumer fads. A shift in family structures will have a profound impact on social relationships outside the family. If individuals substitute activities with parents for those usually undertaken with friends who are not related, these other individuals' choices and relationships also will be affected.

The substantial interdependency in these decisions further complicates the choice of the optimal government policy. Suppose that each particular policy is associated with some distribution of family structures. The policy choice's most immediate effect is its direct influence on household choice. The magnitudes and desirability of these policy impacts are little understood. These uncertainties should discourage policymakers from major attempts to manipulate social behavior, particularly if these policies are not responsive to their performance. The less direct effect of these policies is through their pattern-setting role. If the government distorts choices sufficiently so that a modest number of households choose to divide into separate household units, the incentives for other households to do likewise will be altered, potentially leading to a complete unraveling in the present system of relationships.

The problem of valuing these outcomes is not at all straightforward. Since one's preferred outcome depends on what everyone else is doing, there are severe problems of noncomparability. We need to know much more than we presently do about the nature and strength of individual

---

[3] For a general discussion of this class of issues, see Schelling (1978). The role of such behavior in influencing the employment patterns of the aged is detailed in Viscusi (1979).

preferences and their implications for social welfare to even begin ranking these outcomes in terms of their relative attractiveness. A great deal depends on the nature of the interdependency. If pattern-setting behavior reflects an ephemeral bandwagon effect, then we may feel quite differently than if it derived from more fundamental desires of people to form different kinds of relationships as their peers' actions become altered.

Whether and how the government should undertake an active role in promoting social behavior is unclear. However, as will be argued in the next section, government policies already intrude into this area in quite a significant manner. Moreover, the implications of these impacts are not necessarily favorable.

INCENTIVE EFFECTS OF AID

Any assistance that the elderly choose to receive will increase their welfare and, in effect, make them richer. Some program benefits, such as subsidized housing or food, often will be valued by the aged at less than their dollar cost. Benefits that serve an insurance function, such as the annuities provided by Social Security or the health insurance provided by Medicare, may be valued at more than their actual cost by risk-averse consumers. The income effects generated by these efforts may alter a variety of actions, such as the elderly's decision to work or their social relationships.

These changes in behavior deriving from the fact that program beneficiaries become richer are fairly unobjectionable. Unless it can be shown that too many resources are being transferred to individuals' elder years, the altered behavior can be simply regarded as an optimal change in actions by the elderly in order to enhance their own welfare. Since most individuals augment government aid with savings and earnings of their own, it is doubtful whether society is in danger of making the aged too affluent.[4]

Ideally, assistance should be transferred to individuals on the basis of age or other measures of need that cannot be manipulated. Departures from the idealized situation of lump sum transfers invariably lead to altered actions by the recipient group in an effort to qualify for assistance.

Chief among these disincentives may be the work penalties imposed by Social Security and other income assistance programs. At the program's inception, an individual could not receive any Social Security

[4] See Viscusi (1979) for empirical evidence. Whether or not these savings are large is not consequential. What is important is that the no-savings corner solution is not prevalent.

benefits if he or she had any earnings. These draconian measures were justified in part as an effort to remove the elderly from the labor force in the post-Depression period.[5] Although the earnings test has been repeatedly liberalized, it remains harsh. The aged suffer a 50% marginal penalty on earnings (in addition to their usual taxes) for all earnings above $4500 annually. This penalty continues until all Social Security benefits are exhausted.

There is widespread evidence that individuals with higher levels of Social Security benefits are more likely to retire. This relationship is borne out by the analysis by Boskin (1977) of individual data for workers in their sixties, aggregate analyses of time series and cross-sectional data for various elderly cohorts by Viscusi (1979), and studies of early retirement by both Quinn (1977) and Boskin and Hurd (1977). Although these studies do not distinguish whether it is the income or substitution (i.e., incentive) effect of aid that is primarily responsible, there is a major danger if it is the latter influence that is operative. In that instance, the dependency status of the aged would be partially the result of government policies.

It is important to dispel the traditional argument in support of forced retirement for the aged. Forcing the elderly out of their jobs does not create jobs for the young, but primarily alters the macroeconomic scale of the economy. Short-run gains in employment of younger workers can only be obtained by continually lowering the retirement age—a strategy that would be viable only if the age of death is also reduced.

Present taxpayer restlessness over modest payroll tax increases undoubtedly will become more acute once the tax burden of supporting the elder years of the "baby boom" generation is imposed on the working population. Whereas the levels of Social Security benefits were previously immune from budget-trimming efforts, in 1980, policymakers seriously considered reducing the cost-of-living adjustment in order to balance the federal budget. The prospects for the elderly in terms of in-kind assistance are equally dim as the advent of national health insurance will deprive the elderly of their present privileged status as the principal subsidized consumer group in the health care market. Extrapolating from the post-Medicare experience, one would expect a dramatic increase in medical care costs and a decrease in quality. If the policy response includes rigid cost standards for medical care institutions, one might expect further lowering of the quality of care as well as greater sharing of medical care costs through coinsurance and deductible provisions. Unless the policies for influencing the welfare of the elderly are assessed

[5] This intent of the framers of the Social Security program is discussed by Brown (1972).

and made more effective, there may be a rapid deterioration in the well-being of the aged population.

Concern with work incentives and other effects of policies should not be limited to financial concerns. For example, work is important to the elderly not only for the money it provides. Retirees citing the aspects of work they miss most include the friendships with co-workers and the feeling of being useful in their work (see Shanas *et al.* 1968). A gradual reduction in one's work activity may be preferable to the abrupt transition the aged are now forced to make.

Analysts often attribute the absence of such flexibility in the choice of work hours to economic factors, such as the costs associated with coordinating the work efforts of individuals with shifts of differing length. This tendency to attribute the observed outcome to the market's invisible hand may be unwarranted, owing to the influence of government programs in this area. The Social Security earnings penalty makes work attractive only in very large or very small amounts. Modest reductions in work effort will put the individual in the high marginal tax region in which the financial rewards from work are negligible. The importance of these factors is reflected in the distribution of the hours that the elderly work, which is concentrated in the very low part-time and full-time categories.[6]

Household formation may be influenced directly by Social Security's counterpart for the elderly poor, Supplemental Security Income. That effort reduces one's benefits by one-third if the beneficiary is living in another's house. Due to the strong intergenerational correlation in income status, this provision appears especially pernicious. Even if the aged are not subjected to elderly-in-the-house checks paralleling the man-in-the-house inspections for other welfare beneficiaries, the aged poor may forego potentially beneficial relationships with relatives in order to maintain their meager income status.

In-kind assistance programs have especially great potential for inefficiency when the goods and services provided to the elderly are different from those available to others. Although the modest levels of in-kind assistance limit the extent of this problem, there is a potential danger if, as suggested by the White House Conference on Aging, the elderly push for their fair share of each agency's resources.

The subsidized housing efforts of the U.S. Department of Housing and Urban Development (HUD) illustrate this problem in especially dramatic fashion. In order to reap the government subsidy, the elderly must

---

[6] See Viscusi (1979) for further discussion of the hours data.

live in the housing project apart from their relatives. The very nature of the in-kind transfer has a profound impact on the social relationships of those who receive it. The small role of HUD housing expenditures for the aged in the total aid package for the elderly (under 1%) should not lead one to dismiss this effort as unimportant. The predominantly urban poor elderly who are directly affected may be much more significantly influenced than the modest outlays would suggest.

The considerably larger in-kind assistance provided by Medicare and its companion efforts involve more subtle, but undoubtedly more far-reaching impacts. Since the program's inception, the relative subsidies have favored inpatient care relative to outpatient care. Patients choosing inpatient care incur a deductible amount of $144, after which there is no charge for hospital care until the sixty-first day, when the patient must bear $36 per day until the ninetieth day of care. In contrast, for outpatient care the individual incurs a $60 deductible and must bear 20% of all subsequent costs.

Even if both modes of care were equally costly, the inpatient care would impose fewer out-of-pocket costs on the individual for all care with a total cost above $420. In the usual situation, in which inpatient care is considerably more expensive, the differential costs for society may be quite dramatic. Perhaps the most striking inefficiency is that an individual who has been hospitalized and exceeded his or her deductible faces a marginal cost of zero for inpatient care. The prolonged hospitalizations that result are considerably costlier to society than are outpatient services.

Presumably this bias is justified on the grounds that hospitalized individuals have greater needs and are more deserving of assistance. From the standpoint of efficient utilization of Medicare resources, this policy is clearly misguided, since individuals are encouraged to use relatively more expensive inpatient care whenever there is a choice in treatment modes.

By promoting institutionalized care of the elderly, the relative subsidies for inpatient care may affect the contact the aged who are ill have with their friends and families. This problem appears to be especially acute for the terminally ill, who are deprived of the ability to die with dignity in their homes, and for nursing home residents, who in many instances receive low quality care, in part because the governmental subsidies insulate many of these institutions from competitive pressures.

Although it is easy to cite inadequacies of any in-kind assistance structure, the inherent difficulties in targeting such aid efficiently should not prevent one from examining ways in which these policies can be made more effective. In the next section, I will consider how one might approach these difficulties to promote the interests of the elderly and those of the taxpayers at large.

EFFICIENT TARGETING OF SERVICES

The principal task in designing an optimal cash transfer policy is to develop a program structure that will serve as an annuity for all aged, avoid the problem of adverse work disincentives, and also support the well-being of those most in need. Reconciling these three objectives has been quite difficult. However, the effectiveness of government programs has been enhanced through a diversified policy mix that includes a special income transfer program for the elderly poor—Supplemental Security Income.

The difficulties encountered in designing effective service transfers for the aged are perhaps even more complex. The central problem is that the value of the services to the recipient is unclear. If, for example, medical care were provided free to the aged, there would be no incentive to avoid discretionary expenditures that have little or no effect on one's health status. Moreover, when choosing between alternative modes of care with the same implications for one's health, such as inpatient and outpatient treatment, there would be no incentive for the patient, the doctor, or the hospital to take full account of the ultimate cost to society when making their decisions.

Problems of this type are particularly acute with respect to a subsidized home care option. Many individuals currently receiving nursing home or hospital care might find a government-subsidized home care option more attractive. However, other aged who do not currently receive care also might wish to take advantage of these services. The demand is likely to be especially great if the services are not limited to health care delivery activities that would be desirable only to those in need of care. The provision of meals, assistance with household duties, and perhaps the companionship provided by home care assistants may lead to a substantially more costly health care effort than the current program.

The monitoring difficulties associated with home care are more severe than those usually encountered, although the nature of the problem is quite similar. The fundamental problem is to target the services provided in an efficient manner. For any particular budget level, how should the program best be designed to promote society's objectives?

These concerns can be divided into two broad categories. First, one should attempt to promote individual well-being as it is perceived by the beneficiaries. Other things being equal, one would like to provide the services valued by the elderly themselves. Second, in a publicly supported program, one should attempt to promote the kinds of policies preferred by the taxpayers who support it. The range of government health programs suggests that there is a widespread concern with individual health status and that programs should be directed at improving individual well-being even if the recipient might not have chosen to allocate his or her funds in that manner.

The pivotal question for policy design is how to structure a mechanism for rationing services that best promotes these two concerns. Perhaps the least attractive method of screening out deserving recipients of aid is to make prior institutionalization a precondition for assistance. Such efforts will only distort individual health care choices in much the same manner as Medicare provisions presently encourage needless hospitalizations in efforts to qualify for subsidized nursing home care.

A second possibility is to provide assistance based on ailments that can be monitored. To some extent, distinctions along these lines are already made. Cosmetic surgery and private rooms are excluded from subsidized Medicare coverage. Moreover, dental care is not covered, presumably because it does not affect one's mortality prospects and because much dental care is of a discretionary, cosmetic nature.

Similar restrictions might be imposed when determining eligibility for home care or other services. Thus, the home care option might be made available to those with readily monitored ailments, such as those suffering from terminal illnesses or a disabling stroke. However, individuals omitted from coverage might be regarded as also meriting assistance. These persons include many with ailments whose presence or severity is difficult to verify. Arthritis victims and individuals with back problems are typical examples. Using "monitorable" ailments as a criterion for assistance may be helpful in certifying small segments of the population as meriting assistance, but it will not be completely effective in identifying all individuals for whom medical care would be beneficial and highly valued.

The usual proposal to discourage inefficient utilization of health care services is to employ deductible and coinsurance provisions. All expenditures up to the deductible level are borne by the patient so that the problems involving excessive subsidies from society do not arise. Coinsurance provisions require that the patient bear some fraction of health care costs; this coinsurance rate often varies according to the type of care (e.g., inpatient or outpatient) and the level of expenditure.

The disadvantage of higher deductible and coinsurance rates is that they reduce the risk-spreading function of insurance, partially undermining the principal rationale for such programs. The poor may be especially hard hit by these provisions since they are least able to afford the out-of-pocket expenses needed to receive care.

Here I will propose an alternative approach to rationing medical services. Unlike the usual cost-sharing arrangements, it is able to promote efficient utilization of medical resources without putting the poor at a relative disadvantage.

It is instructive to begin with the preferences of a hypothetical beneficiary. Suppose that the individual is either healthy or ill and that only if he or she is ill will medical care be potentially desirable; additional expenditures may enhance the probability of becoming healthy. The primary difficulty is that one cannot monitor the effect of health care expenditures on the probability of returning to the healthy state. (In a more general framework, the underlying initial health state could also be uncertain.) If health care were fully subsidized, the beneficiary might opt for all available care. As the level of costs shifted to the patient increases, one can be more confident that the expenditures are effective in improving the chance of becoming healthy, but the risk-spreading aspects of insurance are sacrificed.

The hypothetical taxpayer bears the share of costs above the deductible that are not covered by the coinsurance rate. For simplicity, neglect all distributional concerns so that the optimal medical insurance structure can be distinguished from income transfer motivations. In the case of an ill patient receiving treatment, the taxpayer faces a similar lottery since he or she prefers that the individual would become healthy but would like to limit the extent of the public subsidy. The difficulty from the standpoint of the taxpayer is that he or she cannot monitor the functional relationship between the level of health care expenditures and the probability that these allocations will enhance the patient's health.

The structure of the optimal policy design problem is as follows. The government selects the deductible and coinsurance level that will maximize the expected utility of the representative citizen.[7] The taxpayer's well-being is diminished by an increase in his or her contribution to the medical care but is enhanced by the beneficial effect that health care has on the patient's welfare. The deductible and coinsurance provisions affect

---

[7] The mechanics of this problem represent an extension of the model developed by Zeckhauser (1970). The principal difference is that the income of the recipient is allowed to influence the optimal plan structure, and taxpayer preferences with respect to the patient's medical status are recognized.

the medical care decision by the patient, thus influencing the total health care expenditure as well as the public share of any given level of expense. The government is strategic in its plan design since it takes these reactions into account in structuring the optimal policy.

A principal difference with earlier analyses is that the heterogeneity of the beneficiaries is taken into account. Under a wide range of assumptions, one can demonstrate that when placed in identical medical situations, those with higher incomes will choose to spend more on their care.[8] This relationship is also borne out empirically.

As a consequence, the optimal degree of cost sharing will increase as the income level of the beneficiary rises. The reason for this discrepancy is that one can be more confident that, for a given level of expenditure, medical care will enhance the welfare of the poorer recipient. If both rich and poor patients faced the same cost-sharing provisions, wealthier beneficiaries would opt for a greater degree of discretionary medical care.

The usually cited problem of the inordinate burden of cost-sharing provisions on the poor is not necessarily due to a neglect of distributional concerns. Completely apart from equity considerations, the optimal plan structure will vary the degree of cost sharing positively with the beneficiary's income, since the positive income elasticity of demand for medical care affects the informational content (i.e., whether or not the expenditures are productive) of the out-of-pocket expenditures. To avoid work disincentive effects, the wealth measure used could be a lifetime wealth index, such as that used in computing Social Security benefit levels.

No policy alternative will be completely free of shortcomings, since the inability to monitor individuals' health status and the effectiveness of expenditures in enhancing their welfare inevitably leads to a variety of compromises in an effort to hold down program costs while meeting the elderly's needs. In making these tradeoffs, the heterogeneity of elderly beneficiaries should be taken into account when structuring the policy. The benefits will not be targeted efficiently if the information

---

[8] Consider utility functions conditional on one's health, that is $U_1(y)$ = the utility of money y when one is healthy and $U_2(y)$ = the utility of money when one is ill, where $U_1 > U_2$, $U_1' \geq U_2' > 0$, and U_1'', $U_2'' \leq 0$. Let the probability that health care expenditures x make the individual healthy be $p(x)$, where $p' > 0$ and $p'' < 0$. The deductible d and the coinsurance rate c imply that an expenditure of x reduces the consumer's initial assets A to a level $A - d - c(x - d)$ unless the deductible is not exceeded, in which case the individual's wealth is $A - x$. In each of these situations, differentiation of the first-order conditions for the optimal x implies $\partial x / \partial A > 0$. The health care expenditure level chosen increases with one's assets.

conveyed by the expenditures of differently situated elderly citizens is not incorporated in the policy design.

CONCLUSION

Unlike many policy choice problems, not only are the quantitative effects of different policies not fully understood, but the objectives for these policies are also unclear. Our understanding of the effect of different household structures and other relationships on individual welfare is rather meager. Moreover, the extent to which these relationships can be altered by policies is largely unknown, both because the impacts of past policies on the elderly's behavior have not been adequately explored and because there has been no deliberate experimentation with these policies in an attempt to identify particularly effective modes of intervention.

It is almost inevitable that these programs will alter many actions taken by the aged, either because the beneficiaries' wealth is affected or their incentives are altered by assistance. There should be a continuing reexamination of government programs to determine which of these impacts has a substantial, deleterious effect on the aged's welfare and which provisions can be altered to improve the effectiveness of policies.

The analysis of the efficient targeting of assistance also suggested that the changes in the actions taken by the elderly in response to policies are not of interest solely because of the potential inefficiencies that may be involved. The decisions made by the aged often convey important information that can be used in designing a more effective policy.

Consideration of health care choices by the aged, for example, suggests that present policies might be improved by linking the degree of cost sharing to one's income status. This variation in the current approach would be more effective in directing assistance to the individuals for whom government subsidies are most beneficial. The superiority of this approach to current policies would be enhanced if one also wished to express a distributional preference for the elderly poor.

REFERENCES

Becker, G. (1976) *The Economic Approach to Human Behavior*. Chicago: University of Chicago.
Boskin, M. (1977) Social security and retirement decisions. *Economic Inquiry* XV(1):1–25.
Boskin, M., and Hurd, M. (1977) The Effect of Social Security on Early Retirement. National Bureau of Economic Research Working Paper No. 204.

Brown, J. D. (1972) *An American Philosophy of Social Security: Evolution and Issues.* Princeton, N.J.: Princeton University Press.

Coase, R. (1960) The problem of social cost. *Journal of Law and Economics* 3(1).

National Council on Aging (1975) *The Myth and Reality of Aging in America.* Washington, D.C.: Louis Harris and Associates.

Quinn, J. (1977) Microeconomic determinants of early retirement: A cross-sectional view of white married men. *Journal of Human Resources* XII(3):329–346.

Schelling, T. (1978) *Micromotives and Macrobehavior.* New York: W. W. Norton.

Shanas, E., Townsend, P., Wedderburn, D., Friis, H., Miljøl, P., and Stehouwer, J. (1968) *Old People in Three Industrial Societies.* New York: Atherton Press.

Viscusi, W. K. (1979) *Welfare of the Elderly: An Economic Analysis and Policy Prescription.* New York: Wiley-Interscience.

Zeckhauser, R. (1970) Medical insurance: A case study of the tradeoff between risk spreading and appropriate incentives. *Journal of Economic Theory* 2(1):10–26.

chapter 9

Family Roles and Social Security[1]

VIRGINIA P. RENO

There is growing interest in finding a new conceptual framework for providing social security benefits to adults in families. Women's groups, members of Congress, and various advisory groups[2] are exploring alternative ways to take account of family roles in the social security system. It is argued that the current system, which categorizes adults as either workers or dependents of workers, lacks the flexibility to take account of the variation in family economic relationships that occurs over the lifetime. In particular, it is felt that the current system does not take proper account of women's divided work lives between paid employment and unpaid work in the home caring for their families.

As early as 1963, a committee of the President's Commission on the Status of Women recommended modifications in the provisions for dependent wives. The proposed modifications were intended to take ac-

[1] Any views expressed in this chapter are those of the author and do not represent those of the National Commission on Social Security or of the Social Security Administration by whom she has been employed.

[2] Advisory groups that have recently studied retirement benefit programs include the Advisory Council on Social Security, which reported to the Secretary of Health, Education, and Welfare in December 1979; the National Commission on Social Security, which reported to the President and the Congress in January 1981; and the President's Commission on Pension Policy, which reported to the president in early 1981.

count of women's dual roles as workers and as wives of workers by paying a supplemental benefit to those who had filled both roles (Committee on Social Insurance and Taxes 1963). That proposal was not enacted. Other modifications proposed in the 1960s and 1970s were intended to address similar types of issues about fairness between benefits for one-earner couples and two-earner couples. Those plans, like the earlier one, encountered new problems of fairness when couples were compared with single workers, and those plans were not enacted (U.S. Department of Health, Education, and Welfare 1978).

Analysts are now looking into proposals that could take account of the work of unpaid family members in ways that eliminate the need for dependency-based benefits for adults. The intent of such proposals is to provide an independent and portable form of social security protection for each adult family member in her or his own right. A panel of consultants to the Library of Congress studied the social security benefit and financing system as a whole and noted that a natural long-run solution to the problem of benefits for wives and divorced wives would be the creation of individual earnings' records for all adults (Hsiao *et al.* 1976). Broadly based women's groups have espoused a similar goal. The National Commission on the Observance of International Women's Year (1976) and the National Women's Conference (1977) have called on the administration and the Congress to develop a workable plan for covering homemakers in their own right under social security.

The U.S. Department of Health, Education, and Welfare (HEW) released two reports on the subject of family benefits for women (U.S. Department of Health, Education, and Welfare 1978, 1979). The first report analyzed a variety of different proposals that had been made by individuals and groups outside HEW. The second report was completed in response to a Congressional mandate for HEW to study proposals to eliminate dependency as the basis for entitlement to spouse benefits and to provide equal treatment of men and women in any and all respects. The second report presents two comprehensive models for according independent social security protection to all adults—an earnings sharing model and a double-decker model that incorporates many features of the earnings sharing model.

The major proposals for changing family benefits pose different judgments about the economic rights and obligations of individuals within families as well as between family members and society at large. This chapter discusses four of those approaches. Each aims to synthesize the separate types of benefit protection now provided to adults who shift between the paid work force and unpaid work in the home. The first presents an alternative to dependency-based benefits for widowed spouses. The other three present alternative ways to eliminate, or reduce reliance on, dependent spouse benefits.

Inherited Credits for Widowed Spouses. Under this approach, a widowed person could inherit the deceased spouse's social security earnings record and combine it with her or his own for each past year of the marriage. The annual combined credits would be limited to the maximum amount that is taxable under social security and then counted toward an individual worker's benefit in that year. This proposal is a feature of the two comprehensive options in the HEW report (U.S. Department of Health, Education, and Welfare 1979) and was recommended by the 1979 advisory council (Advisory Council on Social Security 1979).

Earnings Sharing. Under this approach, social security credits earned each year by married couples would be divided equally between the husband and wife. This type of proposal is described in detail in the second HEW report (U.S. Department of Health, Education, and Welfare 1979) and in the report of the 1979 advisory council on Social Security.

Contributory Credits for Spouses. Under this approach, some couples would be required to purchase social security credits (at the employee tax rate) to provide an independent record for the lower-earning or unpaid spouse. Couples would need to purchase credits sufficient to ensure that the secondary earner (or homemaker) had credits equal to 50% of the primary earner's credits in each year. The approach was suggested but not fully developed by the Consultant Panel on Social Security (Hsiao *et al.* 1976).

Childcare Dropout Years. Under this approach, a parent would be permitted to drop years of low (or no) earnings when she or he was responsible for the care of a young child. Several versions of this approach are discussed in the report of the 1979 advisory council.

HISTORICAL CONTEXT

The current family benefit structure is built on a framework conceived in the 1930s—a time when the typical family was presumed to be composed of a lifelong breadwinner, a financially dependent housewife, and dependent children. The benefit structure enacted in 1939 reflects that premise. Primary benefits were provided for paid workers. Separate categories of benefits were established for their dependents—wives and children—and for their survivors—widows, children, and aged parents. The 1939 law included a provision to limit the payment of dependents' benefits to women who also qualified for benefits as workers. That provision, which remains in the law today, stipulates that anyone eligible for benefits both as a worker and as a dependent or survivor of another worker receives an amount equal to the larger of the two types of benefits.

Over the years, the categories of dependents' benefits for adults were expanded—both to fill gaps in protection for some widowed and divorced women and to provide more nearly equal treatment between men and women. Widow's benefits were extended in 1956 and 1972 to those widowed a few years before retirement age. In 1967, benefits were extended to widows totally disabled in mid-life. Divorced women, in 1965, were made eligible for the same benefits payable to wives and widows, but under more restrictive requirements. Those requirements were liberalized in 1972 and 1977, but remain stricter than those for wives in intact couples. Husbands and widowers were extended dependents' benefits by incremental changes enacted by Congress in 1950 and 1967 and by recent decisions of the courts, which have found unequal provisions for men and women to be unconstitutional.[3]

These extensions of dependents' benefits have improved protection for certain groups of present or former family members over the years. Now, however, many are questioning whether the basic conceptual framework that separates adult family members into workers and dependents of workers remains appropriate.

SOCIAL CONTEXT

Social changes that prompt a reexamination of social security provisions for adults in families include: the movement of wives into the labor force, the changing perception of women's work in the home, and the rising rate of marital dissolution. These changes taken together in-

[3] The Supreme Court decision in *Weinberger* v. *Wiesenfeld*, 95 S. Ct. 1225 (1975) extended benefits to widowed fathers. The decision in *Califano* v. *Goldfarb*, 97 S. Ct. 1021 (1977) eliminated a special test of dependency that had applied only to husbands and widowers. A federal district court decision in *Oliver* v. *Califano*, N.D. Calif. C-76-2397 (1977) extended dependent's benefits to divorced husbands. A federal district court ruled in *Cooper* v. *Califano*, E.D. Pa. C-78-579 (1978) that husband's benefits should be payable to the father caring for children of a disabled woman under the same conditions that apply to wives.

dicate a mixed picture of family support patterns. On one hand, it seems clear that the dominant family model of the past—a lifelong breadwinner and a lifelong homemaker—no longer fits the majority of families throughout their lifetimes. On the other hand, no easy stereotype emerges to replace the old one. Rather, the trend is toward greater diversity in economic support patterns among families and greater probability that the direction and magnitude of support between family members will change over the lifetime. The trends are noted in the following sections.

Movement of Wives into the Labor Force

At present, about half of married women are in the labor force, and about half are not. Participation rates are lowest for wives with preschool-age children and for those over the age of 55 (Table 9.1). For others, participation rates are well over 50%. A continued rise in the labor force participation of wives is projected for the coming decade. Smith (1979) projects that by 1990 just over half of wives with children under the age of 6 will be in the labor force. Actuarial assumptions used by the Social Security Administration are that women's overall participation rate will rise through the beginning of the twenty-first century and then level off at about 76% of the rate for men (Board of Trustees 1979).

The movement of wives into the labor force means that many more couples are depending on earnings of both partners during at least part

TABLE 9.1
Labor Force Participation of Women, March 1978[a]

	Married husband present	Separated[b]	Widowed	Divorced	Never married
With children under 18					
Under 6	42%	55%	50%	67%	42%
6–13	57	62	59	81	76
14–17	58	62	54	82	[c]
No children under 18					
Women aged					
20–24	81	71	[c]	83	74
25–34	81	80	[c]	91	87
35–44	67	76	67	88	83
45–54	55	63	67	79	75
55 and older	24	31	16	48	34

[a] From Johnson (1979, table E, p.A18–19).
[b] Includes those with husband absent for reasons other than legal separation.
[c] Too few cases to produce reliable estimates.

of their lives. At the same time, the fact that women who were young wives in recent past decades were more likely to stay at home than are today's young wives, and the fact that many wives today and in the coming decade will stay at home when their children are young, mean that married and formerly married women can be expected to have less continuity in their lifetime work careers than is typical of men. One study that simulated lifetime earnings records of people projected to reach retirement age in the year 2000 showed that about 85% of men but only 35% of women would have worked 35 years or more under the social security system (U.S. Department of Health, Education, and Welfare 1979).

Labor force participation represents only part of the picture of women's labor market activity. The wages they receive while employed round out the picture. Here the change from past trends is less striking. According to Nancy S. Barrett:

> Despite the widespread view that a revolution in societal sex roles is taking place, most economists agree that women's progress in the job market—as measured by their earnings and employment opportunities—has not matched the pace of expectations. Although the increased emphasis on paid employment and careers for women and a lessening of sex-role stereotypes point in the direction of an upgrading of women's labor market status, women workers have made relatively little progress toward equality, at least according to the official statistics [1979, pp. 31–32].

The official statistics show that over the past 2 decades median earnings of women working full-time have remained at about 60% of the median earnings for men (Barrett 1979). Within families, the earnings differential between husbands and wives tends to be even wider. In 1977, the median earnings of wives who had any earnings during the year were $5070, while the median earnings of husbands were $13,880 (Table 9.2). In about 10% of couples, the wife's earnings exceeded the husband's, either because he was not employed or because he earned less than she did. Husbands, however, were the primary or sole earners in the large majority of couples. The evidence indicates that policies need to take account of the increasing numbers of wives in the work force, yet recognize that husbands' earnings remain the larger and more continuous source of income for most couples.

Perceptions of the Homemaker Role

Today, nearly half of married women are not in the paid work force. While their numbers are projected to shrink in the future, the importance

TABLE 9.2
Percentage Distribution of the Earnings of Husbands, Wives, 1977[a]

Earnings level	Husbands	Wives
Less than $2,000	5	25
$ 2,000– 3,999	4	17
4,000– 5,999	5	16
6,000– 7,999	7	13
8,000– 9,999	8	11
10,000–14,999	25	⎱14
15,000–19,999	21	⎰ 4
20,000–24,999	12	
25,000 or more	12	
Total	100	100
Total number with earnings (in 1000s)	(40,233)	(25,110)
Median earnings	$13,880	$5,070

	All couples
Only husband had earnings	40
Only wife had earnings	4
Both had earnings	56
Husband earned more than wife	50
Wife earned more than husband	6
Total	100
Total number with earnings (in 1000s)	41,929

[a] From Bureau of the Census (1979, table 28).

attached to the homemaker role by those who fill it and by families who benefit from it is gaining recognition. As more married women are employed outside the home, the work performed by those who do remain at home—particularly when children are young—is increasingly viewed as a job choice in itself, rather than the absence of one. Various studies have aimed to place a dollar value on the work done by homemakers. While few may agree on a precise dollar value, a sense of this value emerges when families forego a second paycheck in order to have a spouse at home—or when they pay more out of pocket for child care or other services in order to have both spouses in the labor market.

When the choice to have a member be a full-time homemaker is viewed as a conscious decision by the family, a decision from which the entire family benefits, then it might seem appropriate for the family to share in the cost of ensuring adequate and secure social security protection for the homemaker's job. On the other hand, when the job of caring for young children is seen as a temporary alternative to paid work, a job that benefits society at large as well as the immediate family, then it might seem appropriate for society at large to ensure that that job does not diminish the adequacy and security of the social security protection available.

Marital Dissolution

Though marriage is still the norm in the United States, changes in marital status throughout individuals' lifetimes are becoming more common. About 80% of men and 75% of women between ages 25 and 64 are married. Yet, the Census Bureau (1976) estimates that of ever-married women between the ages of 26 and 40 in 1975, the first marriage has or will end in divorce for one in three.

A simulation of marital histories for people projected to reach retirement age in the year 2000 estimates that 40% of the men and women in that age cohort will have been divorced, but that only about 18% of the women and 12% of the men will still be divorced at retirement age. Altogether, about one in three of the retirement-age men and women in the simulated population were projected to have been married more than once (U.S. Department of Health, Education, and Welfare 1979).

The high rate of marital dissolution sharpens questions about what constitutes fair treatment under social security when a marriage ends in divorce.

CURRENT BENEFIT STRUCTURE AND ISSUES

This section describes current benefit provisions for workers, widows, wives, and divorced women. Issues raised about current provisions and the responses of alternative approaches are noted. The next section describes new issues that are posed by the alternatives.

Benefits for Workers

Benefits for paid workers are built up over the lifetime based on the worker's average earnings in jobs covered by social security. A retiree's past earnings are indexed to reflect general wage levels near the time he or she reaches retirement age. Table 9.3 shows the full benefits payable at different levels of average indexed earnings for people reaching age 62 in 1980.

Full benefits are paid at age 65; benefits claimed at age 62 are reduced by 20%. As shown, a person who always earned about the average wage

TABLE 9.3
Social Security Benefits for Retired Workers, 1980 Formula

	Benefit at age 65		Benefit at age 62	
Average indexed earnings	Annual amount	As a percentage of earnings	Annual amount	As a percentage of earnings
$ 5,300[a]	$3046	57	$2437	46
6,000	3270	55	2616	44
9,000	4230	47	3384	38
10,600[b]	4742	45	3794	36
12,000	5190	43	4152	35
15,000	5989	40	4791	32
18,000	6439	36	5151	29
24,000	7339	31	5871	24

[a] Represents low-wage worker who always earned about half the average wage.
[b] Represents one who always earned about the average wage.

would be entitled to a full benefit that represents about 45% of his or her average indexed earnings. If he or she claimed reduced benefits at age 62, it would amount to about 36% of his or her average earnings.

THE MEASURE OF EARNINGS TO BE REPLACED

The earnings that are used to compute retirement benefits are averaged over a long and increasing segment of the adult life. For one reaching age 62 in 1980, earnings are averaged over the highest 24 years. For people age 51 or younger in 1980, earnings will be averaged over their highest 35 years. The rationale for the long averaging period is that it ensures that all, or practically all, of a person's taxable earnings can be expected to count toward his or her benefits. However, the long averaging period also means that people who have gaps in their paid careers during which they worked in the home caring for family members will have lower benefits as a result. For example, if a woman worked for 20 years and earned about the average wage (equivalent to $10,600 in Table 9.3) and the averaging period is 35 years, her average indexed earnings would be only about $6000. The full benefit of about $3300 would represent 55% of that average, but only about 31% of her average earnings while she was employed. At age 62, the benefit would represent 25% of her earnings while employed.

WHICH EARNINGS SHOULD BE REPLACED?

The proposals discussed in this chapter aim to improve benefits for those who shift between paid careers and unpaid work in the home by changing the definition of which earnings should be replaced by retirement benefits. Two plans (the inherited credits and earnings sharing plans) shift from the concept of individual to family earnings. One (the child-care dropout years plan) permits certain years to be omitted from an individual's lifetime average. And one (the contributory credits plan) would have couples purchase earnings' credits to fill gaps in one partner's earnings' record.

Any decision about the measure of earnings to be replaced carries with it implicit judgments about fairness—about who should be treated alike and about what characteristics of people's adult roles should make a difference in their retirement benefits. It is the differences in the implicit judgments that distinguish the approaches from each other and from the current system.

Benefits for Widows and Widowers

An aged widow or widower can receive up to 100% of the deceased spouse's benefit if the benefit is claimed at age 65 or later. If the worker had claimed reduced benefits before age 65, that reduction is usually carried over to the survivor's benefits. Also, if the widow(er) claims benefits before she or he reaches age 65, the benefit is reduced to 82.5% of the worker's full benefit at age 62 or to 71.5% at age 60. A totally disabled widow or widower can claim survivor benefits as early as age 50; at that age the benefit is reduced to 50%.

In all cases, a widowed person's benefit as a survivor is offset dollar for dollar against any benefit to which she or he is entitled as a retired worker.

IMPORTANCE OF SURVIVOR PROVISIONS FOR WOMEN

Survivor provisions are important to women for several reasons. First, because husbands typically earn considerably more than their wives, benefits that take account of the husband's earnings are important in providing adequate replacement income when a woman becomes widowed.

Second, widowhood is either a risk or a reality for the large majority of older women. Today about 9 in 10 women aged 65 or older are either widowed (53%) or married (37%) and therefore face the risk of widowhood as they grow older. Of those projected to reach retirement age in the year 2000, about 3 in 4 women are estimated to be either married or widowed.

Third, the types of income with which retirees supplement social security benefits are less likely to be available when a husband dies.

Earnings are a common income supplement for retired couples but are less likely at the more advanced ages when most women are widows (Grad 1979). Pensions, if received by a couple, are likely to belong to the husband. In 1976, only 20% of aged widows received pension income—from either their own employment or that of their husband. The Employee Retirement Income Security Act of 1974 requires that joint and survivor options be offered to retirees. This might increase the number of aged widows in the future who have pensions from their husbands' careers. The joint and survivor options, however, usually stipulate that the worker receive a reduced pension in exchange for the survivor option, and the benefit paid to the survivor is a fraction (not less than 50%) of the retiree's reduced pension. These reductions are consistent with the equity goals of private plans—to provide pensions of equivalent value to workers who do and workers who do not have family members to provide for. These reductions, however, together with the fact that pensions are rarely fully indexed for inflation, sharply limit the adequacy of private pension income for aged survivors.[4]

Prior to 1972, one of the dominant "women's issues" about social security concerned the need for more adequate benefits for aged widows. In response to this concern, the 1972 amendments raised the potential full benefit for widows and widowers from 82.5% to 100% of the deceased worker's full benefit. That change clearly raised benefits for some widows—primarily those who become widowed after their husbands reach age 65. Some widows, however, were unaffected. They include those who are widowed before retirement age and claim benefits at age 60 or 62, and those who receive benefits only as retired workers rather than as survivors of their husbands. Finally, past amendments were not designed to provide survivors of dual-earner couples with benefits that take account of both partners' earnings. Remaining issues about survivor benefits focus on these groups: dual-earner couples; widows who receive retired-worker benefits only; and those who are widowed long before retirement age.

DUAL-EARNER COUPLES AND ONE-EARNER COUPLES

The current system is not designed to provide equal survivor benefits between couples who have had the same total earnings, but have had different mixes of earnings roles between spouses. Because the surviving

---

[4] For example, if a retiree took a 20% reduction to provide a survivor pension equal to 50% of the reduced pension, and the pension was indexed by 3% while the cost of living rose by 8%, the survivor pension payable 10 years after the worker retired would amount to only about 25% of the worker's full pension at retirement.

TABLE 9.4
Social Security Benefits for Aged Widows and Widowers, by Total Earnings of the Couple
and Portion Earned by Each Spouse, 1980 Benefits Formula

Couples' average indexed earnings	Annual full benefit			
	One-earner couple	Dual-earner couples by portion earned by each spouse		
		1/6–5/6	1/3–2/3	1/2–1/2
$ 6,000	$3270	$2950	$2630	$2310
9,000	4230	3750	3270	2790
12,000	5190	4550	3910	3270
15,000	5989	5350	4550	3750
18,000	6439	5989	5190	4230
Percentage less than amount for one-earner couple	—	7–12%	19–25%	29–37%

spouse receives the larger of her or his own retired worker benefit or the deceased spouse's benefit, the survivor's benefit is highest when all of the couple's earnings are on one spouse's record and it is lowest when each spouse earned half of the couple's income. Table 9.4 shows survivor benefit amounts for couples reaching age 62 in 1980.

The survivor's benefit is approximately a third less when both contributed equally to the family's income. The inherited credit approach would base survivor benefits on the couple's combined earnings during their marriage. In that way, benefits for survivors of dual-earner couples could be raised to the amounts shown for survivors of one-earner couples with the same family earnings.

RETIRED-WORKER WIDOWS

Widows who receive benefits as retired workers on their own earnings' records rather than as survivors of their husbands represent a surprisingly large group, and relatively little is known about them.[5] In 1976, widows in the population age 65 and older numbered 6.7 million. In the same year, about 3.2 million aged widows (48%) received social security benefits as widows, and another .9 million (16%) were entitled as retired

[5] Social security program statistics regularly report the numbers and amounts of survivor benefits paid to widows and the ages of widows who receive them. When women receive benefits as retired workers, however, the data on numbers and amounts of benefits are not available by marital status.

workers but received higher benefits as widows. Most of the remaining 39% received retired-worker benefits on their own accounts (U.S. Department of Health, Education, and Welfare 1978). In 1973, the average benefit received by widows who received benefits only on their own accounts was about 15% lower than the average for widows receiving survivor benefits (DelBene 1979).

The inherited credit approach would increase the earnings records and therefore the benefits of retired-worker widows whose husbands had covered earnings before they died. It would be useful to know more about the characteristics of retired-worker widows and about the effect that the inherited credit option would have on their benefits.

Several hypotheses might explain why such a large number of widows receive higher benefits on their own earnings records than on their husbands', yet receive low benefits. Some might have earned more than their husbands throughout their lifetimes, although data on the earnings of husbands and wives indicate this would be a small group (Bureau of the Census 1979). Some might have been married to men whose jobs were not covered by social security. This, too, should be a small group because about 9 in 10 jobs have been covered since the mid-1950s. Some may have been widowed so long before retirement age that the value of social security benefits on their husband's wage record was eroded by economy-wide wage changes since his death.

PEOPLE WIDOWED BEFORE RETIREMENT AGE

If a man dies before age 62, his earnings are indexed by wage changes up to the time of his death, and the survivor benefit based on those earnings is adjusted by price increases between the time of death and the year the widow claims benefits. Therefore, if a widow's husband had died long before she was old enough to claim benefits, her survivor benefit would reflect price increases but not economy-wide wage gains since the husband's death.

Under the inherited credit approach, the deceased worker's earnings would become a part of the survivor's own record that is indexed to reflect prevailing wage rates when the survivor approaches retirement age.

Benefits for Spouses of Retired Workers

The spouse of a retired worker is eligible at age 65 for a benefit equal to 50% of the worker's benefit. If claimed at age 62, the benefit is reduced to 37.5%. Anyone who is eligible for benefits both as a worker and as a spouse of a worker, receives a benefit equal to the larger of the two types of benefits.

In 1976, about 4.7 million married women age 65 and older were living with their husbands. Wife's benefits were paid to 2.3 million (49%). Another .5 million (11%) qualified for retired worker benefits, but their benefits as wives exceeded that amount. Most of the remaining 40% received retired-worker benefits that exceeded their benefits as wives (U.S. Department of Health, Education, and Welfare 1978).

Three kinds of issues are raised about the current provision for spouse benefits. Two question whether the spouse benefit still serves the purpose for which it is intended. One relates to differences in benefit amounts between dual-earner couples and one-earner couples.

DUAL EARNER-COUPLES AND ONE-EARNER COUPLES

Under the current system, couples with the same total earnings credits do not necessarily receive the same total benefits in retirement. A one-earner couple in which one member receives a spouse benefit usually receives a higher benefit than does a couple made up of two earners who, together, earned as much as the paid worker in the one-earner couples. This result is illustrated in Table 9.5, which shows the couple's combined benefits by the portion of family earnings earned by each spouse. This issue implies a different standard of fairness from the one built into the current system: Couples, rather than individuals, with the same cash earnings should have the same benefits when both spouses

TABLE 9.5
Social Security Benefits for Retired Couples by Total Earnings of the Couple and Portion Earned by Each Spouse, 1980 Benefit Formula

Couples' average indexed earnings	One-earner couple	Dual-earner couples by portion earned by each spouse		
		1/6–5/6	1/3–2/3	1/2–1/2
$ 6,000	$4905[a]	$4425[a]	4430	4620
9,000	6345[a]	5625[a]	5580	5580
12,000	7785[a]	6825[a]	6540	6540
15,000	8984[a]	8025[a]	7500	7500
18,000	9658[a]	8983[a]	8460	8460
Percentage less than amount for one-earner couple	—	7–12%	10–16%	6–16%

[a] Dependent spouse benefit payable under present law.

are retired. This standard of fairness is built into the earnings–sharing plan. Under earnings sharing, all couples would receive the benefits shown in the last column of Table 9.5. In contrast, the contributory credit plan does not aim to treat couples with the same earnings as equals. Rather, a one-earner couple is considered to have a higher standard of living because of the homemaker's contribution. The one-earner couple would pay higher taxes to provide credits for the homemaker, and the homemaker's purchased credits together with the breadwinner's earnings credits would yield higher combined benefits than would be received by a dual-earner couple with the same cash earnings. Table 9.6 illustrates the added amount of annual taxes and the increased benefits for the homemaker or lower-earning spouse under this proposal.

SOCIAL ADEQUACY

Benefits for wives of retired workers were enacted in 1939 on the advice of the Advisory Council on Social Security (1938, p. 15). The council recommended the benefits on social adequacy grounds. The council stated:

> The inadequacy of the benefits payable during the years of the old-age insurance program is more marked where the benefits must support not only the annuitant himself, but also his wife. . . . Payment of supplementary allowances to annuitants who have wives over 65 will increase the average benefit in such a manner as to meet the greatest social need with the minimum increase in cost. The Council believes that an additional 50% of the basic annuity would constitute a reasonable provision for the support of the annuitant's wife.

A case could be made today that the provision of spouse benefits no longer effectively fills the original purpose "to meet the greatest social need with the minimum increase in cost." While it remains reasonable to presume that couples need somewhat more income than do unmarried individuals, it is also the case that retired couples have more income from sources other than social security than do aged unmarried women and men. Of those age 65 or older in 1976, about two out of three couples, but only one in three unmarried men and women, had earnings or pensions to supplement social security. In the same year, only 9% of couples had incomes below the poverty threshold, compared with 38% of unmarried women and 27% of unmarried men (U.S. Department of Health, Education, and Welfare 1979). Thus, on grounds of general social adequacy it could be argued that the unmarried aged today have greater unmet needs than do married couples.

TABLE 9.6

Effect of Contributory Credit Option on Couples' Taxes and on Benefits for Low-Earning Spouse

Couple's annual earnings high earner–low earner	Total tax rate: OASDHI & Income Tax		Added tax under option	Benefit for low-earning spouse		
	Present law	Option		Present law amount	Option amount	Percentage increase
$ 9,000						
$ 9,000/0	11	.14	$276	$2136[b]	$2797	31
6,000/3,000	11	.11	0	2316	2316	0
$12,000						
$12,000/0	16	.19	368	2598[b]	3276	26
9,000/3,000	16	.16	92	2316	2797	21
6,000/6,000	16	.16	0	3276	3276	0
$15,000						
$15,000/0	18	.21	460	3004[b]	3757	25
12,000/3,000	18	.19	184	2598[b]	3276	26
9,000/6,000	18	.18	0	3276	3276	0
$18,000						
$18,000/0	19	.23	552	3226[b]	4237	31
15,000/3,000	19	.21	76	3004[b]	3757	25
12,000/6,000	19	.19	0	3276	3276	0
9,000/9,000	19	.19	0	4237	4237	0
$24,000						
$24,000/0	22	.26	736	3676[b]	5196	41
21,000/3,000	22	.24	460	3452[b]	4717	37
18,000/6,000	22	.23	184	3276	4237	0
15,000/9,000	22	.22	0	4737	4237	0

[a] Employee tax of 6.13% for Old-Age, Survivors, Disability and Hospital Insurance (OASDHI) and income tax rates under the 1979 schedule for a married couple with no dependents and using standard deductions.

INCOME SECURITY FOR HOMEMAKERS

If, on the other hand, the spouse benefit is justified as a form of recognition and income security for the spouse who works in the home, then it is argued that this would be more effectively achieved by according social security credits directly to that spouse. The earnings sharing and contributory credit plans take this approach. The earnings sharing plan does so by dividing credits between spouses, thereby lowering the credits on the higher earners record (usually the husband's). The contributory credit plan does so by requiring couples to pay somewhat higher taxes to provide an independent social security record for the spouse at home. The child-care dropout years approach, in contrast, holds harmless gaps in the paid work careers of those who were homemakers when their children were young.

Benefits for Divorced Spouses

If a marriage that ended in divorce lasted at least 10 years, a divorced woman is eligible for the same benefits payable to wives or to widows if the ex-husband is deceased. Relatively few divorced women receive these benefits. In 1978, 25,000 received the wife's benefit and 36,000 received the widow's benefit on their ex-husbands' accounts. In 1976, 87% of the 358,000 divorced women in the population age 65 and older received social security. Most must have been receiving the benefits as retired workers. In the same year, 38% of aged divorced women had incomes below the poverty threshold (Grad 1979).

A number of issues are raised about provisions for divorced women.

Marriage requirement. The marriage requirement, albeit shortened from 20 to 10 years by the 1977 amendments, seems arbitrary. A marriage of 9 years yields no protection while a marriage of 10 years yields spouse and survivor benefits based on the ex-husband's entire work life.

Lack of continuity. The large majority of divorced women are employed after divorce (Table 9.1). Dependents' benefits based on the prior marriage role duplicate, rather than enhance, any social security credits a divorced homemaker may build up on her own record after divorce.

Low benefits. The 50% spouse benefit, which was designed to supplement a worker's benefit, is not adequate to support an unmarried person alone.

Presumption of dependency. The recipient of a spouse benefit is presumed to be financially dependent on the worker's earnings. Therefore the spouse benefit is not paid until the worker retires. Like a wife, a divorced woman must wait until the worker has retired before she receives benefits on his account.

These issues share a common theme—that spouse benefits, which were designed for intact couples, do not seem to be the best way to take account of the divorced woman's previous role. The earnings sharing and the contributory credit approaches would fill gaps in a homemaker's earnings record during marriage. Those credits would then be a permanent and portable basis for old-age benefits if the marriage ends in divorce. The child-care dropout years approach would hold harmless past years of low or zero earnings when a divorced person had been caring for young children.

NEW ISSUES RAISED BY THE PROPOSALS

Each approach raises new issues to be considered in choosing among them or the current system.

Inherited Credit Approach

The inherited credit approach is consistent with the goal built into the current system of providing a secure and adequate old-age income to widowed people. Features that many find attractive in the proposal are summarized below.

- It equalizes benefits between survivors of couples with the same family earnings by raising benefits for survivors of dual-earner couples to the amounts payable to survivors of one-earner couples.
- It synthesizes on one record the separate types of benefits widowed people now may receive as either workers or survivors of workers.
- It updates the survivor's earnings record to reflect prevailing wage levels when the survivor approaches retirement age.
- After credits are inherited, a widowed person would be eligible for benefits under the same provisions that apply to retired workers.

Remaining issues about the approach involve the cost and distributional effects. The inherited credit approach recommended by the 1979 Advisory Council on Social Security is estimated to cost .07% of taxable payroll; that is, the social security tax on employees and employers would need to be raised by .035% in order to pay for it.[6]

Further studies that document the distributional effects of the proposal will be useful in evaluating the extent to which it meets the income security needs of aged widows and widowers. The HEW report (U.S. Department of Health, Education, and Welfare 1979) presents estimates of the effect of the inherited credit proposal on people projected to reach retirement age and claim full benefits in the year 2000. That study showed that 55% of widows and 10% of widowers would have higher benefits under the proposal, while 15% of widows and 9% of widowers would have benefits somewhat lower than present amounts. It would be useful to know more about the characteristics of those groups.

Studies based on actual earnings histories of current retirees could show the effect of implementing the approach in the near future. Such studies could investigate the effects of changes in early retirement provisions that are implicit in the inherited credit approach. Under the current system, widows and widowers first become eligible for benefits at age 60, and receive a 28.5% benefit reduction. If, with inherited credits, they are treated like other workers, they would first become eligible for benefits at age 62, with a 20% benefit reduction.

Earnings Sharing Approach

The earnings sharing approach is based on the principle that marriage is an economic partnership of equals. In line with this principle, earnings' credits of married couples would be divided equally between husbands and wives for each year of their marriage. Features of the earnings sharing approach that many find attractive are summarized below.

- It provides equal benefits to retired couples who have had the same family earnings over their lifetimes.
- It eliminates the concept of dependency in determining benefits for homemakers or low-earning partners in a marriage.
- The 50/50 allocation of social security credits fits with many people's concept of fair treatment at divorce.

Attributes of the earnings–sharing plan that some find problematic are noted on the following two pages.

---

[6] More recent studies indicate that the cost would be considerably higher if the proposal was phased in gradually to ensure that aged widow(er)s would not receive less than the current system provides. See *Development of the Advisory Council's Interim Recommendations on the Treatment of Women under Security*, Office of Policy, Social Security Administration, Department of Health and Human Services, August 1980.

ONE-EARNER COUPLES

The approach achieves the equal benefits between couples with the same earnings by lowering somewhat the benefits for one-earner couples. Some consider this to be equitable and appropriate. Others oppose the reduction. The plan developed for the 1979 advisory council includes a gradual transition feature to phase in the benefit change.

BENEFITS FOR SURVIVING CHILDREN

Under the current system, benefits are payable to surviving children based on a deceased parent's earnings record. Under a pure earnings sharing plan, credits would have been divided equally between the children's parents for each past year of the marriage and, consequently, the children's survivor benefits if the primary earner died would be considerably lower than those payable under current law. The earnings-sharing plan in the HEW report (U.S. Department of Health, Education, and Welfare 1979) and the one developed for the Advisory Council on Social Security (1979) do not apply to the earnings–sharing principle in child survivor cases.

DISABILITY BENEFITS

Under the current system, disability benefits, like retirement benefits, are based on individual earnings' records. The individual record serves as a measure of the earnings loss associated with disability. Benefits to children are also paid on a disabled parent's record. Under a pure earnings sharing model, disability benefits for the primary earner, and children if present, would be considerably lower than under the current system. On the other hand, benefits would be increased (or would be paid where none are now paid) if the secondary earner (or lifelong homemaker) became disabled.

The earnings sharing plan developed for the 1979 advisory council was modified so as not to lower the disability benefits on the primary earner's account. For disability benefit purposes, past credits would be divided between spouses only when the secondary earner or homemaker became disabled. Under this approach, the relationship between disability benefits and earnings loss is weakened, because the homemaker's benefit is based on the past earnings of the nondisabled primary earner who, presumably, would continue working.

Some may consider this to be an equitable consequence of the basic earnings sharing principle—that the low earner or homemaker in a marriage has a right to disability protection based on half the family's earn ings. Others may consider it more fair to retain the earnings loss principle of the current system—in which individual disability benefits are based on the earnings that are lost rather than on the earnings of a nondisabled spouse.

THE FIRST RETIRED SPOUSE

Questions similar to those raised about disability benefits occur under earnings sharing when husbands and wives do not retire at the same time. If the husband who is primary earner retires several years before his wife, should his benefit be based on his own earnings' record, or should it be reduced to the amount based on half of the family's past earnings? If the wife who is secondary earner (or homemaker) is the first to reach retirement age, should her benefit be based on half the family's earnings even if these earnings continue? In all cases in which only one member of an intact couple is eligible for benefits, it is necessary to choose between the earnings replacement principle built into the current system, or the partnership principle of the earnings-sharing approach.

Contributory Credits for Spouses

This type of approach was suggested by the Consultant Panel on Social Security (Hsiao *et al.* 1976). They posed it as an alternative to earnings–sharing, which they felt presented serious problems for determining benefits when only one spouse was eligible. The idea of contributory credits for homemakers has been proposed by others. A bill introduced in the ninety-fourth Congress by Representative Barbara Jordan and Representative Yvonne Burke called for mandatory purchase of social security credits for homemakers. A similar bill (H.R. 1039) was introduced in the ninety-sixth Congress by Representative Margaret Heckler.

The contributory credit plan suggested by the Hsiao panel avoids some of the definitional problems that occur under more general homemaker credit plans (U.S. Department of Health, Education, and Welfare 1978). This plan would require contributory credits only on behalf of married people, and the amount of the credit to be purchased is the difference between the secondary earner's own earnings and half the primary earner's earnings.

This approach has received less attention than the earnings–sharing approach, in part, perhaps, because it lacks the conceptual appeal of the partnership principle inherent in earnings sharing.

Some features similar to the earnings-sharing plan are summarized on page 206.

- It provides an independent and portable social security record for the homemaker or secondary earner.
- At divorce, it ensures that the low-earning party leaves the marriage with credits equal to at least half those of the primary earner.
- When fully phased-in, it would eliminate the need for dependent spouse benefits.

The contributory credit plan avoids lowering the primary earner's benefit Instead it raises taxes for some married couples. Thus, the key issue about the plan involves the distribution of the added tax burden.

THE TAX

Table 9.6 illustrates the amounts of added tax that couples would need to pay under this proposal. In those cases in which added taxes would be paid, higher retirement benefits would result and disability protection would accrue where it is not available under current law. Nonetheless, many couples may feel they would rather forego the added social security protection for the low-earning spouse than pay the added tax.

INTEGRATION WITH THE EARNED INCOME CREDIT

The consultant panel suggested that the "homemaker tax" might be integrated with the earned income credit under the federal income tax so that low-income families would be relieved of part of the added tax burden. The distribution of tax burden under various such options merit further study.

RESPONSE TO FEDERAL INCOME TAX ISSUES

With the increase in dual-earner couples, there is growing pressure to alter federal income tax policies so as to reduce or eliminate the amount by which taxes for dual-earner couples exceed what they would pay as single individuals (Gordon 1979). To permit dual-earner couples to file income tax returns as single individuals would reduce their income tax liability. And it would require an offsetting increase in tax rates for one-earner couples in order to produce the same revenue.

Some believe that it is appropriate for one-earner couples to pay higher taxes in order to take account of the homemaker's productive contribution to the couple's standard of living. If it is felt that the homemaker's contribution should be reflected in the family's tax liability, then there remains a choice between using the federal income tax or the social security tax for this purpose. Under the contributory credit approach the added social security taxes from one-earner couples would provide an independent and portable social security record for the homemaker

Whether such an approach can be designed to achieve acceptable distributional effects on families' taxes and benefits remains a subject for further study.

Child-Care Dropout Years

The child-care dropout years approach is based on the premise that the job of caring for young children is of benefit to society at large, and therefore a parent's years of low or no earnings when children were young should be held harmless in computing social security retirements benefits.

A child-care dropout years provision could be specified in a number of ways. Remaining issues involve the specific details of such a proposal and the consequent effects on the distribution of benefits and costs. Details of a child-care dropout years plan involve the age of children, the number of dropout years allowed, and the parents' earnings level.

AGE OF CHILDREN

Several proposals would allow child-care dropout years only when a child under age 7 is present, on the theory that years when preschool children are present are those in which a parent is most likely to remain at home or to work less than full time. A younger age, say 3 years, would reduce the cost and benefits of the approach. An older age, say 13, would increase them.

MAXIMUM NUMBER OF DROPOUT YEARS

It has been suggested that as many as 20 or as few as 2 dropout years for child care be allowed per person. Relatively little is known about the distributional effects of such different schemes.

PARENTS' EARNINGS LEVEL

Some proposals would allow child-care dropout years only if a parent had practically no earnings in a year. Plans examined by the 1979 Advisory Council on Social Security required that a person earn less than the amount needed for a year of social security coverage ($1040 in 1979). A problem in setting a very low earnings level is that a parent who worked part-time and earned only slightly more than the allowed amount might be worse off than if she or he had not worked at all. This problem could be mitigated by setting the earnings limit in relation to each individual's earnings. For example, a parent could drop a year when a young child was present if earnings in that year were less than her or his average earnings over the rest of the lifetime.

Relatively little is known about the distributional effects of various combinations of provisions for child-care dropout years. How many people would receive more adequate retired-worker benefits in lieu of dependent spouse benefits? How many married, divorced, or single parents would have benefits increase by how much under the alternatives? How many would not be affected, and what are their characteristics?

SUMMARY

The four approaches and the current system pose different judgments about what constitutes fair treatment of family members under social security. The inherited credit approach represents an alternative to dependents' benefits for aged widows and widowers. Under the current system, the aged survivor receives the higher of the benefit based on her or his own earnings or the benefit based on the deceased spouse's earnings. The inherited credit approach reflects the judgment that the couple's past earnings, rather than the individual earnings of either spouse, are the appropriate measure of earnings to replace when a person is both widowed and retired.

The other three approaches aim to provide continuity in social security records of family members so as to eliminate dependents' benefits for spouses or reduce reliance on them. The current system provides a 50% benefit to the spouse of a retired worker, if that benefit exceeds the spouse's own benefit as a worker. The same 50% benefit is provided to a divorced spouse if the marriage lasted 10 years.

Two of the plans, like the current system, use marital status to define family roles. The earnings sharing plan calls for the transfer of social security credits between spouses. The contributory credit plan calls for higher tax payments by some couples. Implicit in both approaches is the view that couples in which one spouse has little or no earnings in a year should bear the cost of providing social security protection to that spouse—either through lower credits for the primary earner or in higher tax payments. Both contrast with the current system, in which society at large shares the cost of providing spouse benefits.

The child-care dropout years approach uses parental status rather than marital status to determine the family role that receives special treatment. It is based on the premise that the parental role is of sufficient value to society at large that society should share the cost of holding harmless a worker's low-earning years during which she or he was responsible for young children.

Choices among the various approaches or the current system will depend in large part on their conceptual appeal. How closely do the value judgments inherent in each approach fit the values of the general public? Informed debate supplemented with survey research will move us closer to a resolution of that question. The desirability of various approaches will also depend in large part on estimates of their distributional effects. How many people in which circumstances would experience a change in benefits or taxes? Empirical studies that apply the various approaches to actual or simulated earnings' histories of individuals and families can provide answers to those questions.

REFERENCES

Advisory Council on Social Security (1979) *Social Security Financing and Benefits, Reports of the 1979 Advisory Council on Social Security*. Washington, D.C.: U.S. Department of Health, Education, and Welfare.

Advisory Council on Social Security (1938) *Final Report*, December 10, 1938, Senate Document 76-4. U.S Congress.

Barrett, N. S. (1979). Women in the job market: Occupations, earnings and career opportunities. Pp. 31–62 in R. E. Smith, ed., *The Subtle Revolution: Women at Work*. Washington, D.C.: The Urban Institute.

Board of Trustees (1979) *Annual Report of the Board of Trustees of the Federal Old-Age and Survivors Insurance and Disability Insurance Trust Funds*, Office of the Actuary, Social Security Administration. Washington, D.C.: U.S. Department of Health, Education, and Welfare.

Bureau of the Census (1979) *Money Income in 1977 of Families and Persons in the United States. Current Population Reports*, Series P-60, No. 118. Washington, D.C.: U.S. Department of Commerce.

Bureau of the Census (1976) *Number, Timing and Duration of Marriage and Divorce in the U.S., June 1975. Current Population Reports*, P-20, No. 297. Washington, D.C.: U.S. Department of Commerce.

Committee on Social Insurance and Taxes (1963) *Report of the Committee on Social Insurance and Taxes*. A Report to the President's Commission on the Status of Women. October 1963. Washington, D.C.: U.S. Government Printing Office.

DelBene, L. (1979) *Studies from Interagency Data Linkages*. Report No. 8. Unpublished tabulations from the Exact Match File, Office of Research and Statistics, Social Security Administration. Washington, D.C.: U.S. Department of Health, Education, and Welfare.

Gordon, N. M. (1978). *The Treatment of Women in the Public Pension Systems of Five Countries*. Working paper 5069-01. Washington, D.C.: The Urban Institute.

Gordon, N. M. (1979) Institutional responses: The federal income tax system. Pp. 201–222 in R. E. Smith, ed., *The Subtle Revolution: Women at Work*. Washington, D.C.: The Urban Institute.

Grad, S., and Foster, K. (1979) *Income of the Population Age 55 and Older, 1976*. Staff Paper #35, Office of Research and Statistics, Social Security Administration. Washington, D.C.: U.S. Department of Health, Education, and Welfare.

Hsiao, W. C., Diamond, P. A., Hickman, J. C., and Moorehead, E. J. (1976) *Report of the Consultant Panel on Social Security to the Congressional Research Service*. Washington, D.C.: Library of Congress.

Johnson, B. L. (1979) *Marital and Family Characteristics of Workers, 1970–1978*. Washington, D.C.: Bureau of Labor Statistics. Reprinted from *Monthly Labor Review* 102(4) April 1979.

National Commission on the Observance of International Women's Year (1976) *To Form a More Perfect Union: Justice for American Women*. Report to the President. Washington, D.C.: U.S. Government Printing Office.

National Women's Conference (1977) *A National Plan of Action*. Resolutions Adopted by the National Women's Conference in Houston, Texas.

Smith, R. E., ed. (1979) *The Subtle Revolution: Women at Work*. Washington, D.C.: The Urban Institute.

U.S. Department of Health, Education, and Welfare (1978) *Report of the HEW Task Force on the Treatment of Women under Social Security*. Office of Legislative and Regulatory Policy, Social Security Administration. Washington, D.C.: U.S. Department of Health, Education, and Welfare.

U.S. Department of Health, Education, and Welfare (1979) *Social Security and the Changing Roles of Men and Women*. Office of Legislative and Regulatory Policy, Social Security Administration. Washington, D.C.: U.S. Department of Health, Education, and Welfare.

chapter 10

The Family in Later Life: Social Structure and Social Policy

ETHEL SHANAS
MARVIN B. SUSSMAN

The family life of old people, especially the patterns of relationships among the elderly, other family members, and bureaucratic organizations, has been intensively reviewed and studied in the last decade (Shanas and Sussman 1977). There are two main reasons for this surge of interest in a previously neglected field of investigation. One is a recognition by scholars of the important role of the family and of kin networks in the life of old people both in the United States and in other industrial countries. The second is that with the increase in the number of old people and the rise in their longevity, legislators and administrators of provider systems in the United States and other countries are confronted with the maintenance and service costs attendant on the care of frail and sick old people. Decision makers, torn between humanitarian and budgetary concerns, have turned to the family as a resource in the care of the elderly.

This chapter focuses on a major problem of older people in the United States: the need for care of the frail and other vulnerable persons among them, in a time when families are changing but traditional conceptions of the family still appear to guide the thinking of decision makers. These traditional views of the family and of the role of old people in the family, reflected in legislation and operating programs, conflict with the real

211

AGING
Stability and Change in the Family

situation of the elderly, creating problems for old people, their family members, and for those who assume responsibility for the care and well-being of older Americans.

The chapter has three parts. It begins with a discussion of family structure and living arrangements of the elderly. *Later life* and the *family* as these terms are used here are defined and described, and the demographic bases of the family structure and living arrangements of the elderly are presented and discussed. These descriptive materials serve as a backdrop for the second section of the chapter, which deals with linkages between older people and their families. Here we consider some of the myths that affect social policies for the elderly: that older people are alienated from their children, that older people are isolated, and that families are unwilling to care for aged sick members. Then we briefly summarize research findings on the proportion of old people in the United States who need health care and supportive social services and consider the significance, both practical and theoretical, of using the family as a link with bureaucracy on behalf of elderly family members. In this section of the chapter we report recent research on the possibilities of the family and the kin network serving as a support system for the frail elderly. The third and final section of the chapter deals with the policy and program implications inherent in such efforts and suggests a research demonstration to test the feasibility of the familly as a social support system.

FAMILY STRUCTURE IN LATER LIFE

A Definition of the Elderly

In the United States, those persons aged 65 and over are officially identified as old people. Such a definition of the elderly, based on calendar age, serves to provide an age floor for government benefits, private and public pension plans, and discounts for goods and services. The population aged 65 and over, however, ranges in age from 65 to over 100, a span of two generations. There are now an estimated 24.1 million persons aged 65 and older, of whom 9 million (37%) are 75 years of age and older (Bureau of the Census 1979). About 2 million persons, roughly 8% of the elderly, are 85 years of age and older. This age group is most likely to be frail and in need of health and social supports. Women outnumber men in the population 65 years of age and older (14.3 million women compared with 9.8 million men). The older the age cohort, the more likely it is to have an excess of women, and among those 85 years of age and over there are two women for every man. Research evidence indicates marked variability among individuals of the same calendar age. Such variability is not usually considered in the determination of social policy, however, and most legislation and programs for the elderly group together all persons aged 65 and over. In this chapter, therefore, we will adopt contemporary usage and describe these persons as "older people," or "the elderly," and that period of life after 65 as "later life."

What Is a Family?

How does one describe or define the family and use such a definition in research and in the formulation of social policy? The task is not an easy one (Sussman 1976). Although the typical American family is usually described as a husband and wife and their offspring, this nuclear family and other pluralistic family structures have existed side by side in this country from the days when the first settlers arrived (Hareven 1975, 1977, Demos 1972). True, there were nuclear families of husband and wife and their issue living in independent households; but there were also three-generation families and extended families composed of persons related by blood or marriage. Boarders who lived in these various households were considered "like family" (Hareven 1975) and were forerunners of a structure that today is described as the "everyday" family (Sussman 1977) or the "neighborhood" family (Ross 1978).

For most older people, the family is that group of individuals to whom they are related by blood or marriage. It includes more than spouse, children, and siblings. The family includes cousins of various degree, in-laws, and a variety of relatives who enter the family network as a need for services, help, or information arises. At traditional family gatherings such as weddings and funerals, the family of the elderly expands. There are many persons present whom the elderly person takes pleasure in identifying and cataloguing into a genealogy. As relatives disperse and return to their homes, whether physically near or distant, the family of the elderly person contracts. The family of the elderly then may be described as a changing network of kin, some biologically and/or physically close to the older person, some biologically and/or physically distant.

Demographic Bases of Family Structure

Elderly persons differ in sex, in age, in marital status, and in whether or not they have children. It is the intermix of these factors—sex, age, marital status, and the presence or absence of children—that determines the structure of an individual's family. The structure of the families of older women is different from the structure of the families of older men. Women outnumber men among those aged 65 and over, they outlive them, and they are more likely than men never to have married, or, if once married, to be widowed or divorced.

All these demographic factors affect the makeup of the old person's family. Among an estimated 23,205,000 persons aged 65 and over in 1977, there were 146 women for every 100 men (Glick 1977). Because women outlive men, the ratio of women to men rises with age. There are 127 women for every 100 men aged 65 to 69, while among the very old, those aged 85 and over, there are 216 women for every 100 men. Because of these differences in life expectancy between the sexes and the fact that widowed men have greater opportunities for remarriage than widowed women, in 1976 it was estimated that there were five times as many older widows as there were older widowers (7.2 million widows compared with 1.4 million widowers).

Older women compared with older men are more likely never to have married or to have a marriage broken by death or divorce. Glick (1977) reports that in 1970, the older woman was 1.5 times as likely as the man her age to be divorced, and 4 times as likely to be widowed. Furthermore, a new type of unmarried woman may now be emerging: the woman who is divorced after the age of 65 and whose prospects of remarriage are slight. While only 3% of all women 65 and over were reported as divorced in the 1970 census, Glick estimates that 12% of all women over 65 in 1975 will eventually be divorced. The number of older persons living together outside marriage is relatively small now, but is representative of a variant family form that is becoming more important. Of an estimated 660,000 persons in such living arrangements in 1976, 84,000 (almost 13%) were persons over 65 years of age. About 2% of all unmarried men aged 65 and over and .5% of all unmarried women in this age group were in this type of arrangement (Glick 1977).

The family structure of old people, besides reflecting their sex, age, and marital status, is also influenced by whether or not they have children. Data on the numbers of living children of older persons are available for the noninstitutionalized elderly (about 95% of all elderly) in national surveys made in 1962 and 1975 (Shanas et al. 1968, Shanas, 1978). Four of every five community residents 65 years of age and over in 1975 had at least one surviving child. Elderly parents reported fewer children overall in 1975 than were reported in 1962. The decline in numbers of children was most apparent among those persons newly reaching the age of 65. Of persons aged 65 to 69 with children, the percentage who had only one child increased between 1962 and 1975 from 21% to 28%, while the percentage of these persons with six or more children decreased from 18% in 1962 to 10% in 1975.

At the same time elderly parents were reporting fewer children, more and more old persons were reporting that they were not only grandparents but also great grandparents. The four-generation family was already becoming common in the United States in 1962. By 1975, more than a third of the elderly, whether or not they had living children, reported that they were great grandparents. The likelihood of being a great grandparent increased with age. Among those aged 65 and 66 with living children, one-fourth were great grandparents. Among those aged 80 and over with living chidren, three-fourths were great grandparents.

The family structure of the elderly, their interaction with other family members, and their living arrangements (as we shall see shortly) rest on a demographic base. The demographic framework within which families exist can be described as having more women than men and an increasing proportion of the unmarried among older women and an increasing proportion of older persons with few or no children. At the same time, increase in the length of life has resulted in the emergence of the four- and even five-generation family in the United States with a person aged 65 or older at its apex.

Living Arrangements of the Elderly

For a family to exist, it is not necessary that its members live under the same roof. Those who do live under the same roof comprise a household. The living arrangements of the elderly in the community reflect, first and most important, their marital status; second, their age; and, finally, whether or not they have children. These same factors, particularly marital status and age, influence whether an old person will live in the community or in an institution. About 95% of the elderly live in the community, and about 5% in nursing homes or homes for aged. Old persons without immediate kin are more likely than their contemporaries to be institutionalized. The institutionalized aged compared with the elderly in the community are three times as likely to have never married and are twice as likely to be widowed (Siegel 1976). The older the person, the more likely he or she is to be institutionalized. About one in every eight persons in the United States aged 80 and over is a resident of an institution.

Marital status is the single most important factor in determining the living arrangements of the elderly in the community (see Table 10.1).

TABLE 10.1
Living Arrangements, Persons Aged Sixty-Five and Over, by Marital Status and Sex: 1975 (Percentage Distribution)[a]

Living arrangements[b]	Unmarried[d]			Married		
	Men	Women	All	Men	Women	All
Living alone	65	67	66	—[e]	—	—
Living with spouse only	—[e]	—	—	82	87	84
Living with married child	8	7	7	2	2	2
Living with unmarried child	6	11	10	12	8	10
Living with siblings or other relatives	14	12	13	5	4	4
Living with others	6	2	3	0	0	0
Total	100	100	100	100	100	100
N = [e]	(560)	(2191)	(2751)	(1755)	(1250)	(3005)

[a] From Shanas 1978.
[b] This is a priority code. When more than one living arrangement was mentioned, the priority for coding use is the same as the order of the categories in the table; for example, when living with married child was mentioned in combination with other living arrangement, the response was coded under living with married child.
[c] The number of cases is weighted. Detailed information on nonresponse is not given in this or subsequent tables since 98% or more of the eligible respondents provided information.
[d] Includes widowed, spearated, divorced, and never married persons.
[e] Data not applicable.

Eight of every 10 married persons in 1975, both men and women, lived in a household with a spouse only, the "couple" family. About 14 of every 100 of the married elderly also had one of their children in the household, and 4 of every 100 had siblings or other relatives in the household. Among unmarried elderly persons (the widowed, separated, divorced, and never-married), living alone was the most common household arrangement for both men and women. Six of every 10 unmarried persons lived alone. About 17 of every 100 unmarried elderly lived with persons who were not their relatives. A detailed analysis of the unmarried elderly that divided the never-married from the separated, widowed, and divorced indicates that fewer of the never-married elderly compared with the separated, widowed, and divorced elderly live alone. As many as one-third of the never-married elderly lived with siblings.

Table 10.2 gives the living arrangements of both the married and unmarried elderly by age group in 1975. Again, marital status is shown to be an overriding factor in the determination of living arrangements among the old. For the married elderly, irrespective of age, the usual pattern was to live in a household with a spouse only. However, among the unmarried elderly, for both men and women, age made a difference

TABLE 10.2
Living Arrangements, Persons Aged Sixty-Five and Over, by Marital Status, Age, and Sex: 1975 (Percentage Distribution)[a]

Living arrangements[b]	Men					Women					All				
	65–69	70–74	75–79	80+	All	65–69	70–74	75–79	80+	All	65–69	70–74	75–79	80+	All
Unmarried persons[c]															
Living alone	75	63	62	56	65	69	69	70	60	67	70	68	68	59	66
Living with married child	4	11	8	10	8	4	5	8	12	7	4	6	8	12	7
Living with unmarried child	6	7	4	9	6	7	11	9	19	11	7	10	8	17	10
Living with others	16	19	26	25	21	20	15	14	10	15	19	16	17	12	16
Total	100	100	100	100	100	100	100	100	100	100	100	100	100	100	100
N[d]	(173)	(156)	(122)	(109)	(560)	(607)	(591)	(435)	(558)	(2191)	(780)	(747)	(557)	(668)	(2751)
Married persons															
Living with spouse only	80	79	87	87	82	86	88	88	88	87	82	83	87	88	84
Living with spouse, married child	1	1	4	1	2	1	2	2	3	2	1	1	4	2	2
Living with spouse, unmarried child	12	14	9	10	12	8	8	8	6	8	10	12	8	8	10
Living with others	7	5	0	2	5	5	2	2	3	4	6	4	1	2	4
Total	100	100	100	100	100	100	100	100	100	100	100	100	100	100	100
N[d]	(717)	(517)	(288)	(232)	(1755)	(628)	(347)	(169)	(107)	(1250)	(1345)	(864)	(457)	(339)	(3005)

[a] From Shanas 1978.
[b] This is priority code. When more than one living arrangement was mentioned. the priority for coding used is the same as the order of the categories in the table; for example, when living with spouse and married child was mentioned in combination with any other living arrangement, the response was coded under living with spouse and married child.
[c] Includes widowed, separated, divorced and never married persons.
[d] The number of cases is weighted.

in their living arrangements. The older the *unmarried* person, the less likely he or she was to live alone. Of those unmarried persons age 65 to 69, 70% lived alone, compared with 59% of those age 80 and over. Among the unmarried elderly, reports of living with a child increase with age. Of those aged 65 to 69, 11% compared with 29% of those 80 and over lived with a child. Of all unmarried men and women over 80, 19% and 31%, respectively, lived with a child.

The living arrangements of older people, like their family structure, reflect demographic differences among them. Married persons live in households separate from children and other relatives. Unmarried persons live alone if it is possible. With advanced age and often associated infirmities, unmarried persons increasingly share a household with their children or with others.

LINKAGES BETWEEN THE ELDERLY AND THEIR FAMILIES

Some Pervasive Social Myths

Having defined what we mean by "elderly" and what we mean by "family," we turn now to a consideration of linkages between the elderly and their families. This section begins with a consideration of some social myths about the elderly. Social myths exist in every society. They encompass those things that everyone knows to be "true," and everyone accepts as fact without either raising questions or asking for evidence. Policymakers, like other people, are either parents or adult chidlren, sometimes both at the same time. Their beliefs about the elderly are often the result of their own experiences with older people. When their experience varies from accepted myth, they are likely to describe their families as "different." Many policymakers seem to have accepted as facts three common myths about old people and their families: first, that older people are alienated from their children; second, that older people, particularly those living alone, are isolated; and third, that families are unwilling or unable to care for their frail elderly members.

Contrary to these myths, the family, defined as that group of individuals related by blood or marriage, is the major resource of its older members for emotional and social support, crisis intervention, and bureaucratic linkages. Using data from three successive nationwide probability surveys of noninstitutionalized persons aged 65 and over made in 1957, 1962, and 1975, Shanas investigated whether older people were alienated from children, whether those living alone were physically isolated, and whether families were caring for frail and sick older members.

She determined the physical proximity of older parents and their children, the frequency with which parents see their children, and the frequency with which older people see siblings or other kin (Shanas 1979). She measured the day-by-day social contacts of old people living alone and determined the proportions of older people who are bedfast and housebound in the community (Shanas 1978). The findings from these surveys indicate that older people are not alienated from children and other relatives, that most old people living alone either had daily visitors or visited other people, and that about twice as many people were bedfast and housebound at home as were in institutions of all kinds.

About four of every five community residents aged 65 and over have living children. While the proportion of persons with children is unchanged over the period of the surveys from 1957 to 1975, the proportion of persons living in the same household with one of their children declined from 36% in 1957 to 18% in 1975. At the same time, however, the proportion of old people living within 10 minutes' walking or driving distance of a child increased, so that the two categories grouped together—the proportions of old people with children who live either with a child or within 10 minutes' distance of a child—have remained fairly constant over 20 years: 59% in 1957, 61% in 1962, and 52% in 1975. The findings indicate that, while old people no longer tend to live in the same household with a child, they now live next door, down the street, or a few blocks away. In 1975, three of every four persons with children lived either in the same household as a child or within a half hour's distance of a child.

Living near adult children is no guarantee that the older parent will see his or her children. In 1975, however, 53% of those persons with children, including those with a child in the same household, saw one of their children the day they were interviewed or the previous day. The proportion of older parents who saw at least one child during the week before they were interviewed has remained stable over almost 20 years: 83% in 1957 and 77% in 1975.

Even though most older people live close to at least one child and see at least one child often, they still may have lost touch with their brothers and sisters or other relatives. In 1975, one-third of all old persons with living brothers and sisters saw at least one of these during the week before they were interviewed. About 3 of every 10 older persons said that they had seen some relative who was neither a brother nor a sister, a child nor a grandchild during the previous week. These relatives were either of their own generation—cousins and in-laws—or of younger generations—nephews and nieces.

The findings of the proximity of older parents to adult children and the frequency of visits between older persons and their children, siblings, and other relatives tell us nothing about the quality of family relations. We do not know whether these meetings are brief or lengthy, friendly and warm or acrimonious and hostile. Every family is different. For some old people and their children and relatives, these meetings may be warm and enriching; for others they may be only a necessary formality to be completed as quickly as possible. Whatever their quality, these interactions between and among the generations do exist. Together with the evidence on family responsibility for the elderly, some of which is presented in this chapter, such findings on the interaction of old people and their children and relatives call into question the myth of family alienation.

Another common belief about the elderly, indeed a paradigm for much research and action, is that the elderly are isolated. The isolated person can be described as someone who suffers from feelings of loneliness and feelings of alienation. In the instance of the elderly, it is commonly assumed that living alone is a concomitant of isolation. Many older persons who live alone, however, like many younger persons who live alone, are neither lonely nor alienated. They feel no special need for more interaction with other persons. Situations that one person might find distressing and conducive to feelings of loneliness might be accepted by another person as quite usual and not at all stress-producing (Tunstall 1966). In identifying the isolated elderly, their psychic feelings and the nature of their interaction with other persons may be more important than whether they live alone or with others.

Survey data for 1975 give some clues as to the physical isolation of the elderly and the extent of the interaction of the elderly with other persons. Old people in general have daily contacts with other persons— only 2% reported no human contact during the most recent weekday before their interview, and 3% reported that they had no human contact during the past Sunday. Three of every 10 older persons live alone. From 6% to 9% of those living alone in 1975 said that they had no interaction with other persons either the previous weekday or Sunday. In contrast, about half of all people living alone, both men and women, said that they had received visitors the previous day and the previous Sunday, and about a third had visited friends (Shanas 1978). The majority of those living alone then report frequent interaction with friends and relatives.

Subjective reports of being "often alone" or of feelings of loneliness differ from the objective reports of human contacts. About 3 of every 10 older persons, irrespective of their living arrangements, said that they were often alone, and the same proportion said that they were often or sometimes lonely. These reports can be compared with the objective reports of human contacts; only 2 or 3 of every 100 persons said that they had no human contact. Old people who lived alone, as might be expected, were the most likely of all elderly to say that they were alone often. As many as 8 of every 10 of those who live alone said they were often alone, despite the fact that those who have children were likely to live close to one child and to see that child often. Unmarried persons—the single, the divorced, and the widowed—whether they lived alone or not, were the most likely of all elderly to say that they were often alone or that they were lonely.

All the indicators of isolation among the elderly, however, whether isolation is perceived as living alone or as reported aloneness or loneliness, are greatest for those persons over the age of 80. The comparisons between these very old and the younger old are striking. The proportion of all old people who lived alone (both the unmarried and the married) was 50% greater among those aged 80 and over than among those aged 65 to 69 (39% compared with 26%); the proportion who said they were often alone is 50% greater among those 80 and over than among the younger aged (44% compared with 30%); and the proportion who said they were often or sometimes lonely is 25% greater among those aged 80 and over than among those 65 to 69 (31% compared with 24%). However, when the very old who were in good health were compared with those in poor health, those aged 80 and more in good health were no more likely than the younger elderly to report subjective feelings of loneliness or to report that they are often alone. The data suggest that it is the frail person among the very old who is likely to experience those psychic feelings that are identified as "isolation." Indeed, it may be that the often-mentioned "isolation" of the aged is not an absence of human contact among them and thus cannot be compensated for by group living or programs of friendly visitors. The isolation of the elderly appears to be an expression of loss, both physical and psychological.

Finally, what of the belief that families are no longer important as a source of care for the elderly? In 1962, 2% of the elderly in the community were reported totally bedfast at home and 6% were reported housebound. That 8% of the elderly bedfast and housebound at home was about twice the proportion of old people in institutions of all kinds. In 1975, about 3% of the elderly were bedfast at home and 7% were housebound. That 10% of the elderly bedfast and housebound at home, just as in 1962, was almost twice the proportion of old people in institutions of all kinds (Shanas 1979). The validity of the survey findings on the family as a caretaker for the elderly is reinforced by other studies. The U.S. General Accounting Office (GAO), summarizing a study in Cleveland, Ohio, that focused on the costs of care, concluded that "the importance of family and friends is evidenced by the fact that greatly or extremely impaired

elderly who live with their spouses and children generally are not institutionalized, whereas those who live alone usually are [Laurie 1978]."
The common beliefs that the elderly are alienated from their children, that old people, particularly those living alone, are isolated, and that families are unwilling or unable to care for elderly members seem not to be applicable to the majority of the American elderly. The persistence of these simplistic social myths as a basis of social policies is a disservice to both older people and their families, as we shall further indicate.

FAMILIES AS LINKS WITH BUREAUCRACY

Before presenting the conceptual issues of linkage and its viability as an explanation of family, bureaucratic organization, and elderly relationships, we will discuss certain pragmatic and empirical concerns related to the health status and care of the elderly. The health status of old people ranges from the completely healthy, independent individual through those with a range of increasingly serious incapacity, to invalids confined to nursing home beds. Socially the life-styles of these persons also vary immensely. As Robert Butler (1977) has noted: "We associate the elderly—particularly the very old, with institutions, but in fact, at any moment in time, only about 6% are there; the other 94% usually prefer to stay out, and generally can care quite well for themselves despite the fact that many suffer some chronic illness or impairment."

During that state of aging between independence and the need for prolonged total care, if such need should arise, there is often a period during which necessary supportive care is best supplied by adult children or other kin. Many families, as previously indicated, now fill this need, often at great family sacrifice. Both these families and others might be more able and willing to provide such care for their elderly kin if various supports were available to ease the burden that such care imposes. In 1962, Shanas foresaw the current situation in which the needs for health care for the elderly would exceed the supply of both public funds and trained personnel. At that time she raised the question of how the family might be better used to meet these needs to the benefit of both the elderly and society in general (Shanas 1962).

Within the past decade, federal health, rehabilitative, and welfare agencies have implicitly followed policies of reversing the trend of providing care and treatment for the aged and chronically ill in isolated, highly bureaucratized, and impersonal institutions. In an effort to relieve the burden on families and to ensure that services go to those old persons who require them, an array of programs at the federal, state, and local levels have developed. For example, there are now at least 134 separate federally sponsored or supported programs providing assistance to older people (Laurie 1977). Programs for the elderly, whatever their sponsorship, have involved various approaches to meet their needs, such as providing financial aid, medical help, nutritional supplements, and/or housing. Such efforts have had mixed results. They often suffer from the common problems of interagency conflict, overlapping services, and high costs for services rendered. Nevertheless, these programs have in common the recognition that a variety of different services and supports may be needed for the elderly, and that a single program cannot hope to provide a total solution.

Robert Benedict, the Commissioner of the U.S. Administration on Aging, has pointed out that "in the neighborhood of 40% of those now 65 and over not in institutions should have some type of supportive service or services to enable them to lead fully independent lifestyles [1978]." Criticizing current programs, Benedict noted that "characteristically so-called service systems are so fractionated as to defy understanding on the part of those who could use them and sometimes to the agencies that undertake to link older people with them [1978]."

While on one hand policymakers lament the alienation of the elderly from their families, on the other hand the effective involvement of families in the exploration of health options available to the elderly and in planning and decision making regarding their health regimens has become a priority item. One reason for this must certainly be the efforts at cost containment as they relate to the elderly. A recent GAO report to the Congress gave some statistics concerning the allocation of funds to the sick elderly. Approximately 60% of the extremely impaired elderly are estimated to live outside institutions. "At all levels of impairment, the value of services provided by families and friends greatly exceeded that cost of services provided by public agencies at public expense [1977]." The report cited Cleveland, Ohio, as an example, noting that "public agencies are currently spending less per person for home services than is spent for institutional care regardless of the levels of impairment [1977, p. 9]." The report concluded that unless the level of impairment is very severe, the cost of institutionalization of the elderly is always greater than providing comparable services and support in a noninstitutional arrangement. Indeed, it has been estimated that between 15% and 30% of the elderly now in long-term care facilities could live in a community setting, given adequate supports (Smyer 1977).

Whether the reasons be cost containment or a recognition of the amount of care now being given the elderly by family members, policymakers are becoming more sympathetic to proposals that suggest new delivery models for health care for the elderly and that provide options for the consumer of services. One such model involves family members in support roles with the prospects of such members functioning as linkages or advocates of aged family members (Rosenmayr 1977, Munnichs 1977, Paillat 1977, Sussman 1971). Knowing the service options and making a choice among them is often beyond the abilities of the elderly individual who needs help. Hence, there is theoretical relevance and practical significance in positing a linking model that places the knowledgeable family representative in an interstitial position between the elderly person and formally organized institutions. In this linking role, family members can communicate, educate, advocate, and facilitate on behalf of elderly relatives with those institutions that control various services, financial support, and health care.

All relationships may be viewed as a series of exchanges. The elderly individual or couple is involved in a series of exchanges with an immediate family or member units of the extended kin network, with service agencies, and with other more formal organizations. Obviously, in order to function in our society, elderly persons link themselves with bureaucratic structures. It is our assumption that in time old people have increasing difficulty and hardship in meeting demands of large-scale dispensers of services. Furthermore, the multiplicity of services to be found in any community, each with a defined focus and each with differing criteria of eligibility, is so great that not all potential clients are aware of the services or economic options available to them nor do they have the skills to implement a chosen option sequence. When the elderly person or couple is integrated into another family unit for the latter to act as a linker or facilitator on behalf of the older person(s), that unit can then enter into an exchange with the more formal organization. Hence the potential importance of family members or linkers with providers of services.

It is assumed here that other members of the family or kin network are more aware of the operations of formal organizations than are elderly kin members. In practice, both elderly people and their families may be ignorant of the structure of formal organizations. Despite such ignorance, in the real world families and organizations operate as a partnership, however uneven. Both primary groups and organizations—such as those that make up the human service system of the United States—operate on the principle of shared functions. The individual needs the primary group to help handle unpredictable events, situations in which there are many contingencies, and those situations in which it is more economic to utilize the family rather than the larger organization. In the human services, the organization is a second line of defense and may or may not be approached for assistance, depending on the primary group's knowledge of existing agency resources, beliefs about using such agencies, and its ability to solve the particular problems of one of its members.

Let us illustrate some such situations that involve families and bureaucracies as they relate to the elderly. These illustrations are not elegant. Instead, they describe common experiences of many older people. Grandfather has wandered away from the house. He has done this before—in fact he does it fairly often. Does one immediately call the police or initially go out to look for him? Your aging mother develops migraines readily. They seem to occur just prior to the time she is to get her social security check. She worries a good deal about the check because she has read in the papers of thefts of such checks and how hustlers and muggers stay around the mailboxes or visit the aged widow on the day the check comes in. Does one call the doctor to treat this condition or does one give her some assurance and suggest that she take whatever medication her physician has already prescribed?

These homely illustrations serve to demonstrate that in the case of the elderly, formal organizations, especially those that provide human services, can be most effectively utilized for their expertise only when called on to handle situations and events beyond the capacities of families. These illustrations also suggest that families may have vast reservoirs of resources, including both technical and nontechnical skills, which are often unidentified.

Economic and Service Supports to Reconstituted Families

President Carter, in proclaiming National Family Week, stated, "All families are important but the extended family, the foster family, the adopted family play a special role by relieving the isolation of those who lack the comfort of a living nuclear family [U.S. President 1978]." We are now prepared to advocate a new family form for the elderly: "functional extended." It is a reconstituted family consisting of two or more generations and its members are bilateral or generationally linked—parents, children, and grandchildren. The family form we are suggesting for the elderly—one that is active in expressing its love, intimacy, solidarity, and social support—is not exclusively a middle-aged child–parent household combination. It is one of elderly relatives residing either in the same household or physically near any family unit, immediate or distant, that makes up their kin network.

The rationale for providing the conditions—economic and social supports—to families so that they can have the option to reconstitute themselves as functional extended units follow

The Increase in the Number and Proportion of Elderly Persons in the United States

The proportion of persons aged 65 and over in our society has increased from 4% in 1900 to 11% in 1977 (23 million). The population aged 65 and over is estimated at 31 million in 2000, between 11% and 13% of the projected population, and at 43 million in 2020, between 12% and 17% of the population. The elderly population itself is aging, and about 44% of the 65 and over group are expected to be 75 and over in the year 2000 (Siegel 1976). The older the person, the more likely he or she is to require supportive services.

The Need to Offset or Neutralize the Pressure to Institutionalize Elderly Persons

About 5% to 6% of the elderly are in long-term care institutions at any one time. About 80% of these institutional residents have been admitted for medical reasons (Bureau of the Census 1978, p. 266). The interests of caretakers and service providers, the needs of a growing number of the elderly for quality care, and the limited economic, social, and psychic resources of families called on to maintain elderly relatives all act to "push" older people into institutions.

The Need to Improve the Quality of Life of All Family Members

Healthy families are a basic goal of public policy and legislation. To achieve this goal requires increasing the options for all members of our society, whether young or old, by means of programs that buttress a family's capability to handle its problems and maintain its integrity as a unit that serves the needs of its members, irrespective of age.

One of the authors of this chapter recently completed two major studies of the feasibility of providing economic and social supports to member units of extended families so that they could incorporate an elderly relative within their household or invite him or her to live nearby without sustaining any loss in their own efforts to achieve their goal of a quality existence (Sussman et al. 1979). The studies were made in

Cleveland, Ohio, and in Winston-Salem, North Carolina. The samples, randomly selected, were 346 family units in Cleveland and 206 in Winston-Salem.

The major findings of these studies indicate that more than 80% of respondents were willing to take an older relative into their household under some circumstances. They preferred that the elderly relative be physically well, yet families indicate a high level of willingness to have even ill and isolated relatives in their households. Overall, families would prefer that the elderly relative live nearby rather than in their household, but they would still be willing to undertake the care of such relatives whether they were in the household or not. Families prefer assistance to help them provide care for elderly relatives in the form of a monthly allowance that they could use to purchase services as needed rather than in the form of special services available to them.

Multivariate and multiple classification analyses indicate that demographic and sociological variables such as race, social class, and life-cycle stage cannot explain the willingness of families to participate in a support program for the elderly. The important correlates of families' willingness to have an older person in the household are situational variables: perception of spouse's willingness; perception of the home's being crowded; the presence of relatives who live close enough to provide help; and personal factors such as positive prior experiences with older people and attitudes toward the elderly. Of all the background variables investigated, only age and duration of marriage, both highly correlated, are related to willingness to have an elderly person live with the respondent. The younger the respondent, the more willing he or she was to share a household with an elderly relative.

In summary, experiential and situational factors rather than demographic characteristics are associated with family willingness to share with and care for an elderly person. Such items as income, race, education, occupation, religious identification, and growing up in an urban or rural area are unrelated to the respondents' willingness to enter into a solidarity "contract" with an elderly relative living nearby. Factors that are related to such willingness are whether the respondent has lived in a household with an elderly person or cared for an older person and whether the respondent feels his or her home is large enough to house an elderly relative.

In a model estimating the probability that different subgroups in the population would be willing to participate in government-supported programs in functional extended families, combinations of individual characteristics and events were delineated. There is a probability of between .90 and 1.00 that two categories of people would be willing to set up a reconstituted family: (1) those who have cared for an older person previously and found the situation to be satisfactory, who are either uncertain or positive that children would be willing to accept this older person, and who express very favorable opinions towards government-supported programs and (2) those who have not lived with an elderly relative but who are either uncertain or positive that children would be willing to accept an older person, who are favorable toward government-supported programs, and who are under 50 years of age. Cooperative and intimate dealings among individuals cannot be based on economic principles alone. One should not underestimate the filial feelings of the middle generation toward the elderly, the almost subconscious need to respond to kith and kin. Such feelings about an elderly member, however, are obviously influenced by the life conditions, aspirations, intrafamily relationships, and current social and economic status of a particular family. The family may wish to do "the right thing," but a variety of conditions may work against it.

THE FAMILY AS A SOCIAL SUPPORT SYSTEM: PROGRAM AND POLICY IMPLICATIONS

The family provides its members with love, intimacy, and solidarity. It is because of these special attributes that it will continue over time as a persistent and viable organizational form regardless of its particular structure. The demands made on the family by its frail elderly members suggest that some families may be shorn of resources and irrevocably damaged as mentally healthy systems if there are unavailable to them sustaining economic resources and service supports.

Studies indicate that families are willing to care for an elderly relative if economic and social supports are provided them. There is some uncertainty, however, that families will really act as they say they will and enter into contracts for taking care of elderly relatives. Program implementation requires careful assessment of existing service arrangements and of financial expenditures for income maintenance as well as the development of regulations, procedures, and settlements. The possibilities of reconstituting household units into functioning extended families with less reliance on formal institutions and agencies requires imaginative experimentation. Demonstrations with appropriate controls and evaluations to measure such outcomes as the quality of life of the older person and what constitutes effective maintenance outside institutions are also recommended.

Complexity is a concomitant of urban industrial societies. For both the elderly person and family members, obtaining knowledge, access, and use of human service resources can be a bewildering and sometimes a degrading experience. The practices of highly organized bureaucratic structures frequently are not attuned to the service preference and needs of those being served. Some critics of human service systems have argued that such organizations exist more for the perpetuation of jobs of providers than for the benefit of the client or patient—the consumer of services. We do not share this pejorative view.

Instead, we see the need for a more effective nexus of elderly persons, families, and bureaucratic service organizations. Informal support networks of elderly persons and network of service providers need to be integrated within a complementary framework. Each system needs the other, since separately they cannot do the necessary mandated or volunteered service tasks. Consequently, a policy that will promote such linkages between systems is suggested.

The nexus between family, elderly member, and bureaucracy is ever present, yet the responsibilities of each to the other is less clear. Should there be a federal public policy mandating that family members support elderly relatives whose resources may be insufficient to meet the costs of care? If, on the other hand, it is affirmed that the government should supersede families in supporting aged dependent members, expanding further its current program of society-wide transfers in the payment of such care and support, should there be a policy of providing reimbursement to families who provide services to the elderly or should the family be given other inducements, such as tax credits? These issues of entitlement and eligibility exacerbate the efforts of families and their elderly relatives to obtain help when needed or to use effectively the available resources. Should there then be a policy wherein all persons aged 65 and over be entitled to available community services, regardless of social class or income?

Our data indicate that the elderly of the twenty-first century will be "in search of a relative" to look after them or to take the appropriate action on their behalf when these older persons cannot function autonomously and independently. The role of the government, then, in the life of these elderly persons and their families needs clarification. Should the agencies of the government mandated to assist the elderly develop a uniform national policy and program of federal support for services to the elderly, allowing for its administration and implementation on the community level? Should such programs be unidirectional from the top downward or multidirectional, with flexibility that would maxmize the input of ideas for policy and program from both families and their elderly members?

The questions we raise in this chapter affect the lives of millions of persons, both the elderly and their families. There are now 24 million older people in the United States, of whom about 1.3 million are institutionalized at any one time. The tentative answers we suggest to some of our questions are based on research findings. Our answers may seem unrealistic, yet they are no more unrealistic than the consequences of some existing programs. The increasing numbers of persons aged 65 and over, the rapidly growing segment of those aged 75 years of age and more, the poor fit between facts and societal myths about the family and the elderly, the existing conflicts between families and bureaucracies, all call for a reevaluation of both policies and programs for this older segment of the American people.

REFERENCES

Benedict, R. (1978) The Family and Long Term Care Alternatives. Paper presented at the 1978 Groves Conference on Marriage and the Family, Washington, D.C., April 28, 1978.

Bureau of the Census (1978) *1976 Survey of Institutionalized Persons*. Current Population Reports. Special Studies, Series P23, No. 79. Washington, D.C.: U.S. Department of Commerce.

Bureau of the Census (1979) *Social and Economic Characteristics of the Older Population*. Current Population Reports. Special Studies, Series P23, No. 85. Washington, D.C.: U.S. Department of Commerce.

Butler, R. M. (1977) Proceedings of the Governor's Conference on the *Quality of Life of Our Senior Citizens*. Raleigh, N.C.: Meredith College, July 6–7, 1977, 33–36.

U.S. President, Carter, J. (1978) Proclamation 4606, "National Family Week," 1978, *Federal Register*, 43, 206, October 24, 1978.

Comptroller General of the United States. (1977) *Report to the Congress, Home Health—The Need for a National Policy to Better Provide for the Elderly*, HRD-78-19, December 30, 1977.

Demos, J. (1972) Demography and psychology in the historical study of family life: A personal report. Pp. 561–570 in P. Laslett with the assistance of R. Wall, *Household and Family in Past Time*. Cambridge, England: Cambridge University Press.

Glick, P. C. (1977) Perspectives on Living Arrangements of the Elderly. A paper presented at the annual meeting of the Gerontology Society, San Francisco, November 20, 1977.

Hareven, T. K. (1975) Family time and industrial time: Family and work in a planned corporation town, 1900–1924. *Journal of Urban History* 1(3):365–389.

Hareven, T. (1977) The last stage: Historical adulthood and old age. *Daedalus*. Proceedings of the American Academy of Arts and Sciences 105(4):13–28.

Laurie, W. F. (1977) The Duke OARS Methodology: Basic research and a practical application. *Center Reports on Advances in Research*, Durham, N.C.: Duke University Center for the Study of the Aging and Human Development 1(2).

Laurie, W. F. (1978) Employing the Duke OARS Methodology in cost comparisons: Home services and institutionalization. *Center Reports on Advances in Research*, 2. Durham, N.C.: Duke University Center for the Study of the Aging and Human Development.

Munnichs, J. (1977) Linkages of older people with their families and bureaucracy in a welfare state, the Netherlands. Pp. 92–116 in E. Shanas and M. B. Sussman, eds., *Family, Bureaucracy and the Elderly*. Durham, N.C.: Duke University Press.

Paillat, P. (1977) Bureaucratization of old age: Determinants of the process, possible safeguards, and reorientation. Pp. 60–74 in E. Shanas and M. B. Sussman, eds., *Family, Bureaucracy and the Elderly*. Durham, N.C.: Duke University Press.

Rosenmayr, L. (1977) The family—a source of hope for the elderly. Pp. 132–157 in E. Shanas and M. B. Sussman, eds., *Family, Bureaucracy and the Elderly*. Durham, N.C.: Duke University Press.

Ross, H. R. (1978) *How to Develop a Neighborhood Family: An Action Manual*. Miami, Florida: Northside Neighborhood Family Services.

Shanas, E. (1962) *The Health of Older People: A Social Survey*. Cambridge, Mass.: Harvard University Press.

Shanas, E. (1978) Final Report. National Survey of the Aged. A Report to the Administration on Aging.

Shanas, E. (1979) Social myth as hypothesis: The case of the family relations of old people. *The Gerontologist* 19(1):3–9.

Shanas, E., Townsend, P., Wedderburn, D., Friis, H., Milhøj, P., and Stehouwer, J. (1968) *Old People in Three Industrial Societies*. New York: Atherton Press; London: Routledge and Kegan Paul.

Shanas, E., and Sussman, M. B., eds., (1977) *Family, Bureaucracy and the Elderly*. Durham, N.C.: Duke University Press.

Siegel, J. (1976) *Demographic Aspects of Aging and the Older Population of the U.S. Current Population Reports, Special Studies*, Series P23, No. 59. Washington, D.C.: U.S. Department of Commerce.

Smyer, M. A. (1977) Differential usage and differential effects of services for impaired elderly. *Center Reports on Advances in Research*. Durham, N.C.: Duke University Center for the Study of the Aging and Human Development, 1(4).

Sussman, M. B. (1971) Family systems in the 1970s: Analysis, policies and programs. *Annals of the American Academy of Political and Social Science*. 396(July):40–56.

Sussman, M. B. (1976) The family life of old people. Pp. 218–243 in R. H. Binstock and E. Shanas, eds., *Handbook of Aging and the Social Sciences*. New York: Van Nostrand Reinhold.

Sussman, M. B. (1977) Family. Pp. 357–368 in *Encyclopedia of Social Work*. Washington, D.C.: National Association of Social Work, Inc.

Sussman, M. B. and Associates (1979) *Social and Economic Supports and Family Environments for the Elderly*, AoA Grant #90-A-316 (3), Typed Script, 142 pages and appendices.

Tunstall, J. (1966) *Old and Alone*. London: Routledge and Kegan Paul.

chapter 11

Long-Term-Care Facilities and Organization Theory: Some Research Suggestions[1]

PATRICK E. CONNOR

More than anything else, this chapter is an open letter to fellow students of organization theory. Its theme is straightforward: Although much research has been conducted and is currently under way in the broad field of aging and in the more narrow area of institionalized care, long-term-care facilities (often called simply nursing homes) are in desperate need of scientific investigation as organizations.[2]

The purpose of this chapter, therefore, is to suggest some research directions organization theorists might fruitfully take. Throughout the chapter I pose some researchable questions. Obviously, the questions do not encompass the entire field of institutionalized health care. I believe they do, however, point to a class of promising scientific problems that so far have gone unaddressed. The questions as posed are for the most part unsophisticated; but, despite their inelegance, they point to five

[1] This chapter is partly based on comments prepared for the Workshop on Stability and Change in the Family. Preparation of the bulk on the chapter was supported by Research Project Grant #11, Center for Business–Government Studies, Willamette University.

[2] There are, of course, facilities providing long-term (or extended) care that are not nursing homes. Retirement homes and homes for the aging are two examples. Frequently, however, discussion of long-term-care facilities is heavily biased toward nursing homes. Unless otherwise noted, therefore, in this chapter the term long-term-care facility refers to nursing homes.

AGING
Stability and Change in the Family

distinct foci of research interest: conceptualizing long-term-care organizations, organizational goals, organization–environment relationships, organization–individual relationships, and definitions and measurement of overall institutional effectiveness.

Many of the questions as well as the accompanying observations and comments are old hat to many of the contributors to these volumes. Gerontologists in particular have been grappling with similar issues for a long time. However, this chapter is not aimed at gerontologists. Its basic premise is, as previously stated, that long-term-care facilities can benefit from organization–theoretic analysis, and organization theorists are largely unfamiliar with the relevant analytical questions. Therefore, this chapter is aimed at organization theorists.

BACKGROUND

In the time that I have spent examining various aspects of nursing home institutions, three points have become clear. First, long-term-care facilities are extremely interesting organizations. Because they are service institutions, they tend to be much messier, analytically, than other enterprises of comparable size (on the order of 50 to 150 employees, typically). Also, they are thoroughly and inextricably connected with various environmental elements: families, many local, state, and federal agencies, community organizations, ownership of all sorts, etc.; the list could go on for several pages. This interconnectedness creates a research arena replete with ill-defined interrelationships.

Second, there is an enormous variety of disciplines involved in the study of long-term-care facilities: sociology, psychology, economics, political science, social demography, and gerontology seem to be the main ones. This variety is well represented, of course, by the contributors to these volumes of the Committee on Aging. Such variety has the obvious advantage of bringing a broad spectrum of viewpoints, analytical perspectives, and methodologies to bear on the subject matter.

Third, despite the wide variety of disciplines noted above, there is almost no research in organization theory being done in the field. Long-term-care facilities have received little analysis by organization theorists. This is unfortunate, because most observers agree that among the things that are wrong with nursing homes, generally inept management ranks very high.

A systematic examination of such organizations from the perspective of organization theory is probably a necessary prerequisite to improved management. As noted earlier, the purpose of this chapter is to suggest some directions such an examination might take.

CONCEPTUALIZING MATTERS

A representative at the national level of an industry association told me recently, "The whole field of nursing home care and management is horribly underconceptualized." This person, a man of somewhat more contemplative bent than many of the nursing home administrators I have interviewed, is concerned that much of what is done to, in, and by long-term-care facilities is based on two concepts. The first involves two contrasting views of long-term care. One, commonly called the medical model, depicts the facility's resident as a patient—a person who is sick and therefore requires medical treatment.

The common alternative to the medical model, known as the personal or social model (Wack and Rodin 1978), depicts the resident quite differently. In this conception, the resident is a person whose home—whose residence—is a long-term-care institution. The implication of this model is straightforward: The person has a variety of interests, drives, wants, and needs. Some of these may be medical, in the traditional sense of the word. Others, however, are not medical—they involve family, feelings of self-worth, community ties, and so forth.

Focusing on the long-term-care organization as the unit of analysis, the medical model promotes a study of nursing operations: the distribution of health care resources over the facility; distribution over three shifts; ambulatory versus bedridden patients, and so on. The social model, on the other hand, focuses analytical attention on such matters as support goals (Gross 1969), the nature of the organizational climate, the quality of residential life, and other dimensions not directly related to medical issues.

In short, the following questions remain open:

1. What is the facility–consumer relationship? Is the consumer a patient, as in a hospital, or a resident, as in a social community?
2. Are different conceptions of that relationship held by administrators, professional staff, consumers, and regulators?
3. Do different conceptions of that relationship produce different levels (and kinds) of health care?

There is a second concept driving analysis of long-term-care facilities. Most people involved in the industry—administrators, nursing directors, and regulators—use a bureaucratic conception of the institution. Nursing home operations are commonly described in terms of hierarchical relationships among staff, technical and administrative specialization of labor, rather clearly specified spheres of competence, explicit norms of conduct, and—it need hardly be said—formal records. Moreover, a strong theme of organizational rationality runs through this description (Weber 1958).

Organization theorists (and organization designers) face an interesting problem. On one hand, the classic bureaucratic form is relatively inappropriate to the delivery of health care. And for care of the elderly, the bureaucratic form may have deficiencies beyond the classic ones. Streib (1977), for example, has described the following charges commonly leveled against the bureaucratic form in long-term care:

- The bureaucratic organization is inaccessible. Location, hours, and psychosocial "distance" contribute to this remoteness.
- The bureaucracy by its nature tends to be cold, impersonal, even indifferent.
- The organization emphasizes efficiency and therefore is often seen as being bogged down with rules, procedures, paperwork, and red tape.

Conversely, there appears to be only slight movement in the long-term-care industry to experiment with alternative forms. As Scott says:

> the movement to provide more services to the elderly is not going to result at this time in the creation of a new round of large-scale public hospitals or long-term care facilities. On the other hand, it does not appear that current professional and organizational arrangements will support the creation of truly decentralized, family-centered service programs [1981, p. 337].

Thus we are left with the following questions:

4. What are alternative conceptualizations of long-term-care organizations?
5. What conceptualizations provide the most theoretical and empirical potential?
6. What alternative designs for organizations are available?
7. What designs have the best potential for delivering quality health care?

Robert Butler opened this workshop by remarking that "the material needs of the elderly are being met; the essential issue is a social one." For me, "social issue" implies, in part at least, social organization. The issue is how best to conceptualize the long-term-care organization. Developing effective institutions probably depends on that conceptualization.

ORGANIZATIONAL GOALS

Some time ago Scott (1966) pointed out that the construct "organizational goals" is a promising area of inquiry for health services research. At that time, he suggested that the process by which goals are established is complicated, rooted in coalition bargaining, and generally not well understood. That description is still valid today.

The notion of goals speaks to the societal function of long-term-care facilities. In particular, there are two, relatively mutually exclusive views used to characterize the goals of long-term-care facilities. Schneider (1979, p. VII-1) has described them well:

> One can raise the issue as to whether the goal . . . is really to promote good quality care or whether it is to prevent poor quality care. Kenneth Clark has said [cf. *Civilization,* Harper and Row 1969] that civilization may be impossible to define—but it is easy to recognize barbarism. Similarly, care of good quality may be beyond our present ability to define for the full range of conditions found in residential health care, or to measure by any cost effective program available. But it is easier to define specific elements of patient care that are clearly below any acceptable standard.

Goals, of course, reflect a variety of demands, bargains, and compromises, stemming from a variety of sources. Within the organization, these sources tend to be implicit or explicit interest groups or coalitions (Cyert and March 1963). Externally based demands stem from the health professions, the community within which the facility is located, and—perhaps most important—from the general public, as expressed in federal and state regulations.

Although little documentation has been produced (one exception: Schneider 1979), it is clear to me that regulations emphasize a goal of bad-care prevention. Regulations specify minimum level-of-care requirements, but welfare reimbursement rates are set in such a way that those requirements become the maximum levels that are reimbursed. The result is obvious: Long-term-care organizations provide care commensurate with their reimbursement; their *de facto* (real, or operating) goal thus becomes one of providing health care at the minimally satisfactory level, avoiding both falling below that level, for regulatory reasons, and rising above it, for resource reasons.[3]

These questions therefore arise:

[3] These comments pertain, of course, not to private, but rather to Medicare and Medicaid support. However, two-thirds to three-fourths of patients in long-term-care facilities are covered by Medicare or Medicaid.

8. What are the operating goals of long-term-care facilities, and how do they differ from those of acute-care institutions (e.g., hospitals)?
9. From where do these goals derive; that is, what are the relative impacts on goal formation by various organizational elements, such as the health professions, regulating requirements, families, and so forth?

Do goals drive actions, or do actions drive goals? Traditional organization and administrative theory has argued the former. Most people's experience, however, as well as some more recent analyses (cf. Pfeffer 1978, Connor 1980) support the latter view. Which view is more accurate for long-term-care facilities? Recently, an advocate for patients rather bitterly told me, "the profit incentive makes it attractive for the facility to keep the patient as long as feasible, with as many services and medicines as possible." If that is true, does a goal of minimal (reimbursable) care explain such action? In general, there seems to be a theoretical need to model goals–action relationships for long-term-care institutions. Organization theorists might consider the following questions:

10. What cause–effect relationships obtain among welfare reimbursement schedules and goals, policies, and actions of long-term-care facilities?
11. How are action outcomes assessed; that is, what criteria are used, and by whom, to judge goal accomplishment?

Finally, organizations pursue a variety of goals, not just those that relate to product (Perrow 1961) or output (Gross 1969). "Support" goals of various types are also important to organizational viability. Environmental adaptation, employee morale, organizational climate, and system maintenance are just a few of the nonoutput dimensions on which we typically see organization resources being spent. For long-term-care facilities, therefore, the following questions suggest themselves:

12. What relative emphases or priorities are assigned to various types of goals?
13. What priorities are reflected by actual organizational activities, that is, by actual resource expenditures?
14. Do these official and actual priority systems or "goal mixes" (Connor and Bloomfield 1977) vary among long-term-care facilities as a function of organizational size, skill level, form of ownership, or other contextual characteristics?

A discussion of organizational goals inevitably leads to an examination of organization–environmental relationships. It is to this aspect of research concerning long-term-care facilities that we now turn.

ORGANIZATIONS AND ENVIRONMENTS

As is true of all organizations, the long-term-care facility is part of a system that includes competitors, suppliers, regulators, allies, and consumers. And as is especially true of health services organizations, long-term-care facilities are intimately connected in a complex community of relationships. Patients' families, social service agencies, hospitals, transportation systems, corporate headquarters, volunteer and advocacy networks, such as the Gray Panthers—all of these groups and organizations interact on a continual basis with the facility and its various members.

There are several questions concerning the relationship of the long-term-care facility (and its quality of care) with its environment. Consider the facility that is part of a chain. Patient advocates tell me that such facility administrators are accountable to a corporate office, removed at some distance from the patient. On the other hand, say the advocates, the administrator of the small, individually owned ("mom and pop") facility is much more directly accountable to the patients and their families. The result is better care in the latter organizations.

Is this hypothesis correct? In other words, extrapolating the patient advocates' assertion a bit:

15. Do administrators use fundamentally different criteria for allocating resources and evaluating performance, as a function of the type of ownership?

Turning to the linkage between the organization and the family or community, several concerns arise. In particular, it is not clear how long-term-care organizations systematically deal with family and community interests and demands. Sussman (1977) has described four mechanisms or processes by which primary groups and formal organizations deal with each other. These he labels accommodation, contest (conflict), exchange, and options. His typology is helpful; still, some questions are suggested:

16. What mechanisms are used to effect family/community linkages with the long-term-care facility?
17. Do alternative mechanisms result in different degrees and kinds of family/community involvement?
18. Do alternative mechanismns result in different degrees and kinds of family/community commitment?
19. Do alternative mechanisms result in different degrees and kinds of patient care?

And what about the nature of the community itself? Several providers (owners and administrators) and advocates have hypothesized to me that the kind of community in which the facility is located—small, close-knit, rural versus large, socially distant, urban—has a pronounced impact on what consumers expect and demand with regard to care. To put their hypothesis into the format of a research question:

20. Do consumer demands and expectations vary in degree and kind as a function of local community characteristics?

An additional issue frequently raised in a discussion of organizational environments is that of environmental enactment. Some time ago, Weick (1969) advanced the idea that organization managers do not react to some objectively perceived environmental condition. Rather, they create their own perceptions, based on their experience, training, role, prejudices, and so forth; that is, they "enact" their environment.

Is this conception of the organizational response accurate for long-term-care facilities? There is persuasive evidence that the elderly person—the customer, if you will—is notably reluctant to initiate action vis-à-vis the organization (Moen 1978). Therefore:

21. How does the long-term-care organization "enact" a reluctant environmental element?

It is reasonable to expect, of course, that not all elderly people are reticent about taking action within the organization. Still, some consumers are no doubt more vulnerable than others and may require organizational intervention into their state. Streib (1977) has commented on this; based on his analysis, the following research questions are suggested:

22. What are the psychosocial–economic characteristics of those elderly people who require organizational intervention?
23. What are the conditions under which the family participates in this intervention? Do different conditions produce different kinds of participation?

Finally, many observers argue that long-term-care facilities are unable to match organizational resources with consumer needs. In a way, this assertion is incredible. Who ever heard of an organization surviving and prospering that did not give its customers what they wanted?

The incredulity is reduced, however, when we recognize that there are two customers. Residents, of course, are an important consumer of the organization's resources. However, the state, specifically through the reimbursement divisions of state and federal government, is another important customer. Thus we find an interesting situation in which, by most estimates, the majority of residents are not matched up with the level of care available in the facility. The obvious question arises:

24. How do specified reimbursement schedules affect otherwise natural consumer–need/organizational–service matches?

As I examine more closely the relationship between regulations and operations of long-term-care facilities (see Connor and Siebler 1979), I become increasingly convinced that reimbursement strongly affects organizational management: goal setting, boundary relationships, client interventions, and so forth. The question, of course, remains: how? In most cases, the lack of match involves a facility that has available many more and varied resources—services and programs—than the resident requires. Hence the call in many quarters today is for alternative mechanisms of extended care (adult day-care centers, for instance).

Over a decade ago, Thompson (1967) described "anticipation" as one stratagem that organizations use to protect their technical cores from environmental uncertainty. The pharmacy is a good example: The pharmacist stocks a large variety of drugs to meet virtually any demand that is presented. Is the long-term-care facility an expanded version of this same phenomenon?

Providers tell me that it is difficult to get a patient defined as requiring "skilled" nursing care and thus have his or her care reimbursed by Medicaid at the higher level. Regulators, on the other hand, tell me that there are actually very few people who require skilled care; however, they say, the provider has a great deal of money tied up in skilled staff and equipment and therefore naturally agitates to maximize the number of patients requiring skilled care. Whatever the cause, the effect is clear: Admissions of patients requiring skilled care have been declining steadily since 1973 (Shanas and Maddox 1976).

25. How do welfare reimbursement standards affect the organization's selection of strategies for managing its environmental uncertainty, especially regarding consumers?

ORGANIZATION–INDIVIDUAL RELATIONSHIPS

Gerontologists seem to know and understand a great deal about aging and its consequences for the individual (see, for example, Riley and Foner 1968, Riley et al. 1969, Binstock and Shanas 1976, Shanas and Sussman 1977). Quite a lot is also known about psychosocio–emotional relationships among elderly, their families, and their communities (and such workshops as this may stimulate continued growth in such knowledge).

Less appears to be known about the relationships between elderly people and institutions. How do institutions affect their residents; and conversely, what impacts do residents have on organizations? The purpose of this section is to pose some researchable questions that relate to these matters.

The first aspect of the organization–individual relationship I want to note concerns human values. Although values have been defined and described in a number of ways by a number of people (see Becker and Connor 1978 for a review), the following is helpful: The term *values* refers to "abstract ideals, positive or negative, not tied to any specific object or situation, representing a person's beliefs about modes of conduct and ideal terminal modes . . . [Rokeach 1968, p. 174]." In short, values may be described as a person's conception of the desirable— either desirable modes of living (instrumental values), or desirable end-states of existence (terminal values).

Thinking about individual's values raises the question of collective values. As we know, social collectivities obviously embody, reflect, and reinforce values. Presumably, different kinds of collectivities or similar kinds of collectivities in different circumstances embody, reflect, and reinforce different sets of values. And so, we have the following sorts of questions:

26. What values do patients bring to the institutional setting?
27. What values are promoted and reinforced by facility management? By the professional staff?
28. Do these "facility" values vary in any systematic way, such as by organizational size, skill level, or form of ownership?
29. Are such values related to the degree and kind of health care received by the patient?
30. Are these facility values different from those reinforced by other organizations with which the elderly deal?
31. Are they different from those embodied, reflected, and reinforced in other stages of patient's lives?
32. If such differences do exist, how do patients, their families, and long-term-care facilities manage them?

Values in and around long-term-care organizations are not the only aspect of the institutional–individual relationship worthy of study. Many behaviors may be uniquely affected by long-term-care organizations. In discussing family aspects of aging, several people have noted the importance of cooperativeness, trust, altruism, companionship, and so forth. In addition, family aspects of aging point to the importance for research on intimacy, sexuality, affection, touching, and sex (see, for example, the chapters in this volume by Whiting, Traupmann and Hatfield, Weiler, and especially Kelley).

33. How do institutional forms—processes, structural properties, and programs—facilitate and constrain these sorts of relationships?

As Kelley points out in his chapter, two-person exchange processes underlie, perhaps in a fundamental way, the marriage relationship. Similarly, multiperson exchange processes are basic to the family.

34. How do institutional forms—processes, structural properties, and programs—facilitate and constrain these sorts of exchanges?

Finally, it is evident that age cohorts are critical to meaningful demographic studies of aging and family issues. Cohorts are obvious sources and reinforcers of important values, attitudes, and bases for attributing meaning. What happens to cohorts when residential care enters the picture? And what happens to the role that cohorts play?

35. Are age cohorts important and, if so, how are they important to behaviors, values, and roles in long-term-care organizations?

To conclude this discussion: When receiving residential care, the elderly become members of organizations that have many community and familial attributes. It seems doubtful that what we know about organizations, such as from the literature on "total institutions" (e.g., Goffman 1961a, 1961b) or adult socialization (see Brim and Wheeler 1966), is sufficient to explain the relationships that develop in such organizations.

ORGANIZATIONAL EFFECTIVENESS

The final subject to be discussed here is the bottom line of organizational functioning: performance. Long-term-care facilities embody performance or effectiveness issues as much as any other type of organization. Three such issues seem interesting.

Meaning of Effectiveness

The first issue pertains to the essential meaning of effectiveness in long-term-care facilities. The view apparently held by virtually everyone connected with long-term care is that a long-term-care facility is performing its societal role satisfactorily if it is providing adequate (i.e., regulation-standard) health care to its residents.

There is no argument, of course, that the provision of appropriate health care is a critical task of long-term-care organizations. In addition, however, privately owned institutions (77% of all long-term-care facilities nationally, National Center for Health Statistics 1977) must produce an acceptable return on investment to their owners if they are to continue operating. Moreover, presumably no facility, whether private, fraternal (e.g., Odd Fellows), church, or state, is different from any other type of organization in that its continued survival and prosperity depend on its meeting support goals as well as output goals.

Providing satisfactory health care is a goal–model of organizational effectiveness; its counterpart, of course, is the natural-systems model (Gouldner 1959, Etzioni 1960). What should be the appropriate conception? In short, long-term-care facilities seem to suffer from a lack of understanding of even how to go about defining organizational effectiveness.

36. How can either a goal model or a systems model of organizational effectiveness be operationalized in long-term-care facilities, bearing in mind such complexities as "satisfactory" health care, return on investment (for some organizations), reimbursement schedules, and community demands?

Campbell has noted that in order to assess an organization's effectiveness,

> one should try to find out if the organization is internally consistent within itself, whether its resources are being distributed judiciously over a wide variety of coping mechanisms, whether it is using up resources faster than it should, and so forth [1976, p. 31].

Following his advice, several dimensions may be identified as reasonably comprising an analytically useful definition of effectiveness (see Connor 1980, Chapter 12 for discussion of these dimensions): efficiency (cost minimization, profit, productivity, turnover, etc.), quality of output (durability of the product, general excellence of the service provided), quality of the work environment (nature of the organizational climate), and organizational responsiveness (long-range adaptability to changing environmental conditions, short-range flexibility in dealing with emergencies or crises). These aspects of the construct of organization effectiveness suggest the following questions:

37. How do long-term-care facilities "score" on such dimensions compared with other health care institutions? Do these scores

vary as a function of organizational size, skill level, form of ownership, proportion of welfare patients/residents?

Values and Effectiveness

I noted earlier that human values may be a factor in the management and operation of long-term-care facilities. Are they related to organizational effectiveness? Recently, a colleague and I used Erikson's (1964) interpersonal/individualistic dimensions to measure 46 nursing home administrators' value orientations. The administrators separated into two groups relatively neatly along the two dimensions (Becker and Connor 1981).

We also asked the subjects to write an essay depicting their conception of the ideal nursing home. The results are striking: The descriptions seem to be of two basic types, following the administrators' placement on the individualistic–interpersonal dimensions. Consider the following two sample descriptions:

"IDEAL NURSING HOME"
Individualistic Value-Orientation

The ideal nursing home is a 90-bed facility located 30 miles from a metropolitan city. The community would have a university and three hospitals and would be at least 50% agribusiness-oriented. There would be at least two other good-quality homes located there. This home would be of recent construction (2–4 years old) and would be a for-profit facility.

"IDEAL NURSING HOME"
Interpersonal Value-Orientation

The ideal nursing home is intensely warm in the radiance of human love and warmth toward the members of the home and to all of those who come into contact in the home. Joy fills the air. It is a place where human needs and companionship are truly met. It is a large home, which seems as a very knitted family. There is a personal relationship between staff and residents.
There is a true beauty and love for the elderly.

It is obvious from these descriptions that these two administrators differ markedly in their conception of what an ideal nursing home organization is. Thus,

38. Do different values relate to different conceptions of organizational effectiveness? To different criteria for assessing organizational performance?

In a similar vein, are administrators' values the only ones relevant to these matters?

39. Do surveyors (inspectors) have values, and therefore conceptions and criteria, significantly different from those of administrators? How about consumers? Regulators? Legislators? Community representatives? Owners?

40. In short, what conceptions and what criteria for assessing performance in long-term-care facilities are used by what parties?

My guess is that these interest groups do have sets of values—and therefore conceptions of organizational performance and criteria for assessing it—that are significantly different from each other. Small wonder that defining and measuring effectivness has proven so difficult.

The Input–Output Problem

The third issue in organizational effectiveness that continues to haunt analysis of long-term-care facilities concerns the problem of measuring inputs (activities) rather than outputs. Consider the following example: For some time, long-term-care facilities in Oregon have been required to honor "patient rights." The measure of compliance with this requirement has been dual: (a) does the patient receive a copy of the patient-rights document; and (b) is the document posted in a "conspicuous place" in the facility. These are clear "input" measures—they measure activity (distributing/posting a document), rather than performance (actual adherence to the spirit and practice of patient rights).

This input–output problem (or process–performance problem, as most people involved with the industry term it) is well recognized by administrators, regulators, and consumers alike. The difficulty is obvious:

41. How does one measure performance in a health services facility— especially when many of the clients will not "get well" in the traditional sense of the phrase?

I have been told by federal regulation writers that attempts are currently under way to articulate regulations that emphasize outputs, or health care performance, rather than activity. How this can be done, retaining meaningful requirements to guide both operators and inspectors, remains an unsolved problem.

CONCLUDING COMMENT

Most of the questions I have posed in this chapter are amenable to empirical investigation, although not necessarily in their current form. Still, there remain some matters that are more conceptual in nature. One that should be mentioned has to do with national policy.

As many observers have noted, our cultural and scientific heritage naturally leads us to think about organizations, their design, and their performance in bureaucratic terms (see, for instance, Presthus 1965). Of ocurse, this tendency is not very original. Indeed, Moses' father-in-law, Jethro, recommended a bureaucratic organization design as a way to solve Moses' time–management problems:

> So Moses hearkened to the voice of his father-in-law, and did all he said. And Moses chose able men out of all Israel, and made them heads over the people, rulers of thousands, rulers of hundreds, rulers of fifties, and rulers of tens. And they judged the people at all seasons: the hard causes they brought unto Moses, but every small matter they judged themselves [Exodus 18, 24–26].

To be sure, since Moses' time there have been some attempts to design fundamentally new forms for formal organizations (see Galbraith 1971, 1974, Khandwalla 1977, Pfeffer 1978, Connor 1980). However, the bureaucratic paradigm is exceedingly difficult to escape. The imperatives of differentiation, specialization, and routinization are incredibly strong. It seems to me, therefore, that if we are to make a useful contribution to the study of long-term-care facilities, organization theorists will need to think especially creatively about the sorts of recommendations for organization design that we produce.

National policy regarding desired extended or residential health care, welfare reimbursement, and overall effective performance is obviously very much in flux. Organization–theoretic analysis of long-term-care institutions, and its attendant design recommendations, can contribute to an improved coherence in that policy.

ACKNOWLEDGMENTS

The support of the Center for Business–Government Studies, Willamette University and that of the center's director, Barbara Karmel, is gratefully acknowledged, as is the assistance of Jane Siebler and Verla Benson.

REFERENCES

Becker, B. W., and Connor, P. E. (1978) On the Status and Promise of Values Research. Paper presented at a meeting of the American Institute for Decision Sciences, St Louis, Missouri.

Becker, B. W., and Connor, P. E. (1981) Values of long-term-care administrators. *The Journal of Long-Term Care Administration*. Vol. IX, no. 2.

Binstock, R. H., and Shanas, E., eds. (1976) *Handbook of Aging and the Social Sciences* New York: Van Nostrand Reinhold Company.

Brim, O. G., Jr., and Wheeler, S. (1966) *Socialization After Childhood: Two Essays*. New York: John Wiley and Sons, Inc.

Campbell, J. P. (1976) Contributions research can make to our understanding of organizational effectiveness. *Organization and Administrative Sciences* 7(Spring Summer):33–44.

Connor, P. E. (1980) *Organizations: Theory and Design*. Chicago: Science Research Associates, Inc.

Connor, P. E., and Bloomfield, S. D. (1977) A goal approach to organizational design. *North-Holland/Tims Studies in the Management Sciences* 5:99–110.

Connor, P. E., and Siebler, J. (1979) Regulation, Deregulation, and Long-Term-Care Facility Management: A Preliminary Report. Paper presented at a meeting of the Gerontological Society, Washington, D.C.

Cyert, R. M., and March, J. G. (1963) *A Behavioral Theory of the Firm*. Englewood Cliffs, N.J.: Prentice-Hall, Inc.

Erikson, E. H. (1964) *Insight and Responsibility*. New York: Norton Press.

Etzioni, A. W. (1960) Two approaches to organizational analysis: A critique and a suggestion. *Administrative Science Quarterly* 5(September):257–278.

Galbraith, J. R. (1971) Designing matrix organizations. *Business Horizons* (February):29–40

Galbraith, J. R. (1974) Organization design: An information-processing view. *Interface* 4:28–36.

Goffman, E. (1961a) *Asylums*. New York: Doubleday.

Goffman, E. (1961b) On the characteristics of total institutions. In Donald Cressey, ed. *The Prison*. New York: Holt, Rinehart, Winston, Inc.

Gouldner, A. W. (1959) Organizational analysis. Pp. 400–428 in R. K. Merton, L. Broom and L. S. Cottrell, eds., *Sociology Today*. New York: Basic Books, Inc.

Gross, E. (1969) The definition of organizational goals. *British Journal of Sociology* 20(September):277–294.

Khandwalla, P. M. (1977) *The Design of Organizations*. New York: Harcourt Brace Jovanovich.

Moen, E. (1978) The reluctance of the elderly to accept help. *Social Problems* 25(3):295–303

National Center for Health Statistics (1977) *1977 National Nursing Home Survey*. Public Health Service, Health Resources Administration. Hyattsville, Md.: National Center for Health Statistics.

Perrow, C. (1961) The analysis of goals in complex organizations. *American Sociological Review* 26(December):854–866.

Pfeffer, J. (1978) *Organizational Design*. Arlington Heights, Ill.: AHM Publishing Corporation

Presthus, R. (1965) *The Organizational Society*. New York: Vintage Books.

Riley, M. W., and Foner, A., eds. (1968) *Aging and Society—Volume One: An Inventory of Research Findings*. New York: Russell Sage Foundation.

Riley, M. W., Riley, J. W., Jr., and Johnson, M. E., eds. (1969) *Aging and Society—Volume Two: Aging and the Professions*. New York: Russell Sage Foundation.

Rokeach, M. (1968) *Beliefs, Attitudes and Values*. San Francisco: Jossey-Bass.

Schneider, D. (1979) Regulation of Long Term Care in New York State—Phase I. Unpublished manuscript. School of Management, Rensselaer Polytechnic Institute, Troy, New York.

Scott, W. R. (1966) Some implications of organization theory for research in health services. *Milbank Memorial Fund Quarterly* 44(October):35–39.

Scott, W. R. (1981) Reform movements and organizations: The case of aging. Pp. 331–345 in S. B. Kiesler, J. N. Morgan, and V. Oppenheimer, eds., *Aging: Social Change*. New York: Academic Press.

Shanas, E., and Maddox, G. L., eds. (1976) *Handbook of Aging and the Social Sciences*. New York: Van Nostrand Reinhold Company.

Shanas, E., and Sussman, M. B., eds. (1977) *Family, Bureaucracy, and the Elderly*. Durham, N.C.: Duke University Press.

Streib, G. F. (1977) Bureaucracies and families: Common themes and directions for further study. Pp. 204–214 in E. Shanas and M. B. Sussman, eds. *Family, Bureaucracy, and the Elderly*. Durham, N.C.: Duke University Press.

Sussman, M. B. (1977) Family, bureaucracy, and the elderly individual: An organizational/linkage perspective. Pp. 2–20 in E. Shanas and M. B. Sussman, eds., *Family , Bureaucracy, and the Elderly*. Durham, N.C.: Duke University Press.

Thompson, J. D. (1967) *Organizations in Action*. New York: McGraw-Hill.

Wack, J., and Rodin, J. (1978) Nursing homes for the aged: The human consequences of legislation-shaped environments. *Journal of Social Issues* 34(4):6–19.

Weber, M. (1958) *From Max Weber: Essays in Sociology*. London: Oxford University Press.

Weick, K. E. (1969) *The Social Psychology of Organizing*. Reading, Mass.: Addison-Wesley.

PART III

CLOSE
RELATIONSHIPS

chapter 12

Love and Its Effect on Mental and Physical Health[1]

JANE TRAUPMANN
ELAINE HATFIELD

What do people mean by *love* and *intimacy*? How long does love last? How important is love in the lives of older Americans? Is love important for their mental and physical health? In this chapter, we will review the evidence that psychologists, social psychologists, sociologists, and experts in aging have begun to collect in an attempt to answer these questions.

DEFINITION OF TERMS: LOVE AND INTIMACY

According to Hatfield and Walster (1978, p. 9), people seem to experience two quite different forms of love—passionate love and companionate love. *Passionate love* is "a state of intense absorption in another. Sometimes lovers are those who long for their partners and for complete fulfillment. Sometimes lovers are those who are ecstatic at

[1] Preparation of this chapter was supported, in part, by a National Institute of Health Grant for Biomedical Research to the University of Wisconsin, Madison, and in part by HEW AOA Grant #90-A-1230 for multidisciplinary research on aging women awarded to the Faye McBeath Institute on Aging and Adult Life, University of Wisconsin–Madison (1977–1979).

AGING
Stability and Change in the Family

finally having attained their partner's love and momentai
fulfillment. A state of intense physiological arousal." *Comp(
is "the affection we feel for those with whom our lives
entwined."

According to a number of theorists, *intimacy* is a multi(
concept (Walster *et al.* 1978, Weiss 1977) that includes evalu
nitive, and behavioral dimensions (Huston 1974), temporal (
of relatedness (Levinger 1974), and involvement–intensity fact(
1970). Hatfield *et al.* (1979, p. 106) provide a conceptual def
intimacy: *Intimacy* is "a relationship between loving people whose liv(
are deeply entwined." They outlined seven characteristics that seem to
distinguish intimate from nonintimate relations: (1) intensity of feelings;
(2) depth and breadth of information exchange; (3) length of relationships;
(4) value of the resources exchanged; (5) variety of the resources exchanged; (6) interchangeability of resources; and (7) unit of analysis:
from "you" and "me" to "we."

Intensity of feelings.   Intimates care about one another. Liking and
passionate and companionate love between intimates are much more
intense than the affection casuals feel for one another. Perhaps not so
obvious is the fact that very often intimate affection is laced with intense
feelings of dislike or even hatred. Whatever intimates feel, they feel
intensely.

Depth and breadth of information exchange.   In casual relationships,
acquaintances usually exchange only the sketchiest of information.
Intimates generally share profound information about each other's personal histories, values, strengths and weaknesses, hopes, fears, and
idiosyncrasies.

Altman and Taylor (1973) provide a painstaking analysis of the "social
penetration" process. They observe that casuals and intimates differ
strikingly in the amount and kind of information they exchange. They
conclude that, with few exceptions, as intimacy progresses, "interpersonal exchange gradually progresses from superficial, nonintimate areas
to more intimate, deeper layers of the selves of the social actors [p. 6]."
The more intimate we are with others, the more information we are
willing to reveal to them and the more we expect them to reveal to us.
(Additional evidence in support of this contention comes from Huesmann
and Levinger 1976, Jourard 1971, Perlmutter and Hatfield 1980, Worthy
et al. 1969.)

Length of relationship.   Casual relationships are usually of short duration. Intimate relationships are expected to endure and generally do
endure over a long period of time. Toffler (1970) cites husband–wife

relationships and parent–child relationships as the most enduring of all relationships. "Til death do us part" is still our cultural ideal of intimates.

Value of resources exchanged. Casuals can please or discomfort us. Intimates can make us ecstatically happy or plunge us into blackest despair. A variety of exchange theorists have observed that as a relationship grows in intimacy, the value of the rewards and punishments a couple can give one another increases (see Aronson 1970, Huesmann and Levinger 1976, Levinger and Snoek 1972).

Many theorists have observed that intimates' rewards are especially potent. Levinger *et al.* (1970) point out that the same reward ("I'm glad I met you") is far more touching when it comes from an intimate than from a casual. In addition, intimates possess a bigger storehouse of rewards than do casuals. People are usually willing to invest far more of their resources in an intimate relationship than a casual one. Thus, intimates are able to provide their partners more valuable rewards (time, effort, intimate information, money, etc.) than are casuals.

Intimates' rewards may be unusually potent—but so are the punishments they can inflict. For example, if a stranger at a party loudly announces that I am a selfish bore, I lose little; I can dismiss his words as those of a shallow person who doesn't really know what kind of person I am. But if my best friend tells me the same thing, I would be crushed—she knows me, and *still* thinks that! Aronson (1970) put it succinctly: "Familiarity may breed reward, but it also breeds the capacity to hurt."

Finally, we should recognize that intimates command one unique and potent punishment: They can threaten to end things.

Variety of resources exchanged. Casuals exchange only a few things. Intimates generally provide one another a great variety of resources (see Donnenwerth and Foa 1974, Foa 1971, Teichman 1971, Turner *et al.* 1971).

Interchangeability of resources. Casuals tend to be limited to exchanging a narrow band of resources. If students lend their notes to their classmates every now and then, they expect to be repaid in kind when they miss a lecture. If a couple is invited to a neighbor's party, they know full well that unless they reciprocate, they will be considered antisocial and unappreciative. But exchanging invitations to parties is all they need to do unless they want the relationship to progress to a deeper level.

In contrast, intimate relationships exist in a variety of contexts. Couples have a wide range of interpersonal resources at their disposal and freely exchange one type for another. Thus, the wife who owes her husband money can pay him back in a number of ways. As Sager (1976) observed, intimates spend much of their time negotiating the terms of their relationship. (Some support for this contention comes from Donnenwerth and Foa 1974, Scanzoni 1972, Turner et al. 1971.)

The unit of analysis: From "you" and "me" to "we." Intimates, through identification with and empathy for their partners, come to define themselves as a unit—as one couple. Examples of this "we-ness" are the joy and pride a father feels at the success and happiness of his child ("That's my boy!"); the distress a wife experiences when her husband has been denied a hoped-for opportunity; the intense pleasure a lover feels while working to make his beloved happy. A variety of theorists have noted that intimates' outcomes often become entwined. Boulding (1973) presents a brilliant elucidation of his point. (Also, see Rubin 1970, Sigall and Landy 1974.)

THE ENDURANCE OF LOVE

When asked about the possibility of love and intimacy lasting over a life-span, social psychologists are negative: Passionate love is characterized by its fragility. Berscheid and Walster (1978) and Hatfield and Walster (1978) reviewed the sparse evidence that existed in 1978 and concluded: "Passionate love is a fragile flower—it wilts in time. Companionate love is a sturdy evergreen; it thrives with contact [p. 125]." Reedy and Birren (1978) would agree with this conclusion.

This conclusion was based on the flimsiest of evidence, however. Hatfield and Walster (1978) could find only two studies that explored the evolution of passionate and companionate love over time: Driscoll et al. (1972) made an intensive study of dating and newlywed college students. They found that early in their relationships, most couples were romantically (passionately?) in love. They reported that as their relationships deepened, however, their feelings began to sound less like passionate love and more like friendship and companionate love. In another study, by Cimbalo et al. (1976), couples who ranged from newlyweds to "long marrieds" were interviewed. (Unfortunately for our purposes, the longest any of these "long marrieds" had been married was 17 years.) These researchers found that the longer a couple had been married, the less passionately they loved one another. Their companionate feelings for one another remained, however.

Some social psychologists are skeptical that even companionate love can last forever. Blood and Wolfe (1960) interviewed a random sample of 900 Detroit women to determine how satisfied they were with their marriages. They found that most couples' marital satisfaction sagged steadily with the passing decades. In the first 2 years of marriage, 50% of wives were "very satisfied" with their marriages; none were notably dissatisfied. Twenty years later, only 6% were still "very satisfied"; 21% were conspicuously dissatisfied (see also Peterson and Payne 1975).

Are social psychologists' negative conclusions justified? Recently, in a series of different studies, researchers interviewed casually and steadily dating couples, newlyweds, and long marrieds about their feelings for their partners. If we examine the trends in these separate studies, it appears that passionate and companionate love may be far heartier than researchers have assumed.

Traupmann et al. (1981c) interviewed 189 college men and women who were dating someone casually or steadily. The dating couples varied in age from 17 to 28. (Their average age was 20.) On the average, they had been going together for 13 months at the time they were interviewed.

Traupmann (1978) and Utne (1978) contacted 284 couples who applied for marriage licenses in Madison, Wisconsin, from August to November 1976. They were able to interview 53 of these newlywed couples shortly after their marriages and then again a year later. At the time of the initial interview, couples had been married 3–8 months. They ranged in age from 16 to 45 (the average bride was 24, the average groom 26). The newlyweds had a variety of occupations—accountants, teachers, farmers, construction workers, and businesspeople; a few were students. Most couples had dated approximately 2 years before marrying.

Traupmann and Hatfield (1981b) contacted a random sample of 480 older women living in Madison, Wisconsin. They interviewed 106 older women about their feelings toward their husbands. Unfortunately for our purposes, they did not interview their husbands. These women ranged in age from 50 to 82. (The average age was 54.) At the time of their interviews, the women had been married from 1 to 59 years. (The average length of marriage was 33 years.)

In the studies we have just described, Traupmann et al. (1981c), Traupmann (1978), Utne (1978), and Traupmann and Hatfield (1981b) assessed couples' positive and negative feelings for one another. The researchers began by explaining what they meant by passionate versus companionate love; they then asked respondents to think back over the last 3 to 6 months and to indicate how they felt about their partners during that period. "What is the level of passionate love that you feel for your partner? That your partner feels for you? What is the level of companionate love that you feel for your partner? That your partner feels for you?" Respondents were asked to indicate their feelings on the following scale: none at all; very little; some; a great deal; a tremendous amount.

The researchers then observed to the respondents that: relationships go through stages; sometimes, for a period, one partner feels seething resentment toward his or her mate and the way he or she is treated. At other times, he or she may feel hostile or depressed. His or her partner may feel the same way. Sometimes we express these feelings, other times, we keep them inside. They asked respondents to think over the last 6 months or so and indicate the levels of resentment, hostility, and depression that they felt toward their partners and that their partners felt toward them. Again, respondents were asked to estimate their feelings on a scale from none at all to a tremendous amount.

Hatfield and Walster (1978) proposed that although passionate love

TABLE 12.1
Steadily dating Couples', Newlywed Couples', and Long Married Women's Feelings for Their Partners

Respondents		(N)	How much passionate love do you feel for your partner?	How much companionate love do you feel for your partner?	How much resentment and hostility do you feel for your partner?	How much depression do you feel about your relationship?
Study 1						
Dating couples						
Men		(70)	3.76	4.03	1.98	2.31
Women		(121)	3.80	4.19	1.98	2.34
Study 2						
Newlyweds						
(Original interview)						
Men		(53)	3.96	4.38	1.63	1.60
	S.D.		(.80)	(.81)	(.68)	(.74)
Women		(53)	3.90	4.72	1.85	1.85
	S.D.		(.69)	(.54)	(.62)	(.77)
Newlyweds						
(1 year later)						
Men		(53)	3.77	4.19	1.74	1.74
	S.D.		(.89)	(.71)	(.62)	(.79)
Women		(53)	3.60	4.57	1.93	1.85
	S.D.		(.77)	(.57)	(.83)	(.91)
F-tests[a]						
Main effect: Sex			.66	11.45***	3.29	1.71
Main effect: Time			10.48**	5.22*	1.78	.77
Interaction: Sex × Time			.56	.06	.02	.77

continued

TABLE 12.1
Continued

Respondents	(N)	How much passionate love do you feel for your partner?	How much companionate love do you feel for your partner?	How much resentment and hostility do you feel for your partner?	How much depression do you feel about your relationship?
Study 3					
Older women					
Women married					
33 years or less					
Women's guesses					
as to their					
husband's feelings	(49)	3.46	4.23	2.57	1.56
S.D.		(.90)	(.72)	(1.17)	(.73)
Women's feelings	(45–46)	3.27	4.24	2.55	1.72
S.D.		(.91)	(.68)	(1.27)	(.96)
Women married					
34 years or more					
Women's guesses					
as to their					
husband's feelings	(57)	3.15	3.96	2.56	1.58
S.D.		(1.11)	(.76)	(1.10)	(.83)
Women's feelings	(51–54)	2.98	3.98	3.06	2.44
S.D.		(.97)	(.73)	(1.03)	(.73)
F-tests[b]					
Main effect: Length of marriage		2.53	3.06*	1.03	.54

[a] d.f. = 1 and 104.
[b] d.f. = 1 and 97.
* $p<.05$
** $p<.01$
*** $p<.001$

declines precipitously over time, companionate loves does not; they took it for granted that men and women could remain friends for a lifetime.

The data from Tables 12.1 and 12.2 and Figures 12.1 and 12.2 lead us to a somewhat different conclusion—over time, both passionate love and companionate love seem to remain fairly high. Couples start out loving their partners intensely. Both steady daters and newlyweds express "a great deal" of passionate love and "a great deal" to "a tremendous amount" of companionate love for their partners. Typically, women still report feeling "some" passionate love and "a great deal"

TABLE 12.2
ANOVA for Ratings of Passionate and Companionate Love

Source	d.f.	Mean square	F
Newlywed sample			
Main effect: Sex	1	1.60	1.77
Subjects/Sex	104	.90	—
Main effect: Time	1	4.57	13.81***
Interaction: Sex × Time	1	.04	.11
Subjects/Sex × Time	104	.33	—
Main effect: Type of Love	1	44.92	62.13***
Interaction: Sex × Type of Love	1	5.90	8.16***
Subjects/Sex × Type	104	.72	—
Interaction: Time × Type of Love	1	.15	.57
Interaction: Sex × Time × Type of Love	1	.15	.57
Subjects/All	104	.27	—
Older women sample			
Main effect: Time Married	1	3.62	4.07
Subjects/Time	94	.89	—
Main effect: Type of Love	1	46.76	92.55***
Interaction: Time/Type of Love	1	.01	.01
Subjects/All	94	.51	—

* $p<.05$.
** $p<.01$.
*** $p<.001$.

of companionate love for their mates even after more than 33 years of marriage.[2] There is some decline, however. Other researchers have assumed that passionate love would decline precipitously while companionate love would remain stable over time. Our results do not support this hypothesis, however. Both passionate love and companionate love appear to decline slightly—and, more important, equally—with time (see Table 12.2).

In the newlywed sample, both passionate and companionate love decline, and decline equally, from Year 1 to Year 2 ($F = 6.65$, 1 and 104 d.f., $p < .05$). There is no evidence, however, that passionate love

[2] It is not really legitimate to compare the Traupmann et al. (1981c), the Traupmann (1978), Utne (1978), and the Traupmann and Hatfield (1981b) studies, since the samples were selected in slightly different ways (i.e., total populations versus random samples) and were run at slightly different times, albeit in the same location—Madison, Wisconsin. Although the data from these studies must be interpreted with caution, they are worth considering, since these are the only studies that have explored the evolution of passionate love and companionate love over time.

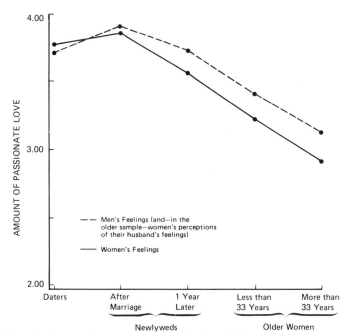

Figure 12.1.   Dating couples', newlywed couples', and older women's passionate love for their partners.

declines any more sharply than does companionate love. (Interaction F = .89, n.s.) (See Hatfield *et al.* [in preparation] for a complete analysis of these data.)

When we compare the feelings of older women, married a relatively short time (1–33 years) with those of older women married a longer time (more than 33 years) we come to exactly the same conclusion. Again, as the means suggest, both passionate love and companionate love do decline slightly from the first to the second quarter-century of marriage (F = 4.07, 1 and 94 *d.f., p* < .05). Again, there is no evidence, however, that passionate love declines any more quickly than does companionate love. (Interaction F = .01, 1 and 94 *d.f.*, n.s.)[3]

Hatfield and Walster (1978) did not speculate as to how intimates' angry or depressed feelings toward one another change with time. It appears that, over time, couples do become somewhat more angry with

---

[3] Of course, one could argue that our conclusion that love declines only slightly with time is overly optimistic. The data we are reporting come from couples whose marriages have survived. Couples who cease to love one another may well divorce at unusually high rates and thus fail to appear in our sample.

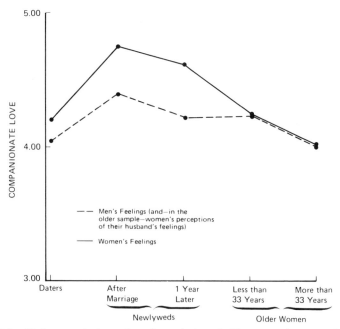

Figure 12.2. Dating couples', newlywed couples', and older women's companionate love for their partners.

one another (see Table 12.1 and Figures 12.3 and 12.4). Newlywed couples report feeling between "none" and "very little" resentment or hostility toward one another. By the time they have been married for 33 years, women express somewhat more anger at their partners—between "very little" and "some."

There is no evidence that there is a significant change in couples' resentment or hostility over time, however. When we look at the newlywed sample, we find that they do not express significantly more anger at one another during the first year of marriage ($F = 1.78$, 1 and 104 *d.f.*, n.s.). When we examine the feelings of older women, we find no evidence that women's anger at their partner increases very much from the first to the second quarter-century of marriage ($F = 1.03$, 1 and 98 *d.f.*, n.s.).

The data on feelings of depression suggest that throughout their lives men and women's intimate relationships remain laced with a small amount of depression. Newlywed couples report feelings between "very little" and "some" depression about their relationships. Older women report feeling between "none at all" and "very little" depression. There is no evidence that either newlyweds or older women's depression

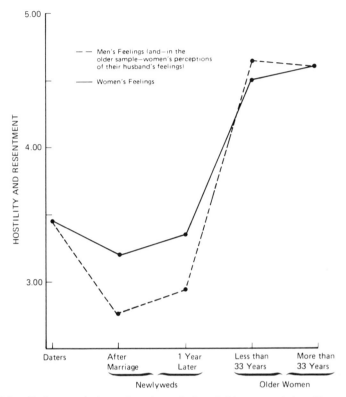

Figure 12.3.   Dating couples', newlywed couples', and older women's hostility–resentment toward their partners.

changes significantly over time. (F = 1.71, 1 and 104 $d.f.$ and .54, 1 and 98 $d.f.$, respectively.)

Overall, the data suggest that social psychologists' assumptions may have been too bleak. Some men and women believe that they stay passionately and companionately in love with their partners throughout their lives. In fact, for most couples, the prospects of love's lasting do seem to be reasonably good. The changes in feelings are small, although statistically significant.

THE IMPORTANCE OF INTIMACY TO
MENTAL AND PHYSICAL HEALTH

Intimacy is generally considered to be a basic human need (see Freud 1922, Maslow 1954). Developmental psychologists have long recognized

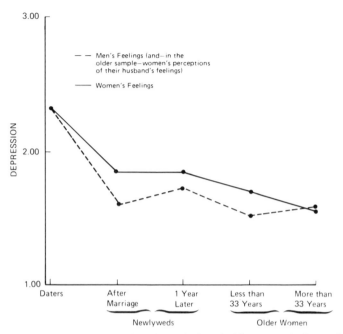

Figure 12.4. Dating couples', newlywed couples', and older women's depression toward their partners.

the importance of love (they use the term *attachment*) in the early development of humans (see Rajecki *et al.* 1978 for a comprehensive review of this literature). Harlow and Harlow's (1965) landmark research with rhesus monkeys demonstrates that contact with a soft, warm mother figure is an essential ingredient in the normal development of primates. Monkeys raised with only wire mothers were fearful, incapable of adequately dealing with stress, and unable to copulate. In the 1950s and 1960s, Bowlby's observations (1969, 1973) of institutionalized infants made it clear that human infants need intimate contact with adults—touching, stroking, hugging, cooing—in order to survive. Infants who were adequately fed but not cuddled became listless, lost weight, and eventually died. It is quite clear, then, that intimate contact is critical for infants and small children.

According to many theorists, one of the major tasks facing adults is the establishment of intimate relations with others (see, for example, Boszormenyi-Nagy 1967, Erikson 1964, Kantor and Lehr 1975, Kaplan 1978). Erikson (1964) has identified the crisis of intimacy versus isolation as the sixth essential stage of human development. Recently, Kaplan (1978) has suggested that adults spend much of their lives resolving the dilemma between their need for closeness and their need for separateness: "All . . . human love and dialogue is a striving to reconcile our longings to restore the lost bliss or oneness with our equally intense need for separateness and individual selfhood. These reconciliations are called *constancy* [p. 27]." In Kaplan's views, the need for intimacy is part of a larger developmental task—that of achieving a sense of self while establishing close nurturant relations (oneness) with others.

Our view is that the experience of a close, loving, tender relationship should make people feel better emotionally and physically on a day-to-day basis. Intimacy, reflected in passionate love, companionate love, and sexual satisfaction, should have a beneficial effect on men's and women's satisfaction with their intimate relationships and be positively related to their mental health and physical health. Figure 12.5 illustrates these interactions.

(In life, causal relations are inevitably entangled. For example, in this model, sexual satisfaction may improve physical health, but the reverse is probably also true—physical health undoubtedly predisposes or indisposes people for sexual relations. However, the simplification reflected in Figure 12.5 is a necessary beginning step in the study of an extremely complex phenomenon.)

Is there any evidence that intimacy is critically important for the physical and mental health of older Americans? Some.

Traupmann *et al.* (1981a) provide some evidence that intimacy may have a critical impact on the mental and physical health of older Americans. As part of a multidisciplinary study of aging women, Traupmann *et al.* interviewed a random sample of 240 women living in five areas of the city of Madison, Wisconsin, in June 1978. The women ranged in age from 50 to 82.

Overall, this group was slightly better off than is the typical older American woman. Their median annual income was approximately $2000 higher than the median income of all older women. The respondents

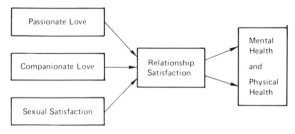

Figure 12.5. Hypothetical relationship between love and mental and physical health: I. (From Traupmann *et al.* 1981a.)

were very highly educated compared with national averages for women in this age group. (There were about 15 women with master's degrees and three with Ph.D.s in the group of 240.) Most of them (over 75%) reported being in very good health. They were a surprisingly physically active group, with 75% reporting that they get some regular physical exercise every day. About one-third of them were working either part-time or full-time.

The 240 women in the sample were asked to describe the most important person in their lives. If the relationship they described were a sexual one, whether or not it was with their husband, they received the intimacy questions; these are the questions on which the data below are based. Of the 240 women, 106 reported an ongoing sexual relationship. For most of these women, it was with their husband; for a few it was with a spouse equivalent. Demographically, they differed very little from the larger group of 240, except in age. The oldest in the sexually active group was 82.

Traupmann et al. (1981a) were interested in the relationship of intimacy and a wide array of other variables to mental and physical health. They proposed a model of this relationship (see Figure 12.6).

The authors assessed the independent variables in a straightforward way: Passionate love and companionate love were assessed as indicated earlier, simply by asking respondents how passionately and companionately they loved their partners. Sexual satisfaction was assessed via two questions: The women were asked how loving and close and how sexually satisfied they felt immediately after a sexual encounter.

Relationship satisfaction was assessed via two questions: Women were asked how satisfied and how happy they were with their relationships.

The authors measured three dependent variables: Satisfaction with life in general, mental health, and physical health. The women's satisfaction with life was assessed via two questions: Women were asked how satisfied and how happy they were with their lives in general. Mental

Figure 12.6. Hypothetical relationships between love and mental and physical health: II. (From Traupmann et al. 1981a.) Asterisks refer to the following p values: * = .05; ** = .01; *** = .001.

health was assessed via a modified version of the Derogatis (1977) SCL-90 Symptoms Check List.[4]

Physical health was assessed by asking women how good their health had been in the preceding year.

Several control variables identified in previous research as important in determining life satisfaction and mental health (see Larson 1978, Pearlin and Johnson 1977)—that is, education, income, respondents' age, spouse's age, and health—were assessed. The authors found only one control variable to be important: financial worry.

Results

What are the components of relationship satisfaction? Passionate love, companionate love, and sexual satisfaction. Traupmann *et al.* found that each of these three components plays an important role in determining the quality of women's close relationships (see Figure 12.6). Passionate love, an intense emotional experience, usually associated with new romance, remains a significant component of older women's intimate lives ($r = .390$, $p < .001$). Though most of these women have been married for more than 30 years, feelings of passionate love still play a role. Companionate love, a more low-keyed emotion, also appears to contribute significantly to the quality of intimacy ($r = .427$, $p < .001$). Finally, the sexual satisfaction these women experience with their partner remains a strong, significant component of the overall satisfaction with their intimate relationship ($r = .376$, $p < .001$). Though about a third of the women refused to answer any questions about their sexuality, those who did felt that sex played a very important role.

To what extent is intimacy related to psychological well being? The results suggest that intimacy is an extremely important contributor to psychological well-being. The correlation between relationship satisfaction and psychological well-being was $-.406$ ($p < .001$). The negative correlation indicates that with an increase in happiness and satisfaction in their relationship, there is a decrease in the number of symptoms of depression, anxiety, and self-consciousness. Thus, as predicted, the quality of intimacy seems to serve as a protection against the depression and anxiety often experienced by middle-aged and older women.

---

[4] This scale consisted of a symptoms checklist for three of nine Derogatis symptom constructs: Anxiety, Depression, and Interpersonal Sensitivity. It was developed by Dr. Marjorie Klein of the Psychiatry Department at the University of Wisconsin specifically for this research.

The results also suggest that women's satisfaction with their intimate relationship is extremely important to their overall sense of well-being. Satisfaction with one's intimate relationships correlated .74 ($p < .001$) with overall life satisfaction (see Figure 12.6). On the average, women were very satisfied with their intimate relationship ($X = 7.23$) and also with their lives in general ($X = 7.02$).

To what extent is the satisfaction women experience in their intimate relationship related to physical health? As can be seen in Figure 12.2, the correlation between how happy they were with their intimate life and how healthy women felt was .239 ($p < .01$). Though the relationship is not so strong as the others, it is remarkably high, considering the many other factors that affect physical health in later life.[5]

Previous literature in aging suggested that the existence of an intimate other is critically important in securing mental and physical health. These data suggest that not merely the existence of an intimate relationship, but the quality of that relationship is an important determinant of mental and physical well-being.

Other Evidence on the Importance of Intimacy

The data from Traupmann *et al.* (1981a) suggest that intimacy is a major concern of adults throughout their lives. Other evidence from several sources buttresses that contention.

Recently, researchers have begun to accumulate additional evidence that suggests that intimacy and mental health may be linked. For example, Larson (1978) and George (1978) found that marriage is critically important in helping older Americans maintain a feeling of subjective well-being. Married people have a lower rate of mental illness than do single people (see Briscoe and Smith 1974, Leff *et al.* 1970, Troll *et al.* 1979).

Brown *et al.* (1975) found that a woman who had a husband or boyfriend who acted as a confidant found it far easier to weather a traumatic event. After an intensely stressful event, only 4% of women having an intimate confidant became psychologically disturbed; 38% of women without confidants did. (Similar results were reported by Lowenthal and Havens 1968.) The loss of a marital partner makes one particularly susceptible to problems. Maddison and Viola (1968), Marris (1958), and

---

[5] As we indicated earlier, these are correlational data. We think it is most likely that intimacy helps maintain mental and physical health. It is of course possible that the relationship works the opposite way—that it is necessary to have good mental and physical health in order to sustain an intimate relationship.

Parkes (1964) found that the newly bereaved were especially likely to have mental problems. A few researchers have suggested that intimacy and mental health might be more strongly correlated for men than for women (see Bernard 1972, Gove 1972).

There is also some evidence that intimacy contributes to the perceived quality of life. People who have someone to share their ideas and feelings with, someone to help them deal with day-to-day problems, are happier than those who do not (see Binstock and Shanas 1976, Birren and Schaie 1977, Cavan 1973, McKain 1969). In a recent review article, Brown and Felton (1978) conclude that a network of close interpersonal ties promotes general life satisfaction and a sense of belonging, worth, and identity. They, too, argue that it is the quality of the individual's interpersonal relationships that is intimately related to well-being.

Recently, researchers have begun to collect data that indicate that intimacy may be related to physical health and longevity. In particular, there appear to be connections between intimacy and the ability to handle stress. According to health statistics, married people are less vulnerable to a long list of diseases and physically disabling conditions than are their peers (Butler 1979, Carter and Glick 1976, Eisenberg 1979, Lynch 1977, National Center for Health Statistics 1976, Somers 1979, Syme 1974). It has repeatedly been observed that those who are married have lower mortality rates than those who are single, widowed, or divorced (Ortmeyer 1974, Price *et al.* 1971).

A supportive marriage seems to increase ability to cope with stressful life events (such as job loss) and to help one avoid psychosomatic symptoms (Cobb 1976, Gore 1978, Kaplan *et al.* 1977, Lowenthal *et al.* 1967, Weiss 1977). In one study of the health consequences of job loss due to factory shutdown, Gore (1978) found that men who had the emotional support of their wives while unemployed had lower cholesterol levels and fewer illness symptoms than did their peers.

The loss of a marital partner is an especially threatening event. Widowhood is tightly linked to increased morbidity and mortality rates. Maddison and Viola (1968), Marris (1958), and Parkes (1964) found that widows have an unusually large number of complaints about their health—especially in the first year following their bereavement.

There is substantial evidence that surviving spouses are at increased risk for death from a variety of diseases (see Berkman and Syme 1979, Clayton 1974, Cox and Ford 1964, Gerber *et al.* 1975, Jacobs and Ostfeld 1977, Kraus and Lillienfeld 1959, Maddison and Viola 1968, Marris 1958, McNeil 1973, Parkes 1964, Rees and Lutkin 1967, Ward 1976, Young *et al.* 1963).

For example, Parkes (1964) found that 213 of 4486 widowers, 55 years of age and older, died within the first 6 months of their bereavement.

This is 40% above the expected rate for that age group. After 6 months, the rates gradually fell back to normal levels. Jacobs and Ostfeld (1977) report that the bereaved are at risk for coronary heart disease and cirrhosis.

In a recent review of the literature on bereavement, Jacobs and Ostfeld (1977) report that, initially, men are harder hit than are women by a spouse's death. However, men remain at risk for only 6 months; women for 2 years. The degree of risk for widowed persons is aggravated by preexisting health problems.

Satariano and Syme (1981) speculate that the stress of bereavement may elevate the risk of death in several ways. It may lead to depression, and the depressed spouse may then neglect his or her own health practices and/or health condition (Belloc 1973, McGlone and Kick 1978). In extreme cases, the depression may lead to drug abuse and/or suicide (Schuckit 1977, Sendbuehler and Goldstein 1977). The stress also may lead to dysfunctions in neuroendocrine balance and, in turn, a reduction in immunity to disease (Timiras 1972).

Haynes *et al.* (1978) found that, among older men and women, marital dissatisfaction and/or marital disagreement were associated with coronary heart disease.

Of course, these data are correlational and must not be interpreted as establishing a casual relationship. Nevertheless, they do suggest that intimacy may be a critical factor in people's lives.

CONCLUSION

In this chapter we reviewed research that indicates that, although for a few couples love does last a lifetime, for most couples passionate and companionate love continue to decline with the passage of time. We then reviewed evidence from a variety of sources that suggests that intimacy may well be critically important in fostering mental and physical health.

Of course, any collection of research always stimulates more questions than it answers. What kinds of people end up with a good relationship? Why are intimacy and mental and physical health so apparently tightly linked? Are passionate and companionate love of differential importance at different stages in a relationship? How important is sex? Does intimacy promote health, or vice versa? How does intimacy promote health? Do those with mates have happier lives? Do they encounter less stress than do others, or is it merely that they have a ready source of help in times of trouble? Is it important to have a mate or would a good neighbor do as well? Are the changes in couples' love for one another over time inevitable consequences of age or simply a reflection of historical change in the importance of love versus practicality as the basis of marriage? We have answered a few questions, but more remain to be explored.

REFERENCES

Altman, I., and Taylor, D. A. (1973) *Social Penetration: The Development of Interpersonal Relationships*. New York: Holt, Rinehart, Winston.

Aronson, E. (1970) Some antecedents of interpersonal attraction. In W. J. Arnold and D. Levine, eds., *Nebraska Symposium on Motivation*. Lincoln: University of Nebraska Press.

Belloc, N. (1973) Relationship of health practices and mortality. *Preventive Medicine* 2:67–81.

Berkman, L. F., and Syme, S. L. (1979) Social networks, host resistance, and mortality: A nine-year follow-up study of Alameda County residents. *American Journal of Epidemiology* 109:186–204.

Bernard, J. (1972) *The Future of Marriage*. New York: World Publishing Co.

Berscheid, E., and Walster, E. (1978) *Interpersonal Attraction*, 2nd ed. Reading, Mass.: Addison-Wesley.

Binstock, R. H., and Shanas, E. (1976) *Handbook of Aging and the Social Sciences*. New York: Van Nostrand Reinhold.

Birren, J. E., and Schaie, K. W. (1977) *Handbook of Psychology*. New York: Van Nostrand Reinhold.

Blood, R. O., and Wolfe, D. M. (1960) *Husbands and Wives: The Dynamics of Married Living*. Glencoe, Ill.: Free Press.

Boszormenyi-Nagy, I. (1967) Relational modes and meaning. In G. H. Zik and I. Boszormenyi-Nagy, eds., *Family Therapy and Disturbed Families*. Palo Alto, Calif.: Science and Behavior Books.

Boulding, K. E. (1973) *The Economy of Love and Fear*. Belmont, Calif.: Wadsworth Publishing.

Bowlby, J. (1969) *Attachment and Loss*, Vol. 1. New York: Basic Books.

Bowlby, J. (1973) Affectional bonds: Their nature and origin. In R. W. Weiss, ed., *Loneliness: The Experience of Emotional and Social Isolation*. Cambridge, Mass.: The M.I.T. Press.

Briscoe, C. W., and Smith, J. B. (1974) Psychiatric illness: Marital units and divorce. *Journal of Nervous and Mental Disease* 158:440–445.

Brown, G. W., Brolchain, M. N., and Harris, T. (1975) Social class and psychiatric disturbance among women in an urban population. *Sociology* 9:225–254.

Brown, P., and Felton, B. J. (1978) Coping with marital disruption in later life: Use of social supports by men and women. Paper presented at the American Ortho-Psychiatric Association meeting, San Francisco.

Butler, R. (1979) Introductory comments presented at the workshop on Stability and Change in the Family. Sponsored by the Committee on Aging, Assembly of Behavioral and Social Sciences, National Research Council.

Carter, H., and Glick, P. C. (1976) *Marriage and Divorce: A Social and Economic Study*. Cambridge, Mass.: Harvard University Press.

Cavan, R. S. (1973) Speculations on innovations to conventional marriage in old age. *The Gerontologist* 13:409–411.

Cimbalo, R. S., Faling, V., and Mousaw, P. (1976) The course of love: A cross-sectional design. *Psychological Reports* 38:1292–1294.

Clayton, P. J. (1974) Mortality and morbidity in the first year of widowhood. *Archives of General Psychiatry* 30:747–750.

Cobb, S. (1976) Social support as a moderator of life stress. *Psychosomatic Medicine* 38(5):300–314.

Cox, P. R., and Ford, J. R. (1964) The mortality of widows shortly after widowhood. *Lancet* 1:163.

Donnenwerth, G. V., and Foa, U. G. (1974) Effect of resource class on retaliation to injustice interpersonal exchange. *Journal of Personality and Social Psychology* 29:785–793.

Driscoll, R., Davis, K. E., and Lipetz, M. E. (1972) Parental interference and romantic love: The Romeo and Juliet effect. *Journal of Personality and Social Psychology* 24:1–10.

Eisenberg, L. (1979) A friend, not an apple, a day will keep the doctor away. *The American Journal of Medicine* 66:551–553.

Erikson, E. H. (1964) *Childhood and Society*. New York: Norton.

Foa, U. G. (1971) Interpersonal and economic resources. *Science* 171:345–351.

Freud, S. (1922) *Group Psychology and the Analysis of the Ego*. London: Hogarth.

George, L. K. (1978) The impact of personality in social status factors upon levels of activity and psychological well-being. *Journal of Gerontology* 33:840–847.

Gerber, I., Rusualen, R., Hannon, N., Battin, D., and Arkin, A. (1975) Anticipatory grief and widowhood. *British Journal of Psychiatry* 122:47–51.

Gore, S. (1978) The effect of social support in moderating the health consequences of unemployment. *Journal of Health and Social Behavior* 19:157–165.

Gove, W. R. (1972) Sex, marital status, and suicide. *Journal of Health and Social Behavior* 13(2):204–213.

Harlow, H. F., and Harlow, M. K. (1965) The affectional systems. In A. Schrier, H. F. Harlow, and T. Stollnitz, eds., *Behavior of Non-Human Primates*, Vol. 2. New York: Academic Press.

Hatfield, E., Nerenz, D., Greenberger, D., and Lambert, P. (in preparation) Passionate and companionate love in newlywed couples: Changes over time.

Hatfield, E., Utne, M. K., and Traupmann, J. (1979) Equity theory and intimate relationships. Pp. 99–103 in R. L. Burgess and T. L. Huston, eds., *Social Exchange in Developing Relationships*. New York: Academic Press.

Hatfield, E., and Walster, G. W. (1978) *A New Look at Love*. Reading, Mass.: Addison-Wesley.

Haynes, S. G., Feinleib, M., Levine, S., Scotch, N., and Kannel, W. B. (1978) The relationship of psychosocial factors to coronary heart disease in the Framingham Study, II prevalence of coronary heart disease. *American Journal of Epidemiology* 197:385–402.

Huesmann, L. R., and Levinger, G. (1976) Incremental exchange theory: A formal model for progression in dyadic social interaction. In L. Berkowitz and E. Walster, eds., Equity theory: Toward a general theory of social interaction. *Advances in Experimental Social Psychology* 9:191–220.

Huston, T. (1974) *Foundations of Interpersonal Attraction*. New York: Academic Press.

Jacobs, S., and Ostfeld, A. (1977) An epidemiological review of the mortality of bereavement. *Psychosomatic Medicine* 39:344–357.

Jourard, S. M. (1971) *Self-Disclosure*. New York: Wiley.

Kantor, D., and Lehr, W. (1975) *Inside the Family*. San Francisco: Jossey-Bass.

Kaplan, B. H., Cassel, J. C., and Gore, S. (1977) Social support and health. *Medical Care* 15(5):47–58.

Kaplan, L. J. (1978) *Oneness and Separateness: From Infant to Individual*. New York: Simon and Schuster.

Kraus, A. S., and Lilienfeld, A. M. (1959) Some epidemiologic aspects of the high mortality rate in the young widowed group. *Journal of Chronic Diseases* 10:207–217.

Larson, R. (1978) Thirty years of research on the subjective well-being of older Americans. *Journal of Gerontology* 33(1):109–125.

Leff, M. J., Roatch, J. R., and Bunney, W. E. (1970) Environmental factors preceding the onset of severe depression. *Psychiatry* 33:293–311.

Levinger, G. (1974) A three-level approach to attraction: Toward an understanding of pair-relatedness. In T. Huston, ed., *Foundations of Interpersonal Attraction*. New York: Academic Press.

Levinger, G., Senn, D. J., and Jorgensen, P. W. (1970) Progress toward permanence in courtship: A test of Kerckhoff-Davis Hypotheses. *Sociometry* 33:427–443.

Levinger, G., and Snoek, J. D. (1972) *Attraction in Relationships: A New Look at Interpersonal Attraction*. Morristown, N.J.: General Learning Press.

Lowenthal, M. F., Berkman, P. L., and Associates (1967) *Aging and Mental Disorder in San Francisco; A Psychiatric Study*. San Francisco: Jossey-Bass.

Lowenthal, M. F., and Havens, C. (1968) Interaction and adaptation: Intimacy as a critical variable. *American Sociological Review* 33:20–31.

Lynch, J. J. (1977) *The Broken Heart: The Medical Consequences of Loneliness*. New York: Basic Books.

Maddison, D., and Viola, A. (1968) The health of widows in the year following bereavement. *Journal of Psychosomatic Resources* 12:297–306.

Marris, R. (1958) *Widows and Their Families*. London: Routledge and Kegan Paul.

Maslow, A. H. (1954) *Motivation and Personality*. New York: Harper.

McGlone, F. B., and Kick, E. (1978) Health habits in relation to aging. *Journal of the American Geriatrics Society* 26:481–488.

McKain, W. (1969) *Retirement Marriage*. Storrs, Conn.: Storrs Agricultural Experiment Station Monograph.

McNeil, D. N. (1973) Mortality Among the Widowed in Connecticut. MPH essay, Yale University.

National Center for Health Statistics (1976) *Differentials in Health Characteristics by Marital Status: United States, 1971–1972*. Vital and Health Statistics, Series 10, No. 104. Washington, D.C.: U.S. Government Printing Office.

Ortmeyer, C. (1974) Variations in mortality, morbidity, and health care by marital status. Pp. 159–188 in C. F. Erhardt and J. E. Berlin, eds., *Mortality and Morbidity in the United States*. Cambridge, Mass.: Harvard University Press.

Parkes, C. M. (1964) The effects of bereavement on physical and mental health: A study of the medical records of widows. *British Medical Journal* 2:274–279.

Pearlin, L. I., and Johnson, J. S. (1977) Marital status, life-strains and depression. *American Sociological Review* 42:704–715.

Perlmutter, M., and Hatfield, E. (1980) Intimacy, intentional metacommunication and second-order change. *American Journal of Family Theory* 8:17–23.

Peterson, J. A., and Payne, B. (1975) *Love in the Later Years*. New York: Association Press.

Price, J. S., Slater, E., and Hare, E. H. (1971) Marital status of first admissions to psychiatric beds in England and Wales in 1965 and 1966. *Social Biology* 18:574–594.

Rajecki, D. W., Lamb, M. E., and Obmascher, P. (1978) Toward a general theory of infantile attachment: A comparative review of aspects of the social bond. *The Behavioral and Brain Sciences* (1).

Reedy, M. N., and Birren, J. E. (1978) How Do Lovers Grow Older Together? Types of

Lovers and Age. Paper presented at the National Gerontological Society Meeting, Dallas, Texas.

Rees, W. D., and Lutkins, S. G. (1967) Mortality of bereavement. *British Medical Journal* 4:13–16.

Rubin, Z. (1970) The measurement of romantic love. *Journal of Personality and Social Psychology* 16:265–273.

Sager, C. (1976) *Marriage Contracts and Couple Therapy*. New York: Brunner/Mazel.

Satariano, W. A., and Syme, S. L. (1981) Life changes and disease in elderly populations: Coping with change. In J. L. McGaugh and S. B. Kiesler, eds., *Aging: Biology and Behavior*. New York: Academic Press.

Scanzoni, J. (1972) *Sexual Bargaining: Power Politics in the American Marriage*. Englewood Cliffs, N.J.: Prentice-Hall.

Schuckit, M. A. (1977) Geriatric alcoholism and drug abuse. *The Gerontologist* 17:168–174.

Sendbuehler, J. M., and Goldstein, S. (1977) Attempted suicide among the aged. *Journal of the American Geriatric society* 25:245–253.

Sigall, H., and Landy, D. (1974) Beauty is talent: Task evaluation as a function of the performer's physical attractiveness. *Journal of Personality and Social Psychology* 29:299–304.

Somers, A. R. (1979) Marital status, health and use of health services: An old relationship revisited. *Journal of the American Medical Association* 241(17):1818–1822.

Syme, S. L. (1974) Behavioral factors associated with the etiology of physical disease: A social epidemiological approach. *American Journal of Public Health* 64:1043–1045.

Teichman, M. (1971) Satisfaction from Interpersonal Relationship Following Resource Exchange. Unpublished doctoral dissertation, University of Missouri at Columbia.

Timiras, P. S. (1972) *Developmental Physiology and Aging*. New York: Macmillan.

Toffler, A. (1970) *Future Shock*. New York: Bantam.

Traupmann, J. (1978) Equity and Intimate Relations: An Interview Study of Marriage. Unpublished doctoral dissertation, University of Wisconsin, Madison.

Traupmann, J., Eckels, E., and Hatfield, E. (1981a) Intimacy in later adult life. Submitted to *The Gerontologist*.

Traupmann, J., and Hatfield, E. (1981b) How important is marital fairness over the lifespan? Submitted to *The International Journal of Aging and Human Development*.

Traupmann, J., Hatfield, E., and Wexler, P. (1981c) Equity and sexual satisfaction in dating couples. *Archives of Sexual Behavior*.

Troll, L. E., Miller, S. J., and Atchley, R. C. (1979) Older couples. Pp. 39–68 in *Families in Later Life*. Belmont, Calif.: Wadsworth Publishing Company.

Turner, J. L., Foa, E. B., and Foa, U. G. (1971) Interpersonal reinforcers: Classification in a relationship and some differential properties. *Journal of Personality and Social Psychology* 19:168–180.

Utne, M. K. (1978) Equity and Intimate Relations: A Test of the Theory in Marital Interaction. Unpublished doctoral dissertation, University of Wisconsin, Madison.

Walster (Hatfield), E., Walster, G. W., and Berscheid, E. (1978) *Equity: Theory and Research*. Boston, Mass.: Allyn and Bacon.

Ward, A. W. (1976) Mortality of bereavement. *British Medical Journal* 1:700–702.

Weiss, L. (1977) Intimacy: An Intervening Factor in Adaptation. Paper presented at the 30th annual scientific meeting of the Gerontological Society, San Francisco.

Worthy, M., Gary, A. L., and Kahn, G. M. (1969) Self-disclosure as an exchange process. *Journal of Personality and Social Psychology* 13:63–69.

Young, M., Benjamin, B., and Wallis, C. (1963) The mortality of widows. *Lancet* 2:454–457.

chapter 13

Marriage Relationships and Aging[1]

HAROLD H. KELLEY

This chapter first presents a view of interpersonal relations derived from the author's recent research and theoretical analysis. The chapter then outlines some of the implications of this view for the changes that might be expected to occur in marriage relationships as their participants become advanced in age. In analyzing the family from an interpersonal perspective, it is appropriate to focus on the husband and wife. In various compelling ways, their relationship marks the beginning and ending of the nuclear family unit. Their relationship is usually the hub around which the rest of the family structure revolves. This focus does not preclude attention to the various other relationships of the marriage partners, with children, kin, work associates, and friends. This analysis of the husband and wife dyad must necessarily take account of its social context and the impact on the marital relationship of age-related changes in that context.

The husband–wife relationship can be viewed in many ways, but from a social–psychological perspective, it must be regarded as a close personal relationship (i.e., as a relationship that is both close and personal).

[1] Preparation of this manuscript was facilitated by National Science Foundation Grant BNS-76-20490.

AGING
Stability and Change in the Family

The two adjectives are used to emphasize that these relationships exist at two levels. To understand them and anticipate how age will affect them, we must consider changes at each level and in the linkage between the two levels.

The two levels, shown in Figure 13.1, are levels at which the husband and wife are interdependent, that is, in control of each other's outcomes—rewards, satisfactions versus costs, dissatisfactions. At what Thibaut and I refer to as the given level, the husband and wife are interdependent in outcomes that are direct and concrete, and they control these outcomes, individually and jointly, through the specific behaviors they enact (Kelley and Thibaut 1978). The given level of interdependence is illustrated by the ways in which each person's outcomes depend on the money, compliments, information, services, and companionship the other provides. At the dispositional level, the husband and wife are interdependent in terms of more symbolic and abstract outcomes, and they control these outcomes by the interpersonal attitudes and values they display. The dispositional level of interdependence is illustrated by the ways in which each person's outcomes depend on the attitudes of love, concern, dominance, and competitiveness the partner displays. As the figure shows and as will be explained, these two levels of interdependence are interlinked in systematic ways, the upper level being derivative from the lower one and the lower one being governed by the upper one. This is not simply a distinction between qualitatively different types of satisfaction and dissatisfaction that exist within interpersonal relationships. It is a theory about the basis of that distinction and about the dynamic processes it implies.

To describe the husband–wife relationship as close is to refer to the fact that they are highly interdependent at the given level (i.e., in the specific things they do and in the direct and concrete consequences of

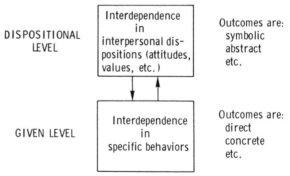

Figure 13.1.   The two levels of interdependence.

their actions). To describe their relationships as personal is to refer to the fact that they are also highly interdependent at the dispositional level (i.e., in the interpersonal attitudes and traits they express and in the abstract or symbolic consequences of these expressions). Relationships become personal when the interpersonal attitudes become important. Relationships may be relatively close without becoming personal. However, relationships that are not close are not likely to become personal.

We may now consider each of these two aspects of the husband–wife relationship in more detail.

MARRIAGE AS A CLOSE RELATIONSHIP

The specific meaning and implications of closeness can be explained by considering the major properties of all interpersonal relationships and then determining how the typical marriage can be characterized in terms of those properties. We may begin with an examination of the properties of interdependence at the given level. Theoretical analysis of the dyad, conducted by means of the payoff or outcome matrix (Kelley and Thibaut 1978), reveals that the given interdependence between two people varies with respect to the following four properties:

1. *Degree of interdependence*: The extent to which each person's satisfaction is dependent on the partner's actions or on their joint actions.
2. *Equal versus unequal dependence:* Given that each person is dependent on the other to some degree, it is possible for the dependence to be equal between the two, or unequal—one person being more dependent than the other.
3. *Commonality versus conflict of interests*: In some dyads, the two persons have common interests: The actions that benefit or satisfy one person tend also to benefit or satisfy the partner. In other dyads the two persons have conflicts of interest about what they, individually and jointly, might do. Most dyads have mixtures of convergent and divergent interests. For example, there may be a common interest in the success of the dyad per se but a conflict of interest about how the resources gained by the dyad will be divided between the two. In these "mixed" cases (often referred to as mixed-motive relationships), the two persons face the complex problem of working together out of concern for their common success while at the same time working "against" each other out of concern for their individual interests.

4. *Dependence on individual versus joint action*: In some dyads, each person depends primarily on what the partner does individually (e.g., on what the partner provides in the way of services and resources). In other dyads, each person depends primarily on what the two do jointly (e.g., on their companionship, joint leisure activities, and coordinated efforts).

The first three of these theoretically derived properties of the dyad are empirically confirmed by a multidimensional scaling study of some 40 interpersonal relationships, reported by Wish, Deutsch, and Kaplan (1976). Their results are also very useful for our present purpose, which is to highlight the properties of the husband–wife relationship. These investigators had their subjects rate a number of kinds of dyads (e.g. close friends, siblings, husband and wife, business rivals, teammates) on a number of semantic differential scales. The results were analyzed by the method of multidimensional scaling known as INDSCAL (Carrol and Chang 1970), which revealed the basic distinctions among the dyads that were implicit in the subjects' ratings.

The analysis yielded four dimensions, three of which are shown in Figure 13.2. The first dimension, "equal versus unequal," is best defined by ratings on "exactly equal power versus extremely unequal power." At the *equal* extreme are the relationships of close friends and business partners (identified in the figure as 1 and 2, respectively) and at the *unequal* extreme, master and servant and parent and child (identified as 3 and 4, respectively, in the figure). Inasmuch as differences in power are closely linked to differences in dependence, discussed shortly, this first dimension corresponds to the theoretical property of equal versus unequal dependence.

The second dimension, "cooperative and friendly versus competitive and hostile," is best defined by ratings on "always harmonious versus always clashing" and "compatible versus incompatible goals and desires." At the *cooperative* extreme are close friends (1) and at the *competitive* extreme are business rivals (5) and personal enemies (6). This dimension clearly corresponds to the theoretically derived property of commonality versus conflict of interest.

The third dimension, "intense versus superficial," is best defined by ratings on "very active versus very inactive" and "intense versus superficial interaction with each other." At the *intense* extreme are husband and wife (7), close friends (1), and parent–child (4) and at the *superficial* extreme are casual acquaintances (8). This dimension corresponds to the theoretical property of degree of interdependence, the intense relationships being ones of high interdependence.

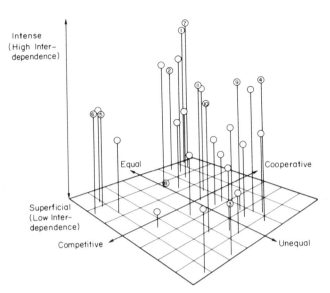

Figure 13.2. The locations of various dyadic relationships in the three-dimensional space. (From M. Wish, M. Deutsch, and S. J. Kaplan, Perceived dimensions of interpersonal relations. *Journal of Personality and Social Psychology* 33:409–420. Copyright 1976 by the American Psychological Association. Reprinted by permission.)

In the three-dimensional space shown in Figure 13.2, we see that the marriage dyad (husband and wife) is located in the intense, cooperative, and equal corner of the three-dimensional space, as shown by the point labeled 7. It is the most intense of the various dyads included in the study, although not quite the most "cooperative" or the most "equal." Clustered very close to it (though not shown in the figure) are also the relationship between fiancé and fiancée and between respondent and respondent's spouse (about half the respondents were married).

We may now see what it means to describe the marriage as "close." It is a relationship of high interdependence. This interdependence is reflected in intense activity and interaction between the husband and wife. This is the essence of closeness. From the evidence summarized in Figure 13.2, we also see that the typical husband–wife relationship was judged by Wish, Deutsch, and Kaplan's respondents to be equal and cooperative. This reflects in part a fact of social life and, in part, an idealized view of marriage. The "fact" is really an hypothesis: Voluntary relationships do not become highly interdependent unless they are moderately cooperative and equal. The Wish, Deutsch, and Kaplan data (not all of which are plotted in Figure 13.2) show that the intense voluntary relationships occur in the extreme cooperative–equal corner of the space.

The intense relationships located elsewhere (e.g., parent and child (4), respondent's mother and respondent as a child (9), and parent and teenager (10)) are almost exclusively nonvoluntary relationships.

Although the ideal marriage may be characterized by equal and cooperative interdependence, as by point 7 in Figure 13.2, it is probably more typical for there to be some conflict and asymmetry in dependence. The respondents' characterizations of the relationship between their mothers and fathers are perhaps more realistic in these respects. As shown by the point labeled 11, that relationship is intense but close to the midpoints of the other dimensions. This is consistent with studies of married couples (e.g., Burgess and Wallin 1953, Gurin *et al.* 1960) that suggest that most husbands and wives experience conflict in their relationships. That inequality in dependence is not uncommon in marriages is implied by studies of decision making in marriage (e.g., Blood and Wolfe 1960). It is reasonable, therefore, to view marriage not as a point but as a sizable zone in Figure 13.2. This zone begins in the cooperative, equal, intense corner of the solid and extends toward the competitive and unequal corners, though maintaining a considerable degree of interdependence.

It will be clear to the reader how the preceding descriptive analysis of marriage, as it compares with other relationships, can be used in studying the effects on marriage of the aging of its members. We will want to know where in this property space a particular marriage is located at the outset. Then we will want to determine the direction in which the aging process moves the marriage. To make predictions about the direction of change and its implications, we will need to take account of what is known about the determinants of a relationship's properties and the implications of those properties for the significant events within the relationship. To these matters we now briefly turn.

PROPERTIES OF INTERDEPENDENCE AND INTERACTION PROCESS

The evidence from Wish *et al.* (1976), summarized in Figure 13.2, is derived from their respondents' perceptions of various relationships rather than from objective measures of those relationships. However, the results are highly consistent with a great deal of other evidence about variations in the properties of dyads. It is clear that the interdependence properties of a dyadic relationship—its location in the space shown in Figure 13.2—are important determinants of the interaction between its members. Much of the last 30 years of research on the dynamics of small groups can be summarized in terms of (a) the determinants of the various properties of interdependence and (b) the effects of the properties on the interaction process. This chapter can only highlight some of the salient conclusions from this research.

With regard to degree of interdependence, the literature on interpersonal attraction identifies the various bases of persons' dependence on each other. One person may be dependent on another because the latter provides concrete resources and services, shares attitudes on important issues, and provides emotional support when needed (Berscheid and Walster 1978). Dependence is reduced if the partner raises the costs (as through conflict behavior) or withholds expected rewarding behaviors (Thibaut and Kelley 1959). A person may also be dependent on another because of what they accomplish as a pair. It will be noted that the distinction between these two sources of dependence (one being interpersonal attraction between the persons and the other being performance of the dyad as a unit) corresponds to the fourth property of interdependence described earlier, whether there is dependence on individual action or on joint action. Research shows that the determinants of dependence are quite different in the two cases (Zander 1979). Interdependence is high in the first case (in which interpersonal attraction and support are involved) when the persons are similar in their values. In the second case (in which joint action on some external task is important), interdependence is high when the dyad is successful and gains outside recognition.

The outstanding dynamic feature of the highly interdependent (and common interest) dyad is mutual influence. This is partly a matter of threat and compliance (persons conform to dyad norms as the price for maintaining the relationship) but it is also partly a matter of desire to be like one another and of ready willingness to listen to and accept one another's ideas. The specific dynamics and the consequences of mutual influence can be rather different when interdependence is based on interpersonal attraction and individual activity as compared with joint task performance. In the first case, there is a common scenario of circular causality in which initial attraction results in mutual influence, which in turn results in heightened similarity, which finally results in a heightening of the interpersonal attraction and interdependence. When dependence is based on successful joint activity, the mutual influence that occurs in the highly interdependent dyad can be either very beneficial to the pair or very detrimental. The crucial factor is whether the uniformity in belief and action that develops within the highly interdependent pair is appropriate or inappropriate to the dyad's tasks. (The negative consequences of strong mutual influence in highly interdependent small, decision-making groups is the focus of Janis's book (1972) on "groupthink.")

Unequal dependence has many possible bases, these being merely asymmetries in one or more of the many factors that render one person dependent on the other. The less dependent person may be more attractive personally, may be more capable of performing valued services, may have greater access to valuable resources, and/or may be more proficient in promoting the dyad's success in its joint ventures. Inasmuch as these are generally things that many other people value, the less dependent person usually has better alternatives to remaining in the dyad.

The essential dynamic feature of the dyad with unequal dependence is an asymmetry in influence, the less dependent member typically exercising more influence than the more dependent one. Again, this is partly a matter of threat and compliance (the less dependent person gets his or her way by threatening to dissolve the relationship) but also a matter of other kinds of influence (deriving from the less dependent individual's personal attractiveness, expertise, and store of information).

In general, there are three possible scenarios for the course of the relationship characterized by unequal dependence. (1) Stable relationship with equitable outcomes: The less dependent person receives privileges and rewards superior to those of the more dependent person, commensurate with the difference in dependence. There is reached an equilibrium in which the satisfactions each person gains from the relationship are inversely proportional to dependence on the dyad. Recent research on equity (Walster et al. 1978b) suggests that dyads are stable to the degree that there is perceived to be an equitable allocation of rewards relative to the members' "investments." (2) The less dependent person leaves the relationship: Sufficient advantages are not provided the less dependent person, so anticipating or being promised superior benefits in other relationships, he or she leaves the dyad. (3) The more dependent person leaves the relationship: This type of disruption occurs when the less dependent person tries to exploit the partner through seeking superior advantages that the more dependent person regards as unfair. The latter often withdraws reluctantly because his or her alternatives are poor, and the withdrawal is accompanied by angry accusations of injustices suffered at the hands of the less dependent person. The evidence from young heterosexual dating dyads suggests that this last scenario is less common than the second one. It is generally the less dependent person who precipitates the breakup (Hill, Rubin, and Peplau 1976). However, little is known on this point as regards marriage relationships.

Whether a relationship is characterized by commonality or conflict of interest depends, of course, on the similarity and compatibility between the two persons in their interests, needs, abilities, etc. The dynamic consequences of these two types of interdependence have to do with conflict and communication (Deutsch 1949). Commonality of interest encourages each person to be open and honest toward the partner and to trust and believe what the partner says. Agreement and coordination are easily achieved and, as already described, there is much mutual influence. In contrast, conflict of interest provides no reason for either person to communicate honestly with the other or to believe anything the other may say. There is little mutual influence and, unless constrained to remain in interaction, the two persons tend to draw apart.

The intermediate or "mixed-motive" relationships, characterized by mixtures of common and conflicting interests, display a dynamic process not found in either extreme type of relationship, namely, negotiation and bargaining. Common interest dyads have no need for bargaining, and dyads characterized by interest conflicts have no basis for bargaining. In the intermediate dyads, there is both a reason to bargain (in the partial conflict of interest) and a basis for bargaining (in the partial commonality of interest). It is the bargaining process that enables the two persons to deal with the difficult dilemmas that arise when they try simultaneously to protect their respective individual interests and to promote their common interests (Kelley 1966). In the course of bargaining, differential dependence on the dyad is recognized and equitably compensated for. In interpersonal relationships, the bargaining process is, of course, quite informal. There are many impediments to successful bargaining, not the least of which is the inability of the two persons to control their emotions and tolerate the high degree of ambiguity that bargaining requires. The conflict associated with bargaining is often exacerbated by differences between the two persons in their approaches to conflict. Conflict about conflict is not uncommon (Kelley 1979), so the very process of resolving certain issues often gives rise to other issues about how the resolution should proceed and about the significance of one another's style of fighting.

One property of interdependence that is revealed by the logical analysis of outcome matrices—dependence on individual versus joint action—is not reflected in any of the dimensions empirically derived by Wish et al. (1976). The probable reason for this is that most relations include both kinds of interdependence. Certainly in the typical marriage, each person is dependent both on the activities and efforts of the partner and on the coordination of their efforts in companionate and joint activities. It is important that these two kinds of dependence be recognized as sources of two kinds of frustration and inefficiency within a dyad. These can be characterized, respectively, as "exchange" problems and "coordination" problems. The distinction is well illustrated (although for larger groups) by Steiner's analysis of group process in problem-solving groups (1972). In analyzing the "process losses" that such groups incur, Steiner distinguishes between (1) losses from inadequate member motivation to make high-quality contributions to the group and (2) losses from poor coordination and temporal programming. In marriages, these have their parallels in the distinction between (1) persons whose personal, egoistic interests and/or laziness interfere with their willingly doing what their partners want and (2) persons who for reasons of work schedules or peculiar diurnal energy cycles have trouble coordinating companionate activities with their partners.

The preceding pages describe the properties of relationships as identified at the *given* level of interdependence (i.e., at the level of specific behaviors and direct, concrete outcomes). We see how marriage is ideally defined in terms of the interdependence properties and how changes in the marriage relationship can be specified in terms of shifts in those properties. From an understanding of the dynamic implications of the properties briefly summarized above, we can make predictions about how the interaction process and scenario of a particular marriage will be affected by changes in its properties.

We must now add some complications to our picture of the dyad. As noted at the outset, a marriage relationship cannot be fully specified at the *given* level of interdependence. It is not only close (i.e., highly interdependent) but also personal. Exactly what this means is our next topic.

MARRIAGE AS A PERSONAL RELATIONSHIP

The distinction between personal and impersonal relationships appear in Wish, Deutsch, and Kaplan's data as a fourth dimension, one they describe as "socioemotional and informal versus task oriented and formal." It is defined by three of their rating scales: pleasure-oriented versus work-oriented, very informal versus very formal, and emotional versus intellectual. At the "socioemotional and informal" end of the scale are the relationships of marriage partners, close friends, siblings, and engaged couples. At the opposite end are, for example, interviewer and job applicant, opposing negotiators, master and servant, and supervisor and employee.

This fourth dimension might be taken to reflect simply a distinction in the kind of outcomes with respect to which persons may be interdependent—socioemotional versus task and intellectual outcomes. The present view is that the distinction means much more than this. The personal relationship (the socioemotional and informal one) is one in which interpersonal dispositions are of great importance to the participants. As shown in Figure 13.1, the two persons are interdependent not only in specific behaviors and concrete outcomes but also in the attitudes and values they express toward each other. Such expressions are typically of very great importance to the participants, hence they often experience high levels of positive and/or negative affect. Most important, the events in such relationships are regulated by these interpersonal dispositions rather than by impersonal, formal rules or by the demands of external tasks.

(To avoid misunderstanding, it should be noted at this point that few relationships are completely impersonal. The tendency to respond to other people in personal terms seems deeply ingrained in most of us. It is difficult to discuss interpersonal relations without reference to their personal features, so some of what we now consider has already been alluded to in the previous discussions.)

Only a brief summary of the relevant facts and ideas can be given here. They are more fully explained in Kelley and Thibaut (1978) and Kelley (1979). Interpersonal attitudes and values are seen as derivative from the problems of interdependence that exist at the given level. Such diverse interpersonal attitudes as considerateness or competitiveness only have meaning as tendencies to view and react to the facts of the given interdependence in certain ways. Through experience with these facts and through practical and moral social training, each individual learns to pay attention to other persons' outcomes in addition to his or her own. In close relationships, he or she learns the advantages of becoming responsive to the partner's outcomes and of freeing his or her behavior from exclusive control by his or her own outcomes and putting it partly under control of the partner's outcomes. [Such responsiveness is shown in much recent social psychological research dealing with such phenomena as altruism, equity (Walster *et al.* 1978a), and competitiveness (McClintock 1972).] Becoming responsive to the other's outcomes involves being prosocial (fair, considerate, responsible) in some instances, but egoistic and even antisocial (competitive, assertive, preemptive) in other instances. Each of these tendencies has its occasional advantages, depending on the opportunities and problems provided by the given interdependence (its commonality versus conflict of interest, equality versus inequality, and outcome control through individual versus joint action) and on the similar or dissimilar tendencies of the particular partner.

Such attitudes as considerateness or assertiveness (to name two) are learned both as strategic procedures to gain good given outcomes and as internalized and generalized values followed in relations with certain other persons and types of persons. In their latter form, as moderately stable dispositions and particularly as they are directed toward a particular partner, they are of enormous importance to that partner. This is especially true in relationships of long duration and extensive interdependence, such as marriage. Because any such relationship inevitably involves some problems of conflict of interest and coordination of joint action as well as opportunities for mutual enhancement versus unilateral exploitation, each person in it is keenly interested in the stable interpersonal dispositions the partner brings to the relationship. Research on couples' sources of satisfaction and dissatisfaction and on their conflicting interpretations of behavior (Kelley 1979) shows what we all know from our everyday experience that such attitudes and traits are of very high importance and are frequently the subject of their interaction. In our marriages and similar relationships, we desire our partners to possess certain interpersonal traits (such as sensitivity, honesty, and initiative) and to hold certain attitudes toward ourselves (such as love, respect, and responsibility). These traits and attitudes are important to us because they guarantee the partner's responsiveness to the total pattern of given interdependence and this responsiveness makes possible the easy resolution of the problems that arise between us.

From the previous discussion, it will be seen that each member of most close relationships will have strong interests in the interpersonal traits and attitudes expressed by both the partner and by the self. Therefore, we may describe the two as being interdependent in their expression of such dispositions. This is what is meant by saying that the relationship becomes "personal," namely, that part of its satisfactions and dissatisfactions derive from the interpersonal dispositions, particularly the attitudes that the two persons are able to display toward each other.

An important point to recognize is that these traits and attitudes are expressed through actions at the *given* level. In their essential meanings, attitudes of love, fairness, competitiveness, dominance, and such are expressed through the ways the person takes account of the partner's outcomes relative to his or her own. Because of the high interest in these attitudes, each person scans the partner's behavior to determine how it relates to the concrete outcomes, and from its deviations from the partner's immediate interests draws inferences about the partner's attitudes. Similarly, each person projects his or her own attitudes by controlling his or her behavior in relation to both sets of outcomes. The broad outlines of these processes are suggested by the ideas and results from research on the attribution process (e.g., Jones *et al.* 1972) and the self-presentation process (Jones and Wortman 1973). Many details remain to be worked out, but it can be stated as a general hypothesis that the traits and attitudes a person can express in a particular relationship depend on the nature of the *given* interdependence. For example, the attributional and presentational opportunities are richest when the interdependence is high and characterized by some degree of conflict of interest.

The fact that marriage partners are interdependent in the interpersonal traits and attitudes they express has several implications for analyzing the effects of aging. In general, we will wish to inquire into changes in interpersonal needs that are produced by the events of aging and changes in the means of satisfying these needs that result from shifts in the interdependence at the given level. Some possible examples of these changes will now be considered.

SOME POSSIBLE EFFECTS OF AGING ON THE MARITAL RELATIONSHIP

Enormous difficulties are encountered in interpreting the existing literature relating to the effects of aging on the marriage relationship. A first set of problems arises from the fact the vast bulk of the research has been cross-sectional, comparing at a given time marriage partners of different ages. This comparison raises the familiar question whether observed age differences may not be due to historical variations in the prevailing cultural norms that governed the formation and structuring of marriage at the different times the relationships developed. Probably more serious is the problem of physical and personality factors related to mortality, particularly that of the husband, and the possible impact of these on the marriage (Troll 1971). If the research linking the Type A personality to myocardial infarction withstands the test of time (e.g., Rosenman *et al.* 1975), it will be very difficult to escape the conclusion that the population of marriage partners at age 70 no longer includes many of those in which, 15 or 20 years earlier, one marriage partner (generally, the husband) assumed most of the responsibility and initiative for the pair's joint activities. Thus, evidence of increasing equalitarianism with age may reflect selective survival of certain types of persons rather than changes in ongoing relationships. A second set of problems arises from the paucity of studies of aging couples. The resulting ambiguity and inconsistency of the facts create a cognitive vacuum that the reviewer's theoretical preconceptions rush to fill. Worse yet, one suspects that one's stereotypes of old age (Bengston 1973) are providing the unstated assumptions that underlie the theoretical interpretations.

Those and other problems require us to proceed with caution. The following comments are to be taken as plausible hypotheses for further research rather than, as they may sometimes seem, credible conclusions from sound research.

Aging is most important as an indicator of the likelihood that certain events will befall a relationship or impinge on its members. If we focus on the later stages of life, from middle to old age, these events include launching the last children (when the parents are around 50), retirement from work (in the sixties), and sickness and disability (from the mid-sixties onward). In addition to these rather sharp changes in the relationship and members, there will be more gradual changes, of needs, abilities, sensibilities, and vigor. Any of these events or changes can be viewed in terms of its likely effect on any aspect of the marriage (i.e., on any point in the model shown in Figure 13.1). Illustrated as follows, the event may affect the marriage at the given level of interdependence, at the dispositional level, and/or in the processes that interlink the two levels.

In view of the many possible ways that an event may impinge on a marriage, it is not reasonable to expect that any particular event, such as child-launching or retirement, will affect all marriages in the same way. It is even less probable that aging per se, encompassing an extremely diverse set of events and trends, will have a main effect on any aspect of marriage. Thus, attempts to find systematic changes related simply to age, without taking account of other factors, seem generally slated for failure. A case in point is the inconsistent set of findings regarding trends in marital satisfaction with advancing age (Stinnett *et al.* 1970). If we consider the consequences of the husband's retirement, for example, it seems likely that the increase in husband–wife interdependence that generally follows from this event will have differing effects on marital satisfaction, depending on the nature and extent of the pre-retirement interdependence. With few prior companionate activities, as in many working-class families, the husband's and wife's spare time interests may have become so divergent that their postretirement relationship is characterized by much conflict of interest and, as a result, little satisfaction. These marriages are to be contrasted with those in which many common leisure interests have developed during the working years, so the time freed by retirement is easily filled with mutually satisfying activities.

Similarly, the effect of launching the last child will depend on the nature of the triadic interdependence prior to the event. Quite different consequences are to be expected if, prior to launching, such diverse configurations exist as the following: (a) the child's activities were a source of conflict between the parents, (b) one parent was deeply dependent on the child for affection, (c) the presence of the child placed a heavy strain on household space and finances, (d) the child formed a coalition with one parent that enabled that parent to control the spouse, or (e) cooperative parental support of the child's social and educational development was an important source of attitudinal satisfaction between husband and wife. The complexities of the analysis of triadic interdependence have not been mentioned here. However, the reader will intuitively understand how these and many such initial conditions can be described by means of interdependence concepts, for example, dependence of parent on child, the child's contribution to degree of parental interdependence, and the child's effect on the level of conflict of interest between the parents. The probable change in the marital interdependence that will result in each case from the child's departure from the home is also fairly obvious. A simple example is that of (c) above, in which the departure may reduce husband–wife conflict over use of financial resources as well as eliminate the coordination problems associated with small living quarters. Instances of this sort would account for expressions of new-found freedoms and improvements in marital satisfaction when the last child leaves home (e.g., Sussman 1955, Rollins and Feldman 1970).

A contrasting scenario for the launching period, described as the transition to the "empty nest" (Spence and Lonner 1971), is one in which the last child's departure removes important sources of satisfaction for one or both parents. The prior dependence on the child may have been at the given level (e.g., pleasant conversational or recreational activities) or at the dispositional level (e.g., the self-expressive satisfactions the mother was able to derive from performing various parenting functions). In traditional families, this prior dependence is likely to have been greater for the wife than for the husband. Accordingly, it is the wife who is more likely to experience an increase in loneliness after the launching (Axelson 1960) and to feel a need for outside activities that substitute for her former parenting activities (Sussman 1955).

These scenarios of the launching period must be qualified in the light of evidence suggesting that the geographical distances between parents and launched children are often rather small and the intergenerational contacts and activities rather frequent. As Sussman (1955) has emphasized, the effect of the children's leave-taking on the needs of the parents must take account of the degree of continuity in the intergenerational relationships. More generally, the effects of launching on parent–child interdependence are highly variable and, consequently, its effects on the parents' own relationship will also be heterogeneous.

There are a number of interesting suggestions in the literature that the intergenerational interdependence often involves an asymmetry in the importance of given versus dispositional rewards. The parents tend to place more importance on dispositional aspects of the interchange (e.g., feelings of closeness, affective ties) and the married children place more importance on the exchange of services and goods (Streib 1965, Sussman 1976). The distinction between the *given* and dispositional levels of interdependence is nicely captured by Bengston and Cutler's (1976) categories of objective solidarity (exchange of help and participation in joint activities) and subjective solidarity (expression of such sentiments as understanding, respect, and affection). These authors summarize evidence indicating that middle-aged children report more intergenerational exchange of the first type and their elderly parents, more of the second type.

Many interpretations can be offered for this generational difference, for example, that evolutionary processes require stronger affective ties to the family of procreation than to the family of orientation; that parents always have more dispositional dependence on the children than the reverse; that with aging, and possibly as a result of growing dependence at the given level, there is increasing concern about other persons' attitudes. Even without being able to evaluate these and other explanations for generational asymmetry, it has important implications for understanding the interaction between elderly parents and their married children. For example, we might anticipate that many interchanges are interpreted differently on the two sides, at the *given* level of concrete rewards by the youngsters but in terms of underlying dispositions (caring, feelings) by the elders.

Although there must be many exceptions, a common effect of retirement is to increase the interdependence between spouses. For the husband, inactivity and the lack of time-filling responsibilities become a major problem (Lipman 1961). He often increases his involvement in household tasks, but whether this becomes a source of satisfaction depends on his prior attitudes about "woman's work" (Troll 1971). This incorporation of the husband into the household routine creates more frequent and new types of coordination problems, as he intrudes on the wife's preexisting activity schedule. The couple is also likely to encounter new conflicts of interests—about when and how to do things, priorities among alternative activities, etc. There is some suggestion in the literature that adjustment after retirement may be easier if the pair manages to coordinate activities in a way that permits household activities to be performed separately rather than jointly (Ballweg 1967). The changes in income and the derivative changes in housing arrangements that often accompany retirement also tend to affect the degree of conflict (e.g., increased conflict over use of the reduced income) and the frequency of coordination problems (e.g., in the use of the limited space in the new small apartment or mobile home).

Aside from the special effects of retirement, advancing age usually brings increasing interdependence to the marriage. The number and kinds of outside social contacts decrease (Bengston 1973) and the sources of pleasurable leisure activities outside the home decline in importance (Gordon et al. 1976). In a situation that is often compared to the earliest years of the marriage, the husband and wife are increasingly thrown upon their own resources. They begin to account for an increasing proportion of one another's social interactions. Companionship and communication become important sources of satisfaction and the main threats to satisfactory interaction are posed by nonmutuality of interests (Stinnett et al. 1972).

There is some evidence suggesting that the husband's dependence on the wife increases at a faster rate than her dependence on him. One study indicates that elderly men derive more satisfaction from their marriages than do their wives (Stinnett et al. 1970). Thurnher (1975) reports that the older women in a cross-sectional sample felt their spouses to be overly dependent. Other research suggests that the wife is more needed as a confidante by the man than he is needed in this role by her (Lowenthal and Haven 1968). This is consistent with other evidence that elderly women more readily establish new close friendships than do elderly men (Powers and Bultena 1976, Lowenthal and Robinson 1976). Thus, when close friends are lost through death or retirement-linked moves, the wife is likely to replace her friends while the husband is likely to be left dependent on the wife for the gratifications of intimate exchange. Accompanying these age-related increments in the husband's dependence there may be age-related decrements in the satisfactions he can provide the wife. Blood and Wolfe (1960) speculate that for reasons of health and vitality, wives maintain for a longer time an interest in keeping active. This is likely to create a conflict over the amount and type of joint activities and eventually to produce a decline in the wife's desire for such activities. Differences in vitality and age (the husband usually being older) may also create the situation in which the husband is not interested in participating in the sexual activity that the wife would enjoy. It is now generally agreed that sexual interest and activity can extend far into the later years of life (Pfeiffer *et al.* 1968, Troll 1971). However, cessation of sexual interaction is reported (by both men and women) as largely due to the man. Declining physical health and the associated concerns play an important part in his loss of interest (Pfeiffer and Davis 1972).

From the husband's increasing dependence, relative to that of the wife, we would expect the wife's influence within the marriage to increase, according to the principle that the less dependent person wields the greater power. Blood and Wolfe's evidence on this point indicates that the wife's power relative to the husband's does increase up to age 60, but then it declines somewhat. These investigators suggest the interesting hypothesis that beyond age 60, the husband's power grows as a result of his increasing scarcity value, inasmuch as different mortality rates produce a sharp drop in the supply of men relative to women.

It is obvious that the severe illness and disability of either spouse create extreme shifts toward unequal dependence. The affected spouse loses in terms of ability to provide rewards for the partner and gains in terms of needs that it is often the partner's lot to satisfy. In general, asymmetries in loss of functions and shifts in needs due to aging will produce shifts toward unequal dependence and heightened conflicts of interest. The traumatic illness or disability is merely a dramatic and tragic instance. One possible interpersonal scenario resulting from illness-based unequal dependence is illustrated by research on the interpersonal consequences of heart attack (e.g., Bilodeau and Hackett 1971, Skelton and Dominian 1973, Croog and Levine 1977). After treatment, the victim (usually, the husband) returns to the home feeling worried, depressed, and helpless. He becomes irritable, demanding, and impatient with his wife. Being deeply concerned to promote his recovery and to avoid another attack, the wife becomes overly protective, seeking to limit his activities and enforce his adherence to what she understands to be the required medical regimen. Her protectiveness heightens the husband's irritability, and this creates a severe internal conflict for her. She feels guilty that she may not be doing enough, angry that her help is not appreciated, and afraid to criticize or create an open conflict. This, of course, is only one of several scenarios to which a shift toward unequal dependence can give rise. However, it reveals the basic dynamics of the newly unequal relationship, namely (1) the dependent person's negative feelings about the situation and ambivalence about the help he or she receives and the compliance he or she is expected to show in return and

(2) the helper's complex feelings about fulfilling their responsibilities to the dependent person, getting proper acknowledgment for the sacrifices they are making, and managing to satisfy some of their own basic needs.

In general, the changes at the *given* level of interdependence, in which the ill or disabled spouse becomes highly dependent on the partner, create a situation to which some major readjustment at the dispositional level must be made. The shift in relative dependence has extensive ramifications in the attitudes the two persons express and the kinds of personal qualities they can exhibit in their interaction. The illness or disability of the one spouse provides the other with the opportunity, and indeed, the moral necessity, to show altruistic concern through self-sacrifice. This creates a possible conflict between sustaining poor *given* outcomes and maintaining the dispositional satisfactions to be derived from the moral and interpersonal aspects of the helping role—a conflict that over a long time period will exact its own psychic toll. The healthy person also has the opportunity, and often the practical necessity, to take over responsibilities and initiatives (in decision making about social and practical matters) previously carried out by the now disabled spouse. If confidently able to assume these functions, the healthy spouse can provide dispositional satisfactions associated with competence and leadership. However, with inadequate preparation to assume them, these responsibilities can become worrisome chores. On the side of the newly dependent person, the spouse's help is almost inevitably a source of ambivalence. On one hand, it is evidence of the partner's loyal devotion and symbolic of the meaning of the marriage bond. On the other hand, the partner's sacrifices will be a source of guilt and, perhaps most significantly, continual reminders of the loss of competence.

The literature on aging shows certain aspects of the interpersonal consequences of increasing inequality of dependence. The research relates to the case in which the aging parents become dependent on their adult children, as for physical care or for financial aid. This situation is seen as creating dissatisfaction and conflict because of the reversal of roles required relative to the earlier time when the children were dependent on the parents (e.g., Adams 1970). The parents have misgivings about accepting care (Litman 1971), possibly for the reason (suggested by Bengston and Cutler 1976) of their reluctance to play out the scenario that reveals their growing dependence. Sussman (1976) summarizes research that highlights the family's conflict between their obligations to the dependent member and the costs of providing help in the activities of daily life. It is suggested that rejection of the disabled member is less likely if that person can regain some ability to contribute to family activities and can reduce the demands made on others.

It seems likely that interpersonal conflict about these matters is exacerbated by uncertainty about the consequences of any particular illness or disability. Illness, disability, and even age itself provide possible reasons for a wide range of changes in behavior, performance, and affect. They therefore inevitably become part of the excuses and justifications that elderly people present for their shortcomings (e.g., forgetting, failure to fulfill responsibilities, demands for services). Inasmuch as people have little experience with these causal factors and, as a consequence, are unsure of their effects, they open the door to tragic attributional conflicts (Orvis *et al.* 1976) in which explanations for aged persons' negative behavior are the subject of fruitless debate.

We have seen in the foregoing some of the ramifications at the dispositional level, in terms of the changes in satisfactions possible there, of increasing dependence at the given level. A different aspect of the dispositional interdependence concerns age-related changes in the dispositional needs that the husband and wife bring to their marriage. Certain of the events associated with aging create new needs in regard to the attitudes and traits that self and partner express in the marriage. For example, the loss of the deferential behavior of his work colleagues that results from the husband's retirement may encourage him to seek analogous attitudinal expressions from the spouse. Under such conditions, the respect the spouse shows may figure prominently in the husband's concerns (Stinnett *et al.* 1970). The problem of gaining such respect may often be complicated by a shift, previously noted, from the wife's greater dependence toward more equal dependence or even, to the husband's greater dependence. The retiring husband's problem of respect will often already have had its parallel in the traditional wife's problem, that with the departure of the last child she lacks an interdependence relationship in which to express certain interpersonal dispositions that she greatly values.

One theme in the aging literature concerns possible general changes in dispositional needs with aging. There is general agreement (e.g., Sussman 1976, Lowenthal and Robinson 1976) that aged persons continue to need intimacy and affection from their interpersonal relations. Beyond that there are a few indications that these needs may increase in importance in the later years. This is one possible interpretation of the generational asymmetry described earlier, that elderly parents place more emphasis on the dispositional aspects of their exchanges with their adult children than the latter do. Kastenbaum and Cameron (1969) present evidence that grandparents are more affected by reduced emotional support than are their children or grandchildren. The investigators' interpretation of this effect points to an age-linked decline in available emotional support rather than an increase in psychological need for it. In this interpretation, as in Bengston and Cutler's ideas (1976), there is the notion that as sources of love and respect decline, elderly people become more concerned about the remaining sources, attach greater importance to them, and become more careful about preserving them and, therefore, more hesitant to draw on them.

A special age-related aspect of changing dispositional interdependence has to do with changes in appearance, vigor, and functioning that can be interpreted in terms of loss of physical attractiveness. If such attractiveness has been highly valued in the relationship, (i.e., if the dispositional interdependence has featured an exchange of attitudes of physical admiration), any change interpreted as loss of the valued attribute will be difficult for the couple to cope with. Asymmetry in such changes is probably more common than symmetry, so the problem is likely to focus on the self-attitudes of one spouse and the manifestations of the partner's evaluations of that spouse. A happy situation is one in which the pair can agree that both are changing ("We're growing old together") and the focus of mutual evaluation can shift to more stable attributes (character, social and religious values, steadfast love, etc.)—if it has not already been there.

It is not only bodily changes that cause the aging person to ask questions about himself or herself and to seek new self-validating responses from the spouse. There is eventually a drastic change in time perspective that stimulates similar questions. As the future becomes foreshortened, the person who has been putting off relationship satisfactions may be stimulated to feel that "it's now or never." For example, the wife who feels she has made sacrifices to promote the husband's career may now assert, "You've had yours. Now it's my turn." The benefits of giving priority to other persons' interests may come into question and prior tendencies altruistically to promote the spouse's satisfaction may be set aside. It seems important on this point to have careful assessment of each person's feelings about overall success in life—whether life goals have been achieved and essential personal responses have been gained from one's family (e.g., whether the "family" itself has been a success) or whether there remain unsatisfied desires that have been temporarily set aside but for which no fulfillment is foreseen without a reorientation to the spouse.

Often stimulated by the shortened time perspective of the elderly is a process of "life review" in which there is extensive reminiscence about earlier events and a potential reevaluation of one's self and relationships (Butler 1963). The interpersonal aspects of this review are not at all clear, but Moriwaki (1973) observes that psychotherapists who work with the aged generally believe that they need social and emotional support during the review process. Whether the spouse is in a good position to provide this support undoubtedly depends on the prior nature of the relationship. Many spouses have their own different versions of the life histories, so a shared review process can easily give rise to a set of irresolvable disagreements about irretrievable facts. Furthermore, old conflicts that have long been sidestepped may be brought to the fore without there being any realistic way currently to deal with them. The elderly couple has a rich stock of significant interpersonal events, real and imagined, to draw on in interpreting past and present behavior. The shared and positive portions of their memories is a treasured resource for review by the happy couple, but the idiosyncratic and negative portions provide a basis for relationship-threatening conflicts.

From the present theoretical perspective, one of the most important human capacities, as it possibly changes with age, is the capacity to be sensitive and responsive to other persons' outcomes. As was argued earlier, such sensitivity and responsiveness are essential to the expression of the interpersonal attitudes that are highly important in a married couples' dispositional interdependence. With advanced aging, there may well be a decline in this capacity, as the individual's preoccupation with his or her own problems and mental life interferes with attention to and concern about others' needs. A change of this sort is suggested by references in the aging literature to "shrinkage of the life space," heightened "preoccupation with inner life," and a decline in "psychological engagement" with the external environment. The evidence for this trend, largely obtained in connection with research on the controversial "disengagement" theory (Cummings and Henry 1961, Shanas 1968) is very meager, so at present it can be considered to be only an interesting hypothesis. If there is a decline in responsiveness to other persons' interests, we would expect to see a corresponding decline in both competitiveness and assertiveness on one hand and cooperativeness, agreeable compliance, and fairness on the other hand.

SUMMARY

The preceding examples illustrate some of the changes in opportunities and occasions for the expression of interpersonal attitudes that accompany changes in the way a husband and a wife are interdependent, both with each other and with other persons. As the interdependence changes at the given level, the spouses' interdependence at the dispositional level may also change. They may have new desires about what attitudes each one displays in the relationship and different means of expressing them. Finally, there may also be changes in the attitude expression and attribution processes by which the given and dispositional levels are linked.

The purpose of this chapter has been to suggest how aging and its effects on the marriage might be examined from the perspective of a social psychological analysis of interpersonal relations. Brevity has made it necessary to summarize the concepts (e.g., properties of interdependence, and levels of interdependence) at a rather general level. An attempt has been made to show the scope of the interdependence analysis and to locate within it the most essential elements to be identified among the complexities of close relationships.

It has been observed that age-related changes in close relationships, as these occur at the given level of interdependence, can be usefully described in terms of vectors that connect initial and terminal locations of the relationship in the property space shown in Figure 13.2. Then, depending on the direction and amount of change in the marriage, we may expect accompanying changes in the interaction process (e.g., shifts in who exercises the greater influence, and changes in the degree of conflict and bargaining). Finally, the changes in the given interdependence produce reverberations at the dispositional level, for example, changes in the kinds of attitudes that are necessary for the smooth functioning of the relationship and in the personal qualities that the husband and wife can express through their interaction.

The interpretations in these terms of research from the aging area has been highly tentative and quite speculative. Yet, it suggests the fruitfulness of examining the aging marriage in terms of interdependence concepts. From this examination, we see that there will often be problems for the aging couple that derive from the increases in their interdependence as their involvement in external activities and relationships declines. Another important set of prolems will arise from the sharp shift toward unequal dependence that comes from illness and disability of one spouse. There is little doubt that the study of elderly couples can contribute much to our understanding of close relationships. The principal reason for this is that although we now know a great deal about the interactional consequences of various configurations of interdependence, we know very little about the transitions from one configuration to another. Thus, for example, the study of drastic changes in the equality of dependence will fill a gap in our understanding of the life history of dyads. It also seems likely that this understanding will be useful in developing ways to ameliorate some of the tragic personal and interpersonal consequences of such changes.

ACKNOWLEDGMENTS

The author is indebted to Edward Carroll for his survey of the literature on age trends in close relationships.

REFERENCES

Adams, B. N. (1970) Isolation, function, and beyond: American kinship in the 1960's. *Journal of Marriage and Family* 32:575–597.
Axelson, L. J. (1960) Personal adjustment in the postparental period. *Marriage and Family Living* 22:66–68.
Ballweg, J. A. (1967) Resolution of conjugal role adjustment after retirement. *Journal of Marriage and Family* 29:277–281.
Bengston, V. L. (1973) *The Social Psychology of Aging.* New York: Bobbs-Merrill.
Bengston, V. L., and Cutler, N. E. (1976) Generations and intergenerational relations: Perspectives on age groups and social change. Chapter 6 in R. H. Binstock and E. Shanas, eds., *Handbook of Aging and the Social Sciences.* New York: Van Nostrand Reinhold.
Berscheid, E., and Walster, E. H. (1978) *Interpersonal Attraction,* 2nd ed. Reading, Mass.: Addison-Wesley.
Bilodeau, C. B., and Hackett, T. P. (1971) Issues raised in a group setting by patients recovering from myocardial infarction. *American Journal of Psychiatry* 128:73–78.
Blood, R. O., Jr., and Wolfe, D. M. (1960) *Husbands and Wives: The Dynamics of Married Living.* New York: Free Press.
Burgess, E. W., and Wallin, P. (1953) *Engagement and Marriage.* Philadelphia: J. B. Lippincott.
Butler, R. N. (1963) The life review: An interpretation of reminiscence in the aged. *Psychiatry* 26:65–76.
Carroll, J. D., and Chang, J. J. (1970) Analysis of individual differences in multidimensional scaling via an *N*-way generalization of "Eckart-Young" decomposition. *Psychometrika* 35:283–319.
Croog, S. H., and Levine, S. (1977) *The Heart Patient Recovers.* New York: Human Sciences Press.
Cummings, E., and Henry, W. E. (1961) *Growing Old: The Process of Disengagement.* New York: Basic Books.
Deutsch, M. (1949) An experimental study of the effects of cooperation and competition upon group process. *Human Relations* 2:199–232.
Gordon, C., Gaitz, C. M., and Scott, J. (1976) Leisure and lives: Personal expressivity across the life span. Chapter 13 in R. H. Binstock and E. Shanas, eds., *Handbook of Aging and the Social Sciences.* New York: Van Nostrand Reinhold.
Gurin, G., Veroff, J., and Feld, S. (1960) *Americans View Their Mental Health.* New York: Basic Books.
Janis, I. L. (1972) *Victims of Groupthink.* Boston: Houghton-Mifflin.
Jones, E. E., Kanouse, D. E., Kelley, H. H., Nisbett, R. E., Valins, S., and Weiner, B., eds. (1972) *Attribution: Perceiving the Causes of Behavior.* Morristown, N. J.: General Learning Press.
Jones, E. E., and Wortman, C. (1973) *Ingratiation: An Attributional Approach.* Morristown, N.J.: General Learning Press.

Hill, C. T., Rubin, Z., and Peplau, L. A. (1976) Breakups before marriage: The end of 103 affairs. *Journal of Social Issues* 32:147–168.

Kastenbaum, R., and Cameron, P. (1969) Cognitive and emotional dependency in later life. Pp. 39–57 in R. A. Kalish, ed., *The Dependencies of Old People*. Ann Arbor, Mich.: Institute of Gerontology.

Kelley, H. H. (1966) A classroom study of the dilemmas in interpersonal negotiations. Pp. 49–73 in K. Archibald, ed., *Strategic Interaction and Conflict*. Berkeley, Calif.: Institute of International Studies, University of California.

Kelley, H. H. (1979) *Personal Relationships*. Hillsdale, N.J.: Erlbaum Associates.

Kelley, H. H., and Thibaut, J. W. (1978) *Interpersonal Relations: A Theory of Interdependence*. New York: Wiley-Interscience.

Lipman, A. (1961) Role conceptions and morale in couples in retirement. *Journal of Gerontology* 16:267–271.

Litman, T. J. (1971) Health care and the family: A three-generational analysis. *Medical Care* 9:67–81.

Lowenthal, M. F., and Haven, C. (1968) Interaction and adaptation: Intimacy as a critical variable. *American Sociological Review* 33:20–30.

Lowenthal, M. F., and Robinson, B. (1976) Social networks and isolation. Chapter 17 in R. H. Binstock and E. Shanas, eds., *Handbook of Aging and the Social Sciences*. New York: Van Nostrand Reinhold.

McClintock, C. G. (1972) Social motivation—a set of propositions. *Behavioral Sciences* 17:438–454.

Moriwaki, S. Y. (1973) Self disclosure, significant others and psychological well-being in old age. *Journal of Health and Social Behavior* 14:226–232.

Orvis, B. R., Kelley, H. H., and Butler, D. (1976) Attributional conflict in young couples. Chapter 16 in J. H. Harvey, W. J. Ickes, and R. F. Kidd eds., *New Directions in Attribution Research*, Vol. 1. Hillsdale, N.J.: Erlbaum Associates.

Pfeiffer, E., and Davis, G. C. (1972) Determinants of sexual behavior in middle and old age. *Journal of American Geriatric Society* 20:151–158.

Pfeiffer, E., Verwoerdt, A., and Wang, H-S. (1968) Sexual behavior in aged men and women. *Archives of General Psychiatry* 19:753–758.

Powers, E. A., and Bultena, G. L. (1976) Sex differences in intimate friendships of old age. *Journal of Marriage and Family* 38:739–746.

Rollins, B. C., and Feldman, H. (1970) Marital satisfaction over the family life-cycle. *Journal of Marriage and Family* 32:20–28.

Rosenman, R. H., Brand, R. J., Jenkins, C. D., Friedman, M., Straus, R., and Wurm, M. (1975) Coronary heart disease in the Western Collaborative Group Study: Final follow-up experience of 8½ years. *Journal of the American Medical Association* 233:872–877.

Shanas, E. (1968) A note on restriction of the life space: Attitudes of age cohorts. *Journal of Health and Social Behavior* 9:86–90.

Skelton, M., and Dominian, J. (1973) Psychological stress in wives of patients with myocardial infarction. *British Medical Journal* 2:101.

Spence, D., and Lonner, T. (1971) The "empty nest": A transition within motherhood. *Family Coordinator* 20:369–375.

Steiner, I. D. (1972) *Group Process and Productivity*. New York: Academic Press.

Stinnett, N., Carter, L. M., and Montgomery, J. E. (1972) Older persons' perception of their marriages. *Journal of Marriage and Family* 34:665–670.

Stinnett, N., Collins, J. E., and Montgomery, J. E. (1970) Marital need satisfaction of older husbands and wives. *Journal of Marriage and Family* 32:428–434.

Streib, G. F. (1965) Intergenerational relations: Perspectives of the two generations on the older parent. *Journal of Marriage and Family* 27:469–476.

Sussman, M. B. (1955) Activity patterns of postparental couples. *Marriage and Family Living* 17:338–341.

Sussman, M. B. (1976) The family life of old people. Chapter 9 in R. H. Binstock and E. Shanas, eds., *Handbook of Aging and the Social Sciences.* New York: Van Nostrand Reinhold.

Thibaut, J. W., and Kelley, H. H. (1959) *The Social Psychology of Groups.* New York: Wiley.

Thurnher, M. (1975) Family confluence, conflict, and affect. Pp. 24–47 in M. F. Lowenthal, M. Thurnher, D. Chiriboga, and Associates. *Four Stages of Life: A Comparative Study of Women and Men Facing Transitions.* San Francisco: Jossey-Bass.

Troll, L. E. (1971) The family of later life: A decade review. *Journal of Marriage and Family* 33:263–290.

Walster, E., Walster, G. W., and Berscheid, E. (1978a) *Equity: Theory and Research.* Boston: Allyn and Bacon.

Walster, E. H., Walster, G. W., and Traupmann, J. (1978b) *Journal of Personality and Social Psychology* 36:82–92.

Wish, M., Deutsch, M., and Kaplan, S. J. (1976) Perceived dimensions of interpersonal relations. *Journal of Personality and Social Psychology* 33:409–420.

Zander, A. (1979) The psychology of group processes. *Annual Review of Psychology* 30:417–451.

chapter 14

Sexual Intimacy in
Aging Marital Partners

WILLIAM GRIFFITT

Most of us take for granted the importance and urgency of sex during
the youthful early stages of intimate relationships between men and
women. Although the available evidence suggests that more and more
people are experiencing coitus prior to marriage (see Griffitt and Hatfield
1981), marriage still provides the only fully legitimate context for sexual
intercourse in our society. Regardless of the extent to which a couple
has been sexually involved previously, marriage provides a setting in
which it is possible to have intercourse with fewer of the nagging doubts
about its morality than characterize the premarital coital involvements
of some young people (Gagnon and Simon 1973, Hunt 1974). Thus, the
significance of marriage is linked, in part, to the role it plays in providing
a socially sanctioned setting for sexual intimacy. This is nicely captured
by George Bernard Shaw's observation that "marriage is popular because
it combines the maximum of temptation with the maximum of opportunity."

Marriage is important to sexual intimacy, but how important is sexual
intimacy to marriage? There is, of course, no single answer to this question, since couples differ widely in the significance they attach to sex
in their relationships. For some, sex is a rather peripheral and mean-
ingless part of marriage (Knox 1979) while for others it is the cement
that holds the marriage together (Scharff 1978). For most couples, how-

AGING
Stability and Change in the Family

ever, the importance of sex in marriage probably falls between these
extremes. For example, Reedy (1978) questioned young adult, middle-
aged, and elderly married couples about the relative importance of
emotional security, respect, helping and playing behaviors, communication, loyalty, and sexual intimacy as sources of marital satisfaction.
Most of the couples studied rated sexual intimacy as fifth (of six) in
importance in their marriages. Regardless of its psychosocial importance,
however, it is clear that most married couples devote little actual time
to intercourse. Even young sexually active married couples spend less
than .5% of their time per year having intercourse (Gagnon 1977).

AGING AND THE IMPORTANCE OF SEX

Despite (perhaps because of) the paucity of evidence concerning the
importance of sexual intimacy relative to other dimensions of life and
relationships (work, parenting, recreation, etc.), it is widely believed that
the importance people attach to sex declines and ultimately disappears
as they age. This belief is based, in part, on a collection of stereotypes
that aging invariably is associated with disappearing capabilities of, frequency of, and interests in sexual activity (Rubin 1965, 1966).

For the most part, the available data do not support these stereotypes.
Reedy (1978) found that sexual intimacy, defined as sexual attraction to
and desire for one's partner along with pleasurable sexual activity in
which feelings of tenderness, warmth, and affection could be expressed
was as important for the elderly as for the younger couples studied.
Many elderly couples cited continued feelings of mutual sexual and physical attraction to their spouses as central to their relationships. Sex, then,
does remain important for at least some elderly couples. As others (Butler
and Lewis 1976, Charatan 1978) have observed, sexual activity for the
elderly may have less of the urgency and focus on physical release than
does that of the young. Nevertheless, for many it continues to serve as
a source of sensual satisfaction, self-esteem, and tension reduction.

AGING AND SEXUAL RESPONSE CAPABILITIES

Central to stereotypes that sex is unimportant to older people are
assumptions that sexual response capabilities disappear with advancing
age. Thus, even if sex remains important to the elderly, aging is thought
to rob them of the physiological capability to perform sexually. Although

there can be little doubt that aging is associated with declining sexual responsiveness (Solnick 1978), the work of Kinsey et al. (1948, 1953) and Masters and Johnson (1966) indicates that, physiologically, most men and women remain fully capable of sexual responses in their later years. Sexual reactions become slower and less intense (Masters and Johnson 1966) but in the absence of specific infirmities they nevertheless continue to be possible.

The declines that do occur are sharper for men than for women. That is, erectile and ejaculatory capacities in men begin a rather steady decline beyond the age of 35 (Kinsey et al. 1948, Solnick 1978) until at 75 nearly half of all men are at least occasionally unable to achieve erection (Kinsey et al. 1948). In contrast, female erotic capacities tend to diminish more gradually (Kinsey et al. 1953, Masters and Johnson 1966). Although there are, of course, many other modes of sexual expression (Butler and Lewis 1976), for those couples who equate sexual intimacy with coitus, erectile failure can seriously interfere with sexual functioning.

AGING AND SEXUAL ACTIVITY

Although most couples continue to regard sex as important and to remain capable of erotic response, there is substantial evidence that, with aging, there is a decline in the percentages of men and women who actually remain coitally active. For example, Kinsey et al. (1948, 1953) found that, up to the age of 40, virtually all married men (99%) and women (98%) continued to have intercourse at least occasionally with their spouses. Beyond 40, however, the percentages of men remaining coitally active began a decline so that at the age of 60 some 6% of men and nearly 20% of women had discontinued marital intercourse. Other more recent studies (Christenson and Gagnon 1965, Pfeiffer et al. 1968, 1972, Verwoerdt et al. 1969) indicate that, beyond the age of 60, fewer and fewer men and women continue coitus, so that by the time they reach their late seventies only about 30% of men and less than 10% of women are coitally active.

Although these data suggest that a substantial number of people "drop out" of active coital involvement with their spouses late in life, it must be emphasized that not all do. Even in their late seventies and beyond, some couples continue to lead active coital lives. Furthermore, even though inactive coitally, many men and women report continued interest in and desire for coitus. To be sure, coital interest and desire decline with age, but not so rapidly as does actual coital involvement.

For example, in one study (Verwoerdt *et al*. 1969) around 30% of men and 10% of women were still coitally active beyond the age of 78, but nearly 60% of men and 20% of women reported continuing desires for coitus. That is, twice as many married men and women at this age desired coitus than were actually having it. This, of course, suggests that coital inactivity at advanced ages may be a source of dissatisfaction for at least some people.

Even among those married people who remain coitally active in their later years, the bulk of the available evidence (Kinsey *et al*. 1948, 1953, Pfeiffer *et al*. 1968, 1972, Verwoerdt *et al*. 1969) suggests that there are rather substantial declines in the frequency with which they have intercourse. Average rates of marital coitus before the age of 30 (two to three times per week) have been reported to be around twice the rates for sexually active couples in their late fifties and beyond (Kinsey *et al*. 1948, 1953).

It should be noted that virtually all studies showing declining incidences and frequencies of marital coitus make use of cross-sectional data, which confound sociocultural changes with age-related changes. At least one recent longitudinal study of married people between the ages of 46 and 71 reveals little decline in coital frequency among those who remain coitally active at all across a time span of 6 years (George and Weiler 1979). In fact, some couples actually showed patterns of increasing frequency of marital coitus across the 6-year period. Data from the same study, however, indicate that, as they age, more and more men and women discontinue engaging in coitus at all. This suggests that the cessation of marital intercourse does not follow lengthy periods of decline but, for most couples is rather abrupt.

ORIGINS OF DECLINING SEXUAL INTIMACY

Other than for obvious reasons such as illness or loss of spouse by death or divorce, why do many couples abandon marital sex as they grow older? Because of increasing agreement that sexual intimacy may contribute in important ways to personal and marital satisfaction in the later years, this question has provoked a great deal of speculation but little research in recent years.

The work of Kinsey *et al*. (1948, 1953) and particularly of Masters and Johnson (1966) indicates that the physiological foundations for sexual expression remain firm for most people throughout their later years. This, of course, suggests that the cessation of marital coitus by physically healthy couples is more often associated with psychosocial rather than biological factors. A number of psychosocial factors leading to sexual decline in the elderly have been identified and may be summarized. Scattered clinical and survey studies suggest that beliefs that sex is unimportant to elderly persons or that aging is associated with inevitable losses of sexual interest or capability are important factors leading to sexual decline (Rubin 1965, 1966, Sviland 1978). As Rubin (1965) notes, such beliefs may lead to a self-fulfilling prophecy in which those who expect decline experience decline. Perhaps of equal importance are various attitudes found in general society and among some elderly that sexual activity in older people is ludicrous, immoral, or in some way unseemly (Rubin 1975, Sviland 1978, Wasow and Loeb 1978). Though the prevalence of such negative attitudes appears to be declining (LaTorre and Kear 1977), where they exist they may serve as formidable obstacles to sexual expression by the elderly (Genevay 1978).

One of the most frequently reported findings is that of a positive association between frequency and enjoyment of sexual activity during the younger years and frequency of sexual activity during the later years (Christenson and Gagnon 1965, Kinsey *et al.* 1948, 1953, Masters and Johnson 1966). That is, those couples who frequently have intercourse and enjoy that intercourse during their younger years continue to lead active marital sex lives as they grow older. Conversely, those whose early relationships are marked by infrequent and unpleasant sexual activity tend to use aging as an excuse for discontinuing intercourse with their spouses as they grow older.

In their in-depth study of relatively small groups of elderly men and women, Masters and Johnson (1966) identified several factors that were associated with declining marital sexual activity. Citing several others as specifically problematic for men (such as performance fears, preoccupation with career, fatigue), they noted that as they age, some men and women become sexually unresponsive to their spouses. Thus, even though they may retain sexual response capabilities and interests in general, some older men and women simply lose sexual interest in their own wives or husbands. Other observers of sexual functioning (Kinsey *et al.* 1948, 1953, Rubin, 1965) have highlighted this factor as significant in leading to declines in marital sex with aging.

The remainder of this chapter is devoted to a consideration of the erotic stimulus value of aging sexual partners as a determinant of sexual involvement among elderly couples. More specifically, focus is placed on the role of perceived sexual attractiveness in the determination and maintenance of sexual responses. Central to that which follows is an assumption that in order to retain some degree of sexual interest in and sexual responsiveness to our sexual partners we must continue to regard them as sexually attractive in some way.

This analysis is based on an informal model of the roles of sexual needs and stimuli as determinants of sexual and emotional responses to potential and actual sex partners (Griffitt 1979). The model consists of four interrelated propositions:

1. Sexual stimuli elicit a variety of feelings that are experienced subjectively as positive and/or negative. We positively evaluate, desire, and approach those sexual stimuli eliciting primarily positive feelings but negatively evaluate, reject, and avoid those sexual stimuli eliciting primarily negative feelings.
2. People are, in part, collections of sex stimuli in the sense that we regard various aspects of others such as their gender, anatomical structures, and physical appearance as relevent to sexuality. Thus, to some extent at least, our sexual perceptions of, evaluations of, and responses to people are influenced by our reactions and feelings concerning their sexually relevant features.
3. Aroused sexual needs, interests, and desires enhance our sensitivity to and, consequently, the perceptual salience of sex stimuli. Thus, the positive and/or negative feelings, behavioral and evaluative reactions evoked by sex stimuli, are intensified by aroused sexual needs.
4. Aroused sexual needs will thus increase our sensitivity to and the salience of the sexual aspects (stimuli) of others and intensify our evaluative and behavioral reactions (positive and/or negative) to them as sexual partners.

While a number of expectations concerning sexual attraction and response may be derived from these relatively simple propositions, two are of primary interest in this context. First is the somewhat obvious (if not socially popular) notion that the perceived sexual and romantic attractiveness of people is positively related to the degree to which they are regarded as physically attractive. The large amount of available data (see Berscheid and Walster 1978) fully support this expectation. These data also suggest that the physical attractiveness of a partner is a more potent determinant of men's responses to women than of women's responses to men.

Sexual attractiveness and physical attractiveness, of course, cannot be equated. Though physical attractiveness is important, a number of additional variables such as mutual needs, attitudes, values, and goals, rewarding interactions, and others influence our feelings of attraction (sexual or otherwise) toward others (Berscheid and Walster 1978, Byrne 1971, Griffitt 1974).

A second and less obvious prediction is that the arousal of sexual interests and desires leads to an intensification of sexual attraction to people perceived as physically attractive and an intensification of sexual aversion to those perceived as physically unattractive. This prediction follows from the proposition that sexual arousal alerts us to and intensifies our reactions to the sexually attractive and sexually unattractive features (stimuli) of others. This prediction has been tested in a recent series of laboratory studies using young college students as subjects. In these studies, we created sexual arousal by exposing men and women subjects to filmed erotica and then assessed their sexual attraction to normatively defined attractive and unattractive people of the opposite sex. We rather consistently found that sexual arousal increased men and women's sexual attraction to normatively attractive people of the opposite sex but decreased their attraction to normatively unattractive people.

These effects also extend to the perceived sexual attractiveness of specifically sexual parts of bodies. For example, sexually aroused men rate female breasts as either more attractive or less unattractive than do men who are not sexually aroused. Similar patterns are found when sexually aroused and nonaroused women respond to attractive and unattractive male buttocks, genitals, and chests. That is, when sexual needs were enhanced, physically attractive people were perceived as more sexually attractive and physically unattractive people as less sexually attractive (Griffitt 1979, Istvan and Griffitt 1978, Weidner et al. 1979).

Taken together, these two expectations and their supporting data suggest several ideas relevant to the effects of aging on marital sexual activity. First, aging in both men and women is generally associated with declining perceived physical attractiveness as it is traditionally defined in our society (Weg 1978). Our standards for beauty are closely linked with youthfulness (Charatan 1978, Genevay 1978, Sontag 1976), and our earliest heterosexual arousal and behavior are experienced and reinforced in the context of youth. Thus, as they age, marital partners may be perceived as less and less sexually attractive and, thus, become weaker sex stimuli to one another.

Second, because they tend to be more sensitive to perceived physical attractiveness cues, men would be expected to lose sexual interest in and responsiveness to their aging wives more quickly than their wives lose interest in them. A related observation often has been made (Huyck 1974, Masters and Johnson 1966, Sontag 1976) that the perceived sexual attractiveness of women is more closely tied to their physical attractiveness than is that of men. Thus, even though men and women may change in physical appearance at comparable rates, the perceived sexual attractiveness of women, as traditionally defined in terms of youthful appearance, declines more rapidly with age than does that of men. This also suggests that men's reactions play a larger role in declining marital sex than do those of women.

Third, since heightened sexual interests and desires tend to intensify aversion to physically unattractive sexual cues, it may well be that sexual activity with an aged sexual partner actually becomes distasteful for some men and women. It should be noted that we are far from a full understanding of the origins of sexual arousal and desires in humans (Griffitt and Hatfield 1981) and for older men and women our knowledge is even less complete. It is clear, however (see earlier discussion), that sexual desires continue to arise late in life for many men and women. Whether these desires are stimulated by physical contacts, fantasies, erotic images in the various media, hormonal processes, contacts with sexually appealing people during everyday activities, or by one's own sexual partner is, to some extent, irrelevant to this analysis. Initially positive or negative responses to sexual cues from a partner will be intensified when one is sexually aroused.

There are surprisingly few data concerning links among aging, physical attractiveness, and sexual intimacy. Most of the data that are available are impressionistic or derived from clinical contacts with sexually dysfunctional couples. Nevertheless, some patterns relevant to the expectations that follow from the model outlined above are apparent.

Virtually all studies in which relevant data have been obtained indicate that in fact the husband more often than the wife is responsible for the cessation of marital intercourse. For example, when asked why they stopped having intercourse, nearly 70% of elderly husbands and wives in two studies (Pfeiffer *et al.* 1968, 1972) placed the "blame" on the husband. Most often both partners agreed that the husband had lost interest in sex with the wife or that he was no longer potent with her. Other studies (Christenson and Gagnon 1965, George and Weiler 1979) have obtained similar findings.

In our society, men are socialized to actively initiate sexual interactions and women are socialized to respond to these initiatives. Furthermore, an erect penis is a virtual necessity for coitus. Thus, either a husband's lack of sexual interest in his wife or his lack of an erection in response to her (or both) effectively eliminates the prospects for coitus in many marriages. It is perhaps because of these related "facts" that most analyses of the reasons for cessation of marital intercourse by physically healthy couples focus on men.

One assumption underlying at least two of these analyses (Kinsey *et al.* 1948, Masters and Johnson 1966) and found in popularized works ("J" 1969, Morgan 1973) is that novelty is an essential element involved in maintaining male sexual interests and responsiveness. It is known that at least some species of male animals become disinterested and unresponsive to their familiar mates following a few copulations within a relatively short period of time but quickly regain interest and responsiveness when a novel female partner becomes available (Clemens 1967). Adult men rather quickly become disinterested in and unresponsive to repeated presentations of explicitly erotic movies, photographs, and literature—but equally quickly regain interest and responsiveness when novel erotic stimuli are introduced (Howard *et al.* 1971).

In studies of actual sexual behavior, it has been observed that married men who are minimally responsive to their wives often are capable of multiple acts of coitus and multiple orgasms when they encounter novel partners at mate-swapping parties (O'Neill and O'Neill 1970).

Kinsey *et al.* (1948) echoed a similar theme by suggesting that marital sexual decline in aging men is

> undoubtedly affected also by psychologic fatigue, a loss of interest in repetition of the same sort of experience, an exhaustion of the possibilities for exploring new techniques, new types of contacts, new situations. Evidence for this is to be found in numerous cases of older males whose frequencies dropped materially until they met new partners, adopted new sexual techniques, or embraced totally new sources of outlet. Under new situations, their rates materially rise, to drop again, however, within a few months, or in a year or two, to the old level [pp. 227, 229].

Reaching a similar conclusion, Masters and Johnson (1966) indicated that a major factor (among others) in the discontinuation of marital coitus is a husband's loss of interest in his partner due to "monotony in a sexual relationship." They note

> The female partner may lose her stimulative effect as her every wish, interest, and expression become too well known in advance of sexual activity, especially if the subconscious male focus has anticipated multiple-partner sexual variation. . . . The complaint of sexual boredom frequently originates in the fact that the female partner has lost sight of the necessity for working at the marital relationship with the same interests in stimulating and satisfying her male partner that she originally may have demonstrated at the outset of marriage [1966, pp. 264–265].

Though each of these analyses focuses primarily on men, it seems clear that sexual boredom is an important factor leading to withdrawal from marital sex by older married women as well. For example, Hite (1976) reported testimonials from a number of older married women revealing that, over the years, their husbands had become less and less stimulating to them as sexual partners. Even though they may have continued to engage in marital intercourse at the insistence of their husbands, many of the women were able to enjoy intercourse and reach orgasm only with the novel partners provided by extramarital relationships. Until more relevant research findings are available, it will be impossible to make definitive statements concerning the importance of boredom-induced unresponsiveness as a factor in marital sexual decline among aging women.

While the monotony of lengthy sexual relationships may well lead many aging men and women to lose erotic interest in and responsiveness to their aging partners, other observations suggest that some older men and women not only become erotically unresponsive to their marital partners, but also actually begin to react with sexual aversion to what they perceive as increasingly unattractive features of appearance. For example, Rubin (1965) cites an early study of men between the ages of 61 and 68 seeking treatment for impotence in sexual intercourse with their wives. Many of the men were impotent only with their wives and could respond effectively with other women. Most attributed their marital impotence to aversive reactions to some aspects of their elderly wife's appearance, including increasing obesity, hypertrophy or atrophy of the breasts, hirsutism, loss of hair, and thickening of the ankles and legs. Data from a number of other sources (Charatan 1978, de Beauvoir 1972, Kaas 1978) indicate that similar factors affect women's reactions to their aging husbands.

If we are to more fully understand the roles played by perceived physical attractiveness and sexual attractiveness in the maintenance of sexual intimacy in aging marital partners, a substantial amount of research is needed. At least three areas in which research is needed are evident.

First, although it is well established that physical attractiveness is an important determinant of sexual attraction among young college students (Berscheid and Walster 1978), virtually no systematic studies have been conducted using older people as subjects or as perceptual targets. One strategy for such research is to examine stereotypic beliefs concerning the sexual attractiveness of people at various ages. For example, in his research, Carducci (1980) is studying stereotypes of the attractiveness of young (18–34), middle-aged (35–59), and older (60 and older) men and women held by young, middle-aged, and older men and women. This study is designed to address heretofore subjectively accepted beliefs that older people are generally viewed as less attractive than younger people. If such stereotypes are actually found, it will be important to identify the personal and social correlates of such stereotypes, the origins and developmental appearance of such steroeotypes, and the consequences of such stereotypes for perceptions of sexual attractiveness and other interpersonal perceptions and beliefs.

Second, beyond some rather rudimentary findings concerning body and facial configurations, little is actually known about what actually contributes to perceptions of physical attractiveness (Beck 1979, Lavrakas 1975, Milford 1978, Wiggins et al. 1968). More particularly, evidence concerning what features of appearance are considered attractive in and by older people is sorely needed.

Third, though some data are available (Christenson and Gagnon 1965, George and Weiler 1979, Pfeiffer et al. 1968, 1972), more specific evidence concerning men's and women's attributions of causes for ceasing marital coitus is needed. That is, even though husbands most frequently "shoulder the blame" for coital cessation, the reasons for their doing so are largely unexplored. Similarly, when wives are responsible for termination of marital sex, their motivations for such action remain unknown.

It seems likely that declines in the erotic stimulus value of aging marital partners is one important psychosocial factor involved in the lowered frequencies and/or cessation of intercourse that characterize the marriages of some middle-aged and elderly couples. This, of course, can be problematic if sex has been an important part of marriage and if one or both partners continue to value and desire sexual intimacy. Among other outcomes, it may become associated with frustration, resentment, loss of self-esteem, extramarital sexual involvements, separation or divorce in search of new, more attractive, and stimulating partners, or simply a somewhat nagging awareness of what it could be like (Charatan 1978, Hite 1976, Rubin 1965).

MAINTAINING SEXUAL INTIMACY

Recognition of a potential problem ideally is associated with suggestions of possible solutions to the problem. The problem identified in this analysis concerns the role of declining erotic stimulus value in aging sexual partners as a determinant of declining marital sexual intimacy among the elderly. Two partially independent factors contributing to declines in erotic stimulus value were discussed, and somewhat separate interventions may be required to deal with each of the factors.

First, it was noted that across the lengthy time spans involved in enduring marriages, sex can become repetitious, boring, and monotonous. As a result, either or both marital partners may lose interest in and become less sexually responsive to their mates. In recent years, there has been increasing recognition of the potentially disruptive effects of monotony on sexual relationships between people at any age. The proposed solution has been relatively straightforward—couples are urged to take every opportunity to introduce some degree of novelty into their sexual interactions. They are encouraged to experiment with new and varied sexual techniques, vary the setting for sex, try new positions, vary the time of day for sex, and so forth (Comfort 1972, "J" 1969, Morgan 1973). According to this view, the necessity for some degree of novelty in sexual relationships increases when married couples continue to seek sexual intimacy as both partners age.

But an incessant search for novelty can itself become tedious and demanding. It may well be that social scientists have created a problem where little problem exists. That is, we have tended to assume that people should continue active coital lives as they grow older. Perhaps, as Butler and Lewis (1976) have suggested, coital performance does, with little detriment or perhaps with some benefit, become secondary to other modes of expressing intimacy as couples age. We must not insist that people continue sexual intercourse regardless of their own mutual preferences. Furthermore, it seems clear that satisfying sexual lives, alone, cannot sustain otherwise unsatisfactory relationships (Scharff 1978).

A second problem noted was that traditional definitions of physical and sexual attractiveness in our society are closely tied to youthful appearance. The inevitable declines in perceived physical attractiveness associated with aging may lead some older couples to become sexually unresponsive to or respond with aversion to their partners. One solution that is often suggested to this aspect of the problem has both agist and sexist overtones: Aging people (particularly women) are urged to devote special attention to their physical appearance and attempt to maintain an aura of youthful beauty. No doubt there is some merit to suggestions that people should avoid becoming overweight and should attempt to maintain acceptable standards of cleanliness and appearance. But the futility of the elderly attempting to match standards of beauty that are so exclusively defined in terms of youth should also be apparent.

It would seem both more reasonable and dignifying to reassess some of our traditional notions concerning standards of attractiveness. Because we are captives of our own society's standards, we tend to overlook the fact that other cultures may have very different views of what is and what is not physically and sexually attractive in a man or woman (Ford and Beach 1951). But broadening our images of attractiveness is, of course, a formidable task and one that might require a lengthy period of time. It would necessitate expanding societal views of physical attractiveness to undermine tendencies in all of us (young and old) to equate attractiveness with youth. On small scales, there seems no doubt that such changes can be accomplished (Genevay 1978, Sviland 1978).

But what about needed changes on the larger society-wide scale? At least two factors seem to contribute to the formation and maintenance of stereotypes of the elderly as sexually unappealing. First is the image of the elderly that is portrayed by the media. Older people are often presented as continually in search of a new and more gentle laxative, a more reliable denture adhesive, or magic elixirs concocted to restore "youthful appearance" to hands, hair, face, or body. Commercial enterprises could (presumably with profit) create more positive and valued images of the elderly. Clothing, automobile, and other types of "sexy" advertisements could be at least partially recast to include older members of society. The prospects for such changes in the media continually improve as the number of elderly citizens approaches the "critical mass" necessary to redirect marketing trends.

Second, once created, stereotypes about the elderly tend to be maintained by the rather pervasive age segregation that exists in our society (Botwinick 1978). Though there may be some advantages to age segregation (Kalish 1975), it is also likely that segregation of the old from the young produced by housing patterns, confinement to nursing homes, and retirement prevents social contacts that might weaken stereotypes and prejudices (Deutsch and Collins 1951). Under some circumstances, increasing exposure to and contact with the elderly would lead to more positive responses and perceptions of the old (Zajonc 1968). Thus, we may want to reevaluate current trends toward widespread development of "elderly only" housing.

Regardless of the ultimate solutions, the potential benefits of freeing the elderly and the young from limited stereotypes of attractiveness and value would certainly include, but extend beyond, enhancing potentials for sexual intimacy in later life.

REFERENCES

Beck, S. B. (1979) Women's somatic preferences. In M. Cook and G. Wilson, eds., *Love and Attraction: An International Conference.* New York: Pergamon.

Berscheid, E., and Walster, E. (1978) *Interpersonal Attraction*, 2nd ed. Reading, Mass.: Addison-Wesley.
Botwinick, J. (1978) *Aging and Behavior*. New York: Springer.
Butler, R. N., and Lewis, M. I. (1976) *Sex After Sixty*. New York: Harper & Row.
Byrne, D. (1971) *The Attraction Paradigm*. New York: Academic Press.
Carducci, B. (1980) Cross-Gender and Cross-Generational Perceptions of Human Sexuality. Unpublished doctoral dissertation, Kansas State University, Manhattan, Kansas.
Charatan, F. B. (1978) Sexual function in old age. *Medical Aspects of Human Sexuality* 12(9):150–165.
Christenson, C. V., and Gagnon, J. H. (1965) Sexual behavior in a group of older women. *Journal of Gerontology* 20:351–356.
Clemens, L. G. (1967) Effect of stimulus female variation on sexual performance of the male deermouse, *peromyscus manifulatus*. Proceedings, 75th Annual Convention, American Psychological Association: 119–120.
Comfort, A. (1972) *The Joy of Sex*. New York: Crown.
de Beauvoir, S. (1972) Joie de vivre. *Harper's Magazine* (January):33–40.
Deutsch, M., and Collins, M. E. (1951) *Interracial Housing*. Minneapolis: University of Minnesota Press.
Ford, C. S., and Beach, F. A. (1951) *Patterns of Sexual Behavior*. New York: Harper.
Gagnon, J. H. (1977) *Human Sexualities*. Glenview, Ill.: Scott, Foresman & Co.
Gagnon, J. H., and Simon, W. (1973) *Sexual Conduct*. Chicago: Aldine.
Genevay, B. (1978) Age kills us softly when we deny our sexual identity. Pp. 9–25 in R. L. Solnick, ed., *Sexuality and Aging*, 2nd ed. Los Angeles: University of Southern California Press.
George, L., and Weiler, S. J. (1979) Aging and sexual behavior: The myth of declining sexuality. Unpublished manuscript. Duke University Medical Center, Durham, North Carolina.
Griffitt, W. (1974) Attitude similarity and attraction. In T. Huston, ed., *Foundations of Interpersonal Attraction*. New York: Academic Press.
Griffitt, W. (1979) Sexual stimulation and sociosexual behaviors. In M. Cook and G. Wilson, eds., *Love and Attraction: An International Conference*. New York: Pergamon.
Griffitt, W., and Hatfield, E. (in press) *Human Sexual Behavior*. Glenview, Ill.: Scott, Foresman & Co.
Hite, S. (1976) *The Hite Report*. New York: Dell.
Howard, J. L., Reifler, C. B., and Liptzin, M. B. (1971) Effects of exposure to pornography. In *Technical Report of the Commission on Obscenity and Pornography*, Vol. 8. Washington, D.C.: U.S. Government Printing Office.
Hunt, M. (1974) *Sexual Behavior in the 1970s*. Chicago: Playboy Press.
Huyck, M. H. (1974) *Growing Older*. Englewood Cliffs, N.J.: Prentice-Hall.
Istvan, J., and Griffitt, W. (1978) Sexual Arousal and Evaluation of Attractive and Unattractive Stimulus Persons. Paper presented at the Midwestern Psychological Association, Chicago.
"J" (1969) *The Sensuous Woman*. New York: Dell.
Kaas, M. J. (1978) Sexual expression of the elderly in nursing homes. *The Gerontologist* 18(4):372–378.
Kalish, R. A. (1975) *Late Adulthood: Perspectives on Human Development*. Monterey, Calif.: Brooks/Cole.
Kinsey, A. C., Pomeroy, W. B., and Martin, C. R. (1948) *Sexual Behavior in the Human Male*. Philadelphia, Pa.: Saunders.
Kinsey, A. C., Pomeroy, W. B., Martin, C. R., and Gebhard, P. H. (1953) *Sexual Behavior in the Human Female*. Philadelphia: Saunders.

Knox, D. (1979) *Exploring Marriage and the Family*. Glenview, Ill.: Scott, Foresman, & Co.

LaTorre, R. A., and Kear, K. (1977) Attitudes toward sex in the aged. *Archives of Sexual Behavior* 6(3):203–213.

Lavrakas, P. J. (1975) Female preferences for male physiques. *Journal of Research in Personality*. 9:324–334.

Masters, W. H., and Johnson, V. E. (1966) *Human Sexual Response*. Boston, Mass.: Little, Brown.

Milford, J. T. (1978) Aesthetic aspects of faces: A (somewhat) phenomenological analysis using multidimensional scaling methods. *Journal of Personality and Social Psychology*. 36:205–216.

Morgan, M. (1973) *The Total Woman*. New York: Pocket Books.

O'Neill, G. C., and O'Neill, M. (1970) Patterns in group sexual activity. *Journal of Sex Research* 6:101–112.

Pfeiffer, E., Verwoerdt, A., and Davis, G. C. (1972) Sexual behavior in middle life. *American Journal of Psychiatry* 128(10):82–87.

Pfeiffer, E., Verwoerdt, A., and Wang, H. S. (1968) Sexual behavior in aged men and women. I. Observations on 254 community volunteers. *Archives of General Psychiatry* 19(December):753–758.

Reedy, M. N. (1978) What happens to love? Love, sexuality and aging. Pp. 184–195 in R. L. Solnick, ed., *Sexuality and Aging*, 2nd ed. Los Angeles: University of Southern California Press.

Rubin, I. (1965) *Sexual Life After Sixty*. New York: Basic Books.

Rubin, I. (1966) Sex after forty and after seventy. Pp. 251–266 in R. Brecher and E. Brecher, eds., *An Analysis of Human Sexual Response*. New York: Signet.

Scharff, D. E. (1978) The power of sex to sustain marriage. *Medical Aspects of Human Sexuality* 12(8):8–25.

Solnick, R. L. (1978) Sexual responsiveness, age, and change: Facts and potential. Pp. 33–47 in R. Solnick, ed., *Sexuality and Aging*, 2nd ed. Los Angeles: University of Southern California Press.

Sontag, S. (1976) The double standard of aging. Pp. 350–366 in S. Gordon and R. W. Libby, eds., *Sexuality Today and Tomorrow*. North Scituate, Mass.: Duxbury Press.

Sviland, M. A. (1978) A program of sexual liberation and growth in the elderly. Pp. 96–114 in R. L. Solnick, ed., *Sexuality and Aging*, 2nd ed. Los Angeles: University of Southern California Press.

Verwoerdt, A., Pfeiffer, E., and Wang, H. S. (1969) Sexual behavior in senescence. II. Patterns of sexual activity and interest. *Geriatrics* 24(2):137–154.

Wasow, M., and Loeb, M. B. (1978) Sexuality in nursing homes. Pp. 154–162 in R. L. Solnick, ed., *Sexuality and Aging*, 2nd ed. Los Angeles: University of Southern California Press.

Weg, R. B. (1978) The physiology of sexuality in aging. Pp. 48–65 in R. L. Solnick, ed., *Sexuality and Aging*, 2nd ed. Los Angeles: University of Southern California Press.

Weidner, G., Istvan, J., and Griffitt, W. (1979) Beauty in the Eye of the Horny Beholdress: Evaluation of Attractive, Medium Attractive, and Unattractive Men by Sexually Aroused Women. Paper presented at the Midwestern Psychological Association, Chicago.

Wiggins, J. S., Wiggins, N., and Conger, J. H. (1968) Correlates of heterosexual somatic preference. *Journal of Personality and Social Psychology* 10:82–90.

Zajonc, R. B. (1968) Attitudinal effects of mere exposure. *Journal of Personality and Social Psychology Monograph Supplement* 9:1–27.

chapter **15**

Aging and Sexuality and the Myth of Decline

STEPHEN J. WEILER

Sexuality in late life is a relatively recent but increasingly popular topic of scientific discussion and systematic research. Research to date has focused primarily on a description of sexual behaviors and some of their demographic, psychological, and physiological correlates. These inquiries have served primarily to dispel myths about the sexuality of older people. The first myth is that of the asexual older person. Numerous studies, beginning with the reports of Kinsey et al. (1948, 1953), demonstrated that sexual interest and activity persist well into late life. A second myth suggests that impotence and sexual involution or the termination of sexual activity and interest, are the expected eventualities for the aging person and that these late-occurring sexual dysfunctions were irreversible. Detailed clinical studies of sexuality in late life, particularly the work of Masters and Johnson (1966, 1970), have demonstrated the lifelong potential for sexual response and the reversibility of sexual disorders occurring later in life.

Even though previous research has dispelled the myth of the asexual and the sexually dysfunctional older person, it has supported the concept of a gradual decline in sexual interest and activity during the last half of adulthood. However, a recent report of longitudinal aging data by George and Weiler (1981) suggests that patterns of sexual activity tend

317

AGING
Stability and Change in the Family

Copyright © 1981 by Academic Press, Inc.
All rights of reproduction in any form reserved.
ISBN 0-12-040003-0 0-12-040023-5(p)

to remain stable in middle and late life, and that the concept of declining sexuality is also a myth.

PREVIOUS LITERATURE: REVIEW AND CRITIQUE

Research on aging and sexuality has come primarily from three sources: the sociological studies of Kinsey *et al.* (1948, 1953); the physiological and clinical studies of Masters and Johnson (1966, 1970); and the Duke University aging studies of Pfeiffer *et al.* (1968, 1969, 1972), Pfeiffer and Davis (1972), and Verwoerdt *et al.* (1969a, 1969b). A few additional reports by Finkle (1959), Freeman (1961), and Newman and Nichols (1960) have also contributed to this relatively small literature.

Kinsey's studies were the earliest to examine the relationship between age and sexuality (Kinsey *et al.* 1948, 1953). These cross-sectional studies indicate that while sexual activity persists in late life, there is a general decline in all measures of sexual activity across the adult age range. This pattern is true for both men and women, although women typically reported lower levels of activity than men at all ages and also indicated that their patterns of sexual activity largely reflect the presence and preferences of a male partner.

A number of other early studies support the basic findings of Kinsey and his colleagues. Finkle *et al.* (1959), for example, reported that 65% of the men age 70 and younger in their sample had engaged in sexual activity within the previous year. Freeman (1961) reported that in a sample of men with an average age of 71 years, 55% indicated that they were sexually active. Both of these studies thus support Kinsey's report that a majority of older men remained sexually active in late life. Newman and Nichols (1960) used cross-sectional data to examine age differences in sexual activity, concluding that there was a gradual decline over the course of adulthood, although some level of sexual activity persisted in late adulthood.

Masters and Johnson's (1966, 1970) clinical studies of the physiology of sexual response included 150 women and 212 men age 50 and older. They reported changes occurring in the sexual response cycle and factors associated with problems of sexual functioning in late life, concluding that the best predictor of the level of sexual activity in old age is the level of sexual activity characteristic in earlier years. Social–psychological factors that relate to sexual responsiveness are also discussed. For women, a secure and warm relationship with a socially appropriate man was the most important factor. For men, a number of factors are discussed as contributing to sexual involution, including monotony in the sexual relationship, concern with economic pursuit, mental and physical fatigue, overindulgence in food or drink, illness of self or spouse, and fear of failure.

In the late 1960s, Pfeiffer and Verwoerdt and their associates (Pfeiffer *et al.* 1968, 1969, Verwoerdt *et al.* 1969a, 1969b) published a series of reports addressing the issue of sexuality in late life. The data included in these reports were taken from a larger, multidisciplinary longitudinal study of aging conducted at Duke University Medical Center. The sample consisted of 260 male and female community volunteers, age 60 and older at the first test date. The sample included both black and white subjects and those who had never married or were widowed as well as those who were partners in intact marriages. The authors focused on the frequency of sexual activity, the degree of sexual interest, sex differences in sexual activity and interest, and patterns of sexual activity over time. They concluded that: sexual activity declines gradually over time for both women and men; sexual interest declines over time, albeit more slowly than sexual activity; men are more sexually active than women although the gap narrows at advanced ages; sexual activity among women is heavily dependent on the availability of a functionally capable, socially sanctioned male partner; and cessation of sexual activity among men and women is most commonly attributed to the male partner.

Pfeiffer and his associates (Pfeiffer *et al.* 1972, Pfeiffer and Davis 1972) later reported data from a second longitudinal study conducted at Duke University Medical Center. This sample consisted of 502 white men and women, aged 46–71 at the first test date. In contrast to the first longitudinal study, this study included middle-aged as well as older subjects. These reports were based on the first wave of data only and were thus based on cross-sectional and retrospective data. The reported results concerning sexual activity and interest and sex differences were similar to those of the earlier study: older persons reported lower levels of sexual interest and activity than younger persons; at all ages, men reported higher levels of interest and activity than women. Data from this study were also examined by a regression analysis for determinants of sexual behavior. For men, many diverse factors were found to influence the extent of sexual activity and interest later in life; the most important included past sexual experience, age, subjective and objective health factors, and social class. Relatively fewer factors were found to account for the extent of sexual activity and interest among women; they were principally marital status, age, and enjoyment derived from sexual experience when younger.

While the studies just reviewed provide an important base of general information concerning sexuality in late life, they typically share a number of methodological problems that compromise the generalizability of the research findings. Each of these problems will be briefly noted.

Sampling Problems. Difficulties with the samples used in previous studies fall into two primary areas: size and representativeness. A number of the previous studies relied on relatively small nubers of subjects. In addition, some of the larger samples that covered a major portion of the adult age range included very few older persons and larger numbers of younger adults.

Even more troublesome is the representativeness of the various samples. The studies by Kinsey and Newman as well as the first Duke longitudinal study, recruited volunteers from the community, drawing chiefly from the memberships of voluntary organizations. Such sampling procedures are unlikely to generate representative cross-sections of the population. Finkle's subjects were clients of an outpatient clinic at a medical school and Freeman depended heavily on referral of subjects from physicians and social workers. Only the second Duke longitudinal study appears to meet the requirements needed to generate a broadly based community cross-section of the population. While this sample also has limitations, they are at least identifiable.

Cross-Sectional versus Longitudinal Data. In order to understand the effects of aging on sexual behavior, longitudinal data are required. The critical problem in cross-sectional studies is that the effects of age and those of cohort membership are inherently confounded. Thus the effects of aging cannot be distinguished from those of differential socialization and the value orientations of particular historical periods. It is generally agreed that significant changes in attitudes toward sexuality have occurred throughout this century, and cohort effects are thus likely to influence the relationship between age and sexual activity in cross-sectional studies.

Virtually all of the previous studies of age and sexuality have relied on cross-sectional data. The first Duke study is the single exception and that sample was small, covering a very narrow age range. The second Duke longitudinal study includes a much broader sample, but previous reports have been based only on cross-sectional analyses using the first round of data.

Statistical Control of Relevant Variables. Previous studies vary widely in the age range of subjects. Several studies sampled virtually the entire adult age range (Masters and Johnson 1966, 1970, Kinsey *et al.* 1948, 1953). Others focused exclusively on late life, but with varying age ranges (Finkle *et al.* 1959, Freeman 1961, Newman and Nichols 1960, Verwoerdt *et al.* 1969a, 1969b, Pfeiffer *et al.* 1968, 1969, Pfeiffer *et al.* 1972, Pfeiffer and Davis 1972). Reports of the relationship between age and sexuality are inevitably influenced by the width of the age range. Marital status is another troublesome variable of studies of aging and sexuality. Patterns of sexual activity have been repeatedly shown to be strongly related to marital status, particularly among women (Kinsey *et al.* 1953, Masters and Johnson 1966, 1970, Pfeiffer *et al.* 1968, Verwoerdt *et al.* 1969a, 1969b). Marital status is also related to age—higher proportions of the elderly, especially women, are widowed. Descriptions of the relationship between age and sexuality that do not pay appropriate attention to marital status are thus likely to incorrectly attribute lower levels of sexual activity among the elderly to age, rather than to lack of a partner.

NEW FINDINGS OF STABILITY

George and Weiler (1980) reported on the completed second longitudinal aging study at Duke University. Their data and analysis avoid the problems in previously reported studies by (a) including randomly selected subjects with an age span of a significant proportion of the adult age range, (b) using longitudinal data and (c) in the analysis, using appropriate statistical controls of confounding factors.

Their subjects were randomly selected from a population of Caucasian, middle-class Americans (from participants of a local health insurance program) and initially consisted of 502 men and women between the ages of 46 and 71. This sample represented the broad middle mass of middle-aged and older individuals who do not experience unusual financial or physical difficulties in adulthood.

The subjects were followed for 6 years during which data were collected on 4 test days at 2-year intervals. The data collected include information concerning economic and social functioning and mental and physical health. The data on sexual behaviors were gathered as part of a self-administered medical history questionnaire and included self-report items about sexual enjoyment, sexual feelings, frequency of sexual relations, awareness or perception of decline in sexual interest or activity, age at which sexual activity stopped (if appropriate) and reason for cessation of sexual activity (if appropriate). These questions were asked at each of the four test dates.

The reported data are based on 278 of the original 502 subjects who both completed all four rounds of data collection and remained married throughout the study period. The 278 subjects used do not differ significantly for demographic variables other than marital status from the original sample of 502, but allow for control of marital status, mentioned as a troublesome variable in previous studies.

The data gathered were analyzed in several ways to overcome previous difficulties in the study of aging and sexuality. When the data were analyzed by age and sex cohorts and controlled for activity versus no-activity by separating out those with no activity, several new conclusions could be drawn.

First, over time, mean levels of sexual activity remained remarkably stable for those subjects in each age–sex group who reported some level of activity. Second, the proportion of subjects in each age–sex group who reported no sexual activity tended to increase over the course of the study. Together, these patterns suggest that individuals in this sample either maintained a stable level of sexual activity or else stopped sexual relations. Third, the data suggest that there were differences in reported levels of sexual activity between men and women (in each age group) and among age groups (for each sex). Finally, comparison of the age–sex groups over time suggested that there were cohort or generational effects operating. For example, by comparing the fourth test date for the men who were initially aged 46–55 with the first test date for the men initially aged 56–65, it was shown the younger cohort exhibited higher levels of sexual activity despite the fact that they were nearly the same age. This pattern held true for each within-sex age comparison.

In order to assess the significance of these patterns, a series of analyses of variance (ANOVA) tests were performed. First, for each of the four test dates, a two-factor analysis of variance was performed to examine the effects of gender and age or cohort. The results indicate that at each measurement, there are significant effects for sex and age cohort. Second, for each of the six age–sex groups, a repeated-measures analysis of variance was performed in order to determine whether the levels of sexual activity of the sexually active subjects significantly differed over the course of the study. The results indicate a significant difference in mean levels of reported sexual activity only for the men who were initially aged 56–65 ($F = 4.14$). The means for the other age–sex groups do not significantly differ across the course of the study. These findings support the evidence of stability in sexual activity among those subjects who continue sexual activity.

Finally, the data were analyzed by classifying subject's individual patterns over the course of the study into a discrete set of patterns. Then tabulations of the various patterns were made. This analysis clearly shows that stable activity is the predominant pattern (58% of the subjects). This does not include subjects who continuously reported no activity (7% of the subjects). Decreasing activity is a relatively uncommon pattern (8% of the subjects). Cessation of sexual activity (the pattern of some activity to no activity) accounts for another significant proportion of the sample (11% of the subjects) and tends to confirm the idea that sexual activity continues stably until it rather suddenly ceases. A small proportion of the subjects (5%) had increasing levels of activity during the study period. Other patterns of a fluctuating nature accounted for the remainder of the subjects' patterns (11%). To summarize these data: During the 6 years of the study period, for individuals between the ages of 46 and 71 at the start of the study, 63% had stable or increasing levels of sexual activity, 7% had continuously absent sexual activity, 11% ceased having sexual activity, and 8% had decreasing levels of sexual activity. Combining these data in a different way, 65% of the subjects had a stable pattern (either present and stable or continuously absent) and 19% had a decreasing pattern (decreasing from some levels to a lower level or to no activity).

This analysis was also reported for the age–sex cohorts and is similar in nature, but with some differences by cohort for patterns for no activity and some differences between men and women of the same age confirming the earlier analyses of variance analyses. Similar analyses of levels of sexual interest and pleasure were reportedly very similar to the patterns of sexual activity, but the specific data are not included.

This study thus is supportive of previous studies' findings that sexual activity continues for older people and that women report significantly lower levels of sexual interest and activity than their male age peers. It is speculated that this is a reflection of the fact that women of these generations in our society tend to be younger than their husbands. Examining an older age cohort of men against a younger age cohort of women (with these cohort age differences roughly equal to the average age differences of spouses) reveals a comparably equal level of sexual activity.

Contrary to previous studies, this data suggests that patterns of sexual behavior tend to remain stable over middle and late life—unless and until there is a cessation of sexual activity. This study also suggests that age cohort rather than age as a reflection of the aging process explains variance of sexual activity among older people.

Thus, this latest contribution to the literature of aging and sexuality includes data and conclusions significantly different from previous studies concerning the actual experience of individuals in the society. The study does seem to offer evidence toward the view of considering decreasing sexual activity as a myth, as the title of this chapter suggests.

IMPLICATIONS OF RECENT FINDINGS

The George and Weiler (1980) study suggests that an earlier accepted belief in the gradually declining sexual activity for older people may be wrong. Their findings suggest that a different pattern—stability until relatively abrupt cessation of sexual activity—is more likely. The study was based on questionnaire data from a longitudinal study of 6 years' duration. The research population was a group of 502 men and women randomly selected from a larger population of Caucasian, middle-class Americans living in a community in the southeastern section of the country (participants in a Durham, North Carolina, health insurance program). Data were analyzed from the 278 participants of the study who contributed data on the four occasions it was collected and who remained married throughout the study.

Because the findings of George and Weiler vary from previous understandings of human sexuality in older people, new psychological and social implications for the older person could be expected. The implications might also be extended to the general understanding of the aging process and sexuality.

The George and Weiler findings suggest that an age-cohort-effect has more relevance to differing levels of sexual activity than age alone. The data also suggest that cohorts of younger people (individuals born later) have higher levels of sexual activity at a given age than older cohorts had at a similar age. Thus one would predict that, as younger cohorts of individuals age, their sexual activity would be greater than expected based on the previous cohorts. This knowledge may have some effect on people's expectations of themselves as they age. The expectation of decline (based partly on previous research findings) may be replaced by the expectation of continued sexual functioning. Together the higher levels of sexual activity for a cohort of individuals and the expectation of sexual continuity by individuals may result in more older individuals who regard their sexuality as a significant aspect of their lives.

The change in expectation regarding continuity of sexual functioning for older people may have effects on sexual dysfunctions. Masters and Johnson (1966) suggest that fear of failure is a prominent factor for sexual involution in men. If a man believes that his sexual activities and functions will gradually decline and then be lost, the first evidences of change in sexual response may lead to anxieties over fear of failure and erectile failures. If the expectation of sexual continuity replaces that of decline and loss, perhaps some instances of sexual dysfunction would be prevented. In addition, the expectation of continued sexual activity may prompt older individuals with sexual dysfunctions to seek therapy for these problems rather than to accept the difficulty as an expected eventuality.

These new data may also change the understanding of what the individual older person experiences regarding change in sexual functioning. Previously, most individuals were thought to gradually decrease sexual functioning until cessation. The new data suggest instead that older people rather abruptly cease sexual activity from a previous stable pattern and that this change occurs for gradually increasing numbers of older people as they age. This abrupt, rather than gradual change, would presumably require a different, perhaps more difficult adjustment for the older person. Such a change would be more likely to threaten personal identity and family relationships and to be experienced as a significant loss. Thus, for a married man or woman who rather suddenly ceases sexual activity aspects of anxiety (from questions of identity and perhaps spouse reaction), guilt (in relation to the spouse's response), and grief reaction may be expected to be more severe than if the change had been gradual.

Previous studies have also shown that for women, sexual activity is dependent on an acceptable and capable partner. Thus the sexual dysfunction, illness, or death of a husband very often determines cessation of sexual activity for his wife. Given new data that suggests that sexual functioning is likely to be stable rather than declining, it is possible that the reaction to the abrupt loss of sexual functioning for such a woman is another significant aspect of her response to her husband's death or illness.

In addition to possible implications for the individual, there are some possible implications regarding the nature of sexuality throughout the life-span. As previously mentioned, these new data suggest that an age–cohort–effect has more relevance to differing levels of sexual activity than age alone. To explain noted decreases in sexual activity by age alone suggests that the process of aging affects sexual functioning. This further suggests that some physiological process accounts for these changes in sexual functioning. To explain differences in sexual activity as an effect of age–cohort suggests that the time when a person was born and was passing through specific developmental phases in life has the more significant effect on later sexual functioning. It follows from this line of logic, then, that the sexual attitudes of the society (which are generally accepted as having changed significantly throughout this century) may have affected individuals at specific periods of development such that decreasing inhibition and increasing sexual interest, pleasure, and activity developed the later one was born. This obviously describes a psychosocial process as a significant determinant of sexual functioning.

From this argument, then, one can assert that levels of sexual functioning in sexually functioning middle-aged and older people are determined more by a psychosocial process than by a physiological process. Masters and Johnson (1966, 1970) have espoused such a view based on their work with sexually dysfunctional older people. Gagnon and Simon (1973) have presented a similar view for the entire life-span. These data certainly support such hypotheses in the middle and late years of life.

CONCLUSIONS

The myths about aging and sexuality are gradually being replaced with what is hoped to be accuracy. It sometimes seems that the nature of the accumulation of knowledge is a two-step-forward, one-step-back process. Previous studies have dispelled the myths of the elderly asexual and sexually dysfunctional person, but have contributed to a belief in gradual declining sexual functioning. More recent studies suggest this too may be a myth, but perhaps in some unseen way contributes to another myth (such as the expectation that all people should continue high levels of sexual activity throughout life). Perhaps the most important lesson for social scientists to learn from this research is to become reasonably skeptical of statistical knowledge and increasingly sensitive to the experience of individuals.

Whatever the specifics turn out to be, it is clear at this time that sexual expression continues late in life and that it continues in the context of the marital unit. Many other questions remain about the nature of sexuality and the relationship of sexual functioning to other aspects of life such as intimacy, marriage, family units, and family functioning. Perhaps through the study of aging these questions can be more clearly addressed and answered.

REFERENCES

Finkle, A. L., Moyers, T. G., Tobenkin, M. I., and Karg, S. J. (1959) Sexual potency in aging males. *Journal of American Medical Association* 170:113–115.
Freeman, J. T. (1961) Sexual capacities in the aging male. *Geriatrics* 16:37–43.
Gagnon, J. H., and Simon, W. (1973) *Sexual Conduct: The Social Sources of Human Sexuality*. Chicago: Aldine-Atherton.
George, L. K., and Weiler, S. J. (1981) Sexuality in middle and late life: The effects of age cohort and gender. *Archives of General Psychiatry*.

Kinsey, A. C., Pomeroy, W. B., and Martin, C. R. (1948) *Sexual Behavior in the Human Male*. Philadelphia, PA: Saunders.

Kinsey, A. C., Pomeroy, W. B., Martin C. R., and Gebhard, P. H. (1953) *Sexual Behavior in the Human Female*. Philadelphia: Saunders.

Masters, W. H., and Johnson, V. E. (1966) *Human Sexual Response*. Boston: Little Brown.

Masters, W. H., and Johnson, V. E. (1970) *Human Sexual Inadequacy*. Boston: Little Brown.

Newman, G., and Nichols, C. R. (1960) Sexual activities and attitudes in older persons. *Journal of the American Medical Association* 173:33–35.

Pfeiffer, E., and Davis, G. C. (1972) Determinants of sexual behavior in middle and old age. *Journal of the American Geriatric Society* 20:151–258.

Pfeiffer, E., Verwoerdt, A., and Davis, G. C. (1972) Sexual behavior in middle life. *American Journal of Psychiatry* 128:82–87.

Pfeiffer, E., Verwoerdt, A., and Wang, H. S. (1968) Sexual behavior in aged men and women. I. Observations on 254 community volunteers. *Archives of General Psychiatry* 19:753–758.

Pfeiffer, E., Verwoerdt, A., and Wang, H. S. (1969) The natural history of sexual behavior in a biologically advantaged group of aged individuals. *Journal of Gerontology* 24:193–198.

Verwoerdt, A., Pfeiffer, E., and Wang, H. S. (1969a) Sexual behavior in senescence— changes in sexual activity and interest of aging men and women. *Journal of Geriatric Psychiatry* 2:163–180.

Verwoerdt, A., Pfeiffer, E., and Wang, H. S. (1969b) Sexual behavior in senescence. II. Patterns of sexual activity and interest. *Geriatrics* 24:137–154.

Stability and Change in the Family
March 22–24, 1979
Annapolis, Maryland

WORKSHOP PARTICIPANTS

Emily Ahern, Johns Hopkins University
Shirley P. Bagley, National Institute on Aging
Richard A. Brown, KOBA Associates, Inc., Washington, D.C.
Robert N. Butler, National Institute on Aging
Patrick E. Connor, Oregon State University
James A. Davis, Harvard University
David Fischer, Brandeis University
Robert W. Fogel, Harvard University
Frank F. Furstenberg, Jr., University of Pennsylvania
William Griffitt, Kansas State University
Gunhild O. Hagestad, Penn State University
Eugene Hammel, University of California, Berkeley
Tamara K. Hareven, Clark University
Elaine Hatfield, University of Wisconsin
Jacquelyne M. Jackson, Duke University Medical Center
Stephen M. Johnson, University of Oregon
Herbert Kaufman, Brookings Institution
Harold H. Kelley, University of California, Los Angeles
Sara B. Kiesler, National Research Council

Melvin L. Kohn, National Institute of Mental Health
Glen Loury, Northwestern University
James G. March, Stanford University
Sidney W. Mintz, Johns Hopkins University
James N. Morgan, University of Michigan
Valerie K. Oppenheimer, University of California, Los Angeles
Jeffrey Pfeffer, Stanford University
Virginia P. Reno, National Commission on Social Security
Matilda W. Riley, National Institute on Aging
David Schneider, University of Chicago
W. Richard Scott, Stanford University
Ethel Shanas, University of Illinois at Chicago Circle
Raymond Smith, University of Chicago
Mark Snyder, University of Minnesota
Marvin B. Sussman, University of Delaware
Jane Traupmann, Wellesley College
Donald J. Treiman, National Research Council
W. Kip Viscusi, Council on Wage and Price Stability, Washington, D.C.
Stephen J. Weiler, New York State University, Stony Brook
Robert S. Weiss, Harvard Medical School
John W. M. Whiting, Harvard University
Carl Whittaker, University of Wisconsin
Aaron Wildavsky, Institute for Policy and Management Research, New York
Robert Willis, New York State University, Stony Brook

appendix B

Reviewers

Vern Bengston, University of Southern California
Lenore Bixby, Washington, D.C.
Ewald W. Buffe, Duke University Medical School
J. Merrill Carlsmith, Stanford University
Robert L. Clark, North Carolina State University
Elizabeth Colson, University of California, Berkeley
James R. Dumpson, New York Community Trust Foundation
Stan Engerman, University of Rochester
Ann Foner, Rutgers University
Frank F. Furstenberg, Jr., University of Pennsylvania
William J. Goode, Stanford University
Alan E. Gross, University of Maryland
John Hagins, Social Security Administration
James S. Jackson, University of Michigan
Theresa Leviton, National Institute of Mental Health
William H. Masters, St. Louis, Missouri
John Modell, University of Michigan
Bernice Neugarten, University of Chicago
Jeffrey Pfeffer, Stanford University
Joan Robertson, University of Wisconsin
Alice K. Rossi, University of Massachusetts
Harold Scheffer, Yale University

James Schultz, Brandeis University
Robert R. Sears, Stanford University
Ethel Shanas, University of Illinois at Chicago Circle
Claudewell S. Thomas, College of Medicine and Dentistry of New Jersey
Charles Tilly, University of Minnesota
Maris A. Vinovskis, University of Michigan
Julian Wolpert, Princeton University

Author Index

Numbers in italics indicate pages on which complete references can be found.

A

Achenbaum, A., 152, *163*
Achenbaum, W., 102, *111*, *164*
Adams, B., 26, 31, *41*, 116, 121, *140*, 293, 298
Aldous, J., 11, 13, 32, *41*
Altman, I., 254, *271*
Anderson, M., 65, 67–69, *79*, 96, 100, 105, 106, 109, *111*, 161, *164*
Ankarloo, B., 19, 22, *41*, 69, *79*
Anspach, D., 120–124, *140*
Aries, P., 23, *42*, 151, *164*
Aronson, E., 255, *271*
Axelson, L., 289, *298*

B

Babchuck, N., 26, 32, *42*
Bahr, H., 32, *42*
Bales, R., 29, *45*
Ballweg, J., 291, *298*

Baltes, P., 13, *42*, 115, *140*
Bane, M., 109, *111*, 118, *140*
Banks, J., 58, 59, 75, *79*
Barrett, N., 190, *209*
Baumert, C., 100, *111*
Beach, F., 313, *314*
Beck, S., 311, *313*
Becker, B., 242, 245, *248*
Becker, G., 49, *79*, 170, *182*
Belloc, N., 270, *271*
Benedict, R., 223, *230*
Bengston, V., 12, 25, 26, 32, 34, 40, *42*, 288, 290, 291, 293, 295, *298*
Berkman, L., 269, *271*
Berliner, J., 109, *111*
Bernard, J., 18, *42*, 269, *271*
Berscheid, E., 256, *271*, 281, *298*, 306, 307, 310, *314*
Bettelheim, B., 26, *42*
Bilodeau, C., 292, *298*
Binstock, R., 241, *248*, 269, *271*

333

Subject Index